Adolescence and Education
Volume 1

GENERAL ISSUES IN THE
EDUCATION OF ADOLESCENTS

Edited by

Tim Urdan
Santa Clara University

Frank Pajares
Emory University

IAP

INFORMATION AGE
PUBLISHING

80 Mason Street • Greenwich, Connecticut 06830 • www.infoagepub.com

*For Jeannine and Ella Sophia,
and Isabel, Jackie, and Afshin.*

Contents

List of Contributors

Lisa Abrams	National Board on Educational Testing and Public Policy, Boston College
Ann A. Battle	University of Maryland
Marguerite Clarke	National Board on Educational Testing and Public Policy, Boston College
Michael Cunningham	Tulane University
Peter Demerath	Ohio State University
Stanford M. Dornbusch	Stanford University
Barbara Finkelstein	University of Maryland
Vinay Harpalani	University of Pennsylvania
Anita Woolfolk Hoy	Ohio State University
Jeanne G. Kaufman	Stanford University
Philip Kaufman	MPR Associates, Inc.
George Madaus	National Board on Educational Testing and Public Policy, Boston College
Carol Midgley	University of Michigan
Stephen Pape	Ohio State University
Paul R. Pintrich	University of Michigan
Gregory Seaton	University of Pennsylvania
Lauren J. Silver	University of Pennsylvania
Margaret Beale Spencer	University of Pennsylvania
Sharon R. Tucker	University of Pennsylvania
Kathryn R. Wentzel	University of Maryland
Akane Zusho	University of Michigan

Foreword

Adolescence is a period of development shaped both by biological unfolding and by societal and cultural norms and expectations. Spanning roughly the second decade of life, the period of adolescence, and the expectations of society for adolescents, has grown and changed dramatically over the last century. Whereas 100 years ago older children and teenagers were once depended on to join the workforce virtually as soon as they were able, today we often expect that our children will not leave school and enter the world of work until they have graduated from high school or, in some cases, completed college. Most American adolescents stay in school until they are at least 18, and about a quarter of them go to college, thereby delaying the adoption of traditionally adult roles until their twenties.

One effect of the increase in the length of time adolescents stay in school, and the number of adolescents that complete at least high school, is an extension of the adolescent period. Sixteen-, seventeen-, and eighteen-year olds, once considered old enough to work full time, are now frequently looked on as too young and inexperienced to begin their careers. They are expected to go to college and viewed as adolescents until they graduate. These changes in adolescence over the last century have created fascinating and difficult questions regarding the education of adolescent students. As adolescence has increasingly been recognized as a period of development distinct from late childhood and early adulthood, prominent scholars have turned their attention to the issue of how to best educate these students. Some have focused on early adolescence (the middle school years); others have examined late adolescence (high school and the transition to college or work). The purpose of this book series, *Adolescence and Education*, is to provide a forum in which research on the education of adolescent students can be presented.

In this inaugural volume, we solicited chapters from leading scholars in a variety of fields related to education. Our aim was to provide a broad overview of several of the most pressing concerns regarding the education of adolescent students. The volume begins with an historical perspective from Barbara Finklestein, who provides background regarding America's changing perceptions of adolescence as a developmental period and how American society has approached the task of educating this age group over time. This is followed by chapters from Carol Midgley and from Sanford Dornbusch and Jeanne Kaufman regarding the organization, purpose, and function of schools designed to serve early and late adolescents. Midgley uses an achievement goal theory lens to analyze middle level schools; Dornbusch and Kaufman consider senior high schools, adopting a more sociological perspective.

The next four chapters explore some of the specific features within school and school life that affect the learning and development of adolescents. Kathryn Wentzel and Ann Battle describe how social relationships during adolescence can influence school experiences, particularly the motivation and achievement of students. Anita Woolfolk Hoy, Peter Demerath, and Stephen Pape describe effective teaching practices for the specific developmental needs and tasks of adolescents. Akane Zusho and Paul Pintrich present an overview of current motivational theories and then apply them to adolescents, focusing on the multiple trajectories that teenage students may take in secondary schools. Marguerite Clarke, Lisa Abrams, and George Madaus, from the National Board on Educational Testing and Public Policy, provide a discussion of assessment practices, especially standardized tests that are proliferating in use across the nation.

The final section of this volume includes two chapters, each addressing a specific problem encountered by many adolescents. Margaret Beale Spencer and her colleagues confront the problem of teen parenting and consider the educational implications of becoming a parent during adolescence from a cultural-ecological perspective. Philip Kaufman, one of the nation's most knowledgeable scholars in the area of school dropouts, having served as lead author of the dropout report for the National Center on Educational Statistics (NCES), explains the often-ignored intricacies of determining how many students fail to complete high school and considers some of the possible causes of dropping out of school.

Together, the chapters in this volume provide an overview of many of the major issues involved in the education of adolescent students, as well as the theories and research related to these issues. Future volumes in the *Adolescence and Education* series will be devoted to more detailed examinations of particular issues, beginning with Volume II, which will focus on academic motivation. As with this inaugural volume, future volumes will continue to draw on the expertise of distinguished scholars to provide readers with the best information about the theories, research, and practice regarding the education of students in the second decade of life.

ACKNOWLEDGMENTS

We are most grateful to the esteemed contributors of chapters for this first volume of *Adolescence and Education*. In addition to writing well-researched and thought-provoking chapters, these scholars were both gracious and patient with our efforts to edit their work and put this volume together. We also appreciate the help of Patricia Brandt. Finally, we would like to thank George Johnson and the staff at Information Age Publishing for giving us the opportunity to edit this series and for their help getting it off the ground.

Tim Urdan and Frank Pajares
Series Editors

CHAPTER 1

Is Adolescence Here to Stay?

Historical Perspectives on Youth and Education

Barbara Finkelstein

INTRODUCTION

A little more than a century ago, adolescence was unrecognized, undiscovered, unknown, and unorganized. Psychologists had not invented it. Physicians had not conceived it. Education reformers had not institutionalized it, social planners had not governed it, and young people had not experienced it (see Demos & Demos, 1969; Holt, 1897; Kett, 1977; Platt, 1969; Schlossman, 1977). Most young people between the ages of twelve and eighteen worked on family farms, engaged in wage labor, and grew up in the company of adults. A handful of relatively high born young people went on to college. Graduation from high school was a privilege of relatively prosperous town dwellers. Legions of new immigrant youth in the cities, attended high schools on occasion and joined what David Nasaw has called a "kiddie labor market." High Schooling was relatively inaccessible to African Americans in the south. A cadre of reluctant and detribalized Native Americans found themselves involuntarily contained in boarding

1

schools. A century ago, young people did not spend elongated periods of time in high schools, nor did they typically congregate in carefully calibrated age cohorts. Their status was relatively undefined. Their lives were relatively unorganized and unpredictable. There was little to distinguish them as a particular class of people, except as physiologically evolving young ones. Strictly speaking, there were no adolescents or juvenile delinquents one hundred and ten years ago. There were few truant officers, no adolescent medical specialists, or predictably available high schools to organize and police the life of young people from the ages of 12–18. Nor were there large numbers of angst-laden, perplexed, or rebellious youth who had the time or disposition to challenge the meaning of adulthood or the direction of society in deeply meaningful ways.

This portrait of adolescent non-being one hundred years ago, suggests that the condition we know today as adolescence is in fact a historically grounded social invention, not a universal state of being. Adolescence acquired a public name in the United States in 1905 when G. Stanley Hall published a book entitled *Adolescence* and imbued it with psychological and moral meaning. Adolescence acquired economic dimension when it provided a rationale for withdrawing young people from a glutted wage labor force and placing them instead in schools. Adolescence acquired political dimension when it served as an intellectual lynchpin for the expansion of high schools to Americanize immigrants, detribalize and civilize Native Americans, credential privileged Americans, and calibrate opportunities for African Americans. Adolescence acquired social meaning as generations of adolescents imbued this stage of life with social, political, and economic inventions of their own making. In short, adolescence has evolved as a historically constructed invention of such exquisite complexity that generations of social, educational, and psychohistorians are still seeking to make sense of it and to discover if it is here to stay.

This essay explores the staying power of adolescence by examining some of the ways in which the inventors of adolescence conceived it, the institutional planners shaped it, the school authorities organized it, and selected groups of students experienced it. By arraying multiple perspectives on the meanings of adolescence, it will perhaps be possible to understand the historical footing on which adolescence has been built and to assess its relative perdurability.

THE INVENTION OF ADOLESCENCE

As historians tell the tale, adolescence is a historically grounded social invention, the product of concerted attempts of socially and morally anxious nineteenth and twentieth-century developmental psychologists, moral

reformers, sociologists, medical specialists, and other emerging professionals, business elites, and social housekeepers to control the socialization of
increasing numbers of detached youth. A newly visible class of young people were, in the view of reformers endangered. They were insufficiently
governed or protected in urban wage labor markets; occupied less central
roles in the political economy of their families; had fewer and less attentive
male authority figures governing the daily conditions of their lives; were
not as yet in the extended custody of school or other public authorities;
and were in possession of habits of association and networks of social relations that were dangerous, unfamiliar, and unregulated.[1]

The inventors of adolescence faced a series of social transformations
which elevated, in their eyes, the status of youth as an important stage in
the life cycle worthy of assiduous attention. They harbored sentiments that
had much in common with old and new testament patriarchs who
entreated parents to recognize youth as a morally transitional life-stage; a
period of time between irresponsible childhood and married adulthood, a
stage during which immature unmarried men and women were particularly subject to sexual temptation, excesses of debauchery, attacks of intem-
perance, and immoderation.[2] The inventors of adolescence also had much
in common with nineteenth century social and moral reformers who had
discovered the vulnerability of childhood and constructed an array of tutorial institutions that would serve as way stations between the dependency of
home, church and neighborhood, and the relative independence associated with wage labor and farm production, civic engagement, and family
responsibility. They inherited templates of educational experience which
they tried to transform in order to rein in what they believed to be the
excesses of jobless and uncontrolled young people with too much free
space, too much free time, too little family government, insufficient moral
training, and too little practical education (Finkelstein, 1997).

They lived during a time when "...urbanization, industrialization, and
immigration threatened the foundations of social order," or so they
believed (Gillis, 1974). They were privy to processes of demographic and
structural transformation that had produced what John Gillis and Joseph
Kett have described as a semi dependent class of "professional bachelors
who would organize themselves into neighborhood gangs, enact various
rituals of social protest, and construct economic and political definition[s]
of brotherhood that positioned them somewhere between dependent
childhood and independent adulthood" (Kett, 1977). The inventors of
adolescence had observed the dissolution of traditional apprenticeship
arrangements and a waning of family authority over the young. They were
familiar with the lure of the cities and the frontier and concerned about
runaway apprentices, defiant college students, and ungovernable street

children who, in different ways, had slipped the regulatory bonds that had held them tight to their families, churches, and local communities.

As we shall see, the architects of adolescence would fundamentally transform traditional concepts of human development as a seamless, imperceptibly blended process through which "Infancy quickly yielded to what we now call childhood, childhood shaded into youth, youth blossomed into maturity, and maturity gave way slowly and irregularly to senescence" (Lassonde, 1994, p. 150). Their guiding intellectual principal was grounded in a belief that adolescence was a particular stage of life with precise age parameters, developmental possibilities, and social requirements. Adolescents, in their view, were pubescent, post menarchic, hormone driven, peer controlled young persons defined not as youth had been traditionally, as persons somewhere midway between childhood dependence and adult maturity, but as developmentally defined, age-specific individuals in possession of particular psychological capacities and cognitive and emotional vulnerabilities.

The essentials of adolescence were articulated in G. Stanley Hall's pioneering work on *Adolescence,* a work of near-Byzantine complexity, but enormous influence during the first two decades of the twentieth century. According to Hall, the development of each adolescent, like the development of the race and the nation, proceeded according to specific principles and time tables. Adolescence was a biologically determined condition, characterized by a rapid spurt of growth in mind, body, and sensibility. It was during this stage of life, as Hall put it, that childhood disintegrates and new portions of "passion and desire spring into vigorous life." Adolescence was a period of unparalleled emotional volatility, a time of "storm and stress..." a stage of enormous energy on the one hand, and lassitude on the other. It was a time of untrammeled passion and ungovernable emotions (Demos & Demos, 1969; Hall, 1904; Ross, 1972).

As the title of G. Stanley Hall's much-cited, influential, and pioneering work on adolescence, *Adolescence: Its Psychology and its Relation to Physiology, Anthropology, Sociology, Sex, Crime, Religion and Education,* would suggest, the construction of adolescence was an important intellectual lynchpin in a particular kind of social project of the early twentieth century, one which reformers hoped could bring the passions of youth under the control of reason and reorganize the structures of authority and networks of association within which young people led their lives. It was a social project grounded in commitments to the value of science and the capacity of the emerging disciplines of developmental psychology, sociology, and medical science to control the pace of social change and guide the cultural practices of parents, teachers, social workers, and assorted other youth workers. It was a social project crafted to normalize the experience of youth by expanding the reach of schools and the authority of teachers, child guidance specialists, youth counselors and by effecting changes in the duration of schooling and the nature of playground, community, and laboring spaces which youths traditionally occupied. It was a social project designed to constrain and regulate the lives of the young and reside authority over their development in carefully organized institutions of formal education (Kett, 1977).

Precise in their definition of adolescence as a stage of life which required protective institutions, special social and political handling, and relentless if benevolent and kindly management, the architects of adolescence turned to high schools and grammar schools as crucibles for the protection and direction of the young. They invented a new category of curable criminality which they called delinquency and also helped to establish the juvenile court and correctional institutions for the labeling, processing and management of troublesome youth (Platt, 1969; Schlossman, 1977). They turned to junior and senior high schools to reconstruct the timing and scheduling of this important life transition, substitute the benevolent authority of teachers for that of employers in factories, mines, plantations, and reservations, and serve as holding agencies for unemployed youth (Fuller, 1983; Modell, Furstenberg, & Hershberg, 1976). They provided psychological justification for universal high school education, not only as an appropriate environment for privileged young people preparing for college, but as a site that could Americanize immigrants, "civilize" Native Americans, and prepare African American youth for relatively low status jobs in an expanding wage economy.

Their concerns resonated with those of earlier nineteenth century reformers who, in the half century from 1830 to 1890, had observed the emergence of a new class of young people who were neither household dependents, journeymen workers, domestically-based apprentices, nor independent married adults, but a relatively autonomous group who were too old to be cloistered within families, but too young to amass wealth, to hold property, to marry, or reproduce. Among them were an emerging class of urban street children who supported themselves "…alternatively from the legitimate street trades (hawking newspapers, tending storefronts and furnaces, (peddling matches or apples), and from outright thievery. They robbed knit stores and bakeries, and pilfered coal and stove wood from neighborhood backyards" (Teeter, 1988, p. 910). Some went to school but were undeterred if not unaffected by the forms of Americanization which they encountered. The architects of adolescence also observed cities overrun by thousands of immigrant youth, transplanted southerners, and previously enslaved persons who, they believed, required formal education, careful socialization, and heavy doses of cultural assimilation (Finkelstein, 1987).

The architects of adolescence also lived during a time when nation-building had been proceeding apace, government power was increasingly consolidated, the potential political power of non-Native Americans, minority ethnic groups, and African American urban dwellers was on the increase, and young people, like the youthful nation of which they were a part, was mired in unknowable possibilities (Meyer, Tyack, Nagel, & Gordon, 1979). As Robert Wiebe (1967) suggested about this era of U.S. History,

> Americans in a basic sense no longer knew who or where they were. The setting had altered beyond their power to understand it, and within an alien context they had lost themselves. In a democratic society, who was master and who servant? In a land of opportunity, what was success? The apparent leaders were as much adrift as their followers. For lack of anything that made better sense of their world, people weighed, counted, and measured it. (pp. 42–43)

The architects of adolescence not only weighed, measured, and counted, but championed the utility of publicly constituted formal educational institutions as important sites for the cultivation and regulation of young people. They were aware of the dangers of the streets and unregulated work spaces. They feared the dissolution of family authority and the emerging influence of peer groups. They observed an educational landscape which, by contemporary standards, was underdeveloped with less than 30% of children between ages 10 and 14 in school and less than 9% over fourteen, in systematically regulated formal school settings.[3]

Facing what they believed to be a dangerous situation or, as Paula Fass has described it, a "degenerating moral order" (Fass, 1977), the framers of adolescence constituted an approach to social planning which they hoped would influence the structure of social relations among and between young people; reorganize their relationship to the world of paid work; enhance the authority and power of educational institutions and agencies, structure environments which prepared young people for orderly civic engagement; and would otherwise bind and direct their energies, passions, and burgeoning sexuality.

FASHIONING YOUTH INTO ADOLESCENCE

In their efforts to organize the social and moral lives of the young and control the socialization of working, immigrant, and minority youth, the inventors of adolescence joined an array of other education reformers in efforts to control the networks of influence surrounding the young, narrow the range of associations, and in these ways keep them out of harm's way—off city streets in the cities, out of dance halls, and movie theaters, and far from the temptations of alcohol, drugs, and sexual encounters—they prepared for the rigors of adult life.

For an array of emerging child care professionals and youth workers, including social workers, representatives of women's club groups, medical professionals, psychologists, urban planners, teachers, and school administrators, high schools created a template for the fashioning of youth into adolescence. The template projected a vision of twelve to eighteen-year-old young people as students who, by attending schools on a sustained and daily basis, would be awash in civilizing educational processes. They envisioned a school in which students not only prepared academically for entrance into college and university, but had opportunities to link academic learning to concepts of everyday life. Schools would become sites of socialization and community building as well as sites for intellectual nurture. The schools could function as laboratories of social change, by inviting students to become community-builders as well as moral beings and good citizens. They could learn to build more virtuous communities by participating and helping to fashion idealized ones within schools.[4] John Dewey (1896) described this vision with clarity and elegance.

> The school is a special social community in which the too complex social environment is reduced and simplified; in which certain ideas and facts concerned with this simplified social life are communicated . . . This simplified social life should reproduce in miniature, the activities fundamental to life as a whole, and thus enable the child, on one side, to become gradually acquainted . . . with the larger community; while upon the other it enables him to individually express himself . . . and thus gain control of his own powers. (p. 418)

Thus constituted on new psychological and pedagogical principles, schools could serve as agencies of resocialization as well as intellectual nurture. They could extricate young people between the ages of twelve and seventeen from the baleful effects of exploitive labor, the influence of street gangs, and what they believed to be the deleterious effects of immigrant, Native American, and African American cultures and traditions. Schools could serve as alternative cultural environments within which students could learn to resist the power of peers, the temptations of the street, and, as appropriate, the moral authority of their families. Situated strategically in the life course, grammar and high schools could become places where young people discovered alternative ways to think, form friendships, identify tradition, and become citizens, or, in a different mode, learn their place in an evolving society. Through an expansion of extracurricular activities—social clubs, drama societies, student government, chaperoned dances, athletics events, and community activities—schools could compete with dance halls, movie theaters, bars, cafes and amusement parks (Odem,

2000). Schools appeared to be the best antidote to the dangers of the city, and the ungovernability of young people. As agencies of adolescent social-ization as well as intellectual cultivation, Robert Hunter (1973), reformer and physician observed of the schools that

> The problems of child life are school problems . . . An awakening to the necessity of assuming the new duties [in schools] should not be delayed, for the yard-less tenement is multiplying, the children must be kept from the fac-tory and the little ones of the street may even be now be counted by the mil-lions. (p. 2202)

In the name of scientific efficiency, humanitarian concern, moral uplift, and social control, the architects of adolescence and other turn-of-the-cen-tury school reformers mounted a campaign to disengage young people from factory, street, field, and tenement and to place larger numbers of them in school. They lobbied for strict child labor laws, and compulsory school attendance for children between the ages of twelve and sixteen. They invented the truant officer, a public official with specialized authority to gather up non-school going young people, label them as "truants," "devi-ants," and "delinquents," send them to the Juvenile Court for triage into specialized child guidance clinics, reformatories, or tutorial environments as appropriate. They invented intelligence tests designed to calibrate the relative potential of each student, identify appropriate curricula, and define standardized testing as a way of sorting and differentiating students in schools. They championed the establishment of manual labor high schools that would prepare less privileged, foreign immigrant minorities, Native Americans, laboring class young people, and African American youth, to acquire skills that would prepare them for expanding handicraft industries, industrial trades, clerical or pink collar industries, and at the same time, dis-engage them from nefarious influences. They conceived of an expansion of the extra curriculum to include a variety of informal social, academic, ath-letic, and community activities that would provide all students with opportu-nities to cultivate self-governing capacities under the eye of adult supervisors, and develop new habits of association for troublesome young people. Ellwood Patterson Cubberley articulated this interest precisely:

> ...an entirely new interest in the extra-curricular activities of youth has been taken by the school. In part this change in attitude has been caused by the new disciplinary problems brought to the school through the recent great popularization of secondary education. (Fass, 1998, p. 96)

The United States Bureau of Education (1918), in their influential tract entitled the "Cardinal Principles of Education," synthesized the fears and the hopes of reformers when they supported universal high school education for young people between the ages of twelve and sixteen.

> …an extended education for every boy and girl is essential to the welfare, and even the existence, of democratic society. The significance of these objectives is becoming more and more apparent under modern conditions in our democracy. These conditions grow out of increased knowledge of science with its rapidly extending applications to all the affairs of life, keener competition with its attendant dangers, closer contacts of peoples of varied racial and religious types, and greater assertiveness of all men and women in control of their own destinies. These and many other tendencies increase the significance of health, worthy home membership, vocation, citizenship, the worthy use of leisure, and ethical character . . . their realization calls for the full period allotted to both the junior and senior high schools.

> Consequently, this commission holds that education should be so reorganized that every normal boy and girl will be encouraged to remain in school to the age of eighteen on full time if possible, otherwise on part time. (pp. 29–30)

ORGANIZING ADOLESCENCE: THE SCHOOLING OF AMERICAN YOUTH

The stage was set for the organization of adolescence. Indeed, the architects of adolescence had done their work well. Historical evidence suggests that schools would emerge as defining contexts for the nurture of youth experience. Serial generations of school reformers would modify rather than fundamentally reconstruct the template of educational experience defined at the start of the century by the inventors of adolescence and the authors of progressivism in education. Like the inventors of adolescence, they have defined adolescence as a biologically determined stage of life, an important and volatile life transition best managed, regulated, and organized by educators in schools. Whether they were progressive reformers in the 1920s and 1930s, new dealers in the 1930s and 1940s, academic conservatives of the 1950s, or mainstream education planners throughout the century, they defined school-going, academic achievement, and participation in school activities as symbols of normality. They regarded dropping-out and school failure as markers of deviance. They have viewed schools as buffers against the destabilizing influences of peer groups, commercial entertainers, dance halls, jazz clubs, pop musicians, alcohol, drugs, and political subversives. Their legacies are visible, stable, institutionalized, and influential.

Over the course of time, more and more young people between the ages of twelve and seventeen would spend more and more time in schools.

Through the commonalities of their shared experience in schools, they would enter into new and more structured forms of association with people of their own age. They would encounter a specialized world of books, print, and socializing, where they could discover worlds outside the family, the church, and the neighborhood under the watchful eye and tutelage of educators. Through the bureaucratic routines of the schools—the schedules of clock and bell, the division of knowledge into subjects, the omnipresence of the report card and the test, the restrictions of movement within and between classrooms, assembly halls and playgrounds, the specification of appropriate verbal behaviors, the gendered division of curricula, the requirements of punctuality, the organization of leisure, and the omnipresence of routine—students would enter into carefully supervised communities.

Notwithstanding the constraining features of most school settings, or perhaps partly because of them, students, if they spent enough time in schools or if they dropped out, appear to have carved out terrains of freedom. The constraining features of schools did not, as we shall see, prevent them from inventing innovative social forms, networks of association, styles of public expression, habits of economic practice, and forms of human connection.

EXPERIENCING ADOLESCENCE

Unfortunately there is a relative paucity of historical work exploring public schools as sites for the cultivation of youth cultures. What little we know suggests that young people have generated a diversity of innovative social practices that have been importantly influenced not only by the practices of educators in school, but by an array of structural conditions that limited and/or enabled them to remain in school for sustained periods of time, finance the hidden costs of schooling, freight the ever-increasing costs of leisure time, balance academic and social requirements, participate in a full range of school activities, make use of schools for economic, social, and political advancement, and control the uses of their own time.

There are glimmers in the historical literature of age-specific youth groups, like that of flappers in the 1920s, bobbysoxers and teenagers in the 1930s and 1940s, "rock and rollers" in the 1950s, and beats and beatle maniacs in the 1960s, for whom schools served as watering holes for the construction of new forms of aesthetic expression, courtship patterns, gender relations, and standards of deportment and behavior. There are also examples in the historical literature of youth cultures which evolved specifically among groups of African American and Native American students who encountered views of their inferiority in the school and generated a diverse range of responses. Some introjected negative characterizations by doing all they could to become like their more privileged counterparts and shed the opprobrium of externally imposed negative identities. Others actively disrupted the culture of the schools, resisted assimilation, and tried to sustain their personal beliefs and traditional cultural habits and values. Still others, after the 1960s engaged in systematic political action that aimed to reorganize the structures of representation and opportunity within the schools.

Yet another vein of historical research has centered around the school life of immigrant children for whom the world of schools has been a world of strangers, a world in which their family names oft times inspired ridicule, where English was a foreign language, the culture of clocks and bells was alien, teachers were strangers, and economic opportunities for their families unstable and discriminatory. These schools, in effect, invited serial generations of first, second, and third generation immigrants to question their identities, to rethink their cultural traditions, to find ways to adapt to the force of unfamiliar circumstance, to reconcile life in family and neighborhood with life in the street and the nation, and somehow invent new identities.

Finally, the historical literatures reveal the evolution of youth-generated social practices that developed outside the orbit of public high schools. They have become known through the diagnostic, moral, and social labels affixed to their members by social scientists, journalists, and consumer marketers. This group inspired fear among adults, but served as important role models for school going young people. "Juvenile delinquents," "gamblers and bums," "transient youth," "zoot suiters," "Pachukos" and V-Girls, emerged in the first half of the century while Rock 'n Rollers, "Dropouts," "push-outs," "hippies," "cats," "beats," and "rebels" set new standards of misbehavior in the 1960s, 1970s, and 1980s.

These four youth-defined, generationally-based practices emerged in specific economic, political, social and demographic circumstances. They began as inventions of schooled young people who, between 1920 and 1950 attended high schools that were culturally, racially, and economically encapsulated. A new and larger school going generation would, in the 1960s and 1970s—amplify, politicize, and enlarge the terrain of social action.

What follows is an exploration of youth cultures as particular groups of young people fashioned them, rather than as reformers imagined or hoped them to be. Because of the relative paucity of secondary historical studies which attend to the role of schools in the forming of youth cultures, or the role of youth cultures in the forming of high school policies and practices, and because the secondary historical literatures rarely focus on the school experiences of immigrants of color, or on African American and Native American minorities, this exploration of youth social practices is necessarily tentative, partial rather than comprehensive, suggestive rather than definitive, in progress rather than fully developed. This article is an interpretive assay through multiple literatures that reveal the contours of youth cultures as young people fashioned and experienced them. It focuses on public rather than private schools, on junior and senior high schools, rather than colleges and universities, unless of course the youth-driven practices of the colleges and universities inspired high school students to import them (Fass, 1981, p. 64). By necessity, we have explored this important intersection by presenting a series of snapshots or vignettes of youth-defined norms and practices, rather than by constructing a traditional historical narrative that documents change in strictly linear ways—an important historical task which compels the attention of future historians.

A substantial portion of this chapter centers on the emergence of youth defined practices from the 1920s, when modern patterns of growing up began to emerge, to the mid 1970s when the outlines of contemporary youth culture had became visible (Modell, 1989, p. 119). During this fifty-year period, high school attendance had become a near universal reality, the number and diversity of college and university students increased exponentially, and the consuming capacity of teenagers had become formidable. It was also during the half century from 1920 to 1970 that teen-age peer groups acquired sufficient economic, political, and cultural power to influence the structure of social relations, standards of behaviors, patterns of spending, the shape of leisure time, and the forms of entertainment that governed their lives. From 1950 to 1975, when almost all young people attended high school for sustained periods of time, a coalition of politically invested youth deepened their political influence and challenged the stratificatory realities within which race, gender, and class relations had been bound. As we shall see, the emergence of youth-generated cultural forms did not happen all at once, nor in the same way for different classes of students.

Over the three decades from 1920 to 1950, more and more students spent more and more time in schools.[5] Within these socially, racially and culturally encapsulated educational institutions, glimmers of youth cultures began to emerge. Among the most visible were those of white middle class students who turned to their peer groups to remake the structure of social relations, transform courting practices, initiate forms of romantic love, extend periods of semi-dependency, and otherwise contribute to a process that delayed parenthood, and re-crafted the terms of their growing up. The period from 1920–1950 was also an era when young Native Americans like their immigrant counterparts, learned to resist the pressures of Americanization in schools. The thirty years between 1920 and 1950 were times when second and third generation white immigrants and Native Americans invented new identities as Americans and as ethnic minorities.

Some imported street and work-defined habits of association into the schools and introduced alternative dating, dressing, and driving habits while others created student countercultures within the school, and still others crafted and mobilized an academic subculture. This thirty-year period was also one during which well born college-going African Americans in historically black colleges in the south and in large urban centers engaged high school young people in youth-generated political campaigns to create access to high schools and equalize the condition of schools. It was also a time when social class divisions within the black community would serve as a focal point for the emergence of a distinct student-generated status system for those who attended junior and senior high schools for sustained periods of time.

Privileged Ones

There have been serial generations of privileged young people who have entered schools in possession of English language skills, high status social standing, prestigious racial characteristics, school-compatible habits of association, and sufficient discretionary time and income to construct social practices that ordered their own social lives, protected their privacy, mediated adult authority, and excluded unwanted outsiders.[6] For middle class youth and prosperous members of the working classes the "…material prosperity of the 1920s provided . . . access to the telephone, family cars, and a certain modicum of 'by rights' discretionary spending . . . (Modell, 1989, p. 70). It was a time when a dance craze had overtaken parts of the nation and dance halls, movie theaters, and automobiles began to transform the uses of leisure for urban dwellers. It was also a time when young people of privilege and relative prosperity discovered "personal gratification," material satisfaction, and individual choice-making as appropriate modes of being. These were times when dropping out of high school was a voluntary activity without negative social or economic consequences for this privileged class of students. If they dropped out, they could become clerks, tellers, salesmen, agents, and were thus able to maintain their socioeconomic status without the effort of long term study (Fass, 1977).

The school life literatures suggest that some groups of school attendees, like those of privileged teen aged young men and women, would help to construct the rules and regulations that governed their social life in schools and in the process restructure the forms of association that governed their lives.

Among the more visible, flamboyant, and influential classes of rebellious young people were those who described themselves as flappers. They were privileged white college-going young women who bridled against the moral and social constraints of a generation of socially conservative Victorian elders and moral fundamentalists (Fass, 1977). They had acquired new status as semi dependent young women with sufficient freedom to escape the confines of family and school government and sufficient time and money to experiment with new forms of aesthetic and sexual expression, social relations, and mental habits. Flappers cut their hair, shortened their skirts, smoke, drank, danced, dieted, and enjoyed jazz. They engaged in the kinds of activities that moral traditionalists labeled as "rude passion, Negro lewdness, sensuous movement" (pp. 19–22). They claimed emotional and sexual emancipation. "Devoted to truth and candor, they refused to accept the counsel of their elders; [claiming that] they had to experience life for themselves and to snatch its pleasures at a hurried pace..." (p. 22). Flappers, as Paula Fass describes them, were hedonistic young women who were less interested in political liberation and women's suffrage or social and economic justice than they were in moral and sexual emancipation. They championed equal sexual freedoms for men and women and as Fass has observed "changed the country's notion of what marriage could be" (pp. 328–329).

Dating, Dancing, Parking, Petting, and Proms

The social practices of flappers, while not reproduced exactly in the high schools of the early twentieth century were reflected in the forms that social relations began to take. Students who could afford to withdraw from wage-earning, remain in schools, carry the costs of extracurricular activities, and commercial entertainment, would invent and/or borrow a variety of rituals that governed group behavior, constituted insiders and outsiders, and created an array of peer-based communities that shaped the forms of association governing relations between boys and girls, young men and young women, and students of different social classes, races, and ethnicities.

The emergence of dating, of clubs and secret societies, team sports, and a variety of extracurricular activities regularized the experience of school going youth, differentiated students across boundaries of social class, race, religion, and gender, and constituted competition, consumption, conformity, and sexuality as important social values.

Dating emerged as a social practice in the 1920s and 1930s and has continued unabated as an important form of social relations in high schools. The invention of dating originated in two other social spaces—among flappers in the colleges and universities and among lower class urban youth, particularly young women, who sought refuge from crowded apartment houses without visiting space (Bailey, 1988; Fass, 1977). Dating was a social practice that linked boys and girls in mutually agreed upon facsimiles of courtship with rules and regulations overseen by age peers rather than parents or teachers, in an informal system of gossip where the rules of restraint were written and rewritten continually (Bailey, 1988; Modell, 1989). Boys would assume the financial burdens of increasingly commercialized leisure time activities while girls could set standards that governed sexual relationships. As Beth L. Bailey (1988) has observed, "the regulations that grew up to govern dating codified women's inequality and ratified men's power. Men asked women out; women were condemned as 'aggressive' if they expressed interest in a man too directly. Men paid for everything, but often with the implication that women 'owed' sexual favors in return. The dating system required men always to assume control, and women to act as men's dependents" (p. 24).

This quasi-contractual form of social practice introduced competition, conformity, and hierarchy into the peer culture of these high school students as indeed it had in the colleges (Fass, 1977). The peer group served as an unrelenting arbiter of status with highest honors going to those material young people who were well endowed with the right kind of paraphernalia, for example, cars, movie money, stylish clothing, nice make-up. As one might expect, young high school students would emerge as a new class of consumers in possession of sufficient discretionary money to attract the attention of marketers. Bobbysoxers and teen-agers emerged in the 1930s and 1940s with identities defined by quality of their possessions: particular kinds of shoes, gym clothes, class rings, life insurance policies, pens, typewriters, Fleishman's yeast (to clean up complexions), yearbooks, access to cars, and more (Palladino, 1996, p. 53). They would become famous for driving "as fast as their little cars could carry them" (p. 52).

As the children of prosperity, these high-school going young people, integrated market values as well as commercial interests into their social practices—a condition which has continued to the present day for substantial numbers of high school students. Indeed, their identities appear to have been importantly shaped by its commercial qualities. As one, oblivious apparently to his economic and social good luck was to remark: "High school bobby-soxers have been subjected to some of the most cruel and prejudicial criticisms ever heaped upon a group of people and we ARE people" he insisted, even if "we like to dance . . . wear dirty saddle-shoes, date, drink cokes, and other normal things" (Palladino, 1996, p. 84).

Fraternities, Sororities, and Social Clubs

Not only did middle class high school students introduce competition, consumption, and popularity into the youth culture of the school, they also created and joined fraternities, sororities, and other secret societies, sponsored an array of extracurricular activities, and emerged as boosters and supporters of high school athletic teams (Graebner, 1987, p. 412).

Through secret societies, fraternities or sororities, curriculum-related literary societies, debating teams, athletic competitions, etc., affluent students created exclusive self-regulating communities, through which they could acquire a modicum of self-government, nurture friendships, expand their own social networks, buffer themselves from unwanted students and adult supervision, and reproduce the social hierarchies of the larger society.

Those involved in secret societies, fraternities and sororities, devised elaborate rites of passage, for example, initiation rituals, hazing periods, pledge "slaves," masters, paddlings, secret codes—all designed to define insiders and outsiders. In spite of organized opposition from an array of progressive reformers, parents, and journalists who viewed the societies as hierarchical, discriminatory, and degrading, fraternities and sororities persisted until the 1950s and so too did the variety of regalia that distinguished their members: rings, pins, sweat shirts, jackets (satin or corduroy, and in colors), insignias (owl, trojan . . .) (Graebner, 1987, p. 417).

School clubs, like fraternities and sororities, also reflected divisions of interest within the student body. In a study of extracurricular activities among high school goers in ten large multiethnic high schools in New York City in the 1930s and 1940s, Paula Fass concluded that school activities "took on a distinctly ethnic cast" (Fass, 1998, p. 97). For example, Black male adolescents dominated track and were sometimes active in basketball. White native, Italian, German and Irish male adolescents played football. " Girls were more typically involved in literary activities and Jewish females dominated. German and native white women were also quite active on the school newspaper, but Italian, black and Irish women were consistently underrepresented, as they were in other publications" (p. 99) While we know very little about the status hierarchies that might have existed, it would stretch credulity to imagine that privileged adolescents in the first half of the century, typically set out to overturn existing racial, ethnic, and socioeconomic hierarchies.

Team Sports and Popularity

The emergence of team sports constitutes one of the more enduring inventions of high school life. In their classic study of "Middletown" a small town in the Midwest, Robert and Helen Lynd, in a gentle critique of school life in this Midwestern town, revealed the growing importance of club life, school spirit, and team sports as motivating activities initiated by and for the young. Pep, rallies, cheer leaders, athletes, school spirit, like the practice of dating, reinforced commitments to competition, conformity, and individual merit (Lynd & Lynd, 1929).

Looked at whole, the world created by privileged high school students from 1900 to 1950, seems to have been a world in which buying power, athletic prowess, sexual knowledge, physical beauty, club membership, and access to a car would define status and prestige. This does not necessarily mean that these students were entirely disengaged from academic study, social service, or political involvement. Nor does it mean that all students were similarly motivated. Rather, it appears that a dominant group carved their identities less around what they knew than what they owned, and set the standards for others to emulate or resist.

FROM IMMIGRANT TO ETHNIC MINORITY: SOUTHERN AND EAST EUROPEAN YOUTH

For the youthful progeny of working class parents who, in the early decades of the twentieth century, "owned little or no property, received little or no formal education, and worked for wages of piece rates at skilled or unskilled jobs" (Nasaw, 1985), attendance at high school was occasional and participation in after school activities unusual, at least until the late 1930s and 1940s when economic opportunities had diminished, new child labor laws were stringently enforced, academic credentials had acquired new importance, and substantial numbers of second and third generation ethnic progeny entered high schools in unprecedented numbers.

Serial generations of eastern and southern European, East Asian, and Latino young people entered public schools where an elaborate machinery of cultural assimilation awaited them. Within these citadels of Americanization, immigrant young people would learn to straddle three alternatively configured worlds: the traditional worlds of their families and churches; the entrepreneurial world of the streets; and the prefabricated academic and social world of the schools.

The schools, by the very nature of their academic and social processes, invited students to question their identities, to rethink their cultural traditions, to find ways to adapt to the force of unfamiliar circumstance, to reconcile life in family and neighborhood with lives in the street and the nation, and somehow invent new identities for themselves.

For this group of young people, earning money and going to school were not mutually exclusive activities. In the early decades of the twentieth century a separate "kiddie labor market" claimed their time outside school hours and the streets as well as the schools provided defining contexts. As David Nasaw (1985) has observed of young working class boys in the early twentieth century, the schools had a part, if only a small one, in broadcasting the requirements for success in rapidly evolving urban centers. "In the movie theaters, on the newspaper pages, in school and on the streets, the children observed that material success appeared to come to those who spoke without accents, who dressed properly, who knew their way around the city…" After all, to be an "Americano [or a Sicilian who behaved like an 'Americanoo'] was a sign that you were getting on in the world" (p. 197).

Young urban entrepreneurs were apparently undeterred by the civilizing rituals of the schools, even those of night schools where the rules and regulations were particularly harsh and intrusive.

> Silence! Silence! Silence! This was the characteristic feature of our existence at the Soup School. You never made an unnecessary noise or said an unnecessary word. Outside in the hall we lined up any size, girls in one line and boys in another without uttering a sound. Eyes front and at attention. Lord help you if you broke the rule of silence . . . The piano struck up a march and from the hall we paraded into assembly . . . We stood at attention as the Bible was read and at attention as the flag waved back and forth, and we sang the same song. I didn't know what the words meant but I sang it loudly with all the rest, in my own way, "Tree Cheers for De Red Whatzam Blu!" But best of all was another song . . . and we sang it with great gusto, "Honest boys who never tread the streets." This was in the days when we not only trod the streets but practically lived in them. (Cavallo, 1973)

Through the crucibles of street and school, thousands of European, Asian, and Hispanic immigrants would learn to speak English, brush their teeth, adopt Americanized names, cultivate a modicum of street smarts, engage in the world of developing commerce, and participate in an evolving youth-specific street culture that distinguished them from their immigrant parents on the one hand, and from their middle class or, as the case might be, white counterparts on the other. As intercultural interlocutors for their families, immigrant youth created a culture that was distinguished not only by their capacity to adapt to the force of social, economic, and political circumstance, but to set themselves as a generation part–straddling the traditional worlds of the family and the cultural and social requirements of the schools (Berrol, 1997).

Their children, second and third generation ethnic minority groups, would enter high schools in the 1930s and 1940s in possession of an array of social habits, communicative styles, and dress codes which might not necessarily mirror those of their more affluent counterparts. There is so little systematic work on the evolving cultures of ethnic minority youngsters in schools before 1960 that we can, at this time, only speculate on the forms and effects they might have had. There are suggestions that some of the students did all that they could to fit themselves into the existing cultures of the school and to blend imperceptibly into the culture created by more privileged students within the schools. This is an important emphasis in the work of James Coleman who, in his pioneering work *The Adolescent Society*, has documented the existence in the 1950s of a powerful, commodity driven youth subculture that compelled allegiance from large majorities of the student body (Coleman, 1961). There are also reasons to believe that some classes of immigrant youth—the progeny of Jewish and Japanese minorities, looked at schools as structures of opportunity, as well as sites of discrimination and elevated the importance of academic learning, created academically-related clubs, and crafted yet another kind of subculture: an academically determined one.

There are also reasons to believe that a substantial minority of working class ethnic-minority youth would craft an alternative subculture that owed as much to their involvement in the streets, the dance halls, and the taverns as it did to their involvement in the schools. When these young people entered schools in the 1930s, 1940s, and 1950s, they were commonly dispatched into specialized vocational tracks, labeled as academic low achievers, and disqualified from college bound program tracks that guaranteed access to higher status professional and corporate jobs. Within the structure of schools, it is possible that they introduced alternatives styles of dress, language use, competed for dates with the most popular girls, or with young women of their own class, modeled different forms of dating and mating, and even dropped out. Working class "cats," wore their hair greased back, listened to underground music—rhythm and blues, and rock and roll—and otherwise announced their alienation from the values of the school and the hegemony of their more affluent counterparts (Palladino, 1996, pp. 114–127). V-Girls dated older men, entertained soldiers, and crossed social class and racial boundaries to form their associations (Austin & Willard, 1998; Bailey, 1998; Espana-Maram, 1998; Garcia, 1998; Kelley, 1998). The evidence of their influence is visible in the anxieties of a generation of adults, who labeled some of their behaviors as delinquent and degenerate, called for the introduction of sex education, driver education, and new forms of "rehabilitation" in the schools (Gilbert, 1986; Hawes, 1997).

All of these manifestations of culture suggest that certain groups of working class young people might have created an alternative youth culture within the schools, redefined the meaning of physical beauty, the uses of discretionary money, the function of cars, and the conduct of gender relations. It was a subculture that emerged in opposition to the hegemony of middle class elite students and degrading educational practices that broadcast a certain level of academic inferiority—their placement in vocational tracks, their use of nonstandard English, their standing as difficult and unmanageable students. The sub culture of their creation, like those of their middle class counterparts, was not consciously political.

African Americans

The realities were different for African American students who, if they went to publicly supported schools at all in the first half of the century did so in a set of parallel educational universes.[7] Some attended racially segregated schools in the South, not uncommonly located on the grounds of historically black colleges, or in legally segregated all-black schools in big cities like Washington, DC, Little Rock, Arkansas, or Baltimore City. Others attended high schools in geographically encapsulated all-black settings in large urban centers in New York, Philadelphia, Los Angeles. Still others, who appear to be relatively prosperous professionals and skilled workers, those whom E. Franklin Frazier has called "upper caste" or "upper class" young people, might have attended all-black schools scattered throughout the country or entered multiethnic high schools in cities and towns where they enrolled in academic rather than vocational tracks (for demographic estimates in different settings, see, Fass, 1989; Franklin, 1979). Still other African American young people acquired their first opportunities to go to secondary schools in the wake of the Great Depression, when the federal government established both the Civilian Conservation Corps and, more importantly for African American young people, the National Youth Administration. A special unit for black young people, directed by Mary Macleod Bethune, established all black Defense Training Schools which, by 1935, had enrolled more than 200,000 students. Finally, there were opportunities for specialized vocational training within the military, which until 1951, sustained segregated units for African Americans (Fass, 1989).

While there are very few studies exploring African American student perspectives and practices within this diverse group of settings in the period from 1900 to 1950, there is reason to believe that youth-generated cultures evolved among a relatively small percentage of African American students who had sufficient means and/or motivation to remain in school for extended periods of time, to prepare for college, and/or generate age-defined social practices. A small, but evocative literature suggests that African American youth practices differed in important ways from those of their white counterparts.

First, there was a political dimension that has not yet, to my knowledge, been documented among white high school cohorts. African American high school students appear to have participated in youth-generated local political initiatives led by African American college and university students (Anderson, 1998, p. 19). Inspired by historic commitments to the liberating power of education, college and university students, in the 1920s and again in the early 1950s joined local political efforts to convince young people to stay in school, go to college, and do what they could to expose discrimination and racial inequalities. College and university students also joined religious leaders and community organizers to end gang fighting on the streets (Morgan, 1995). They led and participated in public demonstrations in 1919 in cities as far flung as New York, Chicago, Charleston, and Philadelphia.

Heightened political sensitivity was not only the product of college and university student initiatives. High school students too were not without political sensibilities. African Americans went to school in settings which broadcast their separate and inferior status. Indeed, racism and discrimination were everywhere evident in the structure of schools. Views of black intellectual inferiority were encoded in the textbooks, the expectations of teachers, and the structure of student life in schools. It was visible as well in the poor quality of buildings and the decaying nature of equipment. Indeed, published historical literatures on black school life suggest that African American youth were indignant about these practices. Some seemed to have invented what we now understand as a politics of identity: One sixteen year old, who went to school in the 1930s called attention to the importance of role models:

> I've often wondered why we didn't study more about Booker T. Washington than George Washington! No matter how much I try, I can never be George Washington. What he did, he did for his own people—what Booker T. Washington did, he did for my people. In school, we seldom ever hear about Negroes. If it wasn't for Negro History week, we'd know a whole lot less. (Frazier, 1967, p. 105)

Another student expressed deep dissatisfaction with the nature of historical representations in school:

> The school system should include a great deal more about Negroes in its curriculum. There's not much use of a Negro becoming famous unless he can stand as an example for others to follow. And to follow such a man, the schools must do their share to keep before Negro children those who have met with success as they've done with Thomas Jefferson, Washington, Lincoln, and others. (Frazier, 1967, p. 110)

The historical literature suggests that racism and discrimination did not necessarily result only in heightened political awareness. Black high school students also constructed a different kind of status system, built among other things, upon caste as well as class. Indeed, there is evidence to suggest that skin color became an important marker of popularity, social status, marriageability, and fitness for further education, even within all black settings. E. Franklin Frazier's exploration of *Negro Youth at the Crossroads,* documents the importance of skin color as well as wealth, dress, athletic ability, leadership capacities, and family background as a basis for popularity, leadership, fitness for marriage, etc.

> When an upper class boy was asked who was the most popular, he answered in this way; He is popular because he dresses well, is a handsome devil, is a star on most of the teams, takes part in almost all the school activities, is an

officer of the cadet unit, has a car, and money. There are very, very few that could meet all those qualifications. To top it all he is a good student and is well liked by the teachers. His father is a popular professional man and that has a lot to do with it. He has one holdback—he isn't quite light enough for some of the students and teachers, but despite that "he's all right." (Frazier, 1967, p. 105)

Color also constituted a basis for club membership and the choice of student leaders. The following description of a cadet core is illustrative: "officers were usually light boys or light-brown skin. Often, they would bawl out dark boys for the same infractions which they would pass over in a light boy. I look upon this as petty abuse and a copy of white psychology toward all Negroes."

Complaints about discriminatory practices visited by light-skinned students on darker ones, punctuate the observations of lower caste young people in black schools, and reveal a form of race-based informal socialization patterns.

They [the lighter boys and girls] don't want to be around you and they act "hinkty." They go around with those that look like they do. The lighter ones stick together most of the time . . . One day I wanted to be with some of them, and they walked away and wouldn't associate with me . . . One day . . . a girl wanted something I had and I wouldn't give it to her . . . She said: "Oh go on away, you old black nigger."

The following oft uttered piece of doggerel, remembered by both upper and lower caste students in Washington, DC and Baltimore also punctuates issues of caste:

If you're light you're all right
If you're Brown, Stick Around,
If you're black, Get Back.

Unlike their white counterparts, African American students did not appear to have cultivated or participated in an elaborate dating system that delayed ultimate sexual gratification until after marriage. John Modell (1989) has suggested that black students "socialized commonly in large mixed-age settings of various sorts" and has documented a certain quality of sexual restraint among "respectable" black girls, who because they married earlier, had no need to cultivate an elaborate system of petting and necking (pp. 90–91).

Beyond the demographic differences between white and black high school students, there were communal habits of association that might have discouraged exclusive, long term relationships between two people, muted tensions between the older and younger generation, and revealed commitments to schooling. As one fifteen-year-old remarked:

> My father has no regular job and I have some more little sisters and a brother. Friends have told me I ought to marry. But I want to go through high school. I haves a good home and very sweet loving parents. There is a boy who loves me and ask me to marry. But I refuse.

For African American students who attended integrated schools as a small student minority, there is evidence to suggest that they were not as deeply involved in the extracurriclum of the schools. Nor were they likely to achieve leadership roles, not at least within the structures of integrated schooling. In fact, some have documented a certain quality of loneliness and disengagement (Fass, 1989, p. 81; Frazier, 1967).

Native Americans

As early as 1900, an emergent native American youth culture evolved in off reservation boarding schools for Native Americans. Designed to "civilize" Native American young people, detach them from the tribal authorities, and immerse them in Americanization processes, boarding schools nonetheless enabled Native American youth to carve particular terrains of freedom and resist the cultural hegemony of nineteenth and early twentieth-century reformers. Indeed, Native American youth would invent themselves as keepers of tradition, agents of cultural resistance, and within their own tribes as carriers of an alien culture to their families. A draconian set of rules called on them to forsake hunting in favor of carpentry, shoemaking, and farming, traditionally considered as women's work in Native American communities. School authorities also required students to forsake their tribal identities, to wear American style clothing, abandon the use of their native languages, and even remain silent at meals" (Coleman, 1984, p. 284). Boarding schools, as Margaret Szasz (1997) has observed, "had a virtual monopoly over the native child for up to nine months in a single year, and sometimes for several years without a break" (p. 351).

Unable to control the force of circumstance in these total institutions, some students ran away. Others clashed with boarding school authorities. Those students who remained, carved alternative sites for the preservation of Native American culture. Relatively unsupervised at night, they shared tribal myths, native stories, and admired Native American heroes and heroines (Bloom, 1998).

Native American youth were sufficiently resistant to find small spaces within which to sustain commitments to the power of tradition and the heroic myths with which they had grown up. In the crucible of these settings, young native Americans discovered their common heritage, learned to protect it, united across boundaries of tribes, together, resisted assimilation, and made boxing their special province, much to the chagrin of education authorities. Gathered together under boarding school roofs from many different tribes and regions of the country, they transformed the circumstances of forced captivity into opportunities to cultivate a "sense of kinship and broader Native American Identity." They were however, without ample power to transform the structural realities which governed their lives in school (West, 1996).

Like their immigrant ethnic counterparts in big cities, Native Americans school goers, would, perforce, blend their identities as both mainstream and Native Americans, and through this means emerge as a generation apart. Don Talyesva, a Hopi who went to a federal boarding school in California, illustrates the kind of cultural dilemma suffered by Native Americans:

> With marriage I began a life of toil and discovered that education had spoiled me for making a living in the desert. I was not hardened to heavy work in the heat and dust and I did not know how to get rain, control winds, or even predict good and bad weather. I could not grow young plants in dry, wind-beaten, and worm-infested sand drifts; nor could I shepherd a flock of sheep through storm, drought, and disease. I might even lead my family into starvation and be known as the poorest man in Oraibi—able-bodied but unable to support a wife. (Szasz, 1997, p. 330)

As we have seen, the contours of at least four distinct youth subcultures had emerged within the crucible of public secondary education during the period from1920 to 1950. There was the subculture created by privileged young people who had transformed the nature of social relations, expanded the boundaries of sexual expression, created innovative forms of leisure time-use, mediated the content of mass culture, set standards of taste that would endure for generations, and inspire a new set of anxieties among social reformers (Gilbert, 1986). There was the dilemma-filled world of immigrant and working class young people who entered school in possession of traditional and sometimes old-world cultural habits, wage-earning experience, and street cultivated entrepreneurial skills. Forced to mediate the quadruple pressures of home, work, street, and school, they blended identities with admixtures of new social practices, aesthetic preferences, academic preoccupations, and for some of them, elaborate counter-cultural repertoires. For African-Americans, the effects of racism and discrimination in schools constituted a defining context for the nurture of a political subculture on the one hand, and an exquisitely calibrated caste-based status system on the other. Finally, the forced involvement of Native-American young people in boarding schools required and inspired the cultivation of habits of heart, mind, and association that not only distinguished them as an age cohort and alienated them from their families, but inspired an age-specific subculture that was deeply countercultural.

Over the quarter-century from 1950 to 1975, students from across the social spectrum—returning veterans of World war II, women workers retired from war-related industries, newly prospering working class, African American, and Native American youth spent more and more time together in high schools, colleges, and universities.[8] They attended schools which were bigger, more comprehensive, and more diverse than high schools of the earlier twentieth century.[9]

When they entered schools, they were in possession of larger stores of discretionary spending money than their prewar counterparts (Modell, 1989, p. 322), and, in the wake of an historic series of court decisions, legislative enactments, local political initiatives, and action in behalf of civil rights, with newly acquired political sensibilities, visions of entitlement, and a sense of generational distinction.

A newly empowered transcultural coalition of young people elaborated an array of political and countercultural repertoires that had been the exclusive preserve of less privileged young people in the earlier decades of the twentieth century. An important focus was on the transformation of schools. Some joined political efforts to desegregate schools. Elite and working class white college students joined black freedom fighters on the front lines of social change and "demanded social justice, not just the privileges of class" (Palladino, 1996, pp. 187–188). Under the auspices of organizations like the National Association for the Advancement of Colored People and the Southern Christian Leadership Conference, college and university students participated in sit-ins in apartment buildings, lunch counters, and schools, and, imbued with principles of nonviolence, went south as freedom riders to reveal and dismantle the discriminatory structures of U.S. life (Urban & Wagoner, 2000, p. 319).

High school students, for their part, mounted campaigns to integrate schools in rural, suburban, and urban public schools. They engaged in school boycotts, joined marches to demand "quality integrated education…," and in large urban high schools, launched efforts to include courses in black history (Franklin, 2000). Native American high school students took time from school to participate in the long march to Wounded Knee, and joined campaigns to return control over public education to tribal authorities (Urban & Wagoner, 2000, p. 319; also personal interviews with Ojibwe and Dakota educators in Minneapolis, March 2001).

Adopting new hair styles and forms of dress, politically inspired African American and Native American high school students symbolized new and proud identities (Kelley, 1998). As one observer suggested: "Today's black students are different from their counterparts of twenty years ago, owing to social changes of many kinds. They have a new race consciousness and feelings of unity..."(Fish, 1970, p. 6). Young women in colleges, universities and high schools also transformed styles of dress, worked to break dress codes that had governed life in schools in the first half of the century, and sought entrance into male dominated courses. There is some work suggesting that gay students "came out" during this period.

> The destiny of being a wife, a mother a teacher, a servant to a man never appealed to me. Who the hell wanted to do that? By being butch I could swagger and strut: I could be abrupt and assertive. I wore my hair in a DA [duck's ass]. When I went to school I combed it into a brush-up so it looked vaguely feminine. I also wore men's clothes—since I was big and they fit me better than women's clothes. (Sears, 1998, p. 179)

The rules and regulations of the high schools also became objects of student protests in the 1960s and 1970s. The rock group Pink Floyd gave voice to these sentiments in their top of the charts favorite "We don't need no education. We don't need no thought control." Movies such as *To Sir with Love* and *Blackboard Jungle* constituted a Hollywood reflection of youth discontent in schools. Some students recognized the structured inequalities of the schools and articulated a form of cross-class sensitivity that was not in evidence in earlier decades of the century.

> High school is used to put people in various slots. It puts black people or poor people into slots—they will be working class. People like us here will go to college and flounder around in the arts. We are not supposed to have any consciousness of what goes on in working kids' minds . . . kids are coming to realize one another's needs and want to break out of this classification system. . . . (Fish, 1970, p. 6)

Publicly voiced complaints about teachers also emerged during this period. "He acts toward us like we're animals..." (Fish, 1970, p. 4). "Us Black students didn't get one demand, not one!" (p. 4). Some school-directed protests turned violent and involved the police. "they [students] invaded the superintendent's office, sprayed Coca-Cola in his face, and blew smoke at him while he awaited help from the police..." (p. 7).

Antiwar sentiments also inspired high school students to protest the Viet Nam war publicly. One of the more successful protests involved a group of Iowa high school students, who had worn black arm bands as a symbol of protest against the war, had a brush with police who sprayed them with mace. The students faced administrative discipline and expulsion for disobeying administrative regulation. They petitioned the federal courts, and in a landmark Supreme Court Decision *Tinker v. DesMoines* (1969), acquired the right to free expression on matters of dress in school (Urban & Wagoner, 2000, p. 338).

The disposition of high school students to reach across social class and race to form new patterns of association was not only reflected in political activities, but in their aesthetic preferences, buying habits, and definition of heroes and heroines as well. Elvis Presley, the Beatles, and Jimmy Hendrix became role models for high school students across the country. As one historian, Grace Palladino (1996), has suggested, "Rock 'n' roll was everything that middle class parents feared: elemental, savage, dripping with sexuality, qualities that respectable society usually associated with depraved classes" (p. 155).

From the 1950s to the mid 1970s, a newly empowered transcultural coalition of young expanded the boundaries of privacy and freedom, acquired real political power, sought to remake the structure of gender relations, and to unravel the degrading affects of assimilation, racism, sexism and homophobia. They became architects of what social commentators have called rebellious, alienated, and countercultural youth practices.

The emergent power, visibility, and dissident quality of youth-cultures was reflected in the appearance in the 1960s and 1970s of a proliferation of books by academic sociologists and psychologists who named and typed the array of youth-generated social forms. There were delinquents, radicals, and Bohemians; college, vocational, academic and nonconformist; professionalist, vocationalist, collegiate, ritualist, academic, intellectual, left activist, and hippy; politically apathetic youth, alienated youth, individualist youth, activist youth, constructivist youth, and antisocial youth (see Braungart, 1975, pp. 265–266; Goodman, 1956; Roszak, 1969). The increasing power of peer groups was also reflected in the proliferation of labels affixed to young people who dropped out of school and elaborated a parallel universe of drugs, sex, and rock n roll.

These classification systems, like the youth cultures which they describe, failed to take account of the existence and stability of classes of young people who sustained social traditions which adolescents had created in the 1930s, 1940s, and early 1950s. Nor did the labels integrate the contours of youth cultures as they evolved among serial generations of new immigrant students who continued to experience the counter pressures of family, school, and peer group. Like immigrant youth before them, they struggled with their identities, aimed to reconcile the traditions of their families with the traditions of a commercially and socially powerful peer culture, became, on occasion politically active, and introduced new social practices to their more mainstream counterparts.

CONCLUSION

The rebellious youth cultures which originated in the 1960s and 1970s have I believed, contributed to a mistaken view of adolescent culture as essentially rebellious, dissident, and countercultural. As we have seen, youth generated social practices are diverse and historically situated. They have emerged out of a crucible of changing economic, demographic, social, political, ideological, and educational circumstances and contingencies.

An historical perspective on adolescence suggests that, as an organized stage of life, adolescence is here to stay. It is stable, not only because it is biologically distinct or psychologically particular, but also because it is embedded in the deep structures of the society. This brief historical foray has suggested that the contours of adolescent subcultures are likely to remain relatively stable unless young people themselves acquire yet more power or invent new realities, or fundamental changes in the economic, political, social, and educational organization of the society evolve.

ACKNOWLEDGMENT

I am deeply indebted to Caroline Eick, a doctoral candidate at the University of Maryland, College Park, for her tireless research efforts and enthusiastic and intelligent participation throughout the preparation of this chapter.

NOTES

1.   An excellent review of historical perspectives can be found in Fuller (1983). See also Gillis (1974), Platt (1969), Schlossman (1977), and Kett (1970).

2.   These sentiments suffuse those books of the Bible which enjoin fathers to instruct their sons in proper conduct toward women, the weak, the intemperate, etc. It is especially clear in "Proverbs, "and "Ecclesiastes."

3.   Going to school was an occasional experience and a highly differentiated one for youth who grew up in the late nineteenth and early decades of the twentieth century. As historian William Reese has noted, "Going to school was often a one-or two-year experience. High schools resembled a pyramid with a very wide base . . . Whether in male, female or coeducational schools, juniors and seniors were rare." Public high schools served both middle and working class students in thousands of neighborhoods across the U.S., but only the more privileged attended on a systematic and sustained basis until graduation. In more isolated rural area schooling proceeded in "broken doses." A system of reformatories emerged for youth labeled as "delinquent." A separate system of federally supported boarding schools served substantial numbers of Native American youth, on a year-round basis. Yet another network of relatively underfinanced and typically segregated grammar schools provided education for young African Americans in teacher education colleges in the plantation south, in selected urban centers, and in an array of

agricultural communities throughout the country. There were also grammar and high schools for Asian students on the west coast, for Mexicans in the South west and for girls, Catholics, for Jews, and German speakers scattered throughout the nation.

4.   By far the most useful work on progressivism in education is that of Lawrence A. Cremin, *The Transformation of the School*, Progressivism in American Education: 1873–1970, later expanded as *American Education: The Metropolitan Experience*. New York: Alfred A.Knopf, 1988.

5.   Historical demographers have documented an increase of 650% in high school enrollment, a considerable bulge in the wake of the Great Depression when scarcities in the urban wage labor market, and urbanizing processes throughout the country, led more young people to withdraw from the labor force and enter schools. Increases continued unabated until world war II when a variety of working and lower class minorities joined the military, National Youth Administration or Civilian Conservation Corps until the wake of World War II, when high schooling became near universal for the first time.

6.   One of the more dramatic developments was the tendency of relatively privileged girls and boys in schools to stay in school into the upper grades. Where as in 1900, only about 8% of persons between 14 and 17 years of age attended high schools, by 1910 the percentage grew to 15%, by 1920 to 32%, by the 1930s in the wake of the Great Depression, to more than half of the high school age population. By the end of the 1950s more than 50% of the privileged population would go on to schools.

7.   It is important to note that high school attendance remained occasional for large numbers of African American youth until after 1950. For example, in Philadelphia, 32% of the black population was enrolled in secondary schools, and almost all took academic or college preparatory courses. A large majority enrolled in all black secondary schools. (Blacks represented only 18.3% of the city population; see, Franklin, 1979).

8.   Between 1940 and 1960, the average number of students per public secondary school increased by nearly 50% between 1946 and 1960 and more than 77% of them were between 14 and 17 years of age. High school retention rates for Native Americans began climbing and by the 1980s and 1990s reached 75%.

9.   To accommodate this growing cadre of students, a coalition of academics, social reformers, government officials, and professional educators invented the comprehensive high school which combined both vocational and academic curricula in a single geographic site.

REFERENCES

Anderson, J.S. (1988). *The education of Blacks in the South, 1860–1935*. Chapel Hill: University of North Carolina Press.

Austin, J., & Willard, M.N. (1998). *Generations of youth: Youth culture and history in twentieth-century America*. New York: New York University Press.

Bailey, B.L. (1988). *From front porch to back seat: Courtship in twentieth century America*. Baltimore: The Johns Hopkins University Press.

Bailey, B. (1998). From panty raids to revolution: Youth and authority 1950–1970 (pp. 187–205). In J. Austin & M.N. Willard (Eds.), *Generations of youth: Youth culture and history in twentieth-century America* (pp. 187–205). New York: New York University Press.

Berrol, S. (1997). Ethnicity and American children. In J. Hawes & N.R. Hiner (Eds.), *American childhood* (pp. 343–377). Westport, CT: Greenwood Press.

Bloom, J. (1998). Rolling with the punches: Boxing, youth culture, and ethnic idfentity at federal Indian boarding schools during the 1930s. In J. Austin & M. Willard (Eds.), *Generations of youth: Youth culture and history in twentieth century America* (pp. 65–81). New York: New York University Press.

Braungart, R.G. (1975). Youth and social movements. In S.E. Dragastin & G.H. Elder (Eds.), *Adolescence in the life cycle: Psychological change and social context.* New York: John Wiley and Sons.

Cavallo, L. (1973). The heart is the teacher. Quoted in S. Cohen (Ed.), *Education in the United States: A documentary history* (Vol. 4, pp. 2153–2155). New York: Random House.

Coleman, J.S. (1961). *The adolescent society: The social life of the teenager and its impact on education.* Glencoe, NY: The Free Press.

Coleman, M. (1984). The responses of Indian children to Presbyterian schooling in the nineteenth-century: An analysis through missionary sources. *History of Education Quarterly, 27*, 473–497.

Demos, J., & Demos, V. (1969, November). Adolescence in historical perspective. *Journal of Marriage and the Family,* (Special Issue).

Dewey, J. (1896). The university school. *University Record, I.*

Espana-Maram, L.N. (1998). Brown 'hordes' in Macintosh suits: Filipinos, taxi dance halls, and performing the immigrant body in Los Angeles, 1930s–1940s. (pp. 118–136). In J. Austin & M.N. Willard (Eds.), *Generations of youth: Youth culture and history in twentieth-century America* (pp. 118–136). New York: New York University Press.

Fass, P.S. (1998). Creating new identities: Youth and ethnicity in New York City high schools in the 1930s and 1940s. In J. Austin & M.N. Willard (Eds.), *Generations of youth: Youth culture and history in twentieth century America* (pp. 95–117). New York: New York University Press.

Fass, P.S. (1989). *Outside in: Minorities and the transformation of American education.* New York: Oxford University Press.

Fass, P.S. (1981). The world of youth: The peer society of the 1920s. In M. Albin & D. Cavallo (Eds.), *Family life in America, 1620–2000.* New York: Revisionary Press.

Fass, P.S. (1977). *The damned and the beautiful: American youth in the 1920s.* New York: Oxford University Press.

Finkelstein, B. (1997). Casting networks of good influence: The reconstruction of childhood in the United States, 1790–1870. In J. Hawes & N.R. Hiner (Eds.), *American childhood: A research guide and historical handbook* (pp. 111–153). Westport, CT: Greenwood Press.

Finkelstein, B. (1987). The schooling of American childhood: 1920–1920. In M.L. Heineger et al. (Eds.), *A century of childhood.* Rochester, NY: Margaret Woodbury Strong Museum.

Fish, K.L. (1970). *Conflict and dissent in the high school.* New York: Bruce Publishing Company.

Franklin, V.P. (2000). Black high school student activism in the 1960s: An urban phenomenon? *Journal of Research in Education, 10*(1), 3–8.

Franklin, V.P. (1979). *The education of Black Philadelphia: The social and educational history of a minority community, 1900–1950.* Philadelphia: University of Pennsylvania Press.

Frazier, E.F. (1967). *Negro youth at the crossroads: Their personality development in the middle states.* New York: Scholar Books.

Fuller, B. (1983, July). Youth job structures and school enrollment, 1890–1920. *Sociology of Education, 56*, 145–156.

Garcia, M. (1998). Memories of El Monte: Intercultural dance halls in post-World War II greater Los Angeles. In J. Austin & M.N. Willard (Eds.), *Generations of youth: Youth culture and history in twentieth-century America* (pp. 157–173). New York: New York University Press.

Gilbert, J.B. (1986). *Cycles of outrage: America's reaction to the juvenile delinquent in the 1950s.* New York: Oxford University Press.

Gillis, J. (1974/1970). *Youth and history: Tradition and change in European age relations, 1970 -present.* New York: Academic Press.

Goodman, P. (1956). *Growing up absurd: Problems of youth in organized soceity.* New York: Vintage Books.

Graebner, W. (1987). Outlawing teenage populism: The campaign against secret societies in the American high school, 1900–1960. *Journal of American History 74*, 411–435.

Hall, G.S. (1904). *Adolescence: Its psychology and its relation to physiology, anthropology, sociology, sex, crime, religion and education* (2 vols.). New York: D. Appleton.

Hawes, J.M. (1997). *Children between the wars: American childhood, 1920 to 1940.* New York: Twayne Publishers.

Holt, L.E. (1897). *The diseases of infancy and childhood: For the use of students and practitioners of medicine.* New York: D. Appleton and Company.

Hunter, R. (1973). An answer to the problems of child life. Quoted in S. Cohen (Ed.), *Education in the United States: A documentary history* (Vol. 4). New York: Random House.

Kelley, R.D.G. (1998). The riddle of the zoot: Macolm Little and Black cultural politics during World War II. In J. Austin & M.N. Willard (Eds.), *Generations of youth: Youth culture and history in twentieth century America* (pp. 136–157). New York: New York University Press.

Kett, J.F. (1977). *Rites of passage: Adolescence in America, 1790 to the present.* New York: Basic Books.

Lassonde, S. (1994). The real, real youth problem. *Reviews in American History, 22*, 150.

Lynd, R.S., & Lynd, H. (1929). *Middletown.* New York: Harcourt, Brace.

Meyer, J., Tyack, D.B., Nagel, J., & Gordon, A. (1979). Public education as nation building in America: Enrollments and bureaucratization in the American States, 1870–1930. *American Journal of Sociology, 85*, 591–613.

Modell, J. (1989). *Into one's own: From youth to adulthood in the United States, 1920–1975.* Berkeley: University of California Press.

Modell, J., Furstenberg, F.F., Jr., & Hershberg, T. (1976). Social change and transitions to adulthood in historical perspective. *Journal of Family History 82*, 1–32.

Morgan, H. (1995). *Historical perspectives on the education of Black children.* Westport, CT: Praeger.

Nasaw, D. (1985). *Children of the city: At work and at play.* Garden City, NY: Anchor Press, 1985.

Odem, M.E. (2000). Delinquent daughters: The age of consent campaign. In P.S. Fass & M.A. Mason (Eds.), *Childhood in America* (pp. 494–499). New York: New York University Press.

Palladino, G. (1996). *Teenagers: An American history.* New York: Basic Books.

Platt, A.M. (1969). *The child savers: The invention of delinquency.* Chicago: University of Chicago Press.

Ross, D. (1972). *G. Stanley Hall: The psychologist as prophet.* Chicago: The University of Chicago Press.

Roszak, T. (1969). *The making of a counter culture: Reflections on the technocratic society and its youthful opposition.* Garden City, NY: Doubleday and Company, Inc.

Schlossman, S.S. (1977). *Love and the American delinquent.* Chicago: University of Chicago Press.

Sears, J.T. (1998). Growing up as a Jewish lesbian in South Florida: Queer teen life in the fifties. In J. Austin & M.N. Willard (Eds.), *Generations of youth: Youth culture and history in twentieth century America* (pp. 173–187). New York: New York University Press.

Szasz, M.C. (1997). Native American children. In J. Hawes & N.R. Hiner (Eds.), *American childhood: A research guide and historical handbook.* Westport, CT: Greenwood Press.

Teeter, R. (1988). Coming of age on the city streets in 19th-century America. *Adolescence 23*(92), 910.

Urban, W., & Wagoner, J. (2000). *American education: A history.* New York: McGraw Hill.

U.S. Bureau of Education. (1918). *Cardinal principles of secondary education, Bulletin No. 35* (pp. 29–30). Washington, DC.

West, E. (1996). *Growing up in twentieth-century America: A history and reference guide.* Westport, CT: Greenwood Press.

Wiebe, R. (1967). *The search for order, 1877–1920.* Westport, CT: Greenwood Press.

CHAPTER 2

A Goal Theory Perspective on the Current Status of Middle Level Schools

Carol Midgley

*The junior high school, by almost unanimous agreement, is the wasteland—
one is tempted to say cesspool—of American education.*
—Silberman (1970)

*If the failure of public education were being investigated today as a criminal proceeding,
indictments could have been handed down months ago to those schools that
teach grades six, seven, and eight.*
—Editorial in *USA Today* (6/29/99)

INTRODUCTION

In this chapter, I use a preeminent motivational theory, achievement goal theory, as the lens through which to examine both the history and current status of middle level schools and middle school reform. Like others, I believe that our knowledge of adolescents' schooling (and all schooling) has been diminished by the lack of a theoretical foundation. As stated by Entwisle (1990), "The dearth of theory contributes to problems at every level; in the absence of theory it is difficult to integrate findings from different studies, to reconcile those that disagree, or to set research priorities"

(p. 222). Goal theory provides a theoretical and empirical foundation upon which to build a science of adolescent schooling. Theory-based principles and models can be tested and revised, using both quantitative and qualitative methods. The applicability of these principles to different groups can be tested and can lead to the refinement of theory. Goal theory is not the only theory and may not even be the "best" theory that can be used to guide our thinking about adolescent schooling. However, goal theory is particularly useful in that it acknowledges the importance of context, and of considering the student-in-context. My colleagues and I have also found that goal theory works well in real school settings, and translates into specific recommendations for providing a more facilitative learning environment for young adolescents (Maehr & Midgley, 1996; Midgley, 1993; Midgley & Edelin, 1998).

I begin this chapter with a brief description of the shift from the junior high school model to the middle school model, beginning in the 1960s. This shift was characterized by a change in grades within school levels more than a change in thinking about what facilitates adolescent learning. I then describe reforms that have been undertaken during the last two decades aimed at providing a learning environment in middle level schools focused on the needs and characteristics of young adolescents. The relevancy of goal theory for examining and assessing the effectiveness of these reforms is discussed. Finally, I offer some suggestions about why middle school reforms are currently under siege, and who and what will shape the nature of middle level schools in the years ahead.

THE SHIFT FROM THE JUNIOR HIGH SCHOOL MODEL TO THE MIDDLE SCHOOL MODEL

Growing dissatisfaction with junior high schools led to the middle school movement in the 1960s. Although supporters of the movement stressed that middle school was a "philosophy and belief about children, their unique needs, who they are and how they grow and learn" (DeVita, Pumerantz, & Wilklow, 1970, p. 25), in reality the movement became identified primarily with a change in grade levels within schools. Sixth graders (and even fifth graders) were moved to middle level schools and ninth graders were moved to high schools. A concern about providing a facilitative environment for young adolescents became, in practice, a reorganization of grade levels without much in the way of changes in philosophy or practice (Gatewood, 1971). Although acknowledging the existence of "exemplary" middle schools with programs consistent with middle school philosophy, Alexander (1988) cited surveys that indicated "a very slow spread of the new features" (p. 109). In 1992 Cuban concluded that ". . . the vast majority of schools housing early adolescents, especially in cities, resemble the junior highs they were supposed to reform" (p. 246).

Research played a relatively minor role in these early efforts to move to the middle school model. In 1977 Joan Lipsitz, in a book reviewing research on schools for early adolescents, concluded that: "The moment one begins to review research on programs in schools, one is in the realm of bombast, ideology, defensiveness, ignorance, emotionalism" (Lipsitz, 1977b, pp. 84–85). Similarly, Wiles and Thompson (1975), in a review of research conducted from 1968 to 1974, stated that "existing research on middle school education is of remarkably low quality" (p . 421).

THE SHIFT TO THE MIDDLE SCHOOL MODEL

Beginning in the 1980s, there was an effort to reform middle schools and a new emphasis was placed on the importance of quality research to guide these efforts. Of particular note, the Carnegie Foundation Task Force on the Education of Young Adolescents (1989) published *Turning Points*. In this document they cited research and called for the fundamental restructuring of middle grades education based on the identified needs of young people at this stage of life. Recommendations included creating small communities for learning where stable, close, mutually respectful relationships with adults and peers are considered fundamental; teaching a core academic program that results in students who are literate and know how to think critically; ensuring success for all students through elimination of tracking by achievement level; and staffing middle schools with teachers who are expert at teaching young adolescents (Carnegie Council, 1989, p. 9). I have talked to middle school administrators and teachers who refer to *Turning Points* as their "Bible." Many middle level schools began to implement at least some of the recommended reforms. In the next section, I describe some of these reforms, using achievement goal theory as the organizing framework.

ACHIEVEMENT GOAL THEORY

Over the past three decades a motivational theory has been evolving that has meaning for young adolescents and middle level schools. This theory has developed within a social-cognitive framework that emphasizes the importance of how students interpret events in classrooms and schools, and process that information. A central tenet of goal theory is that the meaning and purpose of learning and schooling, as construed by students, activates adaptive or maladaptive approaches to learning. The description we often hear from middle school teachers—of students who put little effort into their schoolwork, give up quickly if presented with work they perceive to be difficult, and seem to be disinterested in schoolwork and disinclined to become engaged in learning is an example of a maladaptive approach to learning. These patterns of learning are said to be driven by the goals students pursue in an achievement setting; thus, this conception of motivation is called "achievement goal theory."

A number of researchers have been involved in the development and articulation of goal theory (e.g., Ames, 1992; Dweck, 1986; Maehr, 1989; Nicholls, 1989). They have described two achievement goals in particular: the goal to develop ability (variously labeled a mastery goal, learning goal, or task goal), and the goal to demonstrate ability or to avoid the demonstration of lack of ability (variously labeled a performance goal, ego goal, or ability goal). Although there are some differences among achievement goal theorists regarding the exact nature and functioning of these various conceptualizations of goals, there is considerable overlap (Ames, 1992; Heyman & Dweck, 1992). Mastery goals focus the individual on the task at hand, and relate especially to developing competency and gaining understanding and insight. Performance goals focus the individual on the self, and relate especially to how ability is judged and how one performs, especially relative to others. Although some theorists have described both approach and avoidance components of performance goals (an orientation to demonstrating ability and an orientation to avoiding the demonstration of lack of ability (Dweck & Leggett; 1988; Nicholls, Patashnick, Cheung, Thorkildsen, & Lauer, 1989), until recently most of the research using a goal theory framework has failed to make this distinction. Elliot and Harackiewicz (1996) pointed out this discrepancy between the theory and the research, and used classic motivational theory (e.g., Atkinson, 1974; McClelland, 1951) to provide a rationale for including both the approach and avoidance components in research including performance goals.

Empirical studies have confirmed that these goals are associated with different cognitive, affective, and behavioral outcomes. There has been remarkable consistency, over a host of studies, regarding the relation between mastery goals and adaptive patterns of cognition, affect, and behavior—referred to in this chapter as "patterns of learning" (for reviews see Ames, 1992; Dweck & Leggett, 1988; Pintrich & Schunk, 1996; Urdan, 1997). Examples of adaptive patterns of learning include approaching academic tasks with confidence, using effective learning strategies, and feeling positively about schooling and learning. In addition, recent research assessing both the approach and avoidance components of performance goals is consistent in providing evidence of the maladaptive patterns of learning associated with performance-avoid goals (e.g., Elliot & Harackiewicz, 1996; Middleton & Midgley, 1997; Skaalvik, 1997). Examples of maladaptive patterns of learning include doubting one's academic competency, avoiding challenging and novel tasks, and feeling negatively about schooling and learning. The research on performance-approach goals has been less consistent, but there is evidence that performance goals, in the absence of mastery goals, are associated with less adaptive patterns of learning (Midgley, Kaplan, & Middleton, 2001). Certainly middle school teachers are eager to have students who exhibit adaptive patterns of learning.

USING GOAL THEORY TO COMPARE ELEMENTARY AND MIDDLE LEVEL SCHOOLS

We[1] have used goal theory in research comparing elementary and middle level schools. In a cross-sectional study (Midgley, Anderman, & Hicks, 1995), we found that students at the middle school level espoused mastery goals less and performance goals more than did students at the elementary school level. In addition, middle school teachers and students perceived the school learning environment as less focused on mastery goals and more focused on performance goals than did elementary teachers and students. Elementary school teachers also reported using instructional practices that emphasized mastery goals, and endorsed mastery goals for their students more than did middle school teachers. In a longitudinal study (Anderman & Midgley, 1997), students were more oriented to mastery goals and perceived a greater emphasis on mastery goals in the classroom when they were in fifth grade in elementary school than when they were in sixth grade in middle school. Students perceived a greater emphasis on performance goals after the transition to middle school than before. That students experienced a decreased emphasis on mastery goals and an increased emphasis on performance goals when they made the transition to middle level schools was certainly a cause for concern, given the research cited above. These changes would predict a decrease in adaptive patterns of learning and an increase in maladaptive patterns for students at any stage of life. We suggested that these changes might be particularly harmful for early adolescents. If the emphasis on learning and understanding decreases as students are developing the cognitive ability to grapple with more abstract and complex tasks, opportunities for learning may be lost. If ability comparisons among students become salient as young adolescents are becoming more self-conscious and concerned about how they appear to others, they may engage in strategies that undermine learning in order to protect their self-worth (Covington, 1992). These studies were conducted in the early 1990s in schools that had not implemented middle school reforms.

More recently, we conducted similar studies in three school districts in which some of the recommended middle school reforms had been implemented. In a longitudinal study following students from fifth grade in elementary school to sixth grade in middle school, students no longer perceived an increase in the emphasis on performance goals after the transition (Midgley & Edelin, 1998). This is good news. It may well be that requiring all students to take a core of academic subjects and eliminating the assignment of students to classes based on their ability contributed to this good news. The bad news is that students still perceived a decrease in the emphasis on understanding, mastery, and challenge (a mastery goal structure) when they moved to middle level schools. Less is known about how to create an emphasis on mastery goals in classrooms than how to affect the saliency of performance goals (e.g., Bergin, 1995). At the middle school level, particularly in schools that have not undergone reform, departmentalization, the 40 minute period, the need to cover curriculum, and the emphasis on testing and grades may make it particularly difficult for teachers to communicate mastery goals to students. Later in this chapter I will discuss the need to create a greater emphasis on mastery goals in middle school learning environments, particularly in light of questions that are now being raised about the efficacy of the middle school reforms.

ENHANCING INTERPERSONAL RELATIONSHIPS IN MIDDLE LEVEL SCHOOLS

The other good news does not relate directly to goal theory. Rather, it is in accord with a recommendation in *Turning Points* that "the enormous middle school must be restructured in a more human scale. The student should, upon entering middle grade school, join a small community in which people—students and adults—get to know each other well to create a climate for intellectual development" (Carnegie Council, 1989, p. 37). This recommendation has been taken seriously by many middle school educators. In the reading we have done about middle school reform, in our visits to local middle schools, and in discussions with administrators and teachers, my colleagues and I see evidence that concrete steps have been taken to provide a more caring and connected middle school environment. Others have noted this change as well. Felner and his colleagues (Felner, Jackson, Kasak, Mulhall, Brand, & Flowers, 1997), in their description of more than 100 schools participating in the Illinois Middle Grades Network, reported that students were perceiving more support from teachers and were experiencing greater feelings of connectedness. In a report describing the implementation of the Middle Grades Improvement Program (MGIP) in 16 urban school districts in Indiana, Lipsitz (1997a) wrote:

Even the most jaded of observers agree that there is little question that many of the MGIP schools "feel" better: they are, for the most part, friendlier, warmer, more relaxed, and more respectful. In the best of them there is an energetic calm, more collegiality, and more focused attachments between adults and children. (p. 555)

In our earlier research, we found that both students and observers reported a deterioration in the student/teacher relationship after the transition to junior high school (Feldlaufer, Midgley, & Eccles, 1988). In our more recent research, students' no longer reported a decrease in the quality of student/teacher relationships after the transition to middle school (Midgley, Maehr, Gheen, Hruda, Middleton, & Nelson, 1998), and remarkably, their sense of school belonging increased (Kumar & Midgley, 2001).

It appears that progress has been made regarding promoting positive relationships in middle schools, but the emphasis on learning and understanding, which we conceptualize as a mastery goal structure, still needs attention. We are not alone in coming to this conclusion. Felner and his colleagues (1997), in their description of the schools participating in the Illinois Middle Grades Network, noted that by the second year, most of the participating schools had made considerable progress toward implementing teaming, common planning time, and teacher-based advisory structures. Teaming can allow teachers to spend more time with fewer students, and thus to develop more positive relationships with them. Teaming and common planning time also make it possible for teachers to discuss together how best to meet the needs of students who may be experiencing difficulty. Advisory programs link every student to a teacher who serves as a special advisor, counselor, and friend. Thus, as pointed out by Felner and his colleagues, these changes are important in enhancing students' feelings of connectedness to school. However, they also pointed out that there was little evidence of a change in the quality of instruction. In a recent update on middle school reform, Lipsitz and her colleagues (Lipsitz, Mizell, Jackson, & Austin, 1997) noted that many middle schools are warmer, happier, and more peaceful places for both students and adults. However, they go on to say: "We are frankly concerned that, despite their heavy investment in middle-grades reform, many schools have not progressed beyond the stage of changing climate" (p. 535).

Why is it that many middle schools have been successful in improving interpersonal relationships, but have made little progress in improving the emphasis on mastery goals? Facilitating positive interpersonal relationships can be accomplished, at least in part, by structural changes (forming teacher teams, dividing large schools into smaller units, providing time for advisory programs). Mergendoller (1993), in an introduction to a special issue of *The Elementary School Journal* on middle grades education, argued that many middle schools have made the recommended structural changes and that they often represent "cosmetic fiddling" without resulting in fundamental changes in the purposes, priorities, and functioning of the school (p. 444). Mergendoller and others (e.g., Cuban, 1992) believe that structural changes, without attention to the quality of instruction, have little prospect for improving students' learning. It appears that structural changes have, in many cases, made it possible to create a more caring and responsive school environment. This is important. However, facilitating learning, understanding, and mastery requires more than structural changes.

ENHANCING INTERPERSONAL RELATIONSHIPS *AND* EMPHASIZING MASTERY GOALS IN MIDDLE LEVEL SCHOOLS

Can middle level schools enhance interpersonal relations and feelings of belonging and at the same time expect and promote learning and understanding? We have attended meetings where some parents or middle school teachers pit the relationship dimension against the academic dimension. "We need to focus on promoting achievement and forget about this touchy-feely stuff. Schools are not about feelings, they're about learning." Or "Early adolescents need to feel supported and cared for, the learning will take care of itself." We disagree with both of those hypothetical statements. We do not see this as a case of either/or. Indeed, we suggest that relationships are enhanced when students are truly learning, and learning is enhanced when students are in a caring environment. In truth, this is the message in most middle school reform documents. The real challenge that lies ahead for middle schools is to sustain the positive changes in the relationship dimension while focusing new energy on providing a learning environment in which every young adolescent believes she or he can learn and be successful. If what is valued is effort, hard work, and real understanding, every young person can aspire to that.

The idea that an emphasis on relationships competes with the emphasis on learning in schools is also reflected in the literature (e.g., Phillips, 1997; Shouse, 1996a,b). In a large scale study in 23 middle schools, Phillips (1997) compared the effects of a communitarian climate and an academic climate on middle school students' achievement and absenteeism, describing them as "competing" theories regarding how to improve schools. She found that a communal emphasis was unrelated to math achievement or attendance, whereas an academic emphasis was related to both. She concluded that "researchers, reformers, and educators should begin to question the received wisdom about the benefits of communal schooling" (p. 657). We do not believe that these results point to abandoning efforts to promote a sense of community in schools. Teachers need to understand that they can be both caring *and* intellectually challenging. We continue to believe that a positive interpersonal climate can and should coexist with a strong emphasis on mastery and learning, and would be associated with the most positive outcomes for young adolescents.

Now there is evidence of a reaction against the middle school reforms that have been implemented. Again, the relationship dimension is being pitted against the academic dimension. A recent article in *Education Week* (April 15, 1998) stated that "the middle school model has come under attack for supplanting academic rigor with a focus on students' social, emotional, and physical needs." Are we going to allow the important strides that have been made to develop more positive and supportive relationships in middle schools to be dismantled by those who do not believe that schools can provide both a supportive and academically challenging experience for students? And there is further reason for concern. In a recent discussion of the need to increase the salience of mastery goals in middle level schools we warned: "We do not want our discussion of the need to foster academic excellence in middle schools to be interpreted as an endorsement of rewards for the highest grades, accelerated courses for students who 'qualify,' or programs that promote competition among students. These would all be examples of an emphasis on performance goals" (Midgley & Edelin, 1998, p. 201). Now that warning seems especially appropriate. In the article in *Education Week* cited above, districts are described that have called for "the reintroduction of previously discredited honor rolls, and for core academic classes to be organized according to ability levels."

THE CURRENT EMPHASIS ON STANDARDS, TESTING, AND ACCOUNTABILITY

The attack on middle schools comes at a time when there has been an escalation in the emphasis on standards, testing, and accountability. We do not think this is a coincidence. The question is not whether there should be standards for student learning. Almost all would agree that there should be standards. The debate rather is about the nature of the standards that are set. We make a distinction between standards rooted in mastery goals and standards rooted in performance goals (Midgley et al., 2001). Standards that reflect mastery goals are not less rigorous than standards that reflect performance goals; they are different. Standards that reflect mastery goals are important and necessary. They emphasize deep learning, understanding, the transfer of knowledge, and the development of skills and competencies. The problem comes when there is a need to assess whether a student has achieved these standards. Good middle school teachers, if they have the opportunity to spend a reasonable block of time with their students, can do this. But when there is a massive testing program, such as is the case in many statewide testing programs, there is a movement away from mastery standards to standards that are based on facts and "right answers" that can be assessed with multiple choice questions. In addition, these tests, particularly norm-referenced tests, are used to compare students, teachers, schools, district, and even states. Thus, goal theory is particularly relevant in considering the effects of the movement toward standards, testing, and accountability. In our conversations with middle school teachers, they tell us that the testing and accountability movement has changed their teaching. Rather than promoting thinking and understanding, they feel pressured to teach facts and test-taking strategies. Beane (1999) claims that the standards and testing movement have caused many talented middle school teachers "to scrap their high-quality block-time, integrated, thematic programs and bring back the intellectually impoverished, layer-cake science, history, and mathematics courses" (p. 8). To compound the problem, these practices have the potential to undermine the quality of interpersonal relations in middle schools:

> High stakes testing for accountability can also sabotage the development of a community of learners within and across schools ... teachers subject to rewards and sanctions may begin to treat their students in similarly coercive ways, inhibiting the development of the responsive student-teacher relationships necessary for learning. (Wheelock, 1998, p. 20)

The quote above is from a very interesting book Anne Wheelock (1998) has written about the relevancy of standards-based reform at the middle school level. She points out the perils of moving back to middle school practices that were judged ineffective and even harmful:

> The cost of mistaking old practices for new standards is high. First, because these practices institutionalized narrowly defined and unequal achievement, they are counterproductive to the goals of improved learning for all students. Moreover, these practices, heralded as standards, take a toll in less measurable ways. Taken together, they ensure that schools will remain places where few adolescents dare to excel and where many will feel that *being smart* is fraught with danger. For young adolescents, danger lies in being separated from friends and social circles; it lies in being forced to choose between individual success and group loyalties; it lies in being asked to do work that undermines one's sense of dignity. To avoid these dangers, students may 'tune out,' pretend indifference to learning, or defer from asking questions that invite too much attention from teachers. At the same time, they may hide mistakes that could suggest incompetence. To avoid labels that reflect on their ability, they may dodge difficult assignments or situations that

require hard work, all to circumvent the danger of being judged on the "smartness" continuum. (pp. 183–184)

Her comments are relevant to research we have been conducting in middle schools on strategies young adolescents use to avoid being judged on the "smartness continuum." These studies become particularly meaningful in light of the movement away from recommended middle school reforms and toward practices that emphasize relative ability such as honor rolls based on grades, homogeneous grouping, and special privileges and opportunities for those who receive the highest grades.

THE GOAL STRUCTURE IN MIDDLE SCHOOLS AND THE USE OF STRATEGIES TO PROTECT SELF-WORTH

Covington (1992) has alerted us to strategies students use to protect self worth when the smartness continuum is salient. In our research, this emphasis on relative ability is an important component of what we describe as performance goals. We have conducted a number of studies examining the relation between performance goals and these strategies, including, self-handicapping, avoiding novelty and challenge, and avoiding seeking help in the classroom when it is needed. Self-handicapping involves purposefully withdrawing effort (procrastinating, fooling around with friends instead of studying) so that if subsequent performance is low, those circumstances, rather than lack of ability, will be seen as the cause. These strategies are considered to be "handicapping" because they often undermine performance. In our conversations with middle school educators, they are very familiar with students who engage in self-handicapping. One middle school principal told us that he used to self-handicap when he was an adolescent. "I'd goof off with my friends so that I could use that as an excuse if I didn't do so well." In a series of studies, we found that young adolescents used self-handicapping more when performance goals were salient (Midgley, Arunkumar, & Urdan, 1996; Midgley & Urdan, 1995, 2001; Urdan, Midgley, & Anderman, 1998). Those who suggest that practices and policies that make relative ability salient and thus that promote performance goals, such as ability grouping and the use of honor rolls be reinstituted in middle level schools in order to promote "academic excellence," may need to think about the cost in terms of the increased use of debilitating strategies such as self-handicapping.

We have conducted several studies examining students' reluctance to seek help in the classroom (Middleton & Midgley, 1997; Ryan, Gheen, & Midgley, 1998; Ryan, Hicks, & Midgley, 1997). Students do need help at times, and if they avoid asking for help for fear of looking stupid, this may undermine achievement. Ryan and Pintrich (1997) found that many young adolescents perceived a threat to competence from both teachers and classmates when contemplating seeking help. An orientation to performance goals predicted a perceived threat from both peers and teachers, which in turn predicted the avoidance of seeking help. In another study, Ryan et al. (1998) found that in classrooms where students' perceived more of an emphasis on performance goals, the avoidance of help seeking was greater. In addition, Middleton and Midgley (1997), found that both an orientation to demonstrating ability and an orientation to avoiding the demonstration of lack of ability were correlated positively with help-avoidance. Note that in the quote from Wheelock above, she talks about students who "defer from asking questions that invite too much attention from teachers." If middle schools increase the emphasis on relative ability in response to the emphasis on testing, it may be that more students will avoid asking for help in order to protect their image as able.

We have also examined the relation between early adolescents' perceptions of an emphasis on performance goals in the classroom and the avoidance of novel approaches to learning (Gheen & Midgley, 1999). We found that students' preference to avoid novelty varied significantly across the classrooms in the study. That is, in some classrooms students said they preferred to avoid novel approaches to learning more than in others. In classrooms that were perceived as placing a greater emphasis on performance goals, students were more likely to say they wanted to avoid novel approaches to their school work. Most middle school teachers do not want their students to avoid novel approaches to learning. Unfortunately, that may be the unintended consequence of moving away from many of the middle school reforms that have been undertaken. If middle schools increase the emphasis on relative ability in response to the emphasis on testing, it may be that more students will avoid novel approaches to doing their work and instead approach academic tasks in a "safe" way. This seems most unfortunate in the information age when innovation, risk-taking, and new approaches to thinking and learning are seen as desirable.

EMPHASIZING MASTERY GOALS IN MIDDLE LEVEL SCHOOLS

In many of the studies cited above, mastery goals were related to a lower reported use of avoidance strategies. That is, when students perceived that their classrooms emphasized learning, understanding, and improvement, they were less likely to use these debilitating strategies. As mentioned earlier in this chapter, it has been easier for teachers and schools to reduce the emphasis on performance goals than to increase the emphasis on mastery goals (e.g., Midgley & Edelin, 1998). We learned this when we spent three years collaborating with principals and teachers in a local elementary school and middle school to move toward an emphasis on mastery goals and away from an emphasis on performance goals (Maehr & Midgley, 1996). This experience also affirmed for us that changing the goal structure involves a change in thinking about the purpose of schooling. There needs to be time for teachers to read, talk, debate, and reflect (Urdan, Midgley, & Wood, 1995). But we all know that teachers in this country are not given time to do this kind of thinking and reflecting. We also know that teachers and principals need to work within the constraints imposed on them at the state level, the district level, and by the parents of the students in their schools. When we speak at schools, we assure teachers that we do not have a recipe for change, or a packaged program that we are trying to sell. We talk about a change in thinking about the purposes of learning, and the messages that schools and teachers convey to students about these purposes through policies and practices.

During the course of our collaboration, teachers taught us a lot about mastery goals. I remember a middle school teacher saying to the group: "When we teach a child to ride a bicycle, we don't tell her that she did a good job, but her brother did better. We focus on mastering the task. 'Hold on to the handlebars, pedal faster, look both ways.' Why don't we do that in school?" As the teachers at both the elementary and middle school level began to implement changes, we realized that each school would have a different plan and a different set of priorities. However, they did help us to describe generally the kinds of changes that would represent a movement away from an emphasis on relative performance and competition among students and toward a more mastery-focused learning environment. The list below resulted from our shared understandings.

Another example from this collaborative experience may serve to illustrate the nature of mastery goals in the real world of schools. During our first meeting with our colleagues in the elementary school, they asked us if they were going to have to do away with their honor roll. The "all A" honor roll and the "A and B" honor roll were prominently displayed on the wall outside the principal's office. We assured them that they would decide what actions they wanted to take, and we were there to discuss with them problems they were experiencing and ways to help all students learn. We met weekly and talked about these issues. They began to make small changes in policies and programs, but the honor roll was never mentioned. Arriving for a meeting one afternoon, we noticed that the honor roll had been removed. At the beginning of the meeting, teachers asked us what happened to the honor roll and the principal said that she had removed it, because she "could no longer live with it." Some of the teachers were quite concerned because they knew that the parents of high achieving students

	Move Away From	*Move Toward*
Grouping	Grouping by ability	Grouping by topic, interest, student choice
		Frequent reformation of groups
Competition/	Competition between students	Cooperative learning
Cooperation	Contests with limited winners	
Assessment	Using test data as a basis for comparison	Using test data for diagnosis
	Over-use of standardized tests	Alternatives to tests such as portfolios
Grading	Normative grading	Grading for progress, improvement
	Public display of grades	Involving students in determining their grades
Recognition/	Recognition for relative performance	Recognition of progress, improvement
Rewards/	Honor rolls for high grades	An emphasis on learning for its own sake
Incentives	Over-use of praise, especially for the completion of short, easy tasks	
Student Input	Decisions made exclusively by administrators and teachers	Opportunities for choice, electives
		Student decision-making, self-scheduling, self-regulation
Approaches to the Curriculum	Departmentalized approach to curriculum	Thematic approaches/interdisciplinary focus
		Viewing mistakes as a part of learning
		Allowing students to redo work
		Encouraging students to take academic risks
Academic Tasks	Rote learning and memorization	Providing challenging, complex work to students
	Over-use of work sheets and textbooks	Giving homework that is enriching, challenging
	Decontextualized facts	Encouraging problem solving, comprehension
Remediation	Pullout programs	Cross-age tutoring, peer tutoring
	Retention	Enrichment

believed that the honor roll was very important to their children. They talked about the need all children have for recognition and how they could recognize their students in a way that would convey an emphasis on mastery goals rather than on performance goals. They formulated the following principles of recognition:

1. Recognize individual student effort, accomplishment, and improvement.
2. Give all students opportunities to be recognized.
3. Give recognition privately whenever possible.
4. Avoid using "most" or "best" for recognizing or rewarding—as in "best project" or "most improved." These words usually convey comparisons with others.
5. Avoid recognizing on the basis of absence of mistakes. For example, avoid giving awards for students who get "less than five words wrong on a spelling test."
6. Avoid using the same criteria for all students. For example, avoid giving an award to "all students who get an A on the science test," or "all students who do four out of five projects."
7. Recognize students for taking on challenging work or for stretching their own abilities (even if they make mistakes). This gives a powerful message about what is valued in the classroom.
8. Recognize students for coming up with different and unusual ways to solve a problem or a novel way to approach a task. Again, you are telling students what you value.
9. Try to involve students in the recognition process. What is of value to them? How much effort do they feel they put in? Where do they feel they need improvement? When do they feel successful? How do they know when they have reached their goals?
10. It's O.K. to recognize students in various domains (behavior, athletics, attendance, etc.), but every student should have the opportunity to be recognized *academically*.
11. Try to recognize the quality of students' work rather than the quantity. For example, recognizing students for reading a lot of books could encourage them to read easy books.
12. Avoid recognizing grades and test scores. This takes the emphasis away from learning and problem solving.
13. Recognition must be real. Do not recognize students for accomplishing something they have not really accomplished, for improving if they have not improved, or for trying hard if that is not the case. The important factor is letting students know that they have the opportunity to be recognized in these areas.

One father who regularly attended our meetings told us that he first understood what a mastery goal emphasis was all about when the teachers formulated these principles. We believe these principles are as relevant to the middle school level as to the elementary level. Indeed, as we suggested earlier, the achievement goals that are conveyed by these principles may be especially important for young adolescents because of their increased sensitivity to ability comparisons and their increased capacity to undertake complex and challenging academic tasks.

MIDDLE SCHOOL REFORMS UNDER SIEGE

Now there is a growing awareness that the middle school movement is under siege (Beane, 1999; Bradley, 1998; Erb, 1999; Lewis & Norton, 2000; Tucker & Codding, 1999; Williamson & Johnston, 1996). Some are calling for the abandonment of the middle school model (e.g., Tucker & Codding, 1999). Norton (2000) quotes a senior researcher at the Education Trust who says: "I think we should abandon the whole middle school concept. Middle schools are a disaster" (p. K4). Others have called for a "midcourse correction," pointing out that middle school reforms over the last two decades have attended to organizational issues and to providing an environment in tune with the developmental needs of students, and not enough to "academic issues" (Lewis & Norton, 2000). We would place ourselves in that camp, and ask that middle schools increase the emphasis on mastery goals without abandoning the many important changes that have been made. Others insist that in schools where the recommended reforms have been fully implemented, students are doing better on measures of both academic achievement and social behavior (Felner et al., 1997). Their solution would be to move toward full implementation of the middle school model in all schools. However, we know of some schools where middle school reforms were "fully implemented" but, for the most part, have disappeared. A local school district was one of the first in the country to move to a true middle school model. More than a change in grade levels, administrators and teachers in this district were committed to the middle school reforms suggested in *Turning Points* and supported by research. They spent two years planning for the change. Educators from throughout the nation visited these schools. Today, many of the reforms that were undertaken have been discarded. Teachers who participated in the change effort and believed that they were providing a much better learning environment for young adolescents feel demoralized. Some teachers have told us that they attribute the undermining of the middle school model to a lack of support by parents, and by a school board elected by members of the community. One can perhaps understand why there is dissatisfaction with middle schools that confined their reforms to structural changes, but why would "fully implemented" middle schools be under attack?

I have not conducted any research that bears on this question, but I do believe it is important to try to understand the reasons underlying the attack on reformed middle schools. Certainly there are many reasons. I've done some reading about why seemingly promising educational reforms often disappear within a few years, but can only speculate about why that happens and how it relates to the current status of middle school reform. Critics of the middle school model often make the case that schools in this country are "failing," and middle schools are the weakest link in the educational hierarchy. This is a widely held view, promulgated in particular by the media (note the remarkable quote from a *USA Today* editorial that opens this chapter) and by politicians. I don't recall hearing one politician in the recent election campaign citing the quality of the educational system in this country as one of the reasons for the recent economic prosperity. When our economy was floundering and Japan's was booming, we were barraged with articles and speeches blaming schools and calling for reform. Now our economy is the envy of the world, and a cohort of young people who appear to be particularly creative and productive is fueling much of the boom. Our schools seem to be serving many young people very well.

The widely held belief that our schools are failing seems to arise in particular from international comparisons of test scores. Certainly this is true for middle schools. In almost every document criticizing middle schools, results from the National Assessment of Educational Progress (NAEP) and the Third International Mathematics and Science Study (TIMSS) are cited. The TIMSS study reported that the mathematics achievement of U.S. eighth graders was lower than that of students in many other countries (Silver, 1998), and that eighth graders fared less well in comparison to similar-aged students in other countries than did younger students. However, there is some controversy regarding the way these comparisons are being made and some question whether these comparisons, if they are valid, reflect important differences in mathematics ability (e.g., Bracey, 1997). From a goal theory perspective, one would ask if these tests assess real understanding of mathematical principles.

Berliner (2000) suggests that the Christian Right is systematically attacking any educational reforms that are incompatible with their theories of child rearing. Opportunities for student choice and decision-making, concern with the emotional well being of students, outcomes-based education, the emphasis on connection and understanding in mathematics instruction and on whole language in reading instruction, are just some of the educational practices that are cited for being in direct opposition to the goals of the Christian Right. This group is well organized, well funded, and politically active. But the members of this group represent only about 20% of the U.S. population, and they are certainly entitled to promulgate their views. What is surprising is that many people who are not members of the Christian Right are calling for a return to the basics, the expanded use of standardized tests, retention of low achieving students, rewards and incentives for high achieving students, and major changes in middle level schools. It may be that the Christian Right is involved in the attack on middle schools, but I think it is interesting that their views have met a receptive audience. It appears that many people who have views that differ rather dramatically from those of the Christian Right respond positively to their views on educational reform. These views have more in common with a performance goal orientation than with a mastery goal orientation. Who are these people and why do they endorse these views for schooling in general, and for middle schools in particular?

I believe that many of these people are parents of students currently in school, and are predominantly from the higher socioeconomic classes. These parents, although they may not want the "have-nots" to lose, do want their children to win. It reminds me of a cartoon I once saw depicting two parents outside a school saying "But if all students win, how will we know our children are the best?" In interviews with educated, middle class mothers who were identified as liberals who believed in integrated and inclusive education, Brantlinger, Majd-Jabbari, and Guskin (1996) found that many supported segregated and stratified school structures. They concluded:

> It was evident that the mothers we interviewed wanted to perceive themselves—and be perceived—as liberals, who were just and compassionate people. On the other hand, they harbored illiberal views related to desire for privileged status for their children. (p. 586)

In an article on educational reform, using the case of the junior high school as an example, Cuban (1992) points out that schools, as tax supported institutions, depend on the good will of local constituencies for financial support and, indeed, for their survival. He suggests that schools, therefore, "try to do what their constituencies believe is proper for schools" (p. 248). If local constituencies believe, and he says that they do, that young adolescents should be in a learning environment that is more like the high school than the elementary school (and therefore more oriented to performance goals and less oriented to mastery goals), then that is what the school district will provide. As pointed out by Beane (1999), many upper class parents, who have the most power and whose voices are heard, want middle schools to emphasize a classical, separate subject, college preparatory curriculum that mirrors the high school model, and this is the way they define "academic rigor."

What is it that influences the beliefs of the constituencies that have power? They do not seem to believe the research evidence or perhaps they are unaware of the research evidence. We have been at meetings at which parents claim that those who do educational research can find evidence to support anything they wish to promote. This goes back, in some ways, to my comment at the beginning of this chapter that there is merit in using theory to amass a creditable body of research. But we realize that there will still be those who question its validity. As researchers, we ask what evidence there is that moving back to a junior high school model will enhance student learning? What evidence is there that standardized testing and accountability will improve academic outcomes for all students? What evidence is there that academic rigor and positive interpersonal relationships cannot coexist in middle level schools? What evidence is there that recognizing high achieving students is an effective motivator? We know of no such research, yet that is the premise of many of the critic's attacks on the middle school model.

In contrast to those who discount research, recent articles point to the erroneous interpretation of research by some critics of reform. Whether this is purposeful or not is open to debate. Becker and Jacob (2000) describe efforts by a powerful group of parents and professors of mathematics which, in the view of the authors, manipulated information and played off the public's perceptions of "failing schools" to reverse mathematics reform in California (p. 530). This group produced a "research-based" document that resulted in a massive change in the textbooks that were used, and a $43 million professional development program to retrain teachers in "drill and practice" approaches to mathematics. The revisions were approved with virtually no input from K-12 educators or mathematics education professionals. They concluded by saying that "policy that includes 'teaching for understanding' as its centerpiece has vanished from the California mathematics education landscape, and mastery of procedural skills is now the order of the day" (p. 536). Allington and Woodside-Jiron (1999) provide a detailed description of how a white paper, purportedly based on a synthesis of "rigorous, reliable, and replicable" NICHD-sponsored research, influenced educational policy on the use of phonics for early reading instruction. In their analysis of the research cited in this document, they conclude that none of the recommendations were adequately supported by the research cited. They expressed particular concern about the wide media coverage that the white paper received and the willingness of both politicians and high-ranking education officials to accept the report without questioning its validity. We suggest that the broad media coverage and the widespread acceptance of the unsubstantiated recommendations in both the examples described above may say something about the fit between the vision of education embraced by many powerful middle and upper-middle class parents and the policies that were being advocated. These examples are not specific to middle school reform, but those of us who do research in middle schools should be diligent in preventing the misinterpretation of our research.

Contrasts are often made between the vision of education described above and more "democratic" visions of education. The demise of progressive education and the open classroom movement is illustrative of the short lives of these seemingly effective approaches to education that were based on democratic principles. Will the middle school model be the next victim? Oakes, Quartz, Ryan, and Lipton (2000) studied 16 middle schools engaged in reform efforts modeled after the recommendations from "Turning Points." They describe the commitment by teachers to making their schools "deeply educative, socially just, caring, and participatory" (p. 568). They say that these reforms, similar in many ways to the democratic principles espoused by John Dewey, resulted in cultural and political debates that caused many of the schools to make compromises and some to abandon reform efforts completely:

> Many Americans—typically the most advantaged and powerful—take the common good to mean an aggregate of the actions of self-interested individuals who are free to be guided by such marketplace values as competition and the accumulation of social and material resources. For them, school reform would bring quite different policies and practices—specifically, ones that allow individuals to exercise their preferences, maximize their private and unequal resources, and compete effectively. (pp. 569–570)

Oakes and her colleagues describe in some detail the programs put into place in three middle schools, following principles recommended in *Turning Points*. It seems quite clear that the teachers in one of the schools worked long and hard to achieve a "fully implemented" program. Despite their efforts, many parents were angry and considered the program to be a "hippie-era leftover." They presented a petition to the board of education demanding that the school return to a basic curriculum and traditional teaching.

> Some parents demanded that specific books be read, and others prescribed specific amounts of time for certain lessons. The innovative (math) curriculum became a lightening rod for a group of fathers—many with degrees in science and engineering—who blasted the program as failing to prepare their children for the rigors of the university . . . One school board member summed up the attack: "These people are out for blood. I mean, they're with the 'I pay your salary stuff'." (p. 573)

Oakes and her colleagues do point to progress that was made and reforms that were sustained, but they suggest that attention must be paid to the profound cultural and political challenges that lay at the heart of middle school reform.

Some who might embrace a more democratic model have trouble doing this when it comes to their own children. I heard one of my colleagues say that she opposed cooperative learning, "because my child ends up doing all the work" and another say that he opposed heterogeneous grouping in math "because my child likes challenging math problems." A goal theorist from another university, with a son in high school, told me over lunch that he knew that he should be urging his son to focus on the quality of his academic work, and not to be concerned with how others were doing, but he didn't want him to do anything that might jeopardize his chances of getting into the university of his choice. These colleagues have competed to get into universities and graduate schools, for academic positions, and for tenure. It may be difficult for them to suggest to their children that there may be a better way, even if the research points to that.

Finally, it may also be that these strong feelings are heightened in the case of the schooling of young adolescents. Parents who might espouse a more democratic approach to teaching and learning for younger and older children, may believe that adolescents need to be more closely supervised and controlled. Stereotypes about early adolescents abound. Astroth (1994) suggests that like previous generations, we appear to be suffering from *ephebiphobia*—a word coined from the Greek to signify a fear and loathing of adolescence (p. 412). An editorial about schools, in response to that article, suggests that events such as those in Littleton have exacerbated those fears, and have resulted in a "lock down mentality where adolescents are concerned" (Gough, 2000, p. 482). Hyman and Snook (March 2000) talk about the media's eagerness to sensationalize cases of youth violence and suggest that this "demonization" of youth contributes to the toxicity of schools (p. 490). Years ago I read an article that referred to this as the "zookeeper" view of early adolescent schooling. The idea was that society believes that young adolescents are not quite human, and that middle schools need to contain them and control them until they have passed through this stage (Leet, 1974).

FINAL THOUGHTS

The real question is how school districts are going to respond to the growing dissatisfaction with middle schools by their constituencies, by the media, and by powerful politicians and advocacy agencies. As pointed out by Norton (2000), although there seems to be some agreement that high support and high standards can coexist, "such groups as the National Middle School Association and such standards advocates as the Educational Trust continue to argue about the *best structures and approaches* to achieve the balance" (p. K2) (emphasis added). This is a critical issue, and one that will have a profound influence on the evolution of schools for early adolescents. Will middle schools do away with teaming, advisory groups, small house configurations, and other structures that have allowed them to provide a more supportive and respectful learning environment, even though there is strong research evidence that feelings of connectedness with schools enhance both academic and affective outcomes (e.g., Goodenow, 1993; Resnick et al., 1997; Ryan & Patrick, in press)? Will they revert to practices such as ability grouping, "enriched" courses and special privileges for high achieving students, and honor rolls and societies in emulation of the high school model, even though there is evidence that the messages these practices send to early adolescents can undermine learning? Or are they going to recognize that middle school students have a need to engage in complex, challenging, "rigorous" academic tasks on which learning and understanding are seen as evidence of success rather than comparisons with others? Our data indicate that both teachers and students perceive that the middle school learning environment emphasizes learning, understanding, and improvement less than is the case in elementary schools. This need not be the case. If the same national commitment, media attention, and financial support were put into helping middle school educators provide a mastery-focused learning environment as has been put into the high stakes testing movement, we would be well on our way to providing highly effective middle schools for all young adolescents.

ACKNOWLEDGMENT

The writing of this chapter was funded in part by the Spencer Foundation.
     This chapter builds on issues discussed in Midgley (1993), Midgley and Edelin (1998), and Midgley, Kaplan, and Middleton (2001).

NOTE

1.   Approximately 18 people have participated in this program of research over the past decade and I use the pronoun "we" in this chapter to acknowledge their contribution.

REFERENCES

Alexander, W.M. (1988). Schools in the middle: Rhetoric and reality. *Social Education, 52,* 107–109.

Allington, R.L., & Woodside-Jiron, H. (1999). The politics of literacy teaching: How "research" shaped educational policy. *Educational Researcher, 28,* 4–13.

Anderman, E., & Midgley, C. (1997). Changes in personal achievement goals and the perceived classroom goal structures across the transition to middle level schools. *Contemporary Educational Psychology, 22,* 269–298.

Ames, C. (1992). Classrooms: Goals, structures, and student motivation. *Journal of Educational Psychology, 84,* 261–271.

Astroth, K.A. (1994). Beyond ephebiphobia: Problem adults or problem youths? *Phi Delta Kappan, 75,* 411–413.

Atkinson, J.W. (1974). The mainstreams of achievement oriented activity. In J.W. Atkinson & J.O. Raynor (Eds.), *Motivation and achievement* (pp.11–39). Washington, DC: Winston.

Beane, J.A. (1999). Middle schools under siege: Points of attack. *Middle School Journal, 30,* 3–9.

Becker, J.P., & Jacob, B. (March, 2000). The politics of California school mathematics: The anti-reform of 1997–99. *Phi Delta Kappan,* 529–537.

Bergin, D. (1995). Effects of mastery versus competitive motivation situation on learning. *Journal of Experimental Education, 63,* 303–314.

Berliner, D.C. (2000), *Educational psychology meets the Christian Right: Differing views of children, schooling, teaching, and learning.* http:courses.ed.asu.edu/berlinter/readings/differengh.htm

Bracey, G.W. (1997). *The truth about America_s schools: The Bracey Reports, 1991–1997.* Phi Delta Kappan Educational Foundation.

Bradley, A. (1998, April15). Muddle in the middle. *Education Week, 18,* 38–42.

Brantlinger, E., Majd-Jabbari, M., & Guskin, S.L. (1996). Self-interest and liberal educational discourse: How ideology works for middle-class mothers. *American Educational Research Journal, 33,* 571–597.

Carnegie Council on Adolescent Development. (1989). *Turning Points: Preparing American youth for the 21st century.* Report of the Task Force on Education of Young Adolescents, New York.

Covington, M.V. (1992). *Making the grade: A self-worth perspective on motivation and school reform.* Cambridge: Cambridge University Press.

Cuban, L. (1992). What happens to reforms that last? The case of the junior high school. *American Educational Research Journal, 29,* 227–251.

Darling-Hammond, L. (1997). *The right to learn: A blueprint for creating schools that work.* San Francisco: Jossey-Bass.

DeVita, J., Pumerantz, P., & Wilklow, L. (1970). *The effective middle school.* New York: Parker.

Dweck, C.S. (1986). Motivational processes affecting learning. *American Psychologist, 40,* 1040–1048.

Dweck, C.S., & Leggett, E.L. (1988). A social-cognitive approach to motivation and personality. *Psychological Review, 95,* 256–273.

Elliot, A.J., & Harackiewicz, J.M. (1996). Approach and avoidance achievement goals and intrinsic motivation: A mediational analysis. *Journal of Personality and Social Psychology, 70*, 461–475.

Entwisle, D.R. (1990). Schools and the adolescents. In S. Feldman & G.R. Elliott (Eds.), *At the threshold* (pp. 197–224). Cambridge, MA: Harvard University Press.

Erb, T. (1999). Tucker misses the mark on middle schools. *Middle School Journal, 30*, 2 & 49.

Feldlaufer, H., Midgley, C., & Eccles, J.S. (1988). Student, teacher, and observer perceptions of the classroom environment before and after the transition to junior high school. *Journal of Early Adolescence, 8*, 133–156.

Felner, R.D., Jackson, A.J., Kasak, D., Mulhall, P., Brand, S., & Flowers, N. (1997). The impact of school reform for the middle years: Longitudinal study of a network engaged in Turning Points-based comprehensive school transformation. *Phi Delta Kappan, 78*, 528–532, 541–550.

Gatewood, T. (1971). What research says about the junior high versus the middle school. *North Central Association Journal, 46*, 264–276.

Gheen, M.H., & Midgley, C. (1999, April). *"I'd rather not do it the hard way": Student and classroom characteristics relating to eighth graders' avoidance of academic challenge*. Paper presented at the annual meeting of the American Educational Research Association Meeting. Montreal.

Goodenow, C. (1993). Classroom belonging among early adolescent students: Relationships to motivation and achievement. *Journal of Early Adolescence, 13*, 21–43.

Gough, P.B. (March, 2000). The editor's page: Detoxifying schools. *Phi Delta Kappan*, p. 482.

Heyman, G.D., & Dweck, C.S. (1992). Achievement goals and intrinsic motivation: Their relation and their role in adaptive motivation. *Motivation and Emotion, 16*, 23 -247.

Hyman, I.A., & Snook, P. (March, 2000). Dangerous schools and what you can do about them. *Phi Delta Kappan*, 489–501.

Jones, K., & Whitford, B.L. (December, 1997), Kentucky's conflicting reform principles: High stakes accountability and student performance assessment. *Phi Delta Kappan*, 276–287.

Kumar, R., & Midgley, C. (2000). *The interplay of individual and contextual factors on change in dissonance between home and school across the transition from elementary to middle school*. Manuscript submitted for publication.

Leet, P.M. (1974, April). *Socialization, schooling, and society*. Paper presented at the annual meeting of the American Educational Research Association, Chicago.

Lewis, A.C., & Norton, J. (June, 2000). Middle grades reform: A vision and beyond. *Phi Delta Kappan, 81*, K5.

Lipsitz, J. (1997a). Middle Grades Improvement Program. *Phi Delta Kappan, 78*, 555.

Lipsitz, J. (1977b). *Growing up forgotten: A review of research and programs concerning early adolescence*. Lexington, MA.: Heath.

Lipsitz, J., Mizell, M.H., Jackson, A.W., & Austin, L.M. (1997). Speaking with one voice: A manifesto for middle-grades reform. *Phi Delta Kappan, 78*, 533–540.

Maehr, M.L. (1989). Thoughts about motivation. In C. Ames, & R. Ames (Eds.), *Research on motivation in education, Vol. 3: Goals and cognitions.* New York: Academic Press.

Maehr, M.L., & Midgley, C. (1996). *Transforming school cultures.* Boulder, CO: Westview Press.

McClelland, D.C. (1951). Measuring motivation in phantasy: The achievement motive. In H. Guetzkow (Ed.), *Groups, leadership and men.* Pittsburgh, PA: Carnegie Press.

Mergendoller, J.R. (1993). Introduction: The role of research in the reform of middle grades education. *The Elementary School Journal, 93,* 443–446.

Middleton, M., & Midgley, C. (1997). Avoiding the demonstration of lack of ability: An under-explored aspect of goal theory. *Journal of Educational Psychology, 89,* 710–718.

Midgley, C. (1993). Motivation and middle level schools. In P. Pintrich. & M.L. Maehr, (Eds.). *Advances in motivation and achievement, Vol. 8: Motivation in the adolescent years* (pp. 219–276). Greenwich, CT: JAI Press.

Midgley, C., Anderman, E., & Hicks, L. (1995). Differences between elementary and middle school teachers and students: A goal theory approach. *Journal of Early Adolescence, 15,* 90–113.

Midgley, C., Arunkumar, R., & Urdan, T. (1996). "If I don't do well tomorrow there's a reason:" Predictors of adolescents' use of academic self-handicapping strategies. *Journal of Educational Psychology, 88,* 423–434.

Midgley, C., & Edelin, K. (1998). Middle school reform and early adolescent well-being: The good news and the bad. *Educational Psychologist, 33,* 195–206.

Midgley, C., Kaplan, A., & Middleton, M. (2001). Performance-approach goals: Good for what, for whom, under what circumstances, and at what cost? *Journal of Educational Psychology., 93,* 77–86.

Midgley, C., Maehr, M.L., Gheen, M., Hruda, L., Middleton, M., & Nelson, J. (1998). *The Michigan middle school study: Report to participating schools and districts.* Ann Arbor: University of Michigan Press.

Midgley, C., & Urdan, T. (1995). Predictors of middle school students' use of self-handicapping strategies. *Journal of Early Adolescence, 15,* 389–411.

Midgley, C., & Urdan, T. (2001). Academic self-handicapping and performance goals: A further examination. *Contemporary Educational Psychology., 26,* 61–75

Nicholls, J.G. (1989). *The competitive ethos and democratic education.* Cambridge, MA: Harvard University Press.

Nicholls, J.G., Patashnick, M., Cheung, P.C., Thorkildsen, T.A., & Lauer, J.M. (1989). Can achievement motivation theory succeed with only one conception of success? In F. Halisch & J.H.L. van der Bercken (Eds.), *International perspectives on achievement and task motivation* (pp. 187–208). Amsterdam: Swets & Zeitlinger.

Norton, J. (June, 2000). Important developments in middle-grades reform. *Phi Delta Kappan, 81,* K2–K4.

Oakes, J., Quartz, K.H., Ryan, S., & Lipton, M. (April, 2000). Becoming good American schools: The struggle for civic virtue in education reform. *Phi Delta Kappan,* 568–575.

Phillips, M. (1997). What makes school effective? A comparison of the relationships of communitarian climate and academic climate to achievement and attendance during middle school. *American Educational Research Journal, 34*, 633–662.

Pintrich, P.R., & Schunk, D.H. (1996). *Motivation in education: Theory, research, and application.* Englewood Cliffs, NJ: Prentice-Hall.

Resnick, M.D., Bearman, P.S., Blum, R.W., Bauman, K.E., Harris, K.M., Jones, J., Tabor, J., Beuhring, T., Sieving, R.E., Ireldan, M., Bearinger, L.H., & Udry, J.R. (1997). Protecting adolescents from harm: Findings from the National Longitudinal Study on Adolescent Health. *Journal of the American Medical Association, 10*, 823–832.

Ryan, A.M., Gheen, M.H., & Midgley, C. (1998). Why do some students avoid asking for help? An examination of the interplay among students' academic efficacy, teachers' social-emotional role, and the classroom goal structure. *Journal of Educational Psychology, 90*, 528–535.

Ryan, A.M., Hicks, L., & Midgley, C. (1997). Social goals, academic goals, and avoiding seeking help in the classroom. *Journal of Early Adolescence, 17*, 152–171.

Ryan, A.M., & Patrick, H. (in press). The classroom social environment and changes in adolescents' motivation and engagement during middle school. *American Educational Research Journal.*

Ryan, A.M. & Pintrich, P.R. (1997). Should I ask for help?_ The role of motivation and attitudes in adolescents' help seeking in math class. *Journal of Educational Psychology, 89*, 329–341.

Shouse, R.C. (1996a). Academic press and sense of community: Conflict and congruence in American high schools. *Research in Sociology of Education and Socialization, 11*, 173–202.

Shouse, R.C. (1996b). Academic press and sense of community: Conflict, congruence, and implications for student achievement. *Social Psychology of Education, 1*, 47–68.

Silberman, C.E. (1970), *Crisis in the classroom.* New York: Random House.

Silver, E.A. (March 1998). *Improving mathematics in middle school: Lessons from TIMSS and related research.* http:www.ed.gov.inits/Math/silver.htm.

Skaalvik, E.M. (1997). Self-enhancing and self-defeating ego orientation: Relations with task and avoidance orientation, achievement, self-perceptions, and anxiety. *Journal of Educational Psychology, 89*, 71–81.

Tucker, M.S., & Codding, J.B. (1999). Education and the demands of democracy in the next millennium. In D.D. Marsh (Ed.), *Preparing our schools for the 21st century* (1999 Yearbook) (pp. 25–44). Alexandria, VA: Association for Supervision & Curriculum Development.

Urdan, T. (1997). Achievement goal theory: Past results, future directions. In M.L. Maehr & P.R. Pintrich (Eds.). *Advances in motivation and achievement* (Vol. 10, pp. 99–142). Greenwich, CT: JAI Press.

Urdan, T., Midgley, C., & Anderman, E. (1998). The role of classroom goal structure in students' use of self-handicapping strategies. *American Educational Research Journal, 35*, 101–122.

Urdan, T., Midgley, C., & Wood, S. (1995). Special issues in reforming middle level schools. *Journal of Early Adolescence, 15*, 9–37.

USA Today. (1999, June 29). Education's weakest link.

Wheelock, A. (1998). *Safe to be smart: Building a culture for standards-based reform in the middle grades.* Columbus, OH: National Middle School Association.

Wiles, J.W., & Thompson, J. (1975). Middle school research 1968–1974: A review of substantial studies. *Educational Research, 32,* 421–423.

Williamson, R., & Johnston, J.H. (1999). Challenging orthodoxy: An emerging agenda for middle level reform. *Middle School Journal, 30,* 10–17.

CHAPTER 3

The Social Structure of the American High School

Sanford M. Dornbusch and Jeanne G. Kaufman

INTRODUCTION

American high schools do not exist in a vacuum. What is taught in school, the ways that the material is taught, and how much the students learn are all affected by social structural contexts. Social structure refers to a relatively enduring pattern of social arrangement or relations within a particular social group. The group may be very large or very small. Accordingly, social structure takes on different forms depending on the level of social organization.

This chapter is organized in terms of two levels of social structure: institutional forms that affect the educational process within the larger society of the United States, and the organizational structure of the typical American high school. We will begin at the societal level, where social structure is expressed in integrated patterns of ideologies, norms, and behaviors. The second part of this chapter will deal with the social structure that provides an external context for the appropriate organization of each high school. This context influences the operations of actors within the school and the coordinating mechanisms that produce its visible form.

This chapter, therefore, will limit itself to those properties of the societal and organizational structures that influence teaching and learning. Both of these larger social structures affect the interactions among school boards, school administrators, teachers, counselors, parents, and students. The influence of social structures on teaching and learning is, as we will show, often indirect. For example, social structures affect such student behaviors as part-time employment and participation in extracurricular activities. Those behaviors influence the strength of the bond between the student and the school, which, in turn, affects student investment in learning. Social structures have both direct and indirect influences on what is taught in schools and what is learned by students.

We begin our analysis of the societal social structure by briefly noting the emergence of adolescence as a separate stage of human development. We then relate education to the system of social stratification within the society, noting that education serves as a mechanism of both inheritance and mobility. The allocation of jobs is viewed by both employers and potential employees as closely linked to the level of educational attainment. We note that the United States was the first industrial society to emphasize mass education rather than the education of an elite.

The control of education in the United States is decentralized, with little influence from the federal government. This system of governance has led to enormous variability in the quality of American high schools, with consequent failures to deliver a minimum level of quality in mass education. The variability of schools is masked by the institutionalization of schooling, where almost all schools appear on the surface to have the same form. In addition, the American emphasis on individual differences in ability serves to justify and explain differences in learning among student populations. Recent movements for national standards, accountability, school choice, and charter schools represent reactions to the failure of many schools to fulfill their appropriate function of mass education.

The second part of this chapter examines the organizational structure of high schools. There are two perspectives that shape these organizational structures. First, high schools are organizations embedded in the wider societal structure in ways that affect the extent to which they fulfill their organizational goals. Second, internal structures within the school shape its organizational form. We begin by discussing the mixed nature of high schools. They are neither formal bureaucracies nor organized groups of professionals. This mixed form of organization is associated with the power and the weakness of teachers, the central organizational actors.

The assignment of students to different tracks within the high school is discussed within the context of mass education and of an emphasis on differential ability. There are problems in the assignment of students and in the quality of education in the less academic tracks, problems that are not known to many students and parents. The role of parents in American high schools is less important than in primary education, but lack of social and cultural capital leads to the failure of many parents to act as advocates for their children in secondary education. Finally, the organization of the social world of high school students is examined, with discussions of the emphasis on adolescent freedom, the high proportion of American students with part-time jobs, and the relative prestige of student achievement in athletics, social life, and academic performance.

THE SOCIETAL CONTEXT OF SECONDARY EDUCATION IN THE UNITED STATES

Adolescence

One cannot understand the American high school in its richness and complexity without examining the emergence of adolescence as a major ideological theme. There were sixteen-year-olds in the eighteenth century, but they were viewed as young adults, expected to work and to assume more adult perquisites, responsibilities, and duties. Today, in the United States, that sixteen-year-old is labeled an adolescent, no longer a child, but clearly in an intermediate stage prior to adulthood. Adolescents now are granted considerable freedom to explore divergent roles and identities and are more likely to be excused when they violate societal norms. The shift to the perception of adolescents as a separate stage of human development is related to larger economic forces and to changes in the nature of family life (Modell & Goodman, 1990).

The period of adolescence has been lengthening steadily over the past two hundred years. If adolescence for females begins at menarche, and the age of first menstruation has dropped from 16 to 10 or 11, the adolescent period is thereby stretched. At the other end, the emphasis on college education and even postgraduate training has led some researchers to suggest that the period of adolescence does not end until schooling has ended, at approximately age 25. Without specifying either end of the adolescent period, it is clear that the high school years are central to the stage of adolescence.

Adolescence is viewed as a time of increasing knowledge and developing social skills. The primary arena for the development of those social skills is the high school. Accordingly, life in the high school is about more than education. Students who are performing poorly in academics often report their positive view of school life (Epstein, 1981; Natriello, McDill, & Pallas, 1990). School is where your friends are, and for many students the social life of the school is as important as the educational experience. We will discuss the structure of student interactions and how that structure can influence academic achievement.

Education as a Mechanism of Inheritance and of Mobility

Among the Masai of East Africa, inheriting cattle is the primary way by which the wealth of parents becomes the wealth of children. In modern urban industrial societies, such as the United States, neither land nor cattle are resources available to most families. Money, of course, can be inherited, but most parents are more worried about funding their own retirement than providing cash for the next generation after their death. Accordingly, most parents seek to aid their children economically by investing in their education.

Parents invest in education in diverse ways, not just through direct cash outlays. While some parents choose to pay private school tuition for their children, other parents will base their choice of an area of residence on the quality of the public schools available in that area. If they pay more for housing in that area, they are making an indirect monetary investment in schooling. Parental investment in schooling may take other forms as well, like encouraging students to work hard, assisting with homework, or steering their children to develop friendships with academically-oriented students. Even prior to making decisions about colleges and their tuitions, some parents make major investments in education by keeping the adolescent's part-time work at a minimum.

Most parents want the best possible life for their child, and they see education as closely linked to occupational achievement. Lacking cows, parents try to help each child to get a good education that will lead to a good job and financial independence. Investment in education is the primary mechanism of inheritance for most Americans.

Somewhat paradoxically, education is also viewed as the primary mechanism of social mobility. Those who are less privileged are often encouraged to do well in school and to pursue higher education in order to reach high-status professional and managerial positions. Parents with low-status jobs hope that, blessed with greater educational opportunity, their children will move up the occupational ladder.

The close link between educational and occupational attainments has led to a major theoretical approach to the study of social stratification in the United States. The Wisconsin models of status attainment (Sewell & Hauser, 1975) argue that socioeconomic status indirectly affects educational and occupational attainments through parental and peer influences and educational aspirations (Jencks, Crouse, & Mueser, 1983).

Socioeconomic status is clearly associated with educational attainment. Education is a mechanism for both social mobility and the reproduction of social inequality. The process is at least in part meritocratic, for numerous individuals coming from disadvantaged backgrounds have achieved high educational and occupational status. Yet, it is also true that a person of higher social origin is likely to reach higher levels of attainment than a person of lower social origin.

Theoretical interpretations of the link between schooling and social stratification mirror the same duality. The functional approach views schools as preparing individuals for their future occupations in a knowledge-based society. Schools, according to this perspective, teach the cognitive skills necessary for increasingly sophisticated occupations, and they also provide a rational meritocratic means for selecting able and motivated persons for the highest status positions (Davis & Moore, 1945). The conflict approach, an alternative perspective, emphasizes the ways in which education perpetuates the existing patterns of inequality among groups (Karabel & Halsey, 1977). Tests comparing these two perspectives are inconclusive (Bills, 1983; Oakes, 1982), so that education should be viewed simultaneously as a mechanism for inheritance and for mobility.

Credentialism

The use of educational attainment as a sorting mechanism among job applicants is most appropriate if higher levels of cognitive skills learned in school are related to occupational status and income. But empirical studies indicate that cognitive skills are less related to occupational status and earnings than is the possession of an educational credential. As a higher proportion of the population finishes high school, goes to college, and gets advanced degrees, the educational credentials required for a given occupational status rise correspondingly. The demand for certificates that show graduation from ever-higher educational institutions is not associated with the complexity of the occupation (Hurn, 1978); personnel managers are using educational credentials primarily as a device to shrink the pool of qualified applicants. Indeed, the reliance upon credentials as a sorting mechanism can be problematic. For example, Berg (1970) found that sales personnel with lower levels of education perform better on the job than those with more education. As Gottfredson (1985) suggests, employers typically select workers on the basis of educational levels rather than on their intelligence, even though job performance demands more on intelligence.

The payoff in income for higher education in the United States continues to increase, amounting to a differential of $17,000 per year in 1998, 63% more than the annual income of high school graduates. The payoff for high school graduation is relatively small, only $6,342 (23%) more per year than for those who attended high school and did not graduate (U. S. Census Bureau, 1999a). One result of the differential in payoffs is an increase in the importance of the differences among curricular tracks in American high schools. College-preparatory classes typically are necessary steps to graduation from four-year colleges and to possible postgraduate degrees. In an age of credentialism, tracking in high schools has become a central economic issue.

From Elite to Mass Education

As in all Western societies, the American high school was at first devoted to the education of only a small proportion of the population. Even as primary schools within the public educational system moved toward the provision of opportunities for the masses, American secondary education, whether public or private, was still serving only a small proportion of the population. In 1890, there were 360,000 students enrolled in high school, about 7% of the appropriate age group (Tyack, 1967; U.S. Census Office, 1897). Enrollment was generally reserved for the children of the elite or the upper middle class. Yet, by 1920, 2.5 million children attended secondary school, nearly one-third of the population 14 to 17 (Tyack, 1967). This sharp increase in high school enrollment reflected an extension of the educational philosophy of free schooling to the adolescent period. By 1940, 79% of youth age 14 to 17 were enrolled in high school (U.S. Census Bureau, 1975), and, in 1997, the proportion was nearly 97% (U.S. Census Bureau, 2000).

The continuing spread of secondary education can also be seen in the changing rates of graduation from high school. In 1940, among persons 25 and older, 22% of males and 26% of females had completed high school (U.S. Census Bureau, 1975). By 1998, 83% of adults 25 and older had graduated from high school (U.S. Census Bureau, 2000).

There are a number of reasons why the United States was among the leaders in the development of mass education. Part of the explanation is industrialization and the growth of urban areas. Yet, there are also ideological bases for the increase in mass education. American individualism is associated with an emphasis on meritocracy. In addition, there is an emphasis on equality of opportunity in the United States compared with the aristocratic ideology of western Europe at the end of the nineteenth century. The growing middle class and the vast number of immigrants entering the United States saw schooling as a path to social and economic advancement.

Mandating a higher upper age for compulsory education was also a way to control the adolescents who, not in school, roamed the streets during school hours. There was fear of these unsupervised youth, as well as a desire to control and socialize poor and immigrant children. The public educational system was viewed as a powerful force in assimilating the children of immigrants and protecting society from the threat posed by deviant youth.

The omnipresence of secondary education does not mean that the structure of American high schools has necessarily kept pace with changes in the nature of the students attending secondary schools. First of all, more than half of all high school graduates go on to some form of college (U.S. Census Bureau, 2000). Thus, the academic curriculum that was once appropriate for a minority of high school students is now needed by a majority of students.

Second, the ethnic composition of American high schools has shifted dramatically. In part, the breakdown of a century-old tradition of segregation by race in American schools has led to increased ethnic diversity in the typical high school. In 1940, fewer than 8% of Blacks 25 years and older had graduated from high school (U.S. Census Bureau, 1975), a number that increased to 76% in 1998 (U.S. Census Bureau, 2000). In addition, the "new immigration" of recent years has led to an increase in the proportion of foreign-born students in public high schools. In 1910, about 3% of all high school students were foreign-born (U.S. Census Bureau, 1913); that proportion had more than doubled to almost 7% by 1998 (U. S. Census Bureau, 2000). In the year 2000, California became the first state in which non-Hispanic Whites were a minority. The new immigration is predominantly Latino and Asian. In 1997 51% of the foreign-born population was from Latin America, 27% from Asia, and only 17% (62% in 1970) from Europe (U.S. Census Bureau, 1999b). The shift in areas of origin has already affected enrollment patterns in the elementary grades, and future changes in the composition of American high schools can confidently be predicted. No longer can high schools cater to the higher-status White population and ignore the needs of other groups.

As will be clear in our later discussion of tracking, American high schools have developed ways of organizing their instruction that take into account the increased heterogeneity of the student population, usually to the detriment of disadvantaged students. That organization of curricular offerings is increasingly taken for granted, yet the results for ethnic minorities, immigrant populations, and low-income students are simultaneously viewed as unsatisfactory. We will suggest methods of organizing school curricula that can handle the diversity of student backgrounds and satisfy the needs of both advantaged and disadvantaged students.

An indicator of the extent to which high school graduation has become normative for American youth is the development of a new social problem:

dropouts. The perception of dropping out of high school as a social problem presupposes the assumption of high school graduation as an expected aspect of the education of most American youth. As late as 1925, only 30% of students entering fifth grade would go on to graduate from high school (U.S. Census Bureau, 1975). When most people are not high school graduates, dropping out is not perceived as the problem. But, when 97% attend high school and 83% graduate (U.S. Census Bureau, 2000), the society can turn its concern to those who drop out of the system.

The concern about dropouts is increased by ethnic differences in dropping out. Only 13% of Whites in 1997 dropped out, compared with 17% among Blacks and 27% among Hispanics (U.S. Census Bureau, 2000). Much of the discussion of dropouts centers on the lack of motivation to stay in school among various groups of students. The emphasis is on the payoff for high school graduation in higher adult incomes. That payoff is real, though small.

Dropping out as a social problem is really a subcategory of a larger problem: lack of learning while in school. Those who drop out overwhelmingly come from the students who are not performing satisfactorily in high school. We will discuss later some reasons for their poor performance, but here we stress how little the dropouts were learning in school. A trail-blazing paper by Alexander, Natriello, and Pallas (1985) showed that, among poor-performing students, those who stayed in school to graduate learned only a little bit more of the material taught in class than did those who had dropped out and never were in class. The problem is not dropouts, but lack of learning for so many students who are participating in the American system of mass education.

Ability and Effort

There is a strain toward egalitarianism in the United States, but it does not take the form of expecting equality in results, such as knowledge, status, or income. Accordingly, no one expects that all students will learn equally fast or acquire an equal fund of knowledge. Instead, the goal is equality of opportunity. Each student should have a chance to reach his or her potential. Variability in knowledge gained in high schools is viewed as an expected result of differences in ability.

There are national differences in the emphasis on ability or on effort. In the United States, the focus is on individual differences among students in their levels of ability. In East Asia (China, Japan, Korea, and Taiwan), the emphasis is on differences in the level of effort put out by students (Bennett, 1987; Rohlen, 1983). In the United States, students of high ability usually get higher grades, whereas Japanese teachers try to grade on improvements in ability that reflect an increase in effort (Holloway, 1988). Thus, the grading system is affected by the amount of emphasis on ability or effort.

Comparative studies of the teaching of math in American and in East Asian schools show that the East Asian schools are organized to expect high math performance by all students. Teachers in those schools believe that almost all students can learn the material in math, though perhaps at different rates. Classes are organized in ways that encourage groups of students to learn together and assume that no students need be left behind (Stevenson, 1990). In the United States, where the student body is often drawn from diverse ethnic groups, status differences in the classroom often lead to differences in learning. Interventions to reduce status differences through cooperative learning have been successful in the United States (Cohen & Lotan, 1997), but most classrooms seem to accept the status quo.

In Asian schools, teachers report that clarity of presentation is the primary characteristic of a good teacher. American teachers, on the other hand, believe that the good teacher is one who understands individual differences among students. Variability in performance in the United States is viewed as primarily a product of differences in ability. Failure to keep up with the rest of the class in East Asia is interpreted as indicating a lack of effort by the student. Parents in East Asia often pay for individual tutoring and for schooling on weekends and after the regular school day. The result is more than higher average performance in math—there is lower variability in math performance in East Asia.

When almost all are presumed to have an appropriate capacity for learning, students are encouraged to keep up with the standards set. When individual differences in ability are stressed, teachers will reduce the amount of learning they expect from low-ability students, and low-ability students will put out less effort in arenas where they view themselves as inadequate (James, 1892).

In the United States, the Education Commission of the States has reviewed previous research and concluded that more than 90% of all students are capable of learning the entire curriculum. The American high school is not organized in ways that reflect that perspective. Instead, the ideological emphasis on ability has led to tracks in the organization of the curriculum, a development to be discussed later.

Accountability and Testing

The ideological emphasis on ability has led to a stress on testing in American schools, for purposes of counseling and assignment of individual students. But recently the pressure toward accountability has meant that the tests are designed to evaluate schools as well as students. The pressure is to hold schools accountable for the performance of their students. Schools are now being evaluated on their ability to bring students up to some minimum level of knowledge. Standardized testing is being used to see how much students are learning, and schools will prove they are teaching well through the performance of their students. The quality of each school is now increasingly assessed in terms of standardized tests, not because those tests are necessarily a valid indicator of teaching and learning, but because there is no other agreed-on basis for assessment.

In many ways, the emphasis on standards and testing suggests that Americans are embracing the belief that all children have the potential to reach some level of academic aptitude. It is becoming clearer that differences in academic performance are not entirely based on differences in the intellectual capacity of individual students. Yet, holding schools accountable for bringing their students up to a minimum standard does not reflect a loss of the American faith in ability differentials. It is just that teachers and schools are now being evaluated on the extent to which they can produce students who meet the minimum acceptable level on standardized tests. The discussion now is more likely to concern "failing schools" than failing students.

One should not conclude that the increased emphasis on teachers and schools that are failing to teach appropriately is a sign of a reduced emphasis on ability differentials among students. The concern with passing at a minimum standard, along with more specific graduation requirements, serves to emphasize the lower limit of acceptable school performance. Beyond the minimum standard, however, differences in ability are still emphasized, as will be clear in our discussion of tracking in high schools.

Many educators, and much of the general public, are concerned about "teaching to the test." There is a danger of increased emphasis on rote learning, which can easily be tested, rather than critical and creative skills that are difficult to assess. For students in our better high schools, and for high-performing students in average schools, teaching to the test can often result in students not attaining high levels of academic preparation. Yet, sadly, teaching to the test would be an improvement in numerous schools where the standards are so low that little teaching or learning is taking place. Assessments of schools and of teachers based on the performance of students on standardized tests are imperfect measures of the quality of the teaching process, but they are better than nothing in the many schools and school districts that assume that less-privileged students are not capable of learning high school material. In schools in which the standards are low, and students are not expected to learn much, teaching to the test may increase the quality of the educational experience. In schools with high standards, an emphasis on standardized testing can lead to a decline in the excellence of teaching and learning.

The attempts to assess the quality of schools have led to discussion of a variety of mechanisms to respond to perceived poor performance. Charter schools, publicly supported but operationally independent of the public school system, and vouchers to pay for private-school tuition are both responses to the "school choice" movement. Dissatisfaction with school quality is increasingly based on measured scores on standardized tests. Parents who perceive their children as stuck in unsatisfactory school environments want alternatives to the local school. Children are assigned to a nearby school on the basis of residential location, and that school may be perceived as either substandard in general or not challenging enough for the better students.

Those who want vouchers emphasize the plight of minority and underprivileged students doomed by virtue of attending "failing schools." But most proposals for vouchers include their availability to middle- and upper-class students who want to attend schools that are more challenging than the typical public school. Similarly, charter schools are targeted at different types of students: disadvantaged students whose parents want them in a more academic atmosphere, and students whose parents want them in an environment that emphasizes the highest levels of performance. Unfortunately, few charter schools have had their activities objectively assessed, so, like vouchers, charter schools become a sloganeering topic that pits defenders of the public school system against its attackers.

The movement for standardized testing will certainly change the high schools of the United States. But, given the political atmosphere in which testing is discussed and the lack of accepted judgmental criteria, testing and school choice may lead to both improvements and worsening of the quality of schools.

The Institutionalization of Schooling

Organizations are shaped by their environments. Their adaptation to the environment produces specific forms of organization. In most for-profit organizations, it is the technical environment that shapes the requirements for the performance of tasks. The products or outcomes are to be produced efficiently and effectively. But many organizations are more shaped by the social and cultural environment than by the technical environment (Scott, 1992).

Meyer and Rowan (1977) noted the importance of adaptation to institutionalized environments. These environments specify the task to be performed, the kind of persons who do them, and how they are to be done. The legitimacy of institutionalized organizations arises, not from their rationality, but from their appearing rational.

In these institutionalized organizations, rules for task performance are present, but they are not focused on efficiency or effectiveness. Instead, as in the field of education, performance rules are permeated with cultural value that is independent of their contribution to producing better outcomes (Meyer, Scott, & Deal, 1981). Rules develop to specify the number of days per year of schooling, the number of years of required attendance, and the credentialing of teachers. They may prescribe aspects of the curriculum and the textbooks that may be purchased. The regulation of physical space within schools is even more elaborate, specifying the size of classrooms, window area, number of water fountains, and number of days per week that the cafeteria floor must be cleaned. At the state level, the accreditation of a school system legitimates its elements: districts, facilities, administrators, teachers, pupils, and curriculum (Meyer, 1992)

The implications of the institutionalization of schooling are numerous and powerful. Some of those implications are discussed below in connection with the organization of schooling. In general, the maintenance of the organizational system that has developed in a school becomes a key goal. Organizations that have diffuse goals and less-developed technologies, such as schools, stress institutionalization more than effectiveness and efficiency (Scott, 1995).

Decentralized Control of Schools

Many societies have national school systems, centralizing control in a Minister of Education and exercising control from the center through inspectors and regional administrators (Ramirez & Rubinson, 1979). The senior author of this paper can report that, in 1966, schools in Tours, France, could not turn on their furnaces until it got cold in Paris. The situation in the United States is very different, with the federal government providing only about 7% of the financial support needed to run America's public schools (Johnson, 2000). Instead, education is largely under control of the 50 states, with considerable operating autonomy granted to nearly 15,000 school districts and school boards (Hoffman, 2000). At the head of each school district is a school board, typically elected, which theoretically controls the local schools. The members of the school board, not trained educators, seek to foster educational goals supported by the families in the community, but the school superintendent has autonomy in the exercise of authority (Dornbusch & Scott, 1975; Greene, 1992).

Through the early part of the twentieth century, the main source of educational funding was local taxation. Recently, however, educational authorities in each state, who long have prescribed rules for curricular and facilities, have increasingly become the primary funders (Kirst, 1970). At the level of finances, individual school districts want to receive as much support as possible from the state government. Therefore, there is a lack of accurate measures of school attendance. In high schools, where cutting classes and truancy are frequent, the schools receive much of their aid in terms of average daily attendance. Accordingly, we found that the cutting of classes by students was seldom recorded in the records, and students were counted as present who appeared only for the class each day at which attendance was taken (Massey, Scott, & Dornbusch, 1975). Lack of accurate attendance counts helps the decentralized district obtain financial support from the state government and, to some extent, from the federal government.

Difficulty in Spreading Successful Innovations

Decentralization makes it difficult to spread educational innovations that prove successful. With so many school districts, and with power diffused among school boards, superintendents, principals, and teachers, innovations are numerous, successes are fewer, and interventions that spread widely are not based on demonstrated success in the classroom (Meyer, 1992). The organization of the high school is not closely linked to the actual work processes. High schools are "loosely coupled," showing a tendency to disconnect policies from outcomes and rules from actual activities (March, 1978; Meyer, 1992; Weick, 1976).

Instructional content and the practices of teachers are managed, if at all, at the decentralized local level. There are general controls at a more centralized level, dealing with issues like accreditation, certification of teachers, and the establishment of general curricula. The more central bureaucratic controls, whether federal or state, tend to ignore instructional content and method. Instead, more formal aspects of education, such as inequality within the system for large groups of students, tend to be the stuff of bureaucratic action and political rhetoric. Media attention focuses on school choice, with discussions of school vouchers, charter schools, and public versus private schools. Meanwhile, central bodies dictate rules, but these rules are often not implemented in the classroom. Guidelines for homework, for example, are ignored by many teachers. At the school level, Title I money, federal funds for the improvement of instruction for disadvantaged students, tended to be spread throughout most school systems and not targeted exclusively at the groups supposed to benefit. Loose coupling leads to the instructional side of education being more affected by fashionable educational practice and stories in the mass media than by carefully controlled studies with soundly-based results and implications (Meyer, 1992).

In this context of institutionalization of schools, with little direct control of classroom practices, Tyack and Cuban (1995) note that there is another side to reform changing schools—schools change reforms. Practitioners in the schools typically believe that policymakers do not understand the problems of schools and propose unrealistic reforms. There are occasions when federal and state reform efforts influence classroom practice directly or indirectly. In those circumstances, local schools and teachers adapt innovations to specific circumstances, comply minimally, or even sabotage reforms that are considered undesirable. Since principals and teachers are not in the loop as school reforms are designed and adopted, we should not be surprised at their failure to implement innovations (Tyack & Cuban, 1995).

Variability among American High Schools

School districts, within common institutionalized forms of organization, differ dramatically in the quality of education provided. And within school districts, there can be an equally great disparity between the educational environment in the best local high school and the worst. How bad can a high school be? The valedictorian of a San Francisco Bay Area high school was rejected at the University of California as below their minimum academic standard. Lawsuits against school districts for failing to provide an adequate education typically fail, but that does not mean that the complaints are without merit.

Because of the variability in American high schools and their lack of common standards in grading, selective American colleges and universities typically ask applicants to provide scores on standardized tests, such as those of the College Entrance Examination Board. Those tests, unfairly pilloried because minority students tend to do poorly, do at least as well in predicting college grades for minority students as the tests do in predicting for non-Hispanic White students. The tests seek to predict grades during the freshman year of college, and they do better than chance at that task. The more fundamental problem is not the quality of the testing, but the incredible variability in the quality of American high schools that forces colleges and universities to look beyond grades for an assessment of academic performance.

Stanford University, with which we are affiliated, devotes resources in the admission process in order to overcome the differences among high schools in quality and grading. As part of the selection process when a student applies for admission as an undergraduate, his or her high school grades are used to predict the likely performance in the freshman year of college. Those predicted freshman grades are then adjusted to take into account the grades received by other students from that same high school who previously attended Stanford. If those students did better in their freshman year than was predicted for them, the predicted grades for the current applicant would be raised. If previous students had not done as well as expected, the current applicant would have his or her predicted grade lowered. Of course, this technique assumes few rapid changes in the quality of instruction in a school. It is not an attempt to help or harm any student, but simply a mechanism to adjust for the enormous variability within the universe of American high schools.

Segregated Neighborhoods, Segregated Schools

The composition of the student body is the single best predictor of the quality of the school. If the students in a high school come from families that are better educated, have better jobs, and are richer, that high school is likely to do well as measured by standardized tests taken by its students. That does not mean that school composition directly explains the quality of performance. Rather, the status of the average family affects other variables: the tax base available to the school district, the pressure that parents exert on school personnel, the cultural capital in each home, the social capital that spreads information about the school and schooling, and the level of educational expectations among families and among school personnel. These mediating factors provide the pressures that make it likely that public schools for the advantaged will be superior to public schools for the disadvantaged.

The composition of the student body in a public high school usually directly reflects the composition of the neighborhoods that are part of its catchment area. The variability in school composition that is so great in American high schools is a product of the variability in the neighborhoods from which they draw students. If there were not great differences in social class and ethnicity across neighborhoods, schools would not differ so dramatically in their composition.

It is segregation in housing that drives this phenomenon. Americans accept that rents and home values are a product of the market. The persons who can afford the most desirable residences get their pick of available neighborhoods, while those with the least resources are relegated to the least desirable neighborhoods. Social class differences among communities are known to all, but they are experienced as an inescapable part of the status quo—the rich live where they want, while the poor live where they can.

Segregation by ethnicity is not taken for granted. In recent decades there has been continual pressure to open up neighborhoods for residents of diverse ethnic and racial backgrounds. Given the acceptance of the market, that means that some higher-status Whites are willing to live next to members of minority groups who are also high in income. Because of the great ethnic and racial differences in income in the United States, the result is a continuing pattern of ethnic and racial segregation in housing even as expressed attitudes toward integrated housing have become more favorable.

The impact upon school districts of continuing segregation in housing is clear. To some extent, there has been "White flight," which has led to declines in the enrollment of White students as families seek to avoid participation in integrated schools. The extent of White flight has been exaggerated—the vast majority of Whites left central cities for reasons that were not related to the attendance policies of school districts (Taeuber & Wilson, 1978). African Americans who reside in heavily segregated areas accordingly are high in their preference for school choice, including vouchers.

But, for whatever reason, school integration moved forward rapidly in the South and was limited in some other areas. Today, the level of integration of Blacks and Whites is not controlled by school districts. If all school districts were fully integrated, racial segregation in American high schools would still be very high (Rivkin, 1994). Segregated schools are a product of housing patterns, and residential housing reflects the power of economic factors and ethnic prejudice. Since ethnic and racial segregation in housing has not declined appreciably, high schools are directly affected.

Family socioeconomic status has been found to be more related to school achievement among non-Hispanic Whites than among African American students (Gottfredson, 1981). In an attempt to understand this phenomenon, Dornbusch, Ritter, and Steinberg (1991) examined the ethnic mix in residential communities. They found that, for both non-Hispanic White and African American families, the influence of family statuses on school performance was reduced for students living in a census tract with a substantial proportion of minority residents. The ethnic difference in the influence of family statuses on academic achievement was explained by the high proportion of minority students who live in such minority areas. Therefore, segregated housing has powerful effects on all ethnic groups.

Let us now turn from societal forces affecting American high schools to the organizational structure of the high school.

THE ORGANIZATIONAL CONTEXT OF
AMERICAN HIGH SCHOOLS

A Professional Bureaucracy

As discussed in the earlier section on the institutionalization of school, the organization of schools reflects aspects of the wider society. Two organizational forms that are widespread in Western industrial societies are professions and bureaucracies. In high schools, one observes an uneasy mixture of these two forms, embodying aspects of each. High schools have most of the disadvantages and few of the advantages of both bureaucracies and professions.

Some aspects of schools resemble traditional bureaucracies. There are clear hierarchies of authority, specific jobs are delineated, and merit is supposed to be a factor in filling positions (Bidwell & Quiroz 1991). But schools seldom function as pure bureaucracies. Principals, theoretically in charge of teachers, have few sanctions they can exercise to control teachers, and the power of teachers' unions further restrict their ability to exert authority. Assignment of teachers to schools is also subject to constraints built into the union contract. In Los Angeles, for example, the teachers' union is attempting to preserve the right of teachers with seniority to choose entry into any school with vacancies, regardless of the choices desired by administrators. One result is the inability of school districts to provide enough experienced teachers for those schools that have the least prepared students and the lowest levels of academic performance.

Some school personnel (teachers, counselors, librarians, and nurses) operate as professionals (Hurn, 1978). Teachers, in particular, are licensed by the state and are assumed to have internalized the necessary knowledge to deal with the ever-changing task of teaching (Dornbusch & Scott, 1975). As professionals, teachers are given considerable discretion in the organization of classroom activities (Bidwell & Quiroz, 1991). To some extent, they operate as professionals within a hierarchical bureaucracy (Hall, 1972).

Instruction, the most critical task in the high school, is loosely coupled with the schools' administrative processes (Weick, 1976). Teachers teach behind closed doors, seldom evaluated for the quality of their teaching (Dornbusch, 1976). Once given tenure, so seldom are teachers evaluated by their principals that we once found that teachers liked more those principals who gave them more negative evaluations. It is not that teachers enjoy being criticized, but that they appreciate principals looking at their central task, instruction (Dornbusch & Scott, 1975). Another deficiency of the bureaucratic model in high schools arises from the common practice of departmental organization. Some decision-making rights are assigned to department heads, but they do not exercise much power over teachers and serve mainly as protectors of departmental autonomy against the influence of principals (Worner, 1993). Such protection against bureaucratic control would be reasonable were there a tradition of collegial control or professionalism.

American high schools are a mixed form, a professional bureaucracy. Teacher pay, for example, is distributed on the basis of seniority and educational certificates, and almost never on the basis of merit (Choy, Bobbitt, Henke, Medrich, Horn, & Lieberman, 1993). Even when a state tries to make it easier to lure teachers back from retirement with financial benefits, the legislature worries about whether appointments have to be offered solely on the basis of seniority (Wyatt, 2000). Unions argue that their opposition to merit pay is based on the difficulty of assessing the quality of teaching and on the likely favoritism of administrators (Cramer, 1983; Spillane, 1987), as well as on their view that merit pay will discourage collegiality and teamwork (Feldman, 2000). Recently, some school districts have sought a middle ground in which individual teachers are not given bonuses, but all teachers at schools that improve performance on standardized tests are given extra pay. Such schemes obviously further emphasize the importance of standardized tests.

A trenchant article by Levy (2000) argues that the conditions of the current professional bureaucracy have led to a decline in the quality of teachers recruited in recent decades—a decline that unions are reluctant to acknowledge, that is partly due to low-quality education courses, and that administrators prefer not to mention for fear of reducing confidence in public education. Levy believes that school systems must reduce the bureaucratic hurdles to becoming a teacher, increase teacher pay, and improve working conditions. We would add that increasing opportunities for professional collaboration would increase the autonomy of teachers while simultaneously raising teacher standards.

Even the certification of teachers does not fit the ideal model of a profession. Schools of education are certified, and then all their graduates are granted certification by the state in which they were educated. Individual-level tests might add to the occupation's prestige. In almost all professions, graduation from an accredited school is not enough. Each lawyer, nurse, and accountant must pass a test on his or her knowledge in order to achieve full certification.

The current educational system is certainly not producing enough high-quality teachers. When new teachers were required to take a Pre-Professional Skills Test in Houston, Texas, in the early 1980s, 62% failed. In Dallas, Texas, the superintendent of schools said he was hiring unqualified minority teachers in order to satisfy a desegregation decree and, to avoid reverse discrimination, he was hiring an equal number of unqualified whites. When 202,000 Texas teachers took the Texas Examination of Current Administrators and Teachers in 1986, 99% of graduates of the University of Texas passed, but graduates of smaller colleges had success rates as low as 55%. The state regulatory body in Texas had to expend considerable effort to determine a passing standard that would not fail too many potential teachers and would survive political scrutiny (Shepard & Kreitzer, 1987). Today, in a period when millions of new teachers must be recruited, it is important that the standards of the weaker schools of education be raised. Otherwise, the need for quantity may overwhelm the desire for quality.

Teachers are currently operating autonomously under conditions that demand high levels of skill. Almost all teachers necessarily exercise considerable discretion as they deal with the active task of teaching (Dornbusch & Scott, 1975). They typically operate as individual professionals in a structure that is not concerned with the details of what they teach and how they teach it. Principals lack the time, energy, or sanctioning power to exercise authority over individual teachers (Dornbusch & Scott, 1975), and the teachers seldom exercise collegial control over one another. The relative isolation of each teacher from his or her colleagues prevents the development of a professional culture that seeks to improve performance (Marram, Dornbusch, & Scott, 1972). The public high school is currently a professional bureaucracy that is not conducive to high-level teaching performances, for it is not performing adequately in terms of either bureaucratic or professional criteria.

Tracking

The best high school teachers typically teach classes that contain a high proportion of high-ability students. (Oakes, 1985). In general, the least experienced and non-certificated teachers are assigned to teach classes with lower levels of academic performance and higher levels of classroom disruption. The sorting process by which secondary schools select students for those classes is itself the subject of considerable dispute. Most high schools group students by ability, so that there is considerable between-class variability. In the elementary schools there was ability grouping, but the groups were more often formed within each class.

The high schools do not advertise that they track students, and they do not have formally defined tracks (Oakes, Gamoran, & Page, 1992). Schools, instead, set up classes by ability groups on a subject-by-subject basis. Since students tend to perform similarly across courses, this produces distinct tracks with some level of overlap among students (Gamoran, 1987).

High schools differ on the tracks available (honors, advanced, academic, general, basic, or remedial), on the criteria for assigning students, and on the level of mobility across tracks (Gamoran, 1992; Oakes, 1985; Rosenbaum, 1976). This results in considerable variability in the number of students taking academic (college-preparatory) courses, with the range from 10% to 100%, with an average of 35% (Kilgore, 1991).

In 1917–18, when attendance in high school was not the norm, 69% of all students in American public high schools were taking academic courses (Bureau of Education, 1921). By 1994, as the United States moved away from education for the elite to education for the masses, the proportion of public high school graduates who took predominantly college-preparatory courses was about 32% (U.S. Department of Education, 2000). Thus, the proportion of high school students preparing for college was cut in half as the population in the high school dramatically increased both in number and in heterogeneity. This change means that, though the number of prospective college students has increased, a markedly lower proportion of high school graduates are now eligible for enrollment in four-year colleges and universities. The rise of the community college system is in part a response to this change in the proportion of academically prepared students.

Teachers take into account these ability groupings by class, teaching different material at different speeds in terms of the supposed potential of the students. The instructional agenda accordingly differs by track (Dreeben & Barr, 1988). Movement up in track is hindered by this difference in material covered. To get an "A" in a low-level course does not mean that the student has mastered the material covered in the equivalent high-level course. Moving the student to a high-level course in that subject in the next academic year probably means that he or she must do considerable additional work to make up for prior deficiencies in the content covered. A study of northern California high schools found that, labeling each freshman student as "college-prep" or "not college-prep," about 85% of the students would have the same label when seniors. There is some mobility across tracks, but not very much across the key boundary, which defines who can go to a four-year college (Dornbusch, 1994).

Assignment to a non-college-preparatory track has a powerful impact on learning in high school. Approximately 25% of high school students in 1994 were specializing in vocational concentrations, and 32% in "general" (U.S. Department of Education, 2000). These students typically do not learn sufficient academic material to be eligible for entrance into four-year colleges and universities (Banner, 1999). That lack of learning is not solely a consequence of low ability. When, because of the vagaries of scheduling (taking account of student extracurricular activities and employment as well as the number of classes open at a particular time period), talented students are assigned to low-level math and science courses, they expend less effort, learn less, and get lower grades than if they were in the higher track. The teachers of lower-track classes, on the average, are lower in ability and experience and teach less-demanding courses compared with teachers of higher-track classes (Dornbusch, 1994; Gamoran & Berends, 1987; Oakes, 1987; Rosenbaum, 1980).

Since track assignment can have such powerful effects, inappropriate assignments matter greatly. Research to date indicates that placement of students, particularly those at medium levels of ability, is often arbitrary and difficult to change (Dornbusch, 1994; Tuckman & Bierman, 1971). Because federal and state financing is available for students in special-education classes, there is an incentive to place students in those classes, especially those from disadvantaged minorities ("A special-ed warning," 1998) The term "educationally handicapped" is used as a category within a list of physical and mental disabilities, and it often refers to little more than a failure to learn.

As we have noted, assignments to college-prep or non-college-prep tracks in high school courses tend to be permanent and self-fulfilling. Students deemed less able are taught less and learn less, thus supporting the original image of cognitive inadequacy. We would like to suggest short-term remediation as the substitute for long-term placement. We draw on the work of Farkas (Dornbusch, 2000; Farkas, 1996), who showed that reading disabilities in the early grades could be dramatically overcome by one-to-one assistance from nonprofessional tutors who were appropriately trained. It may seem odd to discuss remediation in early grades in a paper on American high schools, but the senior author has learned from the reaction of the San Francisco School District to his study showing the failure of its high schools to educate minority students. Instead of intervening at the high school level, third- and fourth-grade teachers were given the specific assignment of improving the reading skills of the slow readers. The result was a marked improvement in the reading scores of minority students.

The failure to have basic skills should produce attempts at remediation all through the elementary grades and the years in high school. For example, many disadvantaged students have trouble doing mathematics because they cannot read the problems posed. Such basic skills as reading and arithmetic for example, can be taught at any age if the school invests resources for short-term remediation. The students need not be removed from the standard classrooms, and they need not encounter the stigma of being labeled unteachable or apathetic. Were such short-term approaches made more frequent, the need for assignment of students to the lower tracks in the high school would be reduced. This type of intervention would not attack the interests of the advantaged groups, nor would it reduce in any way the demand for quality advanced courses.

The Role of Families

The single best predictor of the quality of academic life in a high school is the social class composition of the student body. The status of the parents directly and indirectly affects student academic performance, aspirations, and achievement. High school students from lower social classes, disadvantaged minorities, and single-parent households are likely to get low grades in school (Dornbusch, Carlsmith, Bushwall, Ritter, Leiderman, Hastorf, & Gross, 1985; Natriello, McDill, & Pallas, 1990).

In addition to these differences by "status addresses," processes within the family affect adolescent school performance. Authoritative parenting, more common among higher-status families, is associated with high grades (Steinberg, Lamborn, Dornbusch, & Darling, 1992). Single-parent families are more likely to grant too-early autonomy to adolescents, and that lack of parental influence is associated with lower grades in high school (Dornbusch et al., 1985). The high academic performance of Chinese students is partly explained by the emphasis on teaching in the home (Chao, 1994). Finally, the parenting patterns of African Americans, whose adolescents often perform poorly in school, reflect the poverty of the family more than any distinct cultural tradition (McLoyd, Jayaratne, Cebello, & Borquez, 1994). Such processes underlying academic achievement in the high school, such as behavioral control by parents (Dornbusch, Laird, & Crosnoe, 1999), help us to understand how parental statuses get translated into adolescent behaviors.

As students move through adolescence, parents view their role as limited. Whereas parents of students in elementary school view themselves, and are viewed by others, as key actors in the educational process, parents of high school students tend to "let go" and grant more independence to their offspring. Yet, parenting of adolescents appears to continue to have a major impact on school performance in the high school (Astone & McLanahan, 1991; Baker & Stevenson, 1986; Baumrind, 1991; Steinberg, Lamborn, Darling, Mounts, & Dornbusch, 1994; Stevenson & Baker, 1987).

Some of the family influence on adolescent school performance comes from differences in cultural capital (Bourdieu, 1977). Books in the home, political discussions, and cultural activities provide resources for the high school student. Lack of such family resources is associated with the loss of talent, for some students of high academic quality do not expect to be college graduates (Laird, 1999).

Differences in social capital can also influence school performance (Stanton-Salazar & Dornbusch, 1995). Middle-class and upper-class parents are more likely to know about tracking assignments and their significance than are lower-status parents (Useem, 1991, 1992). Mexican-American parents and students seldom call upon school personnel for information and guidance (Stanton-Salazar, 1990/1991).

Not only can parents exercise influence on high school students behind the scenes, but the parents can also act as advocates for their children. At the high school level, teachers do like contacts with parents, but only when they are initiated by the teacher. They resent parent-initiated contacts as "pushy." Despite the prevalence of this view among teachers, parental advocacy does pay off for students, particularly with respect to tracking (Prescott, Pelton, & Dornbusch, 1986).

The Social World of the Students

To this point, we have emphasized the academic function of the high school. Both ideological and organizational patterns have been shown to influence the high school's main task: instruction. Yet, the process of student learning is not entirely dependent on the quality of instruction within a school. Adolescence is a stage in life that demands the development of numerous nonacademic skills. Students and their parents expect the high school to provide a site for the development of social and athletic skills. Students who are doing poorly in their academic courses often report very favorable attitudes toward going to high school, for that is the center of their social world (Natriello, McDill, & Pallas, 1990; Epstein, 1981). Indeed, there is often resistance from parents and students to attempts to increase the level of academic demand in high school (Kralovec & Buell, 2000; Zernike, 2000). Too much homework is seen as a barrier to participation in extracurricular activities, to part-time work, and to an active social life outside of school.

Adolescence is characterized by increased age segregation and reduced contact with adults. Although relations with parents and other adults continue during the high school years, their importance gradually decreases as the importance of friendships with peers increases. High school students still seek advice on educational and career goals from their parents, but the interpersonal world is shared predominantly with their peers. Among their friends, adolescents feel they can express themselves and be understood (Savin-Williams & Berndt, 1990; Youniss & Smollar, 1985).

High school students spend twice as much time with their friends as they do with their parents and other adults (Savin-Williams & Berndt, 1990). When the values of peers conflict with the values of parents, the group that will have more influence on the adolescent is the one that he or she believes is most likely to learn which choice was made (Dornbusch, 1987). Accordingly, given the time adolescents spend with friends, peer values matter.

The values of friends influence numerous aspects of adolescent life, including academic performance in the high school and engaging in deviant activities, such as delinquency and substance use. Yet, parents can play a major protective role by indirection, shaping the choice of friends and reducing adolescent susceptibility to negative peer influences (Chen, 2000). The choice of neighborhood influences the type of school attended, and parental monitoring can shape adolescent activities. Recent portrayal of parental impotence (Harris, 1998) fails to take into account parental ability to buffer the adolescent against inappropriate peer values and behaviors (Crosnoe, Erickson, & Dornbusch, in press; Dornbusch et al., 1999; Erickson, Crosnoe, & Dornbusch, in press). The extent to which peers support academic values is important in affecting academic performance and deviance, but the selection of each adolescent's peer group is not a passive process.

Extracurricular Activities

Extracurricular activities tend to link the high school student to the school, whether those activities are in clubs or sports. There appears to be a consistent relation between engaging in extracurricular activities and staying in school. Accordingly, requiring a decent grade-point-average to participate in extracurricular activities may increase the proportion of students who drop out. Thus, there is sometimes a controversy as to the relative importance of raising academic standards and preventing dropouts.

One form of extracurricular activity, sports, has been the center of considerable research in American high schools. Coleman's (1961) work on the prestige associated with sports achievement was very influential. He stressed that athletic performance brought higher social standing than did academic performance. The symbolic importance of athletic teams, which are typically the only aspect of school life discussed by the general community outside of school, is greater than one would expect. Academic performance is a far better predictor of future occupational achievement and lower deviance than is athletic performance, but the social standards of high school students exalt athletic prowess more than academic skill. Still, in general, students who do well academically are also likely to be doing well in student government, sports, and other extracurricular activities, and they are more likely to be in the most popular "crowd" than those who do poorly in academics. These findings are, in part, the product of differences in social class (Dornbusch, Herman, & Morley, 1996).

In general, high-income students are more likely than low-income students to be involved in extracurricular activities (Brantlinger, 1993). This appears to be true for academic and student government activities and for athletics, except for certain sports, like basketball and football, that have the potential for professional employment (American Institutes for

Research, 1988). Although participation in extracurricular activities is seen as voluntary and open to students of all backgrounds, there are limits on the self-selection process (Quiroz, Gonzalez, & Frank, 1996). Students will be more likely to join clubs or sports teams if doing so is accepted or encouraged by their peer group. Information about how and when to participate is often limited as well. Students get information from their peer groups and from faculty and staff members, who may be less likely to encourage lower-income students to participate. Many schools require minimum-grade-point-averages, and students who are doing poorly in their classes or who have behavior problems may not be eligible or accepted in extracurricular activities. Finally, most extracurricular activities require students to make after-school time commitments. Students who work or take care of younger siblings often cannot participate.

Student Employment

Among all industrial countries in the world, the United States has the highest proportion of high school students who simultaneously are in the labor force. More than 80% of all high school students in the United States have a paid part-time job during the school year (Bachman & Schulenberg, 1992; Light, 1995; Steinberg & Cauffman, 1995).

The percentage employed and the number of hours they work increases with age. One-third of tenth graders and two-thirds of the twelfth-graders reported employment during the school year (Lillydahl, 1990). Among 15-year-olds who worked during the school year, the average number of hours per week was 11. Among 17-year-olds with jobs during the school year, the average was 18 hours of work per week.

Working long hours during the school year, more than 20 hours per week, can have negative repercussions. At that high intensity of part-time work, substance abuse and minor deviance, insufficient sleep and exercise, and reduced educational performance and attainment are more likely. The long hours at work reduce the likelihood of extracurricular activities, whether related to sports or organized clubs (Institute of Medicine, 1998).

CONCLUSION

It seems appropriate that this discussion of the social structure of American high schools starts with larger ideological issues concerning education and adult jobs and ends with a discussion of the social life of high school students. The American high school is a microcosm of the wider society. Numerous diverse forces affect the high school and produce competing views as to what is appropriate or significant in that specific type of organization. Among the issues raised are the influences of the family or of the mass media, the level of concern about the standards of mass education or about ethnic groups left behind, and the image of adolescence as a separate, fun stage of life or as preparation for adulthood. Changes in the structure of American high schools will be part of national changes in institutional ideology and the forms of organization that are deemed appropriate in that educational setting.

REFERENCES

Alexander, K.L., Natreillo, G., & Pallas, A.M. (1985). For whom the school bell tolls: The impact of dropping out on cognitive performance. *American Sociological Review, 50,* 409–420.

American Institutes for Research. (1988). *Report #1: Summary results from the 1987–1988 national study of intercollegate athletes.* Palo Alto, CA: Author.

Astone, N.M., & McLannahan, S.S. (1991). Family structure, parental practices, and high school completion. *American Sociological Review, 56,* 309–320.

Bachman, J.G., & Schulenberg, J. (1992). *Part-time work by high school seniors: Sorting out correlates and possible consequences.* (Monitoring the Future Occasional Paper 32). Institute for Social Research, University of Michigan.

Baker, D., & Stevenson, D.L. (1986). Mother's strategies of children's school achievement: Managing the transition to high school. *Sociology of Education, 59,* 156–166.

Banner, R. (1999, September 8). Critics say graduation exams hurt vocational students. *New York Times,* p. A22

Baumrind, D. (1991). The influence of parenting style on adolescent competence and substance use. *Journal of Early Adolescence, 11,* 56–95.

Bennett, W.J. (1987). Implications for American education. In C.H. Dorfman (Ed.), *Japanese education today* (pp. 69–71). Washington, DC: US Department of Education.

Berg, I.E., with Gorelick, S. (1970). *Education and jobs: The great training robbery.* New York: Praeger.

Bidwell, C.E., & Quiroz, P.A. (1991). Organizational control in the high school workplace: A theoretical argument. *Journal of Research on Adolescence, 1,* 211–229.

Bills, D.B. (1983). Social reproduction and the Bowles-Gintis thesis of a corresponsence between school and work settings. In A.C. Kerckhoff (Ed.), *Research in sociology of education and socialization* (Vol. 4 , pp. 185–210). Greenwich, CT: JAI Press.

Bourdieu, P. (1977). Cultural reproduction and social reproduction. In J. Karabel & A.H. Halsey (Eds), *Power and ideology in education* (pp 487–511). New York: Oxford University Press.

Brantlinger, E.A. (1993). *The politics of social class in secondary schools: Views of affluent and impoverished youth.* New York: Teachers College Press.

Bureau of Education. (1921). *Biennial survey of education, 1916–18* (Vol. IV). Washington, D.C.: Government Printing Office.

Chao, R.K. (1994). Beyond parental control and athoritative parenting style: Understanding chinese parenting through the cultural notion of training. *Child Development, 65,* 1111–1119.

Chen, Z. (2000). The relation between parental constructive behavior and adolescent association with achievement oriented peers: A longitudinal study. *Sociological Inquiry, 70,* 330–381.

Choy, S.P., Bobbitt, S.A., Henke, R.R., Medrich, E.A., Horn, L.J., & Lieberman, J. (1993). *America's teachers: Profile of a profession* (205 pp.). Berkeley, CA: MPR Association.

Cohen, E.G., & Lotan, E.G. (Eds.). (1997). *Working for equity in heterogenous classrooms: Sociological theory in practice.* New York: Teachers College Press.

Coleman, J.S. (1961). *The adolescent society.* New York: Free Press.

Cramer, J. (1983). Merit pay: Challenge of the decade. *Curriculum Review, 22,* 7–10.

Crosnoe, R., Erickson, K.G., & Dornbusch, S.M. (in press). Protective functions of family and school factors on adolescent: Reducing the impact of risky friendships. *Youth and Society.*

Davis, K., & Moore, W.E. (1945). Some principles of stratification. *American Sociuological Review, 10,* 242–249.

Dornbusch, S.M. (1976). Behind closed doors: Failures in evaluating teachers and principals. *Students Review, 1,* 23–24.

Dornbusch, S.M., (1987). Individual moral choices and social evaluations: A research odyssey. In E.J. Lawler & B. Markovsky (Eds.), *Advances in group processes: Theory and research* (Vol. 4, pp. 271–307). Greenwich, CT: JAI Press.

Dornbusch, S.M. (1994). *Off the track.* Presidential Address presented at Biennial Meeting of the Society for Research on Adolescence, San Diego, CA.

Dornbusch, S.M. (2000) Triumph and sadness. *School Psychology Quarterly, 15,* 359–364.

Dornbusch, S.M., Carlsmith, J.M., Bushwall, P.L., Ritter, P.L., Leiderman, P.H., Hastorf, A.H., & Gross, R.T. (1985). Single parents, extended households, and the control of adolescents. *Child Development, 56,* 326–341.

Dornbusch, S.M., Herman, M.R., & Morley, J.A. (1996). Domains of adolescent achievement. In G.R. Adams, R. Montemayor, & T.P. Gullotta (Eds.), *Psychosocial development during adolecsence : Progress in developmental contextualism* (Ch. 6, pp. 181–231). Thousand Oaks, CA: Sage.

Dornbusch, S.M., Laird, J., Crosnoe, R. (1999). Parental and school resources that assist adolescents in coping with negative peer influences. In E. Frydenberg (Ed.), *Young people learning to cope in complex societies* (pp. 277–298). Oxford: Oxford University Press.

Dornbusch, S.M., Ritter, P.L., & Steinberg, L. (1991). Community influences on the relation of faniFly statuses to adolescent school performance differences between African Americans and non-Hispanic whites. *American Journal of Education, 99,* 543–567.

Dornbusch, S.M., & Scott, W.R. (1975). *Evaluation and the exercise of authority.* San Francisco: Jossey-Bass.

Dreeben, R., & Barr, R. (1988) Classroom composition and the design of instruction. *Sociology of Education, 61,* 129–42.

Epstein, J.L. (Ed.). (1981). *The quality of school life.* Lexington, MA: Lexington Books.

Erickson, K.G., Crosnoe, R.C., & Dornbusch, S.M. (in press). A social process model of adolescent deviance: Combining social control and differential association perspectives. *Journal of Youth and Adolescence.*

Farkas, G. (1996). *Human capital or cultural capital? Ethnicity and poverty groups in an urban school district.* Hawthorne, NY: Aldine de Gruyter.

Feldman, S. (2000, September 3), Good for America. *New York Times,* p. WK7.

Gamoran, A. (1987). The stratification of high school learning opportunities. *Sociology of Education, 59,* 185–98.

Gamoran, A. (1992). The variable effects of high school tracking. *American Sociological Review, 57,* 812–28.

Gamoran, A., & Berends, M. (1987). The effects of stratification in secondary schools: Synthesis of survey and ethnographic research. *Review of Educational Research, 57,* 415–435.

Gottfredson, D.L. (1981). Black-white differences in the educational attainment process: What have we learned? *American Sociological Review, 46,* 542–557.

Gottfredson, L.S. (1985). Education as a valid but fallible signal of worker quality: Reorienting an old debate about the functional basis of the occupational hierarchy. In *Research in sociology of education and socialization* (Vol. 5, pp. 123–169). Greenwich, CT: JAI Press.

Greene, K.R. (1992). Models of school board policy-making. *Educational Administration Quarterly, 28,* 220–236.

Hall, R.H. (1972). *Organizations: Structure and process.* Engelwood Cliffs. NJ: Prentice-Hall.

Harris, J.R. (1998). *The nurture assumption: Why children turn out the way they do.* New York: Free Press.

Hoffman, L (2000). *Overview of public and elementary and secondary schools and districts: School year 1998–99* (NCES 2000-333).

Holloway, S.D. (1988). Concepts of ability and effort in Japan and the United States. *Review of Educational Research, 58,* 327–345.

Hurn, C. (1978). *The limits and possibilities of schooling: An introduction to the sociology of schooling.* Boston: Allyn & Bacon.

Institute of Medicine. (1998). *Protecting youth at work : Health, safety, and development of working children and adolescents in the United States.* Washington, DC: National Academy Press.

James W. (1892). *Psychology.* New York: Henry Holt.

Jencks, C., Crouse, J., & Mueser, P. (1983). The Wisconsin model of status attainment: A national replication with improved measures of ability and aspiration. *Sociology of Education, 56,* 3–19.

Johnson, F. (2000). *Revenues and expenditures for public elementary and secondary education: School year 1997–98* (NCES 2000-348).

Karabel, J., & Halsey, A.H. (Eds.). (1977). *Power and ideology in education.* New York: Oxford University Press.

Kilgore, S.B. (1991). The organizational context of tracking in schools. *American Sociological Review, 56,* 189–203.

Kirst, M (1970). *The politics of education at the local, state, and federal levels.* Berkeley, CA: McCutchen.

Kralovec, E., & Buell, J. (2000). *The end of homework: How homework disrupts families, overburdens children, and limits learning.* Boston: Beacon Press.

Laird, J. (1999). *Inflated expectations and lost talent: The relation of social, human and financial capital to unfulfilled educational expectations among adolescents.* Unpublished doctoral dissertation, Stanford University, Stanford, CA.

Levy, H.O. (2000, September 9). Why the best don't teach. *New York Times,* p. A27.

Light, A (1995). *High school employment. National Longitudinal Survey Discussion Paper.* (Report No. NLS 95-27). Washington, DC: U.S. Department of Labor.

Lillydahl, J.H. (1990). Academic achievement and part-time employment of high school students. *Journal of Economic Education, 21,* 307–316.

March, J.G. (1978). American public school administration: A short analysis. *School Review, February,* 86.

Marram, G.D., Dornbusch, S.M., & Scott, W.R. (1972). *The impact of teaming and visibility of teaching on the professionalism of elementary school teachers* (Technical Report No. 33). Stanford, CA: Stanford Center for Research and Development in Teaching.

Massey, G.C., Scott, M.V., & Dornbusch, S.M. (1975). Racism without racists: Institutional racism in urban schools. *The Black Scholar, 7,* 10–19.

McLoyd, V.C., Jayarantne, T.E., Ceballo, R., & Borquez, J. (1994). Unemployment and work interruption among African Americaqn single mothers: Effects of parenting and adolescent socioemotional functioning. *Child Development, 65,* 562–589.

Meyer, J.W. (1992). Organizational factors affecting legalization in education. In J.W. Meyer & W.R. Scott (Eds.), *Organizational environments: Ritual and rationalization* (Ch. 10, pp. 217–232). Newbury Park, CA: Sage.

Meyer, J.W., & Rowan, B. (1977). Institutionalized organizations. *American Journal of Sociology, 83,* 340–363.

Meyer, J.W., Scott, W.R., & Deal, T.E. (1981). Institutional and technical sources of organizational structure: Explaining the structure of educational organizations. In H. Stein (Ed.), *Organization and human services: Cross-disciplinary reflections* (pp. 151–179). Philadelphia, PA: Temple University Press.

Modell, J., & Goodman, M. (1990). Historical perspectives. In S. Feldman & G.R. Elliott (Eds.), *At the threshold: The developing adolescent* (pp. 93–122). Cambridge, MA: Harvard University Press.

Natriello, G., McDill, E.L., & Pallas, A.M. (1990). *Schooling disadvantaged children: Racing against catastrophy.* New York: Teachers College Press.

Oakes, J. (1982). Classroom social relationships: Exploring the Bowles and Gintis hypothesis. *Sociology of Education, 55,* 197–212.

Oakes, J. (1985). *Keeping track: How schools structure inequality.* New Haven, CT: Yale University Press.

Oakes, J. (1987). Tracking in secondary schools: A contextual perspective. *Educational Psychology, 22,* 129–53.

Oakes, J., Gamoran, A., & Page, R.N. (1992). Curriculum differentiation: Opportunities, outcomes, and meanings. In P.W. Jackson (Ed.), *Handbook of research on curriculum* (pp. 570–608). New York: Macmillan.

Prescott, B.L., Pelton, C.L., & Dornbusch, S.M. (1986). Teacher perceptions of parent-school communication: A collaborative analysis. *Teacher Education Quarterly, 13,* 67–83.

Quiroz, P.A., Gonzales, N.F., & Frank, K.A. (1996). Carving a niche in the high school social structure: Formal and informal constraints on participation in the extra curriculum. In *Research in sociology of education and socialization* (Vol. 11, pp. 99–120). Greenwich, CT: JAI Press.

Ramirez, F.O., & Rubinson, R. (1979). Creating members: The political incorporation and expansion of public education. In J.W. Meyer & M.T. Hannan (Eds.), *National development and the world system: Educational, economic, and political change, 1950–1970* (pp. 72–84). Chicago: University of Chidcago Press.

Rivkin, S.G. (1994). Residential segregation and school integration. *Sociology of Education, 67,* 279–292.

Rohlen, T. (1983). *Japan's high schools.* Berkeley: University of California Press.

Rosenbaum, J.E. (1976). *Making inequality: The hidden curriculum of high school tracking.* New York: Wiley.

Rosenbaum, J.E. (1980). Track misperceptions and frustrated college plans: An analysis of the effects of tracks and track perceptions in the National Longitudinal Survey. *Sociology of Education, 53,* 74–88.

Savin-Williams, R.C., & Berndt, T.J. (1990). Friendship and peer relations. In S. Feldman & G.R. Elliott (Eds.), *At the threshold: The developing adolescent* (pp. 277–307). Cambridge, MA: Harvard University Press.

Scott, W.R. (1992). The organization of environments: Network, cultural, and historical elements. In J.W. Meyer & W.R. Scott (Eds.), *Organizational environments: Ritual and rationalization* (Ch. 7, pp. 155–175). Newbury Park, CA: Sage.

Scott, W.R. (1995). *Institutions and organizations.* Thousand Oaks, CA: Sage.

Sewell, W.H., & Hauser, R.M. (1975). *Education, occupation, and earnings.* New York: Academic.

Shepard, L.A., & Kreitzer, A.E. (1987). The Texas teacher test. *Educational Researcher, 16,* 22–31.

A special-ed warning for New York. (1998, December 2). *The New York Times,* p. A30.

Spillane, R.R. (1987). Why Bud Spilane is making merit pay a test of leadership. *Executive Educator, 9*(7), 20–21.

Stanton-Salazar, R.D. (1991). *The role of social and information networks in the formation of educational and occupational expectations among Mexican-origin high scool youth.* (Doctoral dissertation, Stanford University, 1990). *Dissertation Abstracts International, 51,* 3909-A.

Stanton-Salazar, R.D., & Dornbusch, S.M. (1995). Social capital and the reproduction of inequality: Information networks among Mexican-origin high school students. *Sociology of Education, 68,* 116–135.

Steinberg, L., & Cauffman, E. (1995). The impact of employment on adolescent development. *Annals of Child Development, 11,* 131–166.

Steinberg, L., Lamborn, S.D., Dornbusch, S.M., & Darling, N. (1992). Impact of parenting practices on adolescent achievement: Authoritative parenting, school involvement, and encouragement to succeed. *Child Development, 63,* 1266–1281.

Stevenson, H.W. (1990). *Making the grade in mathematics*. Reston, VA: National Council of Teachers of Mathematics.

Stevenson, D.L., & Baker, D.P. (1987). The family-school relation and the child's school performance. *Child Development, 58,* 1348–1357.

Taeuber, K.E., & Wilson, D.R. (1978). Racial segregation among public and private schools. *Sociology of Education, 55,* 133–143.

Tuckman, B.W., & Bierman, M. (1971). *Beyond Pygmalion: Galatea in the schools.* Paper presented at the annual meeting of the American Educational Research Association, New York.

Tyack, D.B (1967). *Turning points in American educational history.* Waltham, MA: Blaisdell Publishing Company.

Tyack, D., & Cuban, L. (1995). *Tinkering toward Utopia: A century of public school reform.* Cambridge, MA: Harvard University Press.

Useem, E.L. (1991). Student selection into course sequences in mathematics: the impact of parental involvement and school policies. *Journal of Research on Adolescence, 1,* 231–250

Useem, E.L. (1992). Middle schools and math groups: parents involvement in children's placement. *Sociology of Education, 65,* 263–279.

U.S. Census Bureau. (1913). *Thirteenth census of the United States taken in the year 1910* (Vol. 1). Washington, DC: U.S. Government Printing Office.

U.S. Census Bureau. (1975). *Historical statistics of the United States: Colonial times to 1970, Part 1.* Washington, DC: U.S. Government Printing Office.

U.S. Census Bureau. (1999a). *Money income in the United States: 1998* (Curent Population Reports, P60-206). Washington, DC: U.S. Government Printing Office.

U.S. Census Bureau. (1999b). *Profile of the foreign-born population in the United States: 1997* (Current Population Reports P23–195). Washington, DC: U.S. Government Printing Office.

U.S. Census Bureau. (2000) *Statistical abstract of the United States, 1999.* Washington, DC: U.S. Government Printing Office.

U.S. Census Office. (1897). *Compendium of the eleventh census, 1890, Part III.* Washington, DC: U.S. Government Printing Office.

U.S. Department of Education. (2000) *Vocational education in the United States: Toward the year 2000* (NCES 2000-029), by K. Levesque, D. Lauen, P. Teitelbaum, M. Alt, & S. Librera. Project Officer: D. Nelson. Washington, DC: U.S. Government Printing Office.

Weick, K. (1976). Educational organization as a loosely coupled systems. *Administrative Science Quarterly, 21,* 1–19.

Worner, G.W.B. (1993). The instructional leadership team: A new role for the department head. *National Association of Secondary School Principals Bulletin, 77*(553), 37–45.

Wyatt, E. (2000, September 15). A back-to-school offer for retirees: Full salary and full pensions. *New York Times,* p. A27.

Younis, J., & Smollar, J. (1985). *Adolescent relations with mothers, fathers and friends.* Chicago: University of Chicago Press.

Zernike, K. (2000, October 10). As homework load grows, one district says 'enough'. *New York Times,* p.A1.

CHAPTER 4

Social Relationships and School Adjustment

Kathryn R. Wentzel and Ann A. Battle

INTRODUCTION

Adolescence is marked by biological, intellectual, and psychological changes that are often accompanied by reappraisals of the self and of relationships with adults and peers. With respect to school-related adjustment, the transition into adolescence is often marked by lower grades and test scores; the degree to which students are interested in learning, value education, and have confidence in their abilities also declines (Braddock & McPartland, 1993; Eccles & Midgley, 1989). These changes often coincide with feelings of alienation with respect to teachers and peers (Harter, 1996), and increased levels of emotional distress (Feldman, Rubenstein, & Rubin, 1988; Rutter, 1986). Although faced with these potentially overwhelming challenges and changes, most young adolescents experience positive and healthy adjustment and transitions to adulthood (Petersen & Ebata, 1987). How, then, might we explain the successful transitions of most adolescents? In the current chapter, we offer the suggestion that adolescent adjustment in the school context is facilitated in part, by the social and emotional supports provided by parents, teachers, and peers.

Recent work on the social nature of motivation and learning provides clear evidence that students can profit from their social relationships with parents, teachers, and peers (Juvonen & Wentzel, 1996). These findings tend to be robust regardless of whether the source of support is a parent, a teacher, or a peer (e.g., Wentzel, 1998), and whether embedded in actual instructional activities (see Tappan, 1998) or expressed in non-academic activities (Wentzel, 1994a). There are two general mechanisms whereby adolescents' adjustment to school and in particular, academic accomplishments, might be influenced by each of these social relationships. First, adults and peers can provide adolescents directly with resources that promote the development of academic competencies. Parents provide academic resources to their adolescent children by virtue of educational opportunities afforded by socioeconomic status and by becoming involved in school-related activities. In the classroom, teachers promote learning through instructional activities and delivery of subject matter. Students frequently clarify and interpret for each other their teacher's instructions concerning what they should be doing and how to do it, provide mutual assistance in the form of volunteering substantive information and answering questions (Cooper, Ayers-Lopez, & Marquis, 1982).

In addition to information and resources related directly to learning, ongoing social interactions teach adolescents about themselves and what they need to do to become accepted and competent members of the school community. In this chapter, we will focus on this second mechanism of influence. We argue that interpersonal relationships can take on motivational significance by creating contexts that are developmentally supportive and conducive to the learning and adoption of socially-valued goals. Moreover, these relationships have the potential to provide personal validation that contributes to emotional health and well-being. Toward this end, we present a general overview of adolescents' relationships with parents, teachers, and peers in relation to academic adjustment at school. We then turn to a discussion of socialization processes and why these relationships might influence levels of academic motivation and performance. The primary purpose of our discussion is to gain additional insight into the role of socialization practices in promoting adolescents' school achievement. Therefore, we will focus on pathways of influence from socialization agent to the child with a recognition that an adolescent's behavior can also have a significant impact on parent, teacher, and peer behavior. In conclusion, we raise unresolved issues and offer suggestions for new areas of inquiry into adolescent development and achievement.

ADOLESCENTS' RELATIONSHIPS WITH PARENTS, TEACHERS, AND PEERS

Relationships With Parents

A hallmark of adolescent development is gaining emotional and psychological independence from the family. Indeed, the amount of time that children spend with their family decreases by almost 20% from fifth to twelfth grade (Larson, Richards, Moneta, Holmbeck, & Duckett, 1996). Despite this move toward independence, most parents remain a central and powerful influence in their adolescents' lives. Indeed, when asked about the sources of interpersonal support in their lives, adolescents typically name their parents as primary sources of emotional support, instrumental help, and even companionship (Furman & Burmester, 1992; Lempers & Lempers-Clark, 1992). The relevance of this ongoing connectedness to parents is reflected in its relation to healthy transitions through adolescence. For instance, positive relationships with parents have been related to adolescents' healthy developmental outcomes such as emotional well-being, and to low levels of self-destructive behavior such as suicide, substance abuse, precocious sexual activity, and antisocial behavior. This appears to be true for most adolescents, regardless of socioeconomic status, race, or family structure (Resnick et al., 1997).

The continuing importance of parents in adolescents' lives is reflected in findings that their influence on academic accomplishments continues throughout the middle and high school years. More specifically, parents facilitate positive academic performance by continuing to promote psychological and intellectual skills that underlie academic success. This is accomplished primarily by transmitting family values about the importance of education (e.g., Bowen & Bowen, 1998; Cooper, Lindsay, Nye, & Greathouse, 1998; Paulson & Sputa, 1996), practicing parenting styles that support both school-related and general psychological adjustment (e.g., Glasgow, Dornbusch, Troyer, Steinberg, & Ritter, 1997), and providing emotional support that buffers against the negative impact of psychological distress (e.g., Fenzel, 2000; Wentzel & McNamara, 1999).

Transmission of Goals and Values

The literature on parenting provides clear and consistent evidence that parents actively communicate to their children goals and expectations concerning academic accomplishments. Moreover, these expectations appear to predict adolescents' academic achievements. For instance, parents' aspirations for their children's educational attainments are related to children's own aspirations for academic success, their intellectual accomplishments, and college attendance (Hess & Holloway, 1984; Hossler

& Stage, 1992; Seginer, 1983). Adolescents with parents who express strong values for education also tend to perform well in school and rate their families higher on scales of achievement orientation than do those with parents who are less expressive of strong educational values (Wood, Chapin, & Hannah, 1988). Moreover, Paulson (1994) found that parental values toward education had more impact on achievement outcomes for adolescents than parental interest in schoolwork, parental involvement in school functions, and levels of parental demandingness and responsiveness (see also Bowen & Bowen, 1998).

The importance of parental valuing of education might be understood best in light of research with immigrant families, who traditionally face many obstacles to academic success, including limited experience with the dominant language, low socioeconomic status, and cultural identity issues, but whose children are often more successful in school than their American peers (Caplan, Choy, & Whitmore, 1991; Kao & Tienda, 1995). Fuligni (1997) found that the relation between academic performance and strong shared values for education among parents, students, and peers was mediated by the students' own attitudes and behavior. Moreover, shared values was a significant correlate of academic achievement for Latino, East Asian, Filipino, and European adolescent immigrants in his study after parent education and socioeconomic status were taken into account.

Parenting Styles

A primary mechanism whereby relationships with parents might influence school adjustment is creation of contexts wherein goals and values are learned and subsequently internalized (see Darling & Steinberg, 1993; Grusec & Goodnow, 1994). In other words, the quality of social interactions and relationships helps to define the contexts wherein learning takes place. In contributing to the nature of learning contexts, social relationships consequently take on motivational significance (see Darling & Steinberg, 1993). It is generally accepted that parents who are the most supportive of their adolescent children are "authoritative" (see Baumrind, 1971, 1991). That is, they are those who enforce firm, yet fair standards for behavior, employ nonthreatening modes of discipline, encourage bidirectional communication, value their children's opinions, recognize the dual rights of parents and children, and strike a balance between parental demandingness (control and supervision) and responsiveness (warmth and acceptance).

In contrast, "authoritarian" parents are less responsive, rarely offering explanations for the rules they impose upon their children, and more demanding, expecting fairly rigid adherence to standards that are set and often using threats of physical punishment to gain compliance. Finally, "permissive" parents are relatively undemanding, employing a lax pattern of discipline that places few behavioral or academic demands on the child.

Some of these parents tend to be highly responsive, encouraging their children to express their individuality within the context of a nurturing relationship, whereas others are particularly neglectful or unresponsive, requiring their children to make decisions without support or expressed interest. Both authoritarian and permissive parenting styles tend to be associated with less favorable patterns of social, psychological, and academic adjustment for adolescents than is authoritative parenting (Baumrind, 1971, 1991).

Of interest for the present discussion is that authoritative parents also have children who score higher on various measures of school adjustment than do parents who are either authoritarian or permissive (Glasgow et al., 1997; Paulson, 1994; Paulson, Marchant, & Rothlisberg, 1998; Steinberg, Lamborn, Darling, & Mounts, 1994). For example, adolescents who perceive low levels of control and responsiveness in parents (i.e., permissive and neglectful) also report having the most difficulty in school, whereas adolescents who perceive their parents as authoritative report the best outcomes (Steinberg et al., 1994). Patterson and his colleagues also have documented significant relations between parenting styles and school success in early adolescent boys, with inconsistent and harsh discipline being associated with the lowest levels of academic achievement (Dishion, 1990; Patterson & Bank, 1990). Similarly, others have linked parenting styles to grades (Paulson, 1994) and effective learning and study strategies (Boveja, 1998). Parenting styles also have been associated with adolescent motivation, with more authoritative styles being related to intrinsic interest (Ginsberg & Bronstein, 1996; Rathunde, 1996), positive goal orientations toward learning (Hokoda & Fincham, 1995), school orientation and perceptions of academic competence (Steinberg et al., 1994), and internal locus of control (Trusty & Lampe, 1997).

For the most part, explanations for why specific parenting styles might promote children's internalization of specific goals have not been the target of empirical investigations. However, a more specific model of parental influence proposed by Ryan (1993) recognizes the importance of parenting styles similar to those identified by Baumrind and speaks directly to the issue of why children adopt and internalize socially valued goals (see also Connell & Wellborn, 1991). Ryan argues that within the context of a secure parent–child relationship in which caregivers provide contingent feedback, nurturance, and developmentally-appropriate structure and guidance, young children develop a generalized positive sense of social relatedness, personal competence, and autonomy when presented with new experiences and challenges. These positive aspects of self development then support the internalization of socially prescribed goals and values, that is, "the transformation of external controls and regulations into internal ones" (Ryan, 1993, p. 29).

Ryan (1993) suggests that goals can be pursued either because of perceived external controls (e.g., threats of punishment), to please others and
therefore, enhance feelings of self-worth (referred to as introjection), or
because the goal has been internalized and therefore, holds personal value
or relevance to the individual (referred to as identification). With respect
to parental influence on goal pursuit, it is likely that parenting characterized by high degrees of controlling and harsh discipline is likely to produce
children who pursue goals valued by parents either because of perceived
external controls (e.g., threats of punishment) or to please them and
therefore, protect positive feelings of self-worth. In contrast, parents who
create a more authoritative learning context are likely to have children
who have internalized parental goals and believe them to hold personal
value and relevance.

One reason that these parenting contexts are likely to lead to such different outcomes is that caregiving characterized by nurturance and emotional support is likely to be instrumental in the development of effective
strategies for coping with emotional distress in new and challenging situations. In support of this notion are findings that adolescents' psychological
distress in the form of low self-esteem, depression, and low emotional well-
being is related to parents' use of harsh and inconsistent discipline
(Armentrout, 1971; Wentzel, Feldman, & Weinberger, 1991), as well as perceived lack of emotional attachment and support from parents (Cumsille
& Epstein, 1994; Feldman et al., 1988; Wentzel & McNamara, 1999; Wenz-
Gross et al., 1997). Interestingly, Fletcher, Steinberg, and Sellers (1999)
found that adolescents who perceived inconsistent parenting (one authori-
tative/one nonauthoritative) had more psychological and somatic symptoms of distress than those from homes with two authoritative parents.
Therefore, the additive effect of warmth and caring from two authoritative
parents might provide an especially strong buffer against stress.

Other studies have linked adolescents' psychological distress and depression to low interest in school (Wentzel, Weinberger, Ford, & Feldman, 1990),
academic problems (Harter, 1990; Wentzel et al., 1990), negative attitudes
toward learning (Dubow & Tisak, 1989), and ineffective cognitive functioning (Jacobsen, Edelstein, & Hoffmann, 1994). In a recent study, emotional
well-being partly explained significant relations between perceived support
from parents and young adolescents' interest in school (Wentzel, 1998).
Together, these studies provide initial evidence that emotional adjustment
might serve as a critical link between perceived social and emotional support
from parents and school-related motivation of adolescents.

Involvement

A concrete example of how parents can nurture their children's academic potential is reflected in the literature on parental involvement in

adolescents' schooling. Beneficial parent involvement comes in many forms. For instance, parents create connections with teachers and school staff, attend school and athletic events in which their children are involved, communicate academic expectations to their children and actively discuss school-related issues, and supervise activities by monitoring behavior and academic progress, checking homework, restricting television, and coordinating educational planning (e.g., Bogenschneider, 1997; Muller, 1995; Paulson et al., 1998).

The importance of parental involvement is reflected in findings that parents who participate in these various activities have children who perform better on a variety of school adjustment measures than parents who do not (Delaney, 1996; Paulsen et al., 1998; Trent, Cooney, Russell, & Warton, 1996; Wentzel, 1998; Wentzel & McNamara, 1999). Of particular interest is that a substantial portion of the positive impact of parental involvement appears to be attributable to direct instruction or encouragement of academic activity by parents through homework (Keith, Keith, Troutman, Bickley, Trivette, & Singh, 1993). However, over-controlling communication from parents about homework can have negative effects on adolescents' achievement. For instance, high levels of parental surveillance, or overly involved, nagging-like inquiries and directives about the completion of homework have been associated negatively with adolescents' intrinsic motivation, academic performance, autonomy, persistence, and satisfaction in doing school work (Ginsburg & Bronstein, 1993).

Researchers have documented a progressive decline in levels of parental involvement over time from middle school to late high school (Milgram & Toubiana, 1999; Paulson & Sputa, 1996). Muller (1998) found that although the actual amount of specific forms of parental involvement (e.g., talking about school, attending events, teacher intervention) might vary somewhat over the course of late middle and high school for boys and girls, the effects of such involvement appear to severely wane as children advance through the later high school grades. The strong correlations between most forms of parental involvement and 8th graders' math scores were modified by 10th grade, and were either zero or modestly negative by senior year of high school. This apparent weakening of the effects of parental involvement, however, might not be particularly detrimental if older adolescents' academic efforts become more self-directed and autonomous.

Some research then, seems to suggest a declining importance of parental involvement in adolescents' academic performance over time, while other studies, particularly those focusing on the effects of involvement with homework, indicate lasting benefits beyond the end of middle adolescence. These contradictory results might reflect the fact that the beneficial effects of parental involvement appear to be derived in conjunction with certain parenting styles. Paulsen et al. (1998) demonstrated that moderate to high demandingness when combined with high responsiveness (i.e., authoritative parenting) has been associated positively with adolescents' perceptions of appropriate or beneficial levels of parental involvement; in turn, these perceptions are related to positive academic outcomes. In contrast, adolescents' who perceive parents to display high demandingness and low responsiveness characteristic of authoritarian parenting also tend to perceive their parents to be only moderately involved and to have significantly lower levels of academic performance.

Our discussion has focused primarily on positive outcomes associated with optimal forms of parent–child relationships. What happens, however, when parent–child relationships are less than optimal? Often, adolescents become increasingly disengaged from their families, develop destructive or antisocial relationships with peers, and fail academically, often dropping out of school altogether (Patterson & Bank, 1989). Some of these at-risk youth, however, are able to develop supportive and positive relationships with teachers and as a result, thrive academically at school despite the odds (Werner & Smith, 1992). Moreover, for all students, having positive relationships with teachers is related to a broad range of positive, health-related behaviors (Resnick et al., 1997). In the following section, the nature of adolescents' relationships with their teachers will be discussed.

Adolescents' Relationships with Teachers

Teachers are rarely mentioned by adolescents as having a significant or important influence in their lives. Adolescents often rate teachers as providing aid and advice but only as secondary sources relative to parents and peers (Furman & Burmester, 1992; Lempers & Lempers-Clark, 1992). However, young adolescents' relationships with and perceptions of teachers appear to change dramatically with the transition from elementary to middle school. During this time, students often report heightened levels of mistrust in teachers, perceptions that teachers no longer care about them, and a decrease in opportunities to establish meaningful relationships with teachers. These reported declines in the nurturant qualities of teacher-student relationships after the transition to middle school also correspond to declines in academic motivation and achievement (Feldlaufer, Midgley, & Eccles, 1988; Harter, 1996; Midgley, Feldlaufer & Eccles, 1989). As students proceed through middle school, they also report that teachers become more focused on students earning high grades, competition between students, and maintaining adult control, with a decrease in personal interest in students. Students who report these changes also tend to report less intrinsic motivation to achieve than students who do not (Harter, 1996).

Studies of teacher characteristics and teacher-student relationships have not been frequent with adolescents in middle and high school. However, like parents, teachers also communicate goals and expectations regarding academic performance and classroom behavior. For instance, teachers tend to have a core set of behavioral expectations for their students. Trenholm and Rose (1981) identified six categories of student behavior deemed necessary for success: appropriate responses to academic requests and tasks, impulse control, mature problem solving, cooperative and courteous interaction with peers, involvement in class activities, and recognition of appropriate contexts for different types of behavior. Moreover, teachers actively communicate these expectations to their students, regardless of their instructional goals, teaching styles, and ethnicity (see also, Hargreaves, Hester, & Mellor, 1975).

The most widely documented influence of teachers on adolescents' school adjustment concerns the degree to which teachers are perceived by students as supportive and caring. At a general level, perceived support from teachers has been related to positive motivational outcomes, including the pursuit of goals to learn and to behave prosocially and responsibly, mastery orientations toward learning, academic interest, educational aspirations and values, and self-concept (Felner, Aber, Primavera, & Cauce, 1985; Goodenow, 1993; Midgley et al., 1989; Wentzel, 1994b, 1997). Moreover, in a recent study of perceived support from teachers, parents, and peers (Wentzel, 1998), perceived support from teachers was unique in its relation to students' interest in class and pursuit of goals to adhere to classroom rules and norms.

Interestingly, middle school students characterize caring and supportive teachers in ways that are similar to authoritative parents. Specifically, they describe caring teachers as those who demonstrate democratic and egalitarian communication styles designed to elicit student participation and input, who develop expectations for student behavior and performance in light of individual differences and abilities, who model a "caring" attitude and interest in their instruction and interpersonal dealings with students, and who provide constructive rather than harsh and critical feedback (Wentzel, 1998). These perceptions are highly consistent with the high levels of demandingness and responsiveness of authoritative parenting referred to earlier. Students' perceptions of teachers along these specific dimensions also predict positive motivational orientations toward school, including students' pursuit of socially-valued goals, interest in schoolwork, and beliefs about personal control. Negative feedback from teachers appears to be a powerful and consistent predictor of students' social behavior and academic performance, with students who perceive teachers as harsh and critical displaying antisocial and uncooperative classroom behavior and earning low grades relative to their peers. These findings underscore the potentially pervasive influence of teachers' negative and highly critical feedback on young adolescents' overall adjustment and success at school.

It could be argued that good teachers simply reinforce the work already accomplished at home, or that students who have adopted the same goals and interests as teachers in turn, motivate teachers to treat them in ways that characterize nurturant and effective parents. However, when compared to perceived support from parents and peers, perceived support from teachers has been found to be unique in predicting young adolescents' interest in class and pursuit of goals to be socially responsible (Wentzel, 1998). Students' perceptions of general levels of support from teachers also predict positive changes in social goal pursuit and academic effort across the middle school years (Wentzel, 1997). Finally, when elementary school teachers are trained to provide students with warmth and support, clear expectations for behavior, and developmentally appropriate autonomy, their students develop a stronger sense of community, increase displays of socially competent behavior, and show academic gains (Schaps, Battistich, & Solomon, 1997). Therefore, a growing body of evidence supports the utility of further investigations of classroom teachers' unique contribution to adolescents' social and academic adjustment to school.

Little is known about teachers' opinions and beliefs about their adolescent students. However, students who are well liked by teachers tend to get better grades than those who are not as well liked (e.g., Hadley, 1954; Kelley, 1958; Wentzel & Asher, 1995). Teachers' preferences for students also appear to reflect the goals that students pursue. When asked to indicate how much they would like to have each of their students in their class again the following year, teachers expressed preferences that were related positively to students' reports of frequent pursuit of goals to be socially responsible as well as to achieve positive evaluations of performance, but not to pursue goals to learn (Wentzel, 1991b). Therefore, even though teacher behaviors that are perceived by students to be authoritative in nature tend to promote positive orientations toward learning, teachers beliefs about students appear to be related most strongly to student behaviors reflecting compliance and conformity to expectations for behavior and performance.

The extant literature on teacher-student interaction just reviewed suggests that like parents, teachers appear to establish contexts that reflect those provided by effective parents. Investigations of continuity of caregiving across home and school contexts are clearly needed in this regard. Findings indicate that certain combinations of students' perceptions of parenting style, teaching style, and school responsiveness are more highly related to school success than are other combinations. Paulson et al. (1998) found that students who perceive congruency across home and school environments, particularly those who see both parents and teachers as authoritative and who believe their school to be a responsive, nurturing environment score higher on measures of academic self concept, feelings about the importance of school, and actual grades than those who perceive incongruent, non-authoritative combinations of parent/teacher styles (neglectful parents/authoritarian teachers) and negative school environments. Therefore, although the process is not completely understood, it is clear that the cross-contextual impact of high academic and behavioral expectations, consistently conveyed in warm and nurturing home and school environments by respectful parents and teachers, is a particularly strong predictor of adolescents' school adjustment patterns.

The notion that teachers, like parents, can promote student achievement by alleviating students' psychological distress has not been studied. In fact, levels of emotional well-being are most often linked to adolescents' relationships with parents and peers rather than to relationships or interactions with teachers (e.g., Wentzel, 1997). It could be that teachers play a relatively minor role in most adolescents' psychological and emotional adjustment. However, it also is possible that teachers have a significant and unique impact on adolescents' emotional well-being but in a fairly constrained manner. It is clear that feeling competent is an integral part of emotional health and contributes to a positive sense of self-worth and well-being (Harter, 1996); one area in which teachers have enormous potential for influencing adolescents' feelings of competence is the academic domain. Indeed, teachers who construct learning situations in which competition, social comparison, and norm-referenced evaluations are valued are likely to set the stage for students to develop low perceptions of academic competence (see Eccles & Midgley, 1989; Harter, 1996). In turn, these perceptions can result in anxious responses to academic challenges, and negative attitudes toward learning in general if students cannot excel relative to their peers. Given the potentially powerful role that a positive attitude toward learning can play throughout the lifespan, a specific and heightened focus on ways in which teachers can influence their students' affective responses to academic success and failure is essential.

Teachers might also be more influential for some adolescents' adjustment to school than to others. Some students who are at-risk for academic problems due to unstable or problematic home life attribute their success to teachers who have served as mentors and often surrogate parents in their lives (Darling, Hamilton, & Niego, 1994). Teachers also might be able to offset the negative impact of low levels of acceptance and rejection from peers. For instance, some middle school students who are rejected by their peers but liked by teachers tend to do well academically over time. In particular, being liked by teachers tends to be a more powerful predictor of students' adoption of school-related goals than a high level of acceptance among peers (Wentzel, 1994b). However, teachers can also exacerbate the negative impact of peer rejection on students in that young adolescents who are disliked by their peers as well as by their teachers are at high risk for academic failure and other school-related problems (Wentzel & Asher, 1995).

Adolescents' Relationships with Peers

Although adults remain central sources of support in adolescents' lives, as children make the transition into adolescence they exhibit increased interest in their peers and a growing psychological and emotional dependence on them for support and guidance (Steinberg, 1990; Youniss & Smollar, 1989). One reason for this growing interest is that many young adolescents enter new middle school structures that necessitate interacting with larger numbers of peers on a daily basis. In contrast to the predictability of self-contained classroom environments in elementary school, the uncertainty and ambiguity of multiple classroom environments, new instructional styles, and more complex class schedules often result in students turning to each other for ways to cope, information, and social support. Therefore, being accepted by and having access to positive support from the larger peer group becomes a central concern of young adolescents.

Types of Peer Relationships

Peer relationships are typically studied in three ways: levels of acceptance and rejection, number and quality of friendships, and group membership. Peer acceptance and rejection is typically assessed along a continuum of social preference (e.g., Who do you like?), or in terms of sociometric status groups (i.e., popular, rejected, neglected, controversial, and average status children). Popular status and high levels of acceptance have been related to successful academic performance, and rejected status and low levels of acceptance to academic difficulties (e.g., Austin & Draper, 1984; DeRosier, Kupersmidt, & Patterson, 1994; Wentzel, 1991a). Findings are most consistent with respect to classroom grades (e.g., Hatzichristou & Hopf, 1996; Wentzel, 1991a), although peer acceptance has been related positively to standardized test scores (e.g., Austin & Draper, 1985) as well as IQ (e.g., Wentzel, 1991a). Moreover, longitudinal studies document the stability of these relations over time (e.g., Wentzel & Caldwell, 1997). An exception to this literature is that in recent studies of middle school students, another group of children has demonstrated particularly positive academic and behavioral profiles (Wentzel, 1991a; Wentzel & Asher, 1995). Identified as sociometrically neglected, these children are neither highly accepted or rejected by their peers. It appears, therefore, that school adjustment is related to acceptance from peers for some students but not others, at least during the middle school years.

Being accepted by peers also has been related positively to motivational outcomes, including satisfaction with school and pursuit of goals to learn and to behave in socially appropriate ways (Wentzel, 1994b; Wentzel & Asher, 1995). In contrast, being rejected by peers has been related to low levels of interest in school (Wentzel & Asher, 1995), and disengaging from school altogether by dropping out (Hymel, Comfort, Schonert-Reichl, & McDougall, 1996). Peer status also has been related to prosocial and socially responsible goal pursuit during middle school (Wentzel, 1991b). Specifically, when compared with average status children, popular children report more frequent pursuit of prosocial goals, neglected students report more frequent pursuit of prosocial and social responsibility goals, and controversial students report less frequent pursuit of responsibility goals. Of additional interest is that students in the different status groups do not seem to differ as a function of goals to learn or to receive positive evaluations of performance.

In addition to being accepted by the general peer group, having friendships also has been related to adolescents' emotional and academic adjustment. Friendships reflect mutually determined dyadic relationships. Research linking adolescent friendships to academic achievement is sparse, although having friends has been related positively to grades and test scores in middle school (e.g., Berndt & Keefe, 1995; Wentzel & Caldwell, 1997), and this appears to be stable over a two-year time span (Wentzel & Caldwell, 1997). For the most part, dyadic friendships in adolescence appear to exert only minimal overt influence on student motivation (see Berndt & Keefe, 1996). However, Berndt and his colleagues (Berndt & Keefe, 1996) argue that when influence does occur, it is likely to support positive behavior such as academic studying, making plans for college, and avoiding antisocial, self-destructive actions (Epstein, 1983).

Of recent interest to researchers of peer relationships is the possibility that the quality of a friendship also might play a role in influencing adolescent adjustment (Hartup & Stevens, 1997). For instance, a friendship can be characterized by positive levels of emotional support, helping, and positive validation of the self, whereas others can be characterized in terms of conflict, betrayal, and antisocial interactions (Parker & Asher, 1993). Although rarely examined, it is likely that the nature of adolescents' close relationships with specific peers can fuel either heightened interest or alienation with respect to school. This possibility is worthy of further empirical investigation.

A final aspect of peer relationships that has been studied in relation to school adjustment is group membership. A distinction between friendship and peer group influence is important given that friendships reflect relatively private, egalitarian relationships whereas peer groups, while often self-selected, are likely to have publicly acknowledged hierarchical relationships based on personal characteristics valued by the group (Brown, 1989; McAuliffe & Dembo, 1994). Typically, adolescent peer groups are characterized in two ways. Peer crowds reflect fairly large, reputation- and status-based collectives of peers who have common interests, values, or attitudes. Most peer crowds are easily recognized by the defining norms or activities of the group. For instance, most schools have groups that students label as "nerds," "jocks," "druggies," "populars," and "loners." Peer networks or cliques are characterized by smaller groups of self-selected friends who interact with each other on a frequent basis (Brown, Morey & Kinney, 1984).

Adolescent crowds are believed to promote identity development by sanctioning specific values, norms, and interaction styles (Brown et al., 1984). Behaviors and interaction styles that are characteristic of a crowd are modeled frequently so that they can be easily learned and adopted by individuals. In this manner, crowds provide prototypical examples of various identities for those who wish to "try out" different lifestyles and can easily affirm an adolescent's sense of self. As adolescents enter high school and the number of crowds increases (Brown et al., 1984), "identities" associated with crowds are more easily recognized and afford the opportunity to try on various social identities with relatively little risk. A specific example of the power of crowd influence is reflected in relations between crowd membership and adolescents' attitudes toward academic achievement. Peer crowds differ in the degree to which they pressure members to become involved in academic activities, with "Jocks" and "Popular" groups providing significantly more pressure for academic involvement than other groups (Brown, 1989). Ethnic group status also appears to be a factor in that White and Asian-American adolescents tend to place value on education, whereas in African-American samples valuing of education is less prevalent (Steinberg, Dornbusch, & Brown, 1992). The reasons for these differences, however, are not well understood.

In contrast to peer crowds, peer networks or cliques are smaller and reflect groups of mutually-determined friendships (Brown, 1989; Cairns, Neckerman, & Cairns, 1989). Peer cliques can also be formed on the basis of common activities such as study groups, athletic teams, or music and arts activities. Peer cliques based on friendships are likely to have similar behavioral styles, for instance those who have similar orientations toward aggression or being cooperative and prosocial, as well as personality styles (Brown et al., 1984). Adolescents belonging to the same friendship network also tend to be similar in terms of levels of emotional stress or psychological well-being (Hogue & Steinberg, 1995).

The function of peer networks is believed to be somewhat different from that of peer crowds (Brown et al., 1984). Peer networks typically provide members with help, support, companionship, and mutual aid typical of close dyadic friendships. Peer networks also play a role in defining social boundaries and status hierarchies that help to maintain social control and enforce conformity to group norms and practices. Social control can be accomplished when adolescents provide each other with positive types of support such as instrumental help and emotional validation. Although adolescents typically depend on each other for this kind of positive support, they also engage in interactions that are often negative and unrewarding and create levels of emotional distress (Cairns et al., 1989; Harter, 1996).

Transmission of Goals and Values

Like adults, students articulate sets of goals that they would like and indeed expect each other to achieve. Although rarely described empirically, these goals provide clear norms for behavior sanctioned by peers. With respect to academic achievement, researchers have documented that classmates provide each other with information concerning normative standards for performance by comparing work and grades (Ruble, 1983) and by modeling academic skills (Schunk, 1987).

Issues concerning the internalization of goals also arise with respect to peer influence. Models of influence based on attachment theory (e.g., Ryan, 1993) would suggest that parent–child relationships are most likely to promote the adoption and internalization of goals, whereas non-familial relationships would not. It often is assumed that adolescent peer groups provide alternative and competing influences to those of parents. Interestingly, however, this is not entirely the case. Although adolescents vary in the extent to which they succumb to peer pressure, adolescents typically follow parental advice when faced with conflicting opinions from parents and peers, especially if decisions involve future plans such as attending and choosing a college (Kandell & Lessor, 1969). As adolescents get older, they tend to make important decisions on their own, independently of advice or pressures from peers or parents (Epstein, 1983).

Exceptions to this pattern are found in adolescents who associate with delinquent gangs. In this case, peers have an enormous amount of influence on individual gang members. However, the strength of gang influence is in large part due to parents who have been ineffective in providing their children with social skills and emotional support (Heath & McLaughlin, 1993). In the case of gang cultures that evolve among children from poor immigrant or ethnic minority groups, economic hardships, cultural discontinuities, and lack of supportive programs in the schools serve to weaken further the role of parents in adolescents' lives. As a result, these adolescents who have become detached from family and school cultures tend to group together into gangs that offer them friendship, emotional support, a sense of security, and protection (Heath & McLaughlin, 1993).

With respect to practice, these findings imply that although peer influence might be strong, it can be superseded. In fact, interventions to offset the often negative influence of peer groups and gangs might be especially successful if children are exposed to interactions with adults who can instill a sense of autonomy, mutuality, warmth, and guidance into their relationships with these children (see Heath & McLaughlin, 1993). Moreover, peer group membership tends to change frequently, suggesting that influence by a particular group might also be fairly transient. Therefore, having access to adult relationships that are stable, responsive, and predictable also should contribute positively to intervention efforts.

Processes of Influence

Explanations for peer influence are not well-articulated and models of family socialization have not been used to understand peer influence on motivation or performance. The link between perceived peer support and motivation (e.g., Wentzel, 1994b, 1998), however, also provides support for a stress-buffering/emotion-regulation model of influence. For instance, students who believe that their peers support and care about them tend to be more engaged in positive aspects of classroom life than students who do not perceive such support.

Perceived social and emotional support from peers has been associated with pursuit of academic and prosocial goals (Felner et al., 1985; Harter, 1996; Wentzel, 1994a, 1997, 1998). Moreover, perceived social and emotional support from peers has been associated positively with prosocial outcomes such as helping, sharing, and cooperating, and related negatively to antisocial forms of behavior (Wentzel, 1994b). Young adolescents who do not perceive their relationships with peers as positive and supportive also tend to be at risk for academic problems (e.g., Goodenow, 1993; Midgley et al., 1989; Phelan, Davidson, & Cao, 1991).

Pressures to conform to peer expectations and standards for performance can heighten feelings of vulnerability (Harter, 1990). It is clear that children are often highly motivated to conform to peer pressures for behavior for fear of rejection or ridicule, especially as they enter into adolescence. Emotional distress has been linked consistently to peer rejection and lack of peer support during this stage of development (e.g., Harter, 1990; Hogue & Steinberg, 1995; Wentzel & McNamara, 1999). Children without friends and who are not accepted by their peers tend to report higher degrees of loneliness and less positive perceptions of self-worth than children who enjoy more positive relationships with peers (e.g., Harter, 1990; Parker & Asher, 1993). Internalized distress also appears to be a defining characteristic of adolescent peer groups (Hogue & Steinberg, 1995; Wentzel & Caldwell, 1997). Therefore, although speculative, it is likely that high levels of emotional distress associated with aspects of peer relationships also might have the potential to generate negative motivational orientations toward school and low levels of academic performance (see Hymel et al., 1996). Without strong and positive interpersonal and emotional coping skills, adolescents who experience these negative feelings are likely to disengage psychologically from school-related activities, including academic pursuits.

SUMMARY AND REMAINING ISSUES

The issues discussed in this chapter provide a foundation for further consideration of ways in which social relationships might influence students' motivation and achievement at school. Although presented as somewhat separate modes of influence, a summary of how the mechanisms of social influence might be integrated into a more comprehensive model is useful. From a developmental perspective, it is reasonable to assume that specific socialization experiences with parents provide the initial social influence on adolescents' school-related goals and values. From early childhood on, parents provide their children with information concerning which outcomes are valued and should be achieved. Specific parenting styles and forms of social interactions also provide contexts that can strengthen the likelihood these goals will be adopted and pursued. The motivational qualities of these socialization contexts are likely to have their greatest impact on children's goal setting by way of their influence on emotional functioning and sense of self. During adolescence, input from teachers and peers contributes to these processes by providing classroom-specific goals and contexts that further promote, or possibly detract from, pursuit of academic excellence.

Most likely, these interpersonal experiences have their most direct and powerful influence in the ways they are perceived and interpreted by adolescents themselves. For instance, parents' and adolescents' perceptions of parenting style do not always agree. In fact, research demonstrates only a modest association between adolescents' and parents' perceptions of parental demandingness and responsiveness (Feldman, Wentzel, & Gehring, 1989; Paulson, 1994). However, adolescents' perceptions of their parents' practices appear to be more powerful predictors of academic outcomes than either the parents' perceptions (Paulson, 1994; Paulson et al., 1998) or observational measures of what is actually going on in the home (Paulson & Sputa, 1996). Although infrequently studied, it is likely that adolescents' perceptions of teachers and peers play a similar role in predicting behavior relative to more objective measures of social interactions.

Although socialization experiences with parents, teachers, and peers were discussed as having relatively independent influence on adolescents, it is important to note that students must often struggle to balance competing socialization influences. Issues of goal coordination are particularly relevant, especially when we consider the potentially negative motivational effects of competing, incongruent goals across family, peer, and classroom contexts often experienced by minority children (Phelan et al., 1991). Children from minority cultures often are expected to adapt to normative expectations for behavior that are inconsistent with those espoused by their families and communities. Ogbu (1985; Fordham & Ogbu, 1986) describes how failing to achieve academically can be interpreted by some minority children as an accomplishment rather than a failure. In such cases, noncompliance with the majority culture's institutional norms and standards for achievement can lead to acceptance within the minority community but social rejection and academic failure at school.

This work underscores the likelihood that adolescence might be a particularly challenging time for minority students as they are consolidating their identities and sense of self (see Spencer, 1999). Issues of race and ethnicity have not been examined extensively in adolescent samples. Limited findings, however, suggest that parents, teachers, and peers might influence minority students in ways that are qualitatively different from ways they influence White, middle-class adolescents (Steinberg et al., 1994). Therefore, continued research on these groups of students is necessary to understand their unique socialization experiences as adolescents. Similarly, most of the work in this area has been conducted with young adolescents as they make their way through middle school. Much less is known about the social lives of high school students. Given that developmental issues with respect to identity, peer relationships, and autonomy are quite unique for this age group, a greater focus on these older students is clearly warranted.

It is worth noting that the underlying purpose of the work on socialization is to understand the impact of parental behavior on children rather than the impact of children's behavior on parents. From a developmental perspective, good parenting is expected to precede the development of competencies by the child; findings from longitudinal studies in the area of educational achievement indicate that parental factors often explain child outcomes rather than the reverse (e.g., Entwistle & Hayduk, 1978). The purpose of the present discussion was to gain additional insight into the role of socialization practices in children's motivation to achieve and, therefore, also has focused on pathways of influence from socialization agent to the child. It is clear, however, that children's behavior can have a significant impact on parent, teacher, and peer behavior. As children grow older and become increasingly autonomous, systems of influence reflecting the joint and interactive effects of children, families, and peers need to be accounted for in explanations of adolescents' motivation and performance at school (Bronfenbrenner, 1989).

It also is likely that other factors might explain associations between adolescents' social relationships and academic accomplishments. For instance, behavioral competence appears to mediate positive relationships between multiple aspects of peer relationships and academic achievement (Wentzel, 1991a, 1997) and between parenting styles and academic performance (Wentzel, 1994a). Therefore, it could be that underlying behavioral and social skills explain both the ability to form positive social relationships and to achieve academically at school. Indeed, social behavior in the form of cooperation, helping, and sharing has been related positively and consistently to positive relationships with adults as well as peers (Wentzel, 1994a,b). Constructivist theories of development also propose that similar forms of positive social interactions can instigate intellectual growth (Piaget, 1965; Youniss & Smollar, 1989); engaging in cooperative interactions and collaborative problem solving can create cognitive conflict that hastens the development of higher-order thinking skills and cognitive structures.

The extant literature indicates that these relations are likely reciprocal and complex, especially with respect to less than optimal outcomes. For instance, social rejection by peers can result in antisocial as well as other maladaptive forms of behavior. However, aggressive and antisocial forms of behavior also appear to be part of a maladaptive cycle of peer rejection, inappropriate behavior, and peer rejection, with behavioral incompetence often instigating initial peer rejection (Dodge, 1986). In some cases this is true of academic achievement as well, with peer rejection appearing after academic difficulties are experienced (Dishion, 1990). Although similar work has not been conducted on teachers, children's relationships with parents can result in similar cycles of inappropriate behavior followed by harsh parenting, escalated child aggression, and finally maladaptive outcomes at school (Patterson & Bank, 1989). It is reasonable to expect that similar patterns of interaction might develop with other adults.

Finally, we have focused on the development of goals and emotion regulation as primary targets of socialization processes. However, other intrapersonal processes are likely to play important mediating roles in linking adolescents' social experiences to academic success. For example, perceptions of ability are likely to have a strong impact on adolescents' motivation to engage in intellectual pursuits (see Eccles, Wigfield, & Schiefele, 1998). The processes by which parents, teachers, and peers influence these beliefs are not well understood. Similarly, it is likely that socialization practices can influence other aspects of adolescent identity, such as peer group allegiance, gender role identification, or avocational interests that also might play a significant role in determining interest in school. Continuing study of how these complex and interrelated processes develop as a function of social experiences is necessary if we are to understand how adolescents can make a successful transition from childhood to adulthood as interested and motivated learners.

REFERENCES

Armentrout, J.A., (1971). Parental child-rearing attitudes and preadolescents' problem behaviors. *Journal of Consulting and Clinical Psychology, 37,* 278–285.

Austin, A.B., & Draper, D.C. (1984). The relationship among peer acceptance, social impact, and academic achievement in middle school. *American Educational Research Journal, 21,* 597–604.

Baumrind, D. (1971). Current patterns of parental authority. *Developmental Psychology Monograph, 4,* (1, Pt.2).

Baumrind, D. (1991). Effective parenting during the early adolescent transition. In P.A Cowan & M. Hetherington (Eds.), *Family transitions* (pp. 111–164). Hillsdale, NJ: Lawrence Erlbaum.

Berndt, T.J., & Keefe, K. (1996). Friends' influence on school adjustment: A motivational analysis. In J. Juvonen & K. Wentzel (Eds.), *Social motivation: Understanding children's school adjustment* (pp. 248–278). New York: Cambridge University Press.

Berndt, T.J., & Keefe, K. (1995). Friends' influence on adolescents' adjustment to school. *Child Development, 66,* 1312–1329.

Bogenschneider, K. (1997). Parental involvement in adolescent schooling: A proximal process with transcontextual validity. *Journal of Marriage & the Family, 59,* 718–733.

Boveja, M.E. (1998). Parenting styles and adolescents' learning strategies in the urban community. *Journal of Multicultural Counseling & Development, 26,* 110–119.

Bowen, N.K., & Bowen, G.L. (1998). The mediating role of educational meaning in the relationship between home academic culture and academic performance. *Family Relations: Interdisciplinary Journal of Applied Family Studies, 47,* 45–51.

Braddock, J.H., & McPartland, J.M. (1993). Education of early adolescents. In L. Darling-Hammond (Ed.), *Review of Research in Education* (p. 135–170). Washington, DC: AERA.

Bronfenbrenner, U. (1989). Ecological systems theory. In R. Vasta (Ed.), *Annals of child development* (Vol. 6, pp.187–250). Greenwich, CT: JAI.

Brown, B.B. (1989). The role of peer groups in adolescents' adjustment to secondary school. In T.J. Berndt & G.W. Ladd (Eds.), *Peer relationships in child development* (pp. 188–215). New York: Wiley.

Brown, B.B., Mory, M.S., & Kinney, D. (1994) Casting adolescent crowds in a relational perspective: Caricature, channel, and context. In R. Montemayor, G.R. Adams, & T.P. Gullotta (Eds.), *Personal relationships during adolescence* (pp. 123–167). Newbury Park, CA: Sage.

Cairns, R.B., Neckerman, H.J., & Cairns, B.D. (1979). Social networks and the shadows of synchrony. In G.R. Adams, R. Montemayor, & T. Gullotta (Eds.), *Biology of adolescent behavior and development* (pp. 275–305).

Caplan, N., Choy, M.H., & Whitmore, J.K. (1991). *Children of the boat people: A study of educational success*. Ann Arbor, MI: University of Michigan Press.

Cooper, C.R., Ayers-Lopez, S., & Marquis, A. (1982). Children's discourse during peer leraning in experimental and naturalistic situations. *Discourse Processes, 5,* 177–191.

Cooper, H., Lindsay, J.J., Nye, B., & Greathouse, S. (1998). Relationships among attitudes about homework, amount of homework assigned and completed, and student achievement. *Journal of Educational Psychology, 90,* 70–83.

Connell, J.P., & Wellborn, J.G. (1991). Competence, autonomy, and relatedness: A motivational analysis of self-system processes. In M.R. Gunnar & L.A. Sroufe (Eds.), *Self processes and development: The Minnesota symposia on child development* (Vol. 23; pp. 43–78). Hillsdale, NJ: Erlbaum.

Cumsille, P.E., & Epstein, N. (1994). Family cohesion, family adaptability, social support, and adolescent depressive symptoms in outpatient clinic families. *Journal of Family Psychology, 8,* 202–214.

Darling, N., Hamiliton, S.F., & Niego, S. (1994). Adolescents' relations with adults outside the family. In R. Montemayor, G.R. Adams, & T.P. Gullotta (Eds.), *Personal relationships during adolescence* (pp. 216–235). Newbury Park, CA: Sage.

Darling, N., & Steinberg, L. (1993). Parenting style as context: An integrative model. *Psychological Bulletin, 113,* 487–496.

DeRosier, M.E., Kupersmidt, J.B., & Patterson, C.J. (1994). Children's academic and behavioral adjustment as a function of the chronicity and proximity of peer rejection. *Child Development, 65,* 1799–1813.

Delaney, M.E. (1996). Across the transition to adolescence: Qualities of parent/adolescent relationships and adjustment. *Journal of Early Adolescence, 16,* 274–300.

Dishion, T. (1990). The family ecology of boys' peer relations in middle childhood. *Child Development, 61,* 874–892.

Dodge, K.A. (1980). Social cognition and children's aggressive behavior. *Child Development, 51,* 162–170.

Dubow, E.F., & Tisak, J. (1989). The relation between stressful life events and adjustment in elementary school children: The role of social support and social problem-solving skills. *Child Development, 60,* 1412–1423.

Eccles, J.S., & Midgley, C. (1989). Stage-environment fit: Developmentally appropriate classrooms for young adolescents. In C. Ames & R. Ames (Eds.), *Research on motivation in education: Vol. 3* (pp. 139–186). New York: Academic Press.

Eccles, J., Wigfield, A., & Schiefele, U. (1998). Motivation to succeed. In W. Damon (Series ed.) and N. Eisenberg (Vol. Ed.), *Handbook of child psychology* (5th ed., Vol. 3). New York: John Wiley.

Entwistle, D.R., & Hayduk, L.A. (1978). *Too great expectations: The academic outlook of young children*. Baltimore: Johns Hopkins University Press.

Epstein, J.L. (1983). The influence of friends on achievement and affective outcomes. In J.L. Epstein & N. Karweit (Eds.), *Friends in school* (pp. 177–200). New York; Academic Press.

Epstein, J.L. (1990). School and family connections: Theory, research, and implications for integrating sociologies of education and family. *Marriage and Family Review, 15,* 99–126.

Feldlaufer, H., Midgley, C., & Eccles, J.S. (1988). Student, teacher, and observer perceptions of the classroom before and after the transition to junior high school. *Journal of Early Adolescence, 8*, 133–156.

Feldman, S.S., Rubenstein, J.L., & Rubin, C. (1989). Depressive affect and restraint in early adolescents: Relationships with family structure, family process and friendship support. *Journal of Early Adolescence, 8*, 279–296.

Feldman, S.S., Wentzel, K.R., & Gehring, T.M. (1989). A comparison of the views of mothers, fathers, and pre-adolescents about family cohesion and power. *Journal of Family Psychology, 3*, 39–60.

Felner, R.D., Aber, M.S., Primavera, J., & Cauce, A.M. (1985). Adaptation and vulnerability in high-risk adolescents: An examination of environmental mediators. *American Journal of Community Psychology, 13*, 365–379.

Fenzel, L.M. (2000). Prospective study of changes in global self-worth and strain during the transition to middle school. *Journal of Early Adolescence, 20*, 93–116.

Fletcher, A.C., Steinberg, L., & Sellers, E.B. (1999). Adolescents' well-being as a function of perceived interparental consistency. *Journal of Marriage and the Family, 61*, 599–610.

Fordham, S., & Ogbu, J.U. (1986). Black students' school success; Coping with "the burden of 'acting white'." *The Urban Review, 18*, 176–206.

Fuligni, A.J. (1997). The academic achievement of adolescents from immigrant families: The roles of family background, attitudes, and behavior. *Child Development, 68*, 351–363.

Furman, W., & Buhrmester, D. (1992). Age and sex differences in perceptions of networks of personal relationships. *Child Development, 63*, 103–115.

Ginsberg, G.S., & Bronstein, P. (1993). Family factors related to children's intrinsic/extrinsic motivational orientations and academic performance. *Child Development, 64*, 1461–1474.

Glasgow, K.L., Dornbusch, S.M., Troyer, L., Steinberg, L., & Ritter, P.L. (1997). Parenting styles, adolescents' attributions, and educational outcomes in nine heterogeneous high schools. *Child Development, 68*, 507–529.

Goodenow, C. (1993). Classroom belonging among early adolescent students: Relationships to motivation and achievement. *Journal of Early Adolescence, 13*, 21–43.

Grusec, J.E., & Goodnow, J.J. (1994). Impact of parental discipline methods on the child's internalization of values: A reconceptualization of current points of view. *Developmental Psychology, 30*, 4–19.

Hargreaves, D.H., Hester, S.K., & Mellor, F.J. (1975). *Deviance in classrooms.* London: Routledge & Kegan Paul.

Harter, S. (1996). Teacher and classmate influences on scholastic motivation, self-esteem, and level of voice in adolescents. In J. Juvonen & K. Wentzel (Eds.), *Social motivation: Understanding children's school adjustment* (pg. 11–42). New York: Cambridge.

Harter, S. (1990). Self and identity development. In S.S. Feldman & G.R. Elliott (Eds.), *At the threshold: The developing adolescent* (pp. 352–387). Cambridge, MA: Harvard University Press.

Hartup, W.W., & Stevens, N. (1997). Friendships and adaptation in the life course. *Psychological Bulletin, 121*, 355–370.

Hatzichristou, C., & Hopf, D. (1966). A multiperspective comparison of peer socio-metric status groups in childhood and adolescence. *Child Development, 67,* 1085–1102.

Heath, S.B., & McLaughlin, M.W. (1993). *Identity and inner-city youth: Beyond ethnicity and gender.* New York: Teachers College Press.

Hess, R.D., & Holloway, S.D. (1984). Family and school as educational institutions. In R.D. Parke (Ed.), *Review of child development research* (*Vol. 7;* pp. 179–222). Chicago: University of Chicago Press.

Hogue, A., & Steinberg, L. (1995). Homophily of internalized distress in adolescent peer groups. *Developmental Psychology, 31,* 897–906.

Hossler, D., & Stage, F.K. (1992). Family and high school experience influences on the postsecondary educational plans of ninth-grade students. *American Educational Research Journal, 29,* 425–451.

Hokoda, A., & Fincham, F.D. (1995). Origins of children's helpless and mastery achievement patterns in the family. *Journal of Educational Psychology, 87,* 375–385.

Hymel, S., Comfort, C., Schonert-Reichl, K., & McDougall, P. (1996). Academic failure and school dropout: The influence of peers. In J. Juvonen & K.R. Wentzel (Eds.), *Social motivation: Understanding children's school adjustment* (pp. 313–345). New York: Cambridge University Press.

Jacobsen, T., Edelstein, W., & Hofmann, V. (1994). A longitudinal study of the relation between representations of attachment in childhood and cognitive functioning in childhood and adolescence. *Developmental Psychology, 30,* 112–124.

Juvonen, J., & Wentzel, K.R. (1996). *Social motivation: Understanding children's school adjustment.* New York: Cambridge University Press.

Kandell, D.B., & Lesser, G.S. (1969). Parental and peer influences on educational plans of adolescents. *American Sociological Review, 34,* 212–223.

Kao, G., & Tienda, M. (1995). Optimism and achievement: The educational performance of immigrant youth. *Social Science Quarterly, 76,* 1–19.

Keith, T.A., Keith, P.B., Troutman, G.C., Bickley, P.G., Trivette, P.S., & Singh, K. (1993). Does parental involvement affect eighth-grade student achievement? Structural analysis of national data. *School Psychology Review, 22,* 474–496.

Larson, R., Richards, M.H., Moneta, G., Holmbeck, G., & Duckett, E. (1996). Changes in adolescents' daily interactions with their families from ages 10 to 18: Disengagement and transformation. *Developmental Psychology, 32,* 744–754.

Lempers, J.D., & Clark-Lempers, D.S. (1992). Young, middle, and late adolescents' comparisons of the functional importance of five significant relationships. *Journal of Youth and Adolescence, 21,* 53–96.

McAuliffe, T.J., & Dembo, M.H. (1994). Status rules of behavior in scenarios of peer learning. *Journal of Educational Psychology, 86,* 163–172.

Midgley, C., Feldlaufer, H., & Eccles, J. (1989). Student/teacher relations and attitudes toward mathematics before and after the transition to junior high school. *Child Development, 60,* 981–992.

Milgram, N., & Toubiana, Y. (1999). Academic anxiety, academic procrastination, and parental involvement in students and their parents. *British Journal of Educational Psychology, 69,* 345–361.

Muller, C. (1995). Maternal employment, parent involvement, and mathematics achievement among adolescents. *Journal of Marriage and the Family, 57*, 85–100.

Muller, C. (1998). Gender differences in parental involvement and adolescents' mathematics achievement. *Sociology of Education, 71*, 336–356.

Ogbu, J.U. (1985). Origins of human competence: A cultural-ecological perspective. *Child Development, 52*, 413–429.

Parker, J.G., & Asher, S.R. (1993). Friendship and friendship quality in middle childhood: Links with peer group acceptance and feelings of loneliness and social dissatisfaction. *Developmental Psychology, 29*, 611–621.

Patterson, G.R., & Bank, C.L. (1989). Some amplifying mechanisms for pathologic processes in families. In M.R. Gunnar & E. Thelan (Eds.) *Systems and development: The Minnesota symposia on child psychology, Vol. 22* (pp. 167–210). Hillsdale, NJ: Erlbaum.

Paulson, S.E. (1994). Relations of parenting style and parental involvement with ninth-grade students' achievement. *Journal of Early Adolescence, 14*, 250–267.

Paulson, S.E., Marchant, G.J., & Rothlisberg, B.A. (1998). Early adolescents' perceptions of patterns of parenting, teaching, and school atmosphere: Implications for achievement. *Journal of Early Adolescence, 18*, 5–26.

Paulson, S.E., & Sputa, C.L. (1996). Patterns of parenting during adolescence: Perceptions of adolescents and parents. *Adolescence, 31*, 369–381.

Peterson, A., & Ebata, A.T. (1987). Developmental transitions and adolescent problem behavior: Implications for prevention and intervention. In K. Hurrlemann (Ed.), *Social prevention and intervention.* New York: deGruyter.

Phelan, P., Davidson, A.L., & Cao, H.T. (1991). Students' multiple worlds: Negotiating the boundaries of family, peer, and school cultures. *Anthropology and Education Quarterly, 22*, 224–250.

Piaget, J. (1965). *The moral judgment of the child.* New York: The Free Press.

Rathunde, K. (1996). Family context and talented adolescents' optimal experience in school-related activities. *Journal of Research on Adolescence, 6*, 605–628.

Resnick, M.D., Bearman, P.S., Blum, R.W., Bauman, K.E., Harris, K.M., Jones, J., Tabor, J., Beuhring, T., Sieving, R.E., Shew, M., Ireland, M., Bearinger, L.H., & Udry, J.R. (1997). Protecting adolescents from harm: Findings from the National Longitudinal Study on Asolescent Health. *Journal of the American Medical Association, 278*, 823–832.

Ruble, D.N. (1983). The development of social comparison processes and their role in achievement-related self-socialization. In E.T. Higgins, D. Ruble, & W. Hartup (Eds.), *Social cognition and social development: A sociocultural perspective* (pp. 134–157). Cambridge University Press: Cambridge.

Rutter, M. (1986). The developmental psychopathology of depression: Issues and perspectives. In M. Rutter, C. Izard, & P. Read (Eds.), *Depression in young people: Developmental and clinical perspectives* (p. 3–30). New York: Guilford.

Ryan, R.M. (1993). Agency and organization: Intrinsic motivation, autonomy, and the self in psychological development. In J. Jacobs (Ed.), *Nebraska symposium on motivation, vol 40* (pp. 1–56). Lincoln, NB: University of Nebraska Press.

Schaps, E., Battistich, V., & Solomon, D. (1997). School as a caring community: A key to character education. In A. Molnar (Ed.), *Ninety-sixth yearbook of the*

National Society for the Study of Education (pp. 127–139). Chicago: University of Chicago Press.

Schunk, D.H. (1987). Peer models and children's behavioral change. *Review of Educational Research, 57*, 149–174.

Seginer, R. (1983). Parents' educational expectations and children's academic achievements: A literature review. *Merrill-Palmer Quarterly, 29*, 1–23.

Spencer, M.B. (1999). Social and cultural influences on school adjustment: The application of an identity-focused cultural ecological perspective. *Educational Psychologist, 34*, 43–58.

Steinberg, L. (1990). Autonomy, conflict, and harmony in the family relationship. In S.S Feldman & G.R. Elliott (Eds.), At the threshold: The developing adolescent (pp. 255–276). Cambridge, MA: Harvard University Press.

Steinberg, L., Dornbusch, S.M., & Brown, B.B. (1992). Ethnic differences in adolescent achievement: An ecological perspective. *American Psychologist, 47*, 723–729.

Steinberg, L., Lamborn, S.D., Darling, N., Mounts, N.S., & Dornbusch, S.M. (1994). Over-time changes in adjustment and competence among adolescents from authoritative, authoritarian, indulgent, and neglectful families. *Child Development, 65*, 754–770.

Tappan, M.B. (1998). Sociocultural psychology and caring pedagogy: Exploring Vygotsky's "Hidden Curriculum." *Educational Psychologist, 33*, 23–33.

Trenholm, S., & Rose, T. (1981). The compliant communicator: Teacher perceptions of appropriate classroom behavior. *The Western Journal of Speech Communication, 45*, 13–26.

Trent, L.M.Y., Cooney, G., Russell, G., & Warton, P.M. (1996). Significant others' contribution to early adolescents' perceptions of their competence. *British Journal of Educational Psychology, 66*, 95–107.

Trusty, J., & Lampe, R.E. (1997). Relationship of high-school seniors' perceptions of parental involvement and control to seniors' locus of control. *Journal of Counseling and Development, 75*, 375–384.

Wentzel, K.R. (1991a). Relations between social competence and academic achievement in early adolescence. *Child Development, 62*, 1066–1078.

Wentzel, K.R. (1991b). Social and academic goals at school: Achievement motivation in context. In M. Maehr and P. Pintrich (Eds.), *Advances In motivation and achievement* (Vol. 7; pp. 185–212). Greenwich, CT: JAI.

Wentzel, K.R. (1994a). Family functioning and academic achievement in middle school: A social-emotional perspective. *Journal of Early Adolescence, 14*, 268–291.

Wentzel, K.R. (1994b). Relations of social goal pursuit to social acceptance, classroom behavior, and perceived social support. *Journal of Educational Psychology, 86*, 173–182.

Wentzel, K.R. (1997). Student motivation in middle school: The role of perceived pedagogical caring. *Journal of Educational Psychology, 89*, 411–419.

Wentzel, K.R. (1998). Social support and adjustment in middle school: The role of parents, teachers, and peers. *Journal of Educational Psychology, 90*, 202–209.

Wentzel, K.R. (1999). Social-motivational processes and interpersonal relationships: Implications for understanding students' academic success. *Journal of Educational Psychology, 91*, 76–97.

Wentzel, K.R., & Asher, S.R. (1995). Academic lives of neglected, rejected, popular, and controversial children. *Child Development, 66,* 754–763.

Wentzel, K.R., & Caldwell, K. (1997). Friendships, peer acceptance, and group membership: Relations to academic achievement in middle school. *Child Development, 68,* 1198–1209.

Wentzel, K.R., Feldman, S.S., & Weinberger, D.A. (1991). Parental childrearing and academic achievement in boys: The mediational role of socioemotional adjustment. *Journal of Early Adolescence, 11,* 321–339.

Wentzel, K.R., & McNamara, C. (1999). Interpersonal relationships, emotional distress, and prosocial behavior in middle school. *Journal of Early Adolescence, 19,* 114–125.

Wentzel, K.R., Weinberger, D.A., Ford, M.E., & Feldman, S.S. (1990). Academic achievement in preadolescence: The role of motivational, affective, and self-regulatory processes. *Journal of Applied Developmental Psychology, 11,* 179–93.

Wenz-Gross, M., Siperstein, G.N., Untch, A.S., & Widaman, K.F. (1997). Stress, social support, and adjustment of adolescents in middle school. *Journal of Early Adolescence, 17,* 129–151.

Werner, E.E., & Smith, R.S. (1992). *Overcoming the odds: High risk children from birth to adulthood.* Ithaca, NY: Cornell University Press.

Wood, J., Chapin, K., & Hannah, M.E. (1988). Family environment and its relation to underachievement. *Adolescence, 23,* 282–290.

Youniss, J., & Smollar, J. (1989). *Adolescents' interpersonal relationships In social context.* In T.J. Berndt & G. Ladd (Eds.), Peer relationships in child development (pp. 300–316). New York: Wiley.

CHAPTER 5

Teaching Adolescents

Engaging Developing Selves

Anita Woolfolk Hoy, Peter Demerath, and Stephen Pape

INTRODUCTION

Adolescence has long been considered a time of transition and becoming. Young students are answering, or at least confronting, identity questions about world view, career direction, interests, gender orientation, values, philosophy of life, and aspirations for the future. As these students are "becoming somebody" they spend hours in classrooms and schools in constant interaction with teachers, peers, ideas, and activities. A challenge for teachers is to engage these students in valuable learning tasks and activities while also supporting the students' emerging identities. In this chapter we explore the implications of engaging students who are in the process of becoming. To frame a consideration of engagement, we look to traditional topics in educational psychology such as self-schemas, self-regulated learning, and motivation, but also to emerging conceptions of identity from sociocultural theories. This sociocultural research on engagement, grounded in anthropology, has focused on how adolescent students' identity formation processes in and out of school affect their willingness to learn. Such perspectives emphasize the importance of students' self-definition processes as well as their own conscious and unconscious efforts to maintain self-worth in their adaptations to school.

First, we consider the student. Again we employ the lenses of psychology and anthropology to better understand the challenges facing students who are learning to regulate their academic behaviors while also deciding who they are and what is important to learn. These challenges raise issues of peer groups, students' possible futures, and power relations in the constructing of identities. Next, we examine several teaching approaches that might promote self-regulation, engagement, and identity construction.

THE STUDENT: PSYCHOLOGICAL PERSPECTIVES ON DEVELOPING SELVES

Psychology has a long and rich tradition of research on the self. Developmental, social, clinical, cognitive, and educational psychology, to name only a few fields, have studied beliefs and conceptions about self and identity. Our interest in examining psychological perspectives on the self is to better understand how conceptions of self might influence learning and motivation in schools and what teachers can do to engage adolescents in learning. Given the vast body of information in psychology, our examination of self and identity must be selective. Thus, we will consider three areas: (a) Eric Erikson's perspective on the development of identity in adolescents, (b) self-schemas including self-concept and self-efficacy and (c) self-regulated learning.

Erikson and Identity

After studying child-rearing practices in several cultures, Erikson (1963, 1968, 1980) concluded that all humans have the same basic needs and that each society must provide in some way for those needs. Therefore, emotional changes follow similar patterns in every society. Erikson saw development as a passage through a series of stages, each with its particular goals, concerns, accomplishments, and dangers. At each stage, Erikson suggested, the individual faces a developmental crisis—a conflict between a positive alternative and a potentially unhealthy alternative. The way in which the individual resolves each crisis will have a lasting effect on that person's self-image and view of society. An unhealthy resolution of problems in the early stages can have potential negative repercussions throughout life, although sometimes damage can be repaired at later stages.

The central issue for adolescents is the development of an identity that will provide a firm basis for adulthood. The individual has been developing a sense of self since infancy. But adolescence marks the first time that a conscious effort is made to answer the now-pressing question, "Who am I?" The conflict defining this stage is identity versus role confusion. Identity refers to the organization of the individual's drives, abilities, beliefs, and history into a consistent image of self. It involves deliberate choices and decisions, particularly about work, values, ideology, and commitments to people and ideas (Marcia, 1987; Penuel & Wertsch, 1995). According to Erikson, if adolescents fail to integrate all these aspects and choices, or if they feel unable to choose at all, role confusion threatens. Schools that give adolescents experiences with real-world work, internships, and mentoring foster identity formation (Cooper, 1998). One such possibility is community service learning, described in a later section.

Since the work of Erikson, many other approaches to understanding identity and "becoming somebody" have emerged. Some of the most influential and valuable perspectives consider the development of a sense of self—sometimes called self-schemas.

Self Schemas

Self-schemas are enduring conceptions of the self that mediate behaviors (Garcia & Pintrich, 1994). These conceptions have four dimensions—affective, temporal, efficacy, and value—that influence how we act within particular situations. For example, high achieving students may have positive self-conceptions and feel efficacious in academic situations, choosing to obtain high levels of competence because their self-schema is one of capability for attaining academic goals. In contrast, low achieving students may have negative self-images, lack efficacy in academic situations, and value the pursuit of athletic prowess, popularity, or recreational activities instead of academic achievement.

Self-Concept

One of the most widely discussed and researched self-schemas is self-concept. Self-concept generally refers to "the composite of ideas, feelings, and attitudes people have about themselves" (Hilgard, Atkinson, & Atkinson, 1979, p. 605). We could consider self-concept to be our attempt to explain ourselves to ourselves, to build a schema that organizes our impressions, feelings, and attitudes about ourselves. But this model or schema is not permanent, unified, or unchanging. Our self-perceptions vary from situation to situation and from one phase of our lives to another.

Self-concept and self-esteem are often used interchangeably, even though they have distinct meanings. Self-concept is a cognitive structure—a belief about who we are. Self-esteem is an affective reaction—an evaluation of who we are. If people evaluate themselves positively—if they "like what they see"—we say that they have high *self-esteem* (Pintrich & Schunk, 1996). Self-esteem, though a popular topic among educators, may or may not have effects on achievement in school, depending on whether school achievement is a source of self-worth to the individual (Bandura, 1997). Self-concept, however, affects learning in school, for example, through course selection. Marsh and Yeung (1997) examined how 246 boys in early high school in Sydney, Australia chose their courses. Academic self-concept for a particular subject (mathematics, science, etc.) was the most important predictor of course selection—more important than previous grades in the subject or overall self-concept. In fact, having a positive self-concept in a particular subject was an even bigger factor in selecting courses when self-concept in other subjects was low. The courses selected in high school put students on a path toward the future, so self-concepts about particular academic subjects can be life-changing influences.

One of the most widely researched self schemas is self-efficacy, a concept that has significant implications for academic learning.

Self-Efficacy

Bandura (1997) defined perceived self-efficacy as "beliefs in one's capabilities to organize and execute the courses of action required to produce given attainments" (p. 3). Self-efficacy is a future-oriented belief about the level of competence a person expects he or she will display in a given situation. Self-efficacy beliefs influence thought patterns and emotions that enable actions in which people expend substantial effort in pursuit of goals, persist in the face of adversity, rebound from temporary setbacks, and exercise some control over events that affect their lives (Bandura, 1986, 1993, 1997). Thus self-efficacy is a primary mechanism that allows humans to be agents, that is, "to intentionally make things happen by one's actions" (Bandura, 2001, p. 2).

Self-efficacy is distinct from other conceptions of self, such as self-concept, self-worth, and self-esteem, in that it is *specific to a particular task.* Self-efficacy has to do with self-perceptions of competence rather than actual level of competence. This is an important distinction because people regularly overestimate or underestimate their actual abilities, and these estimations may have consequences for the courses of action they choose to pursue or the effort they exert in those pursuits. Over or underestimating capabilities also may influence how well they use the skills they possess. For example, Bouffard-Bouchard, Parent, and Larivee (1991) found junior and senior high school students with the same level of skill development in mathematics differed significantly in their ability to solve math problems, depending on the strength of their efficacy beliefs. Adolescents with higher efficacy more consistently and effectively applied what they knew;

they were more persistent and less likely to reject correct solutions prematurely. In most cases, slightly overestimating one's actual capabilities has the most positive effect on performance.

Self-efficacy is a critical factor in self-regulated learning. A consideration of self-regulation brings us closer to understanding teaching and schooling for adolescents.

Self-Regulation

Today, people change jobs an average of seven times before they retire. Many of these career changes require new knowledge and skills (Weinstein, 1994). Thus, one goal of teaching should be to free students from the need for teachers so the students can continue to learn independently throughout their lives. To continue learning independently throughout life, students must be self-regulated learners. Self-regulated learners have a combination of academic learning skills and self-control that makes learning easier, so they are more motivated; in other words, they have the *skill* and the *will* to learn (McCombs & Marzano, 1990; Murphy & Alexander, 2000).

Learning to regulate one's behaviors, emotions, and motivations is a life long task beginning in infancy. The task of developing self-regulation for learning becomes even more important during adolescence when academic learning becomes more difficult and schooling becomes more complex, with multiple teachers, assignments, and deadlines every week. Self-regulated behavior has been shown to correlate with academic achievement, to be distinct from general ability, and to be teachable (Zimmerman & Risemberg, 1997). Furthermore, self-regulated behavior has been shown to explain achievement in spite of circumstances that often lead to desperation and failure.

To be self-regulated, students need *knowledge* about themselves, the subject, the task, the learning strategies, and the contexts in which they will apply their learning. Expert students probably understand that different learning tasks require different approaches on their part. A simple memory task, for example, might require a mnemonic strategy while a complex comprehension task might be approached by means of maps of the key ideas (these strategies are described in a later section). Also, self-regulated learners know that learning often is difficult and knowledge is seldom absolute—there usually are different ways of looking at problems as well as different solutions (Pressley, 1995; Winne, 1995).

Expert students not only know what each task requires, they also can apply the strategy needed. They can skim or read carefully. They can use memory strategies or reorganize the material. As they become more knowledgeable in a field, they apply many of these strategies automatically. In short, they have mastered a large, flexible repertoire of learning strategies and tactics. Finally, self-regulated learners know how to protect themselves from distractions—where to study, for example, so they are not interrupted. They know how to cope when they feel anxious, drowsy, or lazy (Corno, 1992; Snow, Corno, & Jackson, 1997).

To regulate one's emotions, behaviors, and cognitive processes in academic situations requires a store of domain (academic subject) specific knowledge, clear goals, supportive attributions, appropriate self-schemas, and useful strategies. Fourteen categories of strategies have been identified: self-evaluating; organizing and transforming; goal setting and planning; seeking information; keeping records and monitoring; environmental restructuring; self-consequences; rehearsing and memorizing; seeking peer, teacher, and adult assistance; and reviewing tests, notes, and texts (Zimmerman & Martinez-Pons, 1986, 1990). Goals, attributions, and self-schemas are particularly important when teaching adolescent populations because, in order to learn to be self-regulated, students must be helped to set realistic goals and monitor their progress toward these goals. This involves self-efficacy and other self-beliefs.

The Structure of Self-regulated Learning

Zimmerman (2000) presents a cyclical phase structure of self-regulated learning that includes (a) forethought, (b) performance or volitional control, and (c) self-reflection. Forethought involves the ability to analyze tasks and includes self-motivation beliefs. Students must believe in their capabilities to accomplish a task, must expect positive outcomes from engaging in the task, must value the potential outcomes, and have appropriate goal orientations (e.g., learning vs. performance goal orientation) before they will engage in the task. Performance and volitional control involves self-control of attention and other aspects of behavior through techniques such as self-instruction, imagery, and task strategies (example strategies are described below). Success during performance is dependent upon self-observation; self-reflection is crucial to self-regulation. Based on observations of progress toward accomplishing a task, self-regulated students adjust their behaviors and emotions accordingly. Self-judgments of progress include causal attributions. Students who attribute failure to external stable factors will not persist effectively toward the attainment of goals that are perceived to be out of their control.

The Development of Self-regulated Learning

Development of self-regulation involves four stages: observation, emulation, self-control, and self-regulation (Zimmerman, 2000). Following the observation of strategic behaviors, the learner practices specific aspects of these performances through imitation. Once competent in carrying out particular strategies, students begin to implement them in isolation. It is not until the final stage, self-regulation, when students make choices about the implementation of these behaviors in particular situations that one can say they are truly self-regulated. This sequence is similar to the process of internalization of higher-level functioning proposed within a Vygotskian perspective (Rohrkemper, 1989). In order for students to become self-regulated, they must have the opportunity to observe strategic behavior and to practice these behaviors.

Promoting Self-Regulation: Examples from Research

The developmental sequence proposed by Zimmerman (2000) and self-schemas have particularly important implications for the teaching of adolescents. Students need to observe the control of behaviors and emotions; they need to be explicitly taught how to analyze tasks; and they need to be motivated to accomplish goals they have set for themselves. The models of instruction discussed in later sections of this chapter, cognitive apprenticeships, cooperative learning, problem-based learning and anchored instruction, and service learning, provide potential examples for teaching adolescents to become self-regulated within academic situations. Several areas of research that have pointed toward effective classroom interventions are particularly instructive in these areas.

Self-Monitoring

Schunk and his colleagues (e.g., Schunk & Gunn, 1986) have investigated the influence of self-monitoring and task strategies on self-efficacy, and the role of self-efficacy on mathematical development. Students who were taught to monitor their progress in the use of appropriate task strategies were found to increase in self-efficacy beliefs, which has been shown to mediate and directly influence such outcomes as mathematical problem solving (Pajares & Miller, 1994). Students with poor histories in mathematics need to be taught how to monitor their progress in using specific strategies to accomplish tasks, which in turn affects their efficacy beliefs for attempting these tasks in the future.

Attribution Retraining

Attribution retraining studies (e.g., Borkowski, Weyhing, & Carr, 1988) have been successful in helping adolescents to adopt and use strategic behavior. These interventions train students to attribute successful performance to the use of a strategy and failure to the lack of strategy use, internal unstable attributions, rather than to intelligence or the lack there of, an internal stable attribution. When students attribute success to strategic behavior, they are more likely to maintain strategy use and to use strategies in the future (Borkowski et al., 1988).

Learning Disabled Students

Another line of research that is instructive in developing self-regulated learners among adolescents involves learning disabled students. Although these students are often depicted as inactive or inefficient, Butler (1998) has shown that they may be assisted to be more active in their learning through intensive work. Her empirically validated intervention model, Strategic Content Learning (SCL), involves scaffolding students' self-regulated behaviors while they work on a task of their own choosing. Students analyze the demands of the task, state the requirements of the task, and set goals for its completion. Through this analysis, the demands of the academic situation are made explicit for the students. The teacher might perform this analysis out loud for the students as in cognitive apprenticeships (Collins, Brown, & Newman, 1989). Strategies are not predetermined but are built from the students' existing knowledge. Students are encouraged to select strategies in their repertoire to accomplish the task and/or to problem-solve possible strategies. Strategy use is monitored for effectiveness and adjusted through the help of the tutor.

Self and Identity: Lessons for Teachers

Adolescents often come to learning situations with poor self-schemas. Histories of poor academic performance may result in negative academic self-images, low self-efficacy, and poor motivation. Each of these factors greatly reduces the potential that students will regulate their own behaviors and makes the teaching of adolescents particularly daunting. A challenge for teaching is to help adolescents move toward a sense of self that supports learning, responsibility, and connection to society. A strong sense of self-efficacy for learning and self-regulation would serve adolescents well as they assume increasing career and family responsibilities in a rapidly changing, unpredictable world. Skills and attitudes of self-regulation should be taught directly and practiced in a range of arenas so that adolescents enter adulthood with the skill and will to continue learning and adapting throughout their lives. But do teachers actually focus on teaching students how to learn? Sirotnik's (1983) study of middle and high school teachers indicates such instruction seldom is provided. It is strange that educators value life-long learning yet seldom directly teach adolescents how to learn. In a later section on teaching we will examine strategies based on general principles of how to learn, remember, and solve problems.

BECOMING SOMEBODY: A VIEW OF ADOLESCENCE FROM ANTHROPOLOGY

In the past, anthropologists tended to focus on cultural influences (e.g., Mead, 1973) or psychological predispositions (e.g., Cohen, 1964) in their cross-cultural understandings of adolescence. Researchers studying adolescence today see it as a universal physiological, psychological, and social stage in the developmental process that occurs at or near puberty. Although this period includes transitions in sexual maturity, relationships with parents and peers, psychological functioning, and identity formation, as well as adoption of different formal roles, the specific nature of these shifts ultimately is shaped, expressed, and given meaning by local cultural traditions and world views (Schlegel & Barry, 1991). For example, anthropologists have described a great diversity of adolescent initiation practices in many societies that have the common goals of fostering changes in individual's identity and role and strengthening their allegiance to core social values (Spiro, 1965; Whiting, Kluckholn, & Anthony, 1958).

Anthropologists historically have seen education itself as a process of cultural *transmission*—teaching young humans "how to think, act and feel appropriately" (Spindler, 1967). More recent perspectives have focused on cultural *acquisition*, thereby seeking to understand the extent to which learners have, indeed, "caught" what has been "taught" (Wolcott, 1994). Implicit in such views is that learning always occurs in a cultural context and involves the integration of new with extant knowledge. It is for this reason that anthropologists of education generally regard schooling as a *calculated intervention* with the overall learning process (Spindler, 1982); the students' primary task in school is to "become somebody" (Wexler, 1992). Instructional and curricular influences in school as well as non-instructional influences such as family, employment, extracurricular activities, media influences, and peer-group affiliations shape these processes of self-creation.

Identity and Peers

Studies in diverse cultures have shown that peers play a major role in shaping students' attitudes, values and actions with regard to education (Coleman, 1961; Harris, 1995; Heath & McLaughlin, 1993). Indeed in his comprehensive study of student life in a rural high school, Cusick found that students' "most active and alive moments" seemed to occur not when they were engaged with the subject matter, but rather in their own small group interactions during the school day (Cusick, 1973, p. 58). Peer influence seems to originate in cognitive, affective, and social changes that reach their peak during puberty in early adolescence (Berndt, Laychak, &

Park, 1990). During this period individuals experience an increased tendency to affiliate with others and to compare and evaluate themselves in relation to them. Peers and smaller friendship groups gradually define values and accepted behaviors through processes such as giving assistance, modeling, imitation, labeling, exclusion, ostracism, sanctions, and occasionally, physical assault (Brown, 1989; Fordham & Ogbu, 1986).

The effects of peer influence depend on the attitudes and values of the people with whom students spend most of their time (Berndt et al., 1990). Often these pressures motivate students to remain in school and finish their course of study. For example, it has been shown that peers can function as educational resources: high-achieving students positively influence the academic achievement of their initially low-achieving friends over time (Epstein, 1983). However, peers can also restrain high achievement, reject academic aspirations, and turn to other activities to display competence and success (MacLeod, 1995). In sum, by developing their own notions of what success is, how schooling fosters success, and how much deviance will be tolerated, peer cultures can circumscribe a powerful school ideology for students. Students' valuations of schooling, and ultimately their willingness to learn, are embedded in relationships between their cultural/ethnic backgrounds and the school environment (Kohl, 1991)—which we examine next.

Culture, Power, and Engagement

A starting point for much of the research on culture and schooling is an analysis of how students from different cultural and class backgrounds are affected by the institutionalized individualism of Western-style schools with their emphases on competition, autonomy, and meritocracy (Carnoy & Levin, 1985; Stanton-Salazar, 1997). Researchers have shown how cultural discontinuities between home and school can help explain the performance difficulties of some adolescent students in school. In particular, *compatibility* (or continuity) between dominant home cultural patterns and school practices often yields in-school success, whereas *incompatibility* (or discontinuity) often fosters tension, conflict, and performance difficulties (Heath, 1983). In addition, scholars have demonstrated how tensions over appropriate gender role in home and school can affect the academic experiences and outcomes of students (Gibson, 1982; Orenstein, 1994).

More critical perspectives on academic engagement seek to understand the roles of power, politics, and ideology in students' responses to schooling. Such perspectives are informed by *practice* theory in an attempt to understand how systemic structures construct actors/actresses and how these agents respond to the structures (Collier & Yanagisako, 1989; Ortner, 1984). Ogbu's multi-level analyses, for example, have shown how specific groups' experiences with dominant social, political, and economic structures shape their cultural models of schooling. Such models include folk explanations for the role of schooling in "getting ahead." These models can be either *additive* (nonthreatening to a group's identity) or *subtractive* (threatening to a group's identity). For example, immigrant minorities tend to adopt a cultural model that leads them to accept the mainstream wisdom that school achievement leads to getting ahead (additive). But the historical experiences of nonimmigrant minorities such as African-Americans often lead them to adopt a more skeptical (subtractive) cultural model that includes the notion of a glass ceiling—success in school may not lead to success as adults in the wider society. Students with such orientations may develop oppositional identities in school that can pose barriers to academic success (Ogbu, 1990).

In addition, adolescent students' academic engagement may be shaped by the models of personhood that are implicit in their homes and schools (Phelan, Davidson, & Yu, 1998; Rival, 1996). Indeed, students from more communalistic home environments may accentuate identities grounded in their homes to preserve self-worth in competitive and alienating school environments (Cummins, 1997; Deyhle, 1995). Levinson, for example, showed that for students in a Mexican secundaria, adopting a schooled identity created "a perception of difference where there had been none before—thereby imperiling students' potential solidarity with other members of their community" (1996, p. 231). Similarly, many of the high school students studied by Fordham (1996; Fordham & Ogbu, 1986) perceived academic success as "acting white," and those studied by Demerath (1996) saw this kind of success as "acting extra." These adolescent students experienced pressures in school to conform to a dominant culture as a threat, and consequentially disengaged from their academics, resisted school personnel, and celebrated oppositional identities, although not all researchers agree with this interpretation. For example, Spencer, Noll, Stoltzfus, and Harpalani (2001) describe African American adolescents who show high self-esteem and achievement goals in combination with high Afrocentricity.

So it appears that implicit in many adolescent students' approaches to school are dilemmas regarding what constitutes an educated person and the value of such an identity (Levinson, Foley, & Holland, 1996). Critical ethnographers such as Levinson and colleagues have shown how many subordinated students respond to inherited material conditions by actively drawing on their own cultural, ideological, and historical resources. In the process, their *cultural productions*[1] can inadvertently lead to their disengagement from school (Fine, 1991; Levinson et al., 1996) to critiques of dominant cultural forms (Solomon, 1992; Wagner, 1998), and also to school success (Davidson, 1996; Goto, 1997; Hemmings, 1996; O'Connor, 1997). Much of this work describes the experiences of students who come from historically dominated, colonized, or enslaved groups (see Osborne, 1996). Many of these students disengage from or resist schooling practices when they do not trust that the school will further their own interests (Erickson, 1987; Holland & Eisenhart, 1988).

Culture and Identity: Lessons for Teachers

Research suggests that students do better in school when they feel strongly anchored in the identities of their families, communities, and peers (Deyhle, 1995; Gibson, 1997; Mehan, Hubbard, & Villanueva, 1994). Teachers therefore need to connect meaningfully with their adolescent students: establish trusting relationships with them, and, to the extent possible, reference their out-of-school experiences and knowledge in the classroom (Phelan et al., 1998; Stanton-Salazar, 1997). Teachers should also be aware of the powerful influences students can exert on one another and use institutionally-sanctioned peer groups to build cultures of learning in school (Mehan et al., 1994; Slavin, 1995).

The challenge for teachers of adolescent students from minority backgrounds is to help them manage their lives in multiple worlds (New London Group, 1996; Stanton-Salazar, 1997). School practices that can contribute to these ends include *culturally relevant teaching*, which Ladson-Billings (1994) asserts comprises the following tenets: Students whose educational, economic, social, political, and cultural futures are most tenuous are helped to become intellectual leaders in the classroom. Students are apprenticed in a learning community rather than taught in an isolated and unrelated way. Students' real-life experiences are legitimized as they become part of the "official" curriculum. Teachers and students participate in a broad conception of literacy that incorporates both literature and oratory. Teachers and students engage in a collective struggle against the status quo. Teachers are cognizant of themselves as political beings (1994, pp. 117–118).

Culturally relevant pedagogy rests on three propositions. First, students must experience academic success. "Despite the current social inequities and hostile classroom environments, students must develop their academic skills. The ways those skills are developed may vary, but all students need literacy, numeracy, technological, social, and political skills in order to be active participants in a democracy" (Ladson-Billings, 1995, p. 160).

Second, as they become more academically skilled, students must still retain their cultural competence. Culturally relevant teachers use the students' culture to improve learning (Ladson-Billings, 1995). For example, one teacher used non-offensive rap music to teach about literal and figurative meaning, rhyme, alliteration, and onomatopoeia in poetry. Another brought in a community expert known for her sweet potato pies to work with students. Follow-up lessons included investigations of George Washington Carver's sweet potato research, numerical analyses of taste tests, marketing plans for selling pies, and research on the educational preparation needed to become a chef.

Third, students should develop a critical consciousness to challenge the status quo. In addition to developing academic skills while retaining cultural competence, excellent teachers help students "develop a broader sociopolitical consciousness that allows them to critique the social norms, values, mores, and institutions that produce and maintain social inequities" (Ladson-Billings, 1995, p. 162). For example, in one school students were upset that their textbooks were out of date. They mobilized to investigate the funding formulas that allowed middle-class students to have newer books, wrote letters to the newspaper editor to challenge these inequities, and updated their texts with current information from other sources.

Other researchers also call on teachers to help their students develop this kind of critical consciousness (Delpit, 1995), critical framing ability (New London Group, 1996) or boundary strategy (Deyhle, 1995). More specifically, Delpit (1995) asserts that teachers should make explicit the rules and codes for participating in the culture of power (including ways of talking, writing, dressing, and interacting) so that those students who do not have knowledge of them may enhance their life-chances.

In the following section we examine several teaching strategies that support self-regulation, identity development, connection, cultural competence, and engagement.

TEACHING THOSE WHO ARE BECOMING: STRATEGIES TO PROMOTE ENGAGEMENT AND IDENTITY

How can both psychological and anthropological conceptions of adolescence, self, and identity guide our thinking about teaching? We begin by examining ways of helping students become more self-regulated in their learning through the direct teaching of learning strategies. Then we turn to cognitive apprenticeships that teach thinking and problem solving in the social context of a master/apprentice relationship. Problem-based learning is another approach that situates learning, this time in authentic and meaningful dilemmas that give a reason for learning. Next we turn to cooperative learning to explore how social support, collaboration, and dialogue can encourage learning. Finally we examine community service learning. This approach—with its emphasis on developing a sense of agency and connections with society—is consistent with anthropological perspectives on identity and sociocultural influences on the self.

Promoting Self-Regulation in Every Class

Learning strategies are ideas for accomplishing learning goals, a kind of overall plan of attack. Learning tactics are the specific techniques that make up the plan (Derry, 1989). Several principles have been identified.

- Students must be exposed to a number of *different strategies,* not only general learning strategies but also very specific tactics, such as the graphic strategies described later in this chapter.
- *Teach conditional knowledge* about when, where, and why to use various strategies (Pressley, 1986). Although this may seem obvious, teachers often neglect this step, either because they do not realize its significance or because they assume students will make inferences on their own. A strategy is more likely to be maintained and employed if students know when, where, and why to use it.
- Students may know when and how to use a strategy, but unless they also *develop the desire to employ these skills,* general learning ability will not improve. Several learning strategy programs (Dansereau, 1985) include a motivational training component.
- *Direct instruction in schematic knowledge* is often an important component of strategy training. In order to identify main ideas—a critical skill for a number of learning strategies—students must have an appropriate schema for making sense of the material. Table 1 summarizes several tactics for learning declarative (verbal) knowledge and procedural skills (Derry, 1989).

Table 1.   Examples of Learning Tactics

	Examples	*Use When?*
Tactics for Learning Verbal Information	1. Attention Focusing	
	• Making outlines, underlining	With easy, structured materials; for good readers
	• Looking for headings and topic sentences	For pooer readers; with more difficult materials
	2. Schema Building	
	• Story grammars	With poor text structure, goal is to encourage active comprehension
	• Theory schemas	
	• Networking and mapping	
	3. Idea Elaboration	
	• Self-questioning	To understand and remember specific ideas
	• Imagery	

Table 1.   Examples of Learning Tactics (Cont.)

	Examples	Use When?
Tactics for Learning Procedural Information	1. Pattern Learning	
	• Hypothesizing	To learn attributes of concepts
	• Identifying reasons for actions	To match procedures to situations
	2. Self-instruction	
	• Comparing own performance to expert model	to tune, improve complex skills
	3. Practice	
	• Part practice	When few specific aspects of a performance need attention
	• Whole practice	To maintain and improve skill

Source: Based on "Putting Learning Strategies to Work," by S. Derry, 1989, *Educational Leadership 47*(5), pp. 5–6.

Deciding What Is Important

As indicated in the first entry in Table 1, learning begins with focusing attention—deciding what is important. But distinguishing the main idea from less important information is not always easy. Often students focus on the "seductive details" or the concrete examples, perhaps because they are more interesting (Dole, Duffy, Roehler, & Pearson, 1991; Gardner, Brown, Sanders, & Menke, 1992). Finding the central idea is especially difficult if you lack prior knowledge in an area and the amount of new information provided is extensive. Teachers can give students practice in using signals in texts such as headings, bold words, outlines, or other indicators to identify key concepts and main ideas. Teaching students to summarize material can be helpful too.

Summaries

Creating summaries can help students learn, but students have to be taught how to summarize (Byrnes, 1996; Dole et al., 1991; Palincsar & Brown, 1989). Jeanne Ormrod (1999, p. 333) suggests these techniques for helping students create summaries:

- Begin doing summaries of short, easy, well-organized readings. Introduce longer, less organized and more difficult passages gradually.
- For each summary, ask students to find or write a *topic sentence* for each paragraph or section, identify *big ideas* that cover several specific points, find some *supporting information* for each big idea, and delete any *redundant information* or unnecessary details.

- Ask students to compare their summaries and discuss what ideas they thought were important and why—what's their evidence?

Two other study strategies that are based on identifying key ideas are *underlining* texts and *taking notes*.

Underlining and Highlighting

Underlining, highlighting, and note taking are probably the most commonly used strategies among high school and college students. Yet few students receive any instruction in the best ways to take notes or underline, so it is not surprising that many students use ineffective strategies. One common problem is that students underline or highlight too much. It is far better to be selective. In studies that limit how much students can underline—for example, only one sentence per paragraph—learning has improved (Snowman, 1984). In addition to being selective, students also should actively transform the information into their own words as they underline or take notes. Teach students not to rely on the words of the book. Encourage them to note connections between what they are reading and other things that they already know. Draw diagrams to illustrate relationships. Finally, look for organizational patterns in the material and use them to guide underlining or note taking (Irwin, 1991).

Taking Notes

Research indicates that taking notes serves at least two important functions:

1. Taking notes focuses attention during class and helps encode information so it has a chance of making it to long-term memory. In order to record key ideas in your own words, you have to translate, connect, elaborate, and organize. Even if students don't review notes before a test, taking them in the first place appears to aid learning, especially for those who lack prior knowledge in an area. Of course, if taking notes distracts them from actually listening to and making sense of the lecture, then note taking may not be effective (DiVesta & Gray, 1972; Kiewra, 1989; Van Meter, Yokoi, & Pressley, 1994).
2. Notes provide extended external storage that allows students to return and review. Students who use their notes to study tend to perform better on tests, especially if they take many high quality notes—more is better as long as the students are capturing key ideas, concepts, and relationships, not just intriguing details (Kiewra, 1989).

Van Meter et al. (1994) concluded that understanding is served when students match notes to their anticipated use and make modifications in strategies after tests or assignments; use personal codes to flag material that is unfamiliar or difficult; fill in holes by consulting relevant sources (including other students in the class); record information verbatim only when a verbatim response will be required; and generally are strategic about taking and using notes.

To help students organize their note taking, some teachers provide matrices or maps, such as the one in Figure 1. When students are first learning to use these maps, teachers often fill in some of the spaces for

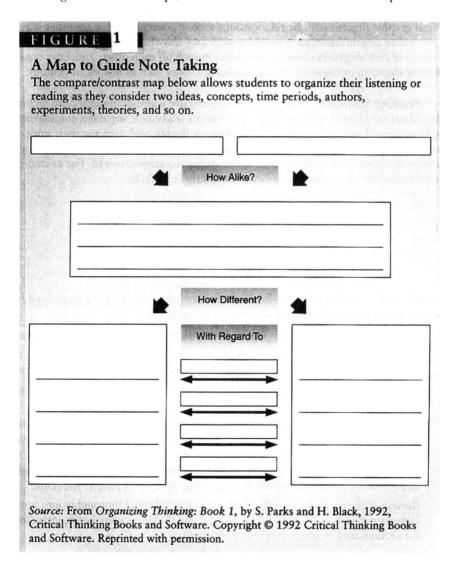

FIGURE 1

A Map to Guide Note Taking

The compare/contrast map below allows students to organize their listening or reading as they consider two ideas, concepts, time periods, authors, experiments, theories, and so on.

How Alike?

How Different?

With Regard To

Source: From *Organizing Thinking: Book 1*, by S. Parks and H. Black, 1992, Critical Thinking Books and Software. Copyright © 1992 Critical Thinking Books and Software. Reprinted with permission.

Figure 1.   A map to guide note taking.

them. Also, it is helpful for students to exchange their filled-in maps and explain their thinking to each other.

Visual Tools for Organizing

To use underlining and note taking effectively students must identify main ideas. In addition, effective use of underlining and note taking depends on an understanding of the organization of the text or lecture—the connections and relationships among ideas. Some visual strategies have been developed to help students with this key element. There is evidence that creating graphic organizers such as maps or charts is more effective than outlining in learning from texts (Robinson, 1998). Armbruster and Anderson (1981) taught students specific techniques for diagramming relationships among ideas presented in a text. Mapping these relationships by noting causal connections, comparison/contrast connections, and examples improved recall. Davidson (1982) suggested that students compare one another's maps and discuss the differences. There are other ways to visualize organization such as Venn diagrams showing how ideas or concepts overlap or tree diagrams showing how ideas branch off of each other. Timelines organize information in sequence and are useful in classes such as history or geology. Software such as Inspiration or MindMaps also allows students to map relationships.

Mnemonics

Mnemonics are systematic procedures for improving memory and have helped medical students learn the names of bones and organs for years. Many mnemonic strategies use imagery (Atkinson et al., 1999; Levin, 1994). If students need to remember information for long periods of time, an acronym may be the answer. An acronym is a form of abbreviation—a word formed from the first letter of each word in a phrase, for example HOMES to remember the Great Lakes (Huron, Ontario, Michigan, Erie, Superior). Another method forms phrases or sentences out of the first letter of each word or item in a list, for example, Every Good Boy Does Fine to remember the lines on the G clef—E, G, B, D, F. Because the words must make sense as a sentence, this approach also has some characteristics of chain mnemonics, methods that connect the first item to be memorized with the second, the second item with the third, and so on. In one type of chain method, each item on a list is linked to the next through some visual association or story. Another chain-method approach is to incorporate all the items to be memorized into a jingle like "i before e except after c."

The mnemonic system that has been most extensively applied in teaching is the keyword method. The approach has two stages. To remember a foreign word, for example, students first choose an English word, preferably a concrete noun, that sounds like the foreign word or a part of it. Next, they associate the meaning of the foreign word with the English word through an image or sentence. For example, the Spanish word *carta* (meaning "letter") sounds like the English word "cart." Cart becomes the keyword: students imagine a shopping cart filled with letters on its way to the post office, or make up a sentence such as "The cart full of letters tipped over" (Pressley, Levin, & Delaney, 1982).

One problem, however, is that the keyword method does not work well if it is difficult to identify a keyword for a particular item. Many abstract words and ideas that students need to remember do not lend themselves to associations with keywords (Hall, 1991). Also, vocabulary learned with keywords may be more easily forgotten than vocabulary learned in other ways, especially if students are given keywords and images instead of being asked to supply the words and images. When the teacher provides the memory links, these associations may not fit the students' existing knowledge and may be forgotten or confused later, so remembering suffers (Wang & Thomas, 1995).

Reading Strategies

Effective learning strategies and tactics should help students focus attention, invest effort (elaborate, organize, summarize, connect, translate) so they process information deeply, and monitor their understanding. There are a number of strategies that to support these processes in reading. Many use mnemonics to help students remember the steps involved. For example, one strategy for any grade above later elementary is READS:

R   *Review* headings and subheadings
E   *Examine* boldface words
A   *Ask*, "What do I expect to learn?"
D   *Do* it—Read!
S   *Summarize* in you own words. (Friend & Bursuck, 1996).

READS is similar to another well-known strategy called **PQ4R** or Preview, Question, Read, Reflect, Recite, Review (Thomas & Robinson, 1972).

A strategy that can be use in reading literature is **CAPS**:

C   Who are the *characters?*
A   What is the *aim* of the story?
P   What *problem* happens?
S   How is the problem *solved?*

There are literally hundreds of strategies that can be taught in middle schools and high schools. Ours has been a brief and selective look. The point for teachers is to teach subject-appropriate learning strategies directly and support strategic learning through coaching and guided practice. We will examine a few more strategies when we consider cognitive apprenticeships in the following section.

Cognitive Apprenticeships

Knowledge gained in school often is stripped from the contexts in which the knowledge might be used, and students are not afforded the insights of expertise. That is, students are provided tasks to complete and abstractions to learn without situations that make the information to be learned meaningful and without experts' tools for performance. Geometry students are often presented with clean, step-by-step proofs that don't make explicit the thinking necessary to construct such a proof. Novice problem solvers are often provided instruction in specific problem-solving strategies and solved problems without a window on the complex thinking that is involved with using these strategies and solving such problems. As a result, knowledge within the domain often remains inert because the control of its application is hidden from view. The crucial cognitive and metacognitive strategies and processes are not made explicit, thus preventing students from learning how to work as an expert within a domain (Brown, Collins, & Duguid, 1991; Collins et al., 1989).

Cognitive apprenticeship models of teaching draw on examples from traditional forms where apprentices learn specific methods for carrying out a task through modeling, scaffolding, coaching, and fading (Collins et al., 1989; Collins, Brown, & Holum, 1991). A main tenet of this model of teaching is "making thinking visible." By talking aloud as the teacher or student completes tasks, learners are able to observe the actual thinking that is necessary to accomplish the performance, which provides the "means of building a conceptual model of a complex target skill" (Collins et al., 1989, p. 457). Observing expert performances of cognitive processes makes them explicit, and through the alternation of expert performance and novice practice, novices begin to be capable of monitoring their progress toward the use of these strategies. That which was tacit is made explicit. Slowly, as novices begin to take on the behaviors of the expert through the teacher's coaching and scaffolding, the teacher begins to withdraw or fades this assistance.

A second tenet of cognitive apprenticeships is that learning must be situated within contexts that make the skills meaningful for students—"conceptual and factual knowledge are exemplified and situated in the contexts of their use" (Collins et al., 1989, p. 457). In traditional apprenticeships, skills are embedded within contexts of application. "When tasks arise in the context of designing and creating tangible products, apprentices naturally understand the reasons for undertaking the process of apprenticeship" (Collins et al., 1991, p. 9). A third tenet results from the fact that in traditional apprenticeships skills are inherent in the final product. For example, individual skills of tailoring are necessary and apparent in light of the final product—the tailored suit. Within schools, the goal is to transfer learned skills to varying contexts. Thus, the student must learn to generalize thinking skills, to distinguish between exemplars where the skill is appropriate and where it is not appropriate, and to apply the skill in novel situations.

Elements of a Cognitive Apprenticeship

There are many cognitive apprenticeship models, but most share six features:

1. Students observe an expert (usually the teacher) *model* the performance.
2. Students get external support through *coaching* or tutoring (including hints, feedback, models, and reminders).
3. Conceptual *scaffolding* is provided and then gradually faded as the student becomes more competent and proficient.
4. Students continually *articulate* their knowledge—putting into words their understanding of the processes and content being learned.
5. Students *reflect* on their progress, comparing their problem solving to an expert's performance and to their own earlier performances.
6. Students are required to *explore* new ways to apply what they are learning—ways that they have not practiced at the master's side.

As students learn, they are challenged to master more complex concepts and skills and to perform them in many different settings (Shuell, 1996).

Apprenticeships are powerful teaching and learning opportunities and can be beneficial to both master and apprentice. More knowledgeable guides provide models, demonstrations, and corrections, as well as a personal bond that is motivating. The performances required of the learner are real and important and grow more complex as the learner becomes more competent (Collins et al., 1989, 1991). In addition, both the new comers to learning and the old timers contribute to the community of practice by mastering and remastering skills—and sometimes improving these skills in the process (Lave & Wenger, 1991).

A Cognitive Apprenticeship in Reading: Reciprocal Teaching

The goal of reciprocal teaching is to help students understand and think deeply about what they read (Palincsar, 1986; Palincsar & Brown, 1989). To accomplish this goal, students in small reading groups learn four strategies: summarizing the content of a passage, asking a question about the central point, clarifying the difficult parts of the material, and predicting what will come next. These are strategies that skilled readers apply almost automatically, but poor readers seldom do. To use the strategies effectively, poorer readers need direct instruction, modeling, and practice in actual reading situations—elements of a cognitive apprenticeship teaching model.

First, the teacher introduces these strategies, perhaps focusing on one strategy each day. The teacher explains and models each strategy and encourages students to practice. Next, the teacher and the students read a short passage silently. Then the teacher again provides a model by summarizing, questioning, clarifying, or predicting based on the reading. Everyone reads another passage, and the students gradually begin to assume the teacher's role. Often the students' first attempts are halting and incorrect. But the teacher gives clues, guidance, encouragement, and support in doing parts of the task such as question stems, models, and other scaffolding to help the students master these strategies. The goal is for students to learn to apply these strategies independently as they read so they can make sense of text.

Applying Reciprocal Teaching

Research on reciprocal teaching has shown some dramatic results. Although reciprocal teaching seems to work with almost any age student, most of the research has been done with younger adolescents who can read aloud fairly accurately, but who are far below average in reading comprehension. After 20 hours of practice with this approach, many students who were in the bottom quarter of their class moved up to the average level or above on tests of reading comprehension. Based on the results of several studies, Palincsar has identified three guidelines for effective reciprocal teaching (Harvard University, 1986):

1.   Shift gradually. The shift from teacher control to student responsibility must be gradual.
2.   Match demands to abilities. The difficulty of the task and the responsibility must match the abilities of each student and grow as these abilities develop.
3.   Diagnose thinking. Teachers should carefully observe the "teaching" of each student for clues about how the student is thinking and what kind of instruction the student needs.

In reciprocal teaching, Palincsar and Brown have made four significant contributions to education. First, they reminded us that procedures for fostering and monitoring comprehension must be taught—not all students develop these strategies on their own. Second, they focused on four rather than 40 or more strategies, as some sources have suggested. Third, they emphasized practicing these four strategies in the context of actual reading—literature and texts. Finally, they refined and developed the idea of scaffolding and gradually moving the student toward independent and fluid reading comprehension (Rosenshine & Meister, 1994).

A Cognitive Apprenticeship in Learning Mathematics

Schoenfeld's (1989) teaching of mathematical problem solving is another example of the cognitive apprenticeship instructional model. Through the analysis of verbal protocols, Schoenfeld (1987) investigated differences between novice and expert problem solvers. He found that novice problem solvers began ineffectual solution paths, based predominantly on exploration of the problem solution, and continued these paths although they were not leading toward a solution. In comparison, expert problem solvers began with reading and analyzing the problem, but then moved toward solutions using various other cognitive processes such as planning, implementing, and verifying, altering their behavior based on judgments of the validity of their solution processes.

Schoenfeld (1989) asks three important questions to improve performance of small groups of students: What are you doing, why are you doing it, and how will success in what you are doing help you find a solution to the problem? These questions help students control the processes they use and build their metacognitive awareness. Schoenfeld (1987) describes the type of instruction he feels will help students learn to think mathematically:

> Problem sessions begin when I hand out a list of questions ... Often one student has an "inspiration" ... At times X is reasonable, and at times not. My task is not to say yes or no, or even to evaluate the suggestion. Rather it is to raise the issue for discussion ... Typically a number of students respond [that they haven't made sense of the problem]. When we have made sense of the problem, the suggestion [X] simply doesn't make sense ... When this happens, I step out of my role as moderator to make the point to the whole class: If you make sure you understand the problem before you jump into a solution, you are less likely to go off on a wild goose chase. (p. 201)

This monitoring of problem understanding and problem-solving helps students begin to think and act as mathematicians. Throughout this process, Schoenfeld repeats his three questions (What are you doing? Why? How will this help?). Each of these components is essential in helping students to be aware of and to regulate their behaviors.

Bringing together the approach of cognitive apprenticeship with the concept of self-regulated learning described earlier in this chapter, we suggest that effectively teaching adolescents mathematics involves developing the thinking patterns of expert mathematicians. To do this we need to make our thinking available to the students; help the students develop positive concepts of themselves as mathematicians; help them to attribute success and failure to their behaviors rather than to stable aspects of their beings; and help them analyze tasks, set goals for completing these tasks, and monitor their progress in using strategies that will help them complete these tasks. To help them develop as mathematicians, we need to act as mathematicians, allowing them to understand that hard thinking with peers, sometimes over extended time periods, is necessary to solve important questions within situated learning experiences.

Problem-Based Learning and Anchored Instruction

An instructional model that combines aspects of the cognitive apprenticeship and cooperative learning instructional models is problem-based, situated instruction as exemplified in the Jasper Series (Cognition and Technology Group at Vanderbilt [CTGV], 1992). The Jasper Series was designed to teach mathematics. Problem-based learning attempts to provide contextualized learning environments in which knowledge might be generated rather than passively absorbed. The Vanderbilt group calls its problem-based approach *anchored instruction*. The anchor is a rich, interesting situation. This anchor provides a focus—a reason for setting goals, planning, and using mathematical tools to solve problems. The intended outcome is to develop knowledge that is useful and flexible, not information that is memorized but seldom applied, often called inert knowledge (Whitehead, 1929).

Even though the Jasper situations are complex and lifelike, the problems can be solved using data embedded in the stories presented. For example, in one adventure, Jasper sets out in a small motorboat, headed to Cedar Creek to inspect an old cruiser he is thinking of buying. Along the way Jasper has to consult maps, use his marine radio, deal with fuel and repair problems, buy the cruiser, and finally determine if he has enough fuel and time to sail his purchase home before sundown. Often the adventures have real-life follow-up problems that build on the knowledge developed. In one adventure, after designing a playground for a hypothetical group of children, students can tackle building a real playhouse for a preschool class. Based on videodisc scenarios with embedded real-world problems, students are motivated to learn the mathematics and problem-solving skills that are needed to solve these problems. This occurs through "repeated opportunities to engage in in-depth exploration, assessment, and revision of their ideas over extended periods of time" (CTGV, 1992, pp. 292–293).

There are 12 different adventures. Research indicates that students as young as fourth grade and as old as high school can work with the adventures (CTGV, 1990). Students are highly motivated as they work in groups to solve the problems; even group members with limited math skill can contribute to the solutions because they might notice key information in the videotape or suggest innovative ways to approach the situation. Jasper students and matched control groups increased in content knowledge over a year at the same rates, Jasper students outperformed control groups in problem solving, showed less anxiety, saw mathematics as a domain relevant and useful to their lives, and were more likely to appreciate complex challenges (CTGV, 1992).

The Jasper Series is one example of problem-based learning. More generally, the teacher's role in problem-based learning is summarized in Table 2.

Table 2.   The Teacher's Role in Problem-Based Learning

Phase	Teacher Behavior
Phase 1 Orient students to the problem	Teacher goes over the objectives of the lesson, describes important logistical requirements, and motivates students to engage in self-selected problem-solving activity.
Phase 2 Organize students for study	Teacher helps students define and organize study tasks related to the problem.
Phase 3 Assist independent and group investigation	Teacher encourages students to gather appropriate information, conduct experiments, and search for explanations and solutions.
Phase 4 Develop and present artifacts and exhibits	Teacher assists students in planning and preparing appropriate artifacts such as reports, videos, and models and helps them share their work with others
Phase 5 Analyze and evaluate the problem-solving process	Teacher helps students to reflect on their investigations and the processes they used.

Source: From Classroom Instruction and Management (p. 161), by R.I. Arends, New York: McGraw-Hill, Copyright © 1997 McGraw Hill. Reprinted with permission.

Example of Problem-Based Learning in a Math Class

Mathematics students enter their classroom to find materials and a piece of paper containing a simple statement: "Using the materials listed below, create something to weigh objects accurately." The students look confused at first but are eager to examine the materials provided: a dowel, a large spring, two types of nails, "S" hooks, a plastic "cup," wire, and pliers. Groups of students discuss their ideas for several minutes before the whole class is brought back together to discuss their understanding of the problem and issues they might have, and to brainstorm ideas. Once all groups of students indicate they understand the parameters of their task and have discussed their initial ideas, the students are set about their task.

As the students work on their constructions, the instructor walks from group to group asking questions similar to those proposed by Schoenfeld (1989): What has your group decided to do? How will this help you to weigh something? As the instructor visits with each group, she realizes that two distinct models, a spring scale and a balance, are being created, but she had only anticipated the creation of a spring scale. How will she be able to help the students understand the ideas of proportional reasoning and linear relationships (i.e., the relationship between the weight of an object and the length of the stretched spring)? With quick thought she realizes that each of these solutions can help her to draw out related and equally important mathematical concepts. The balance scale can be used to examine ideas of ratio, the beginning knowledge needed to fully understand the mathematics of the spring scale. This more sophisticated model will help her students move further toward their understanding of proportional reasoning.

On the second day, the students are asked to discuss their creations with the whole class. This discussion includes strengths and weaknesses of the design and the mathematics the students needed to understand to calibrate their scales. The groups that constructed a balance scale quickly begin talking about the relationship between the two types of nails: "five of the small nails equals the weight of the large nail." The instructor takes advantage of this opportunity to review the concept of ratios and standard units of measurement. The remaining groups begin to discuss the relationship between the length of the spring and the number of nails it takes to stretch the spring a particular length. Again the ideas of ratio, standard unit of measurement, and proportional reasoning, as well as linear relationships are discussed. Using this as an opportunity to incorporate technology, the instructor collects the data from each of these groups in the list function on her graphing calculator. The students begin a discussion of the relationship between various weights (i.e., numbers of nails) and the length of the stretched spring. Both groups are finally asked to weigh several objects ranging in mass.

Although this problem was not completely authentic, this scenario serves as a bare example from which several elements of problem-based learning may be illustrated. The problem presented was ambiguous resulting in two different solutions. This ambiguity caused an additional level of complexity for the teacher, but it also presented an additional context in which to review an important mathematical concept. In addition, groups of students were motivated to examine important mathematical content while participating in the solution of a problem. Finally, technology was used as a tool to illustrate the data and to facilitate the development of statements about the relationship between weight and the length of the stretched spring.

Cooperative Learning

A number of the strategies discussed thus far involve group work. Collaboration and cooperative learning have a long history in American education. In the early 1900s, John Dewey criticized the use of competition in education and encouraged educators to structure schools as democratic learning communities. These ideas fell from favor in the 1940s and 1950s, replaced by a resurgence of competition. In the 1960s, there was a swing back to individualized and cooperative learning structures, stimulated in part by concern for civil rights and interracial relations (Webb & Palincsar, 1996).

Today, evolving constructivist perspectives on learning fuel interest in collaboration and cooperative learning. Two characteristics of constructivist teaching—complex, real-life learning environments and social interaction (Driscoll, 1998)—are consistent with the use of cooperative learning structures. As educators focus on learning in real contexts, there is more interest in situations where elaboration, interpretation, explanation, and argumentation are integral to the activity and where others support learning (Webb & Palincsar, 1996).

Theoretical Underpinnings of Cooperative Learning

Advocates of different theories of learning find value in cooperative learning, but not for the same reasons. In terms of academic learning goals, information processing theorists suggest that group discussion can help participants rehearse, elaborate, and expand their knowledge. As group members question and explain, they have to organize their knowledge, make connections, and review—all processes that support information processing and memory. Advocates of a Piagetian perspective assert that the interactions in groups can create the cognitive conflict and disequilibrium that lead an individual to question his or her understanding and try out new ideas—or, as Piaget (1985) said, "to go beyond his current state and strike out in new directions" (p. 10). Educators who favor Vygotsky's (1978) theory suggest that social interaction is important for learning because higher mental functions such as reasoning, comprehension, and critical thinking originate in social interactions and are then internalized by individuals. Students can accomplish mental tasks with social support before they can do them alone. Thus cooperative learning provides the social support and scaffolding that students need to move learning forward. Table 3 summarizes the functions of cooperative learning from different perspectives, and describes some of the elements of each kind of group.

Table 3.   Different Forms of Cooperative Learning for Different Purposes

Different forms of cooperative learning (Elaboration, Piagetian, and Vygotskian) fit different purposes, need different structures, and have their own potential problems and possible solutions.

Considerations	Elaboration	Piagetian	Vygotskian
Group size	Small (2–4)	Small	Dyads
Group composition	Heterogeneous/ homogeneous	Homogeneous	Heterogeneous
Tasks	Rehearsal/integrative	Exploratory	Skills
Teacher role	Facilitator	Facilitator	Model/guide
Potential problems	Poor help-giving	Inactive	Poor help-giving
	Unequal participation	No cognitive conflict	Providing adequate time/dialogue
Averting Problems	Direct instruction in help-giving	Structuring controversy	Direct instruction in help-giving
	Modeling help-giving		Modeling help-giving
	Scripting interaction		

Source: From "Learning from Peers: Beyond the Rhetoric of Positive Results," by A.M. O'Donnell and J. O'Kelly, 1994, *Educational Psychology Review, 6,* p. 327. Copyright © 1999 by Plenum Publishing Corporation. Reprinted with permission.

In terms of interpersonal or social goals, research indicates that cooperative learning can have positive effects. Based on an extensive review of the research, Slavin (1995) concluded that cooperative learning had a positive impact on interracial friendships, prejudice reduction, acceptance of disabled students, self-esteem, peer support for academic goals, altruism, empathy, social perspective-taking, liking fellow classmates and feeling liked, sense of responsibility and control over learning, and time on task. Explanations for these positive effects are grounded in early work in social psychology. Positive effects often are attributed to the process of working toward common goals as equals, which was shown in laboratory studies to increase liking and respect among individuals from different racial or social groups (Allport, 1954), and to the motivation growing from the praise and encouragement of peers working toward a common goal (Deutsch, 1949). Thus cooperative strategies have been touted as particularly useful in combating the detrimental social effects of cliques in middle school and high schools, the negative effects of competition on student self-esteem, and the alienation of students who are not members of popular social groups (Aronson, in press; Aronson & Patnoe, 1997).

Elements of Cooperative Learning

David and Roger Johnson (1999) list five elements that define true cooperative learning groups.

1. Students *interact face-to-face* and close together, not across the room.
2. Students experience *positive interdependence*—they need each other for support, explanations, and guidance.
3. Students are held *individually accountable* for learning, even though they work together and help each other.
4. Students cooperate because *collaborative skills* are necessary for effective group functioning. Often these skills, such as giving constructive feedback, reaching consensus, and involving every member, must be taught and practiced before the groups tackle a learning task.
5. Students monitor *group processes* and relationships to make sure the group is working effectively and to learn about the dynamics of groups. They take time to ask, "How are we doing as a group? Is everyone working together?"

O'Donnell and O'Kelly (1994) note that determining the size of a group depends in part on the purpose of the group activity. If the purpose is for the group members to review, rehearse information, or practice, larger groups (about 4 to 5 or 6 students) are useful. But if the goal is to encourage each student to participate in discussions, problem solving, or computer learning, then groups of 2 to 4 members work best. Also some research indicates that when there are just a few girls in a group, they tend to be left out of the discussions unless they are the most able or assertive members. By contrast, when there are only one or two boys in the group, they tend to dominate and be "interviewed" by the girls unless these boys are less able than the girls or are very shy. In general, for very shy and introverted students, individual learning may be a better approach (Webb & Palincsar, 1996).

In practice, the effects of learning in a group vary, depending on what actually happens in the group and who is in it. If only a few people take responsibility for the work, these people will learn, but the nonparticipating members probably will not. Students who ask questions, get answers, and attempt explanations are more likely to learn than students whose questions go unasked or unanswered. In fact, there is evidence that the more a student provides elaborated, thoughtful explanations to other students in a group, the more the *explainer* learns. Giving good explanations appears to be even more important for learning than receiving explanations (Webb & Palincsar, 1996). In order to explain, students have to organize the information, put it into their own words, think of examples and analogies (which forges connections between prior knowledge and new information), and test understanding by answering questions. These are excellent learning strategies (O'Donnell & O'Kelly, 1994).

Some teachers assign roles such as reporter or discussion manager to students to encourage cooperation and full participation. Such roles should be assigned with engagement and learning in mind. In groups that focus on practice, review, or mastery of basic skills, roles should support persistence, encouragement, and participation. In groups that focus on higher-order problem solving or complex learning, roles should encourage thoughtful discussion, sharing of explanations and insights, probing, brainstorming, and creativity. Teachers must be careful, however, not to communicate to students that the major purpose of the groups is simply to do the roles in order to avoid having roles become ends in themselves (Woolfolk Hoy & Tschannen-Moran, 1999).

Jigsaw

An early format for cooperative learning, *Jigsaw*, emphasized high interdependence. This structure was invented by Elliot Aronson and his graduate students in 1971 in Austin, Texas: "…as a matter of absolute necessity to help defuse a highly explosive situation" (Aronson, in press). The Austin schools had just been desegregated by court order. White, African American, and Hispanic students were together in classrooms for the first time. Hostility and turmoil ensued with fistfights in corridors and classrooms. Aronson's answer was the Jigsaw classroom.

In Jigsaw, each group member was given part of the material to be learned by the whole group and became an "expert" on his or her piece. Students had to teach each other, so everyone's contribution was important. A more recent version, Jigsaw II, adds expert groups where the students who have the same material from each learning group confer to make sure they understand their assigned part and then plan ways to teach the information to their learning group members. Next, students return to their learning groups, bringing their expertise to the sessions. In the end, students take an individual test covering all the material and earn points for their learning team score. Teams can work for rewards or simply for recognition (Aronson & Patnoe, 1997; Slavin, 1995).

In his first test of Jigsaw, Aronson reports that teachers "spontaneously told us of their great satisfaction with the way the atmosphere of their classrooms had been transformed. Adjunct visitors (such as music teachers and the like) were little short of amazed at the dramatically changed atmosphere in the classroom" (Aronson, in press). Students expressed less prejudice, were more confident, liked school better, and had higher scores on objective examinations. The overall improvements in test scores came mostly from increases in minority group children—Anglo students maintained their previous levels of performance. These findings are consistent with recent research on cooperative learning, as reviewed by Slavin (1995).

Reciprocal Questioning

Another cooperative approach, *reciprocal questioning,* can be used with a wide range of ages and subjects because it requires no special materials or testing procedures. After a lesson or presentation by the teacher, students work in pairs or triads to ask and answer questions about the material (King, 1994). The teacher provides question stems (see Figure 2), then students are taught how to develop specific questions on the lesson material using the generic question stems. The students create questions, then take

Reciprocal Questioning Prompt Cards to Guide Dialogue

After studying materials or participating in a lesson, pairs of students use the "Prompt Cards" below to develop questions and then share answers.

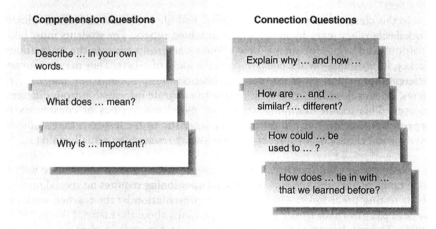

Source: From "Guiding Knowledge Construction in the Classroom: Effects of Teaching Children How to Question and How to Explain," by A. King, 1994, *American Educational Research Journal, 31,* p. 345. Copyright © 1994 by the American Educational Research Association. Adapted with permission.

Figure 2.   Reciprocal questioning prompt cards to guide dialogue.

turns asking and answering. This process has proved more effective than traditional discussion groups because it seems to encourage deeper thinking about the material. Questions such as those in Figure 2, which encourage students to make connections between the lesson and previous knowledge or experience, seems to be the most helpful.

Scripted Cooperation

Dansereau and his colleagues have developed a method for learning in pairs called *scripted cooperation*. Students work together on almost any task, including reading a selection of text, solving math problems, or editing writing drafts. In reading, for example, both partners read a passage, then one student gives an oral summary. The other partner comments on the summary, noting omissions or errors. Next, the partners work together to elaborate on the information—create associations, images, mnemonics, ties to previous work, examples, analogies, and so on. The partners switch roles of summarizer and listener for the next section of the reading, and then continue to take turns until they finish the assignment (Dansereau, 1985, O'Donnell & O'Kelly, 1994).

What Can Go Wrong: Misuses of Group Learning

Even though cooperative learning has been widely advocated by educators (Howey, 1996), research indicates that it is not a universal panacea for learning. As Eliot Aronson, the inventor of the jigsaw classroom, notes:

> But simply assigning students to work together in groups to produce a joint report does not guarantee true cooperation. Unstructured attempts to encourage cooperation in the classroom usually fail to accomplish their ultimate goal and might even backfire if not carefully designed. Most often the group dynamics of an unstructured "cooperative" situation mirror the larger competitive classroom dynamic. The one or two most able or most motivated students put themselves forward to do most of the work while simultaneously resenting the fact that they are carrying the load for the entire group. And the less able or less motivated students end up doing little, learning little, and feeling inadequate. These so-called cooperative groups are cooperative in name only. (Aronson, in press)

Without careful planning and monitoring by the teacher, group interactions can hinder learning and reduce rather than improve social relations in classes. For example, if there is pressure in a group for conformity—perhaps because rewards are being misused or one student dominates the others—interactions can be unproductive and unreflective. Misconceptions might be reinforced or the worst, not the best, ideas may be combined to construct a superficial understanding (Battistich, Solomon, & Delucci, 1993). Also, the ideas of low status students may be ignored or even ridi-

culed while the contributions of high status students are accepted and reinforced, regardless of the merit of either set of ideas (Anderson, Holland, &
Palincsar, 1997). McCaslin and Good (1996) list several other disadvantages of group learning. Students often value the process or procedures
over the learning. Speed and finishing take precedence over thoughtful-
ness and learning. Socializing and interpersonal relationships may take
precedence over learning. Students may simply shift dependency from the
teacher to the "expert" in the group—learning is still passive and what is
learned can be wrong. Status differences may be increased rather than
decreased. Some students learn to "loaf" because the group progresses
with or without their contributions. Others are even more convinced that
they are helpless to understand without the support of the group.

Community Service Learning

The practice of engaging young people in some sort of education-
related community service activity is gaining widespread currency throughout the United States. A recent survey reported that 15% of the 130 largest
school districts in the U.S. require some sort of service district-wide, and
44% have at least one school requiring service (National and Community
Service Coalition, 1995). The appeal of community service learning lies in
its ability to close the gap between schools and the communities that sur-
round them provide positive identity-defining experiences for adolescents
(Yates & Youniss, 1999), and to remedy the lack of social connectedness
and purpose that many adolescents currently experience (Claus & Ogden,
1999).

According to Howe (1997), community service learning activities may
include the following features:

- Working together to plan and implement service activities.
- Adjusting activities to fit the needs of people who often are different
  from the learner—different in age, cultural background, and view-
  points about daily living.
- Reflecting on the meaning of these activities in the lives of both the
  server and the served.
- Providing opportunities to learn how to work effectively in groups
  and assume increasing responsibilities in such relationships.
- Helping others in ways that develop "habits of the heart."

Community service learning is seen primarily as a way to make school
learning more relevant and meaningful for students by giving them occasion to critically reflect and act upon difficult social problems. More specifically, developmental psychologists have found that participation in

community service learning can promote political-moral development in diverse youth. Through developing an explicit linkage between students' selves and society, service learning projects enable adolescents to experience their own agency through working with others in need, thereby seeing themselves as political and moral agents, rather than as merely compliant and decent citizens (Youniss & Yates, 1997).

Furthermore, community service learning can help adolescents think in new ways about their relationships with people that are unlike them. Service learning experiences can lead adolescents to become more tolerant of difference, and be a part of the postmodern imperative to build "communities of difference" (Tierney, 1993). Finally, researchers assert that service learning experiences foster an "ethic of care," originating in feminist epistemology, that can result in a growing commitment to confront difficult social problems (Rhodes, 1997). In this sense, student involvement in community service learning can motivate and empower adolescents to critically reflect on their role in society and to act on it with a sense of agency and purpose (Claus & Ogden, 1999).

Yates and Youniss' (1999) description of a mandatory service-learning program at an urban parochial high school illuminates several components and outcomes of successful service-learning experiences. This program was required for juniors at the school and was part of a year-long course on social justice. Students think about the moral implications of current events such as homelessness, poverty, exploitation of immigrant laborers, and urban violence. As part of the class, students were required to serve four times (approximately 20 hours) at the same inner-city soup kitchen. Yates and Youniss administered questionnaires at the beginning and end of the course, and ran discussion groups and collected student essays after each trip to the soup kitchen. These data sources enabled them to identify 10 program characteristics that led this service-learning course to have a "profound positive impact" on many of its students:

1. The service activity is meaningful.
2. Helping others is emphasized.
3. The program is part of an articulated ideology.
4. Activities are performed as a group rather than individually.
5. Reflective opportunities with peers are provided.
6. Program organizers serve as models and integrators.
7. Site supervisors serve as models.
8. Participants' diversity is acknowledged.
9. Feeling a part of history is encouraged.
10. Acceptance of personal and social responsibility is encouraged (1999, p. 50).

Yates and Youniss asserted that this program promoted identity development through its integration of service, curriculum, and school activities. More specifically, they reported that students emerged from the course with, "a deeper awareness of social injustice, a greater sense of commitment to confront these injustices, and heightened confidence in their abilities overall" (Yates & Youniss, 1999, p. 64).

CONCLUSIONS

In this chapter we began with the assumption that a key task for adolescents in every culture is to "become somebody"—to establish an identity that will guide life choices and meet challenges. Psychological perspectives emphasize the formation of self-schemas that organize beliefs about the meaning, value, and capabilities of the self. The sense of self-efficacy, a future-oriented belief about the level of competence a person expects he or she will display in a given situation, is a key factor in human agency—the capacity to make things happen through personal actions. To be an agent in your own intentional learning is to be a self-regulated learner. Thus it is not surprising that theories of self-regulated learning also include a key role for self-efficacy beliefs. From anthropological perspectives, human agency has been defined as

> ...the realized capacity of people to act upon their world and not only to know about or give personal or intersubjective significance to it. That capacity is the power of people to act purposively and reflectively, in more or less complex interrelationships with one another, to reiterate and remake the world in which they live, in circumstances where they may consider different courses of action possible and desirable, though not necessarily from the same point of view. (Inden, 1990, p. 23)

We suggest that helping adolescents to develop the skill and will to be agents in learning throughout life should be a goal of teaching. The approaches we have outlined move from direct instruction in learning strategies and tactics to community service learning that helps adolescents to become agents in real and valuable service to others. Important elements in many of these approaches include structuring graduated practice in increasingly real setting, providing models—not just of skill but of commitment, social connection and support, challenge, and tasks that have meaning and authenticity.

NOTE

1.   According to Paul Willis, cultural production is "The active, collective use and explorations of received symbolic, ideological, and cultural resources to explain, make sense of and positively respond to 'inherited' structural and material conditions" (1983, p. 112).

REFERENCES

Aboud, F., & Skerry, S. (1984). The development of ethnic identification: A critical review. *Journal of Cross-Cultural Psychology, 15,* 3–34.

Allport, G. (1954). *The nature of prejudice.* Cambridge, MA: Addison-Wesley.

American Association of University Women. (1991). *Shortchanging girls, shortchanging America.* Washington, DC: AAUW.

Anderson, C.W., Holland, J.D., & Palincsar, A.S. (1997). Canonical and sociocultural approaches to research and reform in science education: The story of Juan and his group. *The Elementary School Journal, 97,* 359–384.

Armbruster, B.B., & Anderson, T.H. (1981). Research synthesis on study skills. *Educational Leadership, 39,* 154–156.

Aronson, E. (in press). Building empathy, compassion and achievement in the jigsaw classroom. In J. Aronson & D. Cordova (Eds.), *Improving education: Classic and contemporary lessons from psychology.* Mahwah, NJ: Erlbaum.

Aronson, E., & Patnoe, S. (1997). *Cooperation in the classroom: The Jigsaw method.* New York: Longman.

Atkinson, R.K., Levin, J.R., Kiewra, K.A., Meyers, T., Atkinson, L.A., Renandya, W.A., & Hwang, Y. (1999). Matrix and mnemonic text-processing adjuncts: Comparing and combining their components. *Journal of Educational Psychology, 91,* 242–257.

Bandura, A. (1986). *Social foundations of thoughts and action: A social cognitive theory.* Englewood Cliffs, NJ: Prentice-Hall.

Bandura, A. (1997). *Self-efficacy: The exercise of control.* New York: W.H. Freeman and Company.

Bandura, A. (2001). Social cognitive theory: An agentic perspective. *Annual Review of Psychology, 52,* 1–26.

Bandura, A., Barbaranelli, C., Caprara, G.V., & Pastorelli, C. (1996). Multifaceted impact of self-efficacy beliefs on academic functioning. *Child Development, 67,* 1206–1222.

Battistich, V., Solomon, D., & Delucci, K. (1993). Interaction processes and student outcomes in cooperative groups. *Elementary School Journal, 94,* 19–32.

Berndt, T.J., Laychak, A.E., & Park, K. (1990). Friends' influence on adolescents' academic achievement motivation: An experimental study. *Journal of Educational Psychology, 82,* 664–670.

Borkowski, J.G., Weyhing, R.S., & Carr, M. (1988). Effects of attributional retraining on strategy-based reading comprehension on learning-disabled students. *Journal of Educational Psychology, 80,* 46–53.

Bouffard-Bouchard, T., Parent, S. & Larivee, S. (1991). Influence of self-efficacy on self-regulation and performance among junior and senior high-school age students. *International Journal of Behavioral Development, 14*, 153–164.

Brown, B. (1989). The role of peer groups in adolescents' adjustment to secondary school. In T.J. Berndt (Ed.), *Peer relationships in child development* . New York: Wiley.

Brown, J.S., Collins, A., & Duguid, P. (1991). Situated cognition and the culture of learning. *Educational Researcher, 18*, 32–42.

Butler, D. (1998). The strategic content learning approach to promoting self-regulated learning: A report of three studies. *Journal of Educational Psychology, 90*, 682–697.

Byrnes, J.P. (1996). *Cognitive development and learning in instructional contexts.* Boston: Allyn & Bacon.

Carnoy, M., & Levin, H. (1985). *Schooling and work in the democratic state.* Stanford, CA: Stanford University Press.

Claus, J., & Ogden, C. (1999). Service learning for youth empowerment and social change: An introduction. In J. Claus & C. Ogden (Eds.), *Service learning for youth empowerment and social change.* New York: Peter Lang.

Cohen, Y.A. (1964). *The transition from childhood to adolescence.* Chicago: Aldine.

Cognition and Technology Group at Vanderbilt. (1992). The Jasper series as an example of anchored instruction: Theory, program description, and assessment data. *Educational Psychologist, 27*(3), 291–315.

Coleman, J.S. (1961). *Adolescent society.* Glencoe, NY: Free Press.

Collier, J.F., & Yanagisako, S.J. (1989). Theory in anthropology since feminist practice. *Critical Anthropology, 9*(2).

Collins, A., Brown, J.S., & Holum, A. (1991). Cognitive apprenticeship: Making thinking visible. *American Educator, 15(3),* 6, 8–11, 38–46.

Collins, A., Brown, J.S., & Newman, S.E. (1989). Cognitive apprenticeship: Teaching the crafts of reading, writing, and mathematics. In L.B. Resnick (Ed.), *Knowing, learning, and instruction: Essays in honor of Robert Glaser* (pp. 453–494). Hillsdale, NJ: Lawrence Erlbaum.

Cooper, C.R. (1998). The weaving of maturity: Cultural perspectives on adolescent development. New York: Oxford University Press.

Corno, L. (1992). Encouraging students to take responsibility for learning and performance. *The Elementary School Journal, 93*, 69–84.

Cummins, J. (1997). Minority status and schooling in Canada. *Anthropology & Education Quarterly, 28*(3), 411–430.

Cusick, P. (1973). *Inside high school: The students' world.* New York: Holt Rinehart & Winston.

Dansereau, D.F. (1985). Learning strategy research. In J. Segal, S. Chipman, & R. Glaser (Eds.), *Thinking and learning skills. Vol. I: Relating instruction to research.* Hillsdale, NJ: Erlbaum.

Davidson, A.L. (1996). *Making and molding identity in schools.* Albany: State University of New York Press.

Davidson, J. (1982). The group mapping activity for instruction in reading and thinking. *Journal of Reading, 26*, 52–56.

Delpit, L. (1995). *Other people's children: Cultural conflict in the classroom.* New York: The New York Press.

Demerath, P. (1996). Social and cultural influences on the decline in Manus School Certificate Examination performance: Student dilemmas and adaptations. *Papua New Guinea Journal of Education, 32*(1), 55–64.

Derry, S.J. (1989). Putting learning strategies to work. *Educational Leadership, 47*(5) 4–10.

Deutsch, M. (1949). An experimental study of the effects of cooperation and competition upon group processes. *Human Relations, 2*, 199–231.

Deyhle, D. (1986). Break dancing and breaking out: Anglos, Utes, and Navajos in a border reservation high school. *Anthropology and Education Quarterly, 17*, 111–127.

Deyhle, D. (1995). Navajo youth and Anglo racism: Cultural integrity and resistance. *Harvard Educational Review, 65*(3), 403–444.

DiVesta, F.J., & Gray, G.S. (1972). Listening and notetaking. *Journal of Educational Psychology, 63*, 8–14.

Dole, J.A., Duffy, G.G., Roehler, L.R., & Pearson, P.D. (1991). Moving from the old to the new: Research on reading comprehension instruction. *Review of Educational Research, 61*, 239–264.

Driscoll, M.P. (1998). *Psychology of learning for instruction* (2nd ed.) Boston: Allyn & Bacon.

Epstein, J.L. (1983). The influence of friends on achievement and affective outcomes. In J.L. Epstein & N. Karweit (Eds.), *Friends in school: Patterns of selection and influence in secondary schools.* New York: Academic Press.

Erikson, E.H. (1980). *Identity and the life cycle* (2nd ed.). New York: Norton.

Erickson, F. (1987). Transformation and school success: The politics and culture of educational achievement. *Anthropology and Education Quarterly, 18*(4), 335–356.

Fine, M. (1991). *Framing dropouts.* Albany: State University of New York Press.

Fordham, S. (1996). *Blacked out: Dilemmas of race, identity, and success at Capital High.* Chicago: University of Chicago Press.

Fordham, S., & Ogbu, J.U. (1986). Black students' school success: Coping with the "burden of acting White". *The Urban Review, 18*, 176–206.

Friend, M., & Bursuck, W. (1996). *Including students with special needs: A practical guide for classroom teachers.* Boston: Allyn & Bacon.

Garcia, T., & Pintrich, P.R. (1994). Regulating motivation and cognition in the classroom: The role of self-schemas and self-regulatory strategies. In D.H. Schunk & B.J. Zimmerman (Eds.), *Self-regulation of learning and performance: Issues and educational applications* (pp. 127–153). Hillsdale, NJ: Lawrence Erlbaum.

Gardner, R., Brown, R., Sanders, S., & Menke, D.J. (1992). "Seductive details" in learning from text. In K.A. Renninger, S. Hidi, & A. Krapp (Eds.), *The role of interest in learning and development.* Hillsdale, NJ: Erlbaum.

Gibson, M. (1982). Reputation and respectability: How competing cultural systems affect students' performance in school. *Anthropology and Education Quarterly, 8*(1), 3–27.

Gibson, M. (1997). Complicating the immigrant/involuntary minority typology. *Anthropology & Education Quarterly, 28*(3), 431–454.

Gist, M., & Mitchell, T. (1992). Self-efficacy: A theoretical analysis of its determinants and malleability. *Academy of Management Review, 17,* 183–211.

Goto, S.T. (1997). Nerds, normal people, and homeboys: Accommodation and resistance among Chinese American students. *Anthropology & Education Quarterly, 28*(1), 70–84.

Hall, J.W. (1991). More on the utility of the keyword method. *Journal of Educational Psychology, 83,* 171–172.

Harris, J.R. (1995). Where Is the child's environment? A group socialization theory of development. *Psychological Review, 102*(3), 458–489.

Harvard University. (1986, March). When the student becomes the teacher. *Harvard Education Letter, 2*(3), 5–6.

Heath, S.B., & McLaughlin, M.W. (Eds.). (1993). *Identity & inner city youth: Beyond ethnicity and gender.* New York: Teachers College Press.

Hilgard, E.R., Atkinson, R.L., & Atkinson, R.C. (1979). *Introduction to psychology* (7th ed.). New York: Harcourt Brace Jovanovich.

Holland, D., & Eisenhart, M. (1988). Women's ways of going to school: Cultural reproduction of women's identities as workers. In L. Weis (Ed.), *Class, race, and gender in U.S. education* (pp. 266–301). Albany: State University of New York Press.

Howe, H. (1997). Foreword. In J. Schine (Ed.), *Service learning: Ninety-sixth yearbook of the National Society for the Study of Education* (Vol. 1,). Chicago: University of Chicago Press.

Inden, R. (1990). *Imagining India.* Oxford: Blackwell.

Irwin, J.W. (1991). *Teaching reading comprehension* (2nd ed.). Boston: Allyn & Bacon.

Johnson, D., & Johnson, R. (1999). *Learning together and alone: Cooperation, competition, and individualization* (5th ed.). Boston: Allyn & Bacon.

Kiewra, K.A. (1989). A review of note-taking: The encoding storage paradigm and beyond. *Educational Psychology Review, 1,* 147–172.

King, A. (1994). Guiding knowledge construction in the classroom: Effects of teaching children how to question and how to explain. *American Educational Research Journal, 31,* 338–368.

Kohl, H. (1991). *I won't learn from you: The role of assent in learning.* Minneapolis: Milkweed.

Ladson-Billings, G. (1994). *The dreamkeepers: Successful teachers of African American children.* San Francisco: Jossey-Bass.

Ladson-Billings, G. (1995). But that is just good teaching! The case for culturally relevant pedagogy. *Theory Into Practice, 34,* 161–165.

LaFontaine, J. (1985). *Initiation.* Middlesex: Penguin.

Lave, J., & Wenger, E. (1991). *Situated learning: Legitimate peripheral participation.* Cambridge, MA: Cambridge University Press.

Levin, J.R. (1994). Mnemonic strategies and classroom learning: A twenty-year report card. *Elementary School Journal, 94,* 235–254.

Levinson, B.A. (1996). Social difference and schooled identity at a Mexican Secundaria. In B.A. Levinson, D.E. Foley, & D.C. Holland (Eds.), *The cultural production of the educated person.* Albany: State University of New York Press.

Levinson, B.A., Foley, D.E., & Holland, D.C. (Eds.). (1996). *The cultural production of the educated person.* Albany: State University of New York Press.

McCaslin, M., & Good, T. (1996). The informal curriculum. In D. Berliner & R. Calfee (Eds.), *Handbook of educational psychology* (pp. 622–670). New York: Macmillan.

MacLeod, J. (1995). *Ain't no makin' it: Leveled aspirations in a low-income neighborhood.* Boulder, CO: Westview.

Marsh, H.W., & Yeung, A.S. (1997). Coursework selection: Relation to academic self-concept and achievement. *American Educational Research Journal, 34,* 691–720.

McCombs, B.L., & Marzano, R.J. (1990). Putting the self in self-regulated learning: The self as agent in integrating skill and will. *Educational Psychologist, 25,* 51–70.

Mead, M. (1973). *Coming of age in Samoa: A psychological study of youth for western civilization:* William Morrow & Co.

Mehan, H., Hubbard, L., & Villanueva, I. (1994). Forming academic identities: Accomodation without assimilation among involuntary minorities. *Anthropology & Education Quarterly, 25*(2), 91–117.

Murphy, P.K., & Alexander, P.A. (2000). A motivated exploration of motivation terminology. *Contemporary Educational Psychology.*

National and Community Service Coalition. (1995). *Youth volunteerism: Here's what the survey says.* Washington D.C.

New London Group. (1996). A pedagogy of multiliteracies: Designing social futures. *Harvard Educational Review, 66*(1), 60–92.

O'Connor, C. (1997). Dispositions toward (collective) struggle and educational resilience in the inner city: A case analysis of six African American high school students. *American Educational Research Journal, 34*(1), 593–629.

O'Donnell, A.M., & O'Kelly, J. (1994). Learning from peers: Beyond the rhetoric of positive results. *Educational Psychology Review, 6,* 321–350.

Ogbu, J. (1990). Cultural model, identity and literacy. In R.S.J. Stigler, & G. Herdt (Ed.), *Cultural psychology: Essays on comparative human development* . Cambridge: Cambridge University Press.

Ormrod, J.E. (1999). *Human learning* (3rd ed.). Upper Saddle River: NJ: Merrill/ Prentice-Hall.

Orenstein, P. (1994). *School girls: Young women, self-esteem, and the confidence gap.* New York: Anchor.

Osborne, A.B. (1996). Practice into practice: Culturally relevant pedagogy for students we have marginalized and normalized. *Anthropology & Education Quarterly, 27*(3), 285–314.

Pajares, F., & Miller, M.D. (1994). Role of self-efficacy and self-concept beliefs in mathematical problem solving: A path analysis. *Journal of Educational Psychology, 86*(2), 193–203.

Palincsar, A.S. (1986). The role of dialogue in providing scaffolded instruction. In J. Levin & M. Pressley (Eds.), *Educational Psychologist, 21,* 73–98 (Special issue on learning strategies).

Palincsar, A.S., & Brown, A.L. (1989). Classroom dialogues to promote self-regulated comprehension. In J. Brophy (Ed.), *Advances in research on teaching* (Vol. 1, pp. 35–67). Greenwich, CT: JAI Press.

Peneul, W.R., & Wertsch, J.V. (1995). Vygotsky and identity formation: A sociocultural approach. *Educational Psychologist, 30,* 83–92.

Phelan, P., Davidson, A., & Yu, H.C. (Eds.). (1998). *Adolescents' worlds: Negotiating family, peers, and school.* New York: Teachers College Press.

Piaget, J. (1985). *The equilibrium of cognitive structures: The central problem of intellectual development.* (T. Brown & K. L. Thampy, Trans.) Chicago: University of Chicago Press.

Pintrich, P.R., & Schunk, D.H. (1996). *Motivation in education: Theory, research, and applications.* Columbus, OH: Merrill.

Pressley, M. (1986). The relevance of the good strategy user model to the teaching of mathematics. In J. Levin & M. Pressley (Eds.), *Educational Psychologist, 21,* 139–161 (Special issue on learning strategies).

Pressley, M. (1995). More about the development of self-regulation: complex, long-term, and thoroughly social. *Educational Psychologist, 30,* 207–212.

Pressley, M., Levin, J., & Delaney, H.D. (1982). The mnemonic keyword method. *Review of Research in Education, 52,* 61–91.

Rhodes, R.A. (1997). *Community service and higher learning: Explorations of the caring self.* Albany: State University of New York Press.

Rival, L. (1996). Formal schooling and the production of modern citizens in the Ecuadorian Amazon. In B. Levinson, D. Foley, & C. Holland (Eds.), *The cultural production of the educated person: Critical ethnographies of schooling and local practice.* Albany, NY: State University of New York Press.

Robinson, D.H. (1998). Graphic organizers as aids to test learning. *Reading Research and Instruction, 37,* 85–105.

Rohrkemper, M. (1989). Self-regulated learning and academic achievement: A Vygotskian view. In B.J. Zimmerman & D.H. Schunk (Eds.), *Self-regulated learning and academic achievement: Theory, research, and practice* (pp. 143–167). New York: Springer.

Rosenshine, B., & Meister, C. (1994). Reciprocal teaching: A review of the research. *Review of Educational Research, 64,* 479–530.

Scales, P., & McEwin, C.K. (1994). *Growing pains: The making of America's middle school teachers.* Columbus, OH: National Middle School Association and the Center for Early Adolescence.

Schlegel, A., & Barry, H. (1991). *Adolescence: An anthropological inquiry.* New York: The Free Press.

Schoenfeld, A.H. (1987). What's all the fuss about metacognition? In A.H. Schoenfeld (Ed.), *Cognitive science and mathematics education* (pp. 189–215). Hillsdale, NJ: Lawrence Erlbaum.

Schoenfeld, A.H. (1989). Teaching mathematical thinking and problem solving. In L.B. Resnick & L.E. Klopfer (Eds.), *Toward the thinking curriculum: Current cognitive research* (pp. 83–103). Alexandria, VA: ASCD.

Schunk, D.H., & Gunn, T.P. (1986). Self-efficacy and skill development: Influence of task strategies and attributions. *Journal of Educational Research, 79,* 238–244.

Shavelson, R.J., & Bolus, R. (1982). Self-concept: The interplay of theory and methods. *Psychology, 74,* 3–17.

Shuell, T. (1996). Teaching and learning in a classroom context. In D. Berliner & R. Calfee (Eds.), *Handbook of educational psychology* (pp. 726–764). New York: Macmillan.

Sirrotnik, K.A. (1983). What you see is what you get. *Harvard Educaitonal Review, 54*, 16–32.

Slavin, R.E. (1995). *Cooperative learning* (2nd ed.). Boston: Allyn & Bacon.

Snow, R.E., Corno, L., & Jackson, D. (1996) Individual differences in affective and cognitive functions. In D. Berliner & R. Calfee (Eds.), *Handbook of educational psychology* (pp. 243–310). New York: Macmillan.

Snowman, J. (1984). Learning tactics and strategies. In G. Phye & T. Andre (Eds.), *Cognitive instructional psychology*. Orlando, FL: Academic Press.

Solomon, R.P. (1992). *Black resistance in high school: Forging a separatist culture.* Albany: State University of New York Press.

Spencer, M.B., Noll, E., Stoltzfus, J. & Harpalani, V. (2001) Identity and school adjustment: Revisiting the "Acting White" assumption. *Educational Psychologist, 36*, 21–30.

Spindler, G. (1982). *Doing the ethnography of schooling: Educational anthropology in action.* New York: Holt, Rinehart and Winston.

Spindler, G.D. (1967). The transmission of culture. In A.R. Beals (Ed.), *The transmission of culture.* New York: Holt, Rinehart and Winston.

Spiro, M.E. (1965). *Children of the Kibbutz.* New York: Schocken.

Stanton-Salazar, R.D. (1997). A social capital framework for understanding the socialization of racial minority children and youths. *Harvard Educational Review, 67*(1), 1–40.

Thomas, E.L., & Robinson, H.A. (1972). *Improving reading in every class: A sourcebook for teachers.* Boston: Allyn & Bacon.

Tierney, W.G. (1993). *Building communities of difference: Higher education in the twenty-first century.* Westport, CT: Bergin and Garvey.

Van Metter, P., Yokoi, L., & Pressley, M. (1994). College students' theory of note-taking derived from their perceptions of note-taking. *Journal of Educational Psychology, 86*, 323–338.

Vygotsky, L.S. (1978). *Mind in society: The development of higher mental process.* Cambridge, MA: Harvard University Press.

Wagner, J. (1998). Power and learning in a multi-ethnic high school: Dilemmas of policy and practice. In **Y.Z. a. E. Trueba** (Ed.), *Ethnic identity and power: Cultural contexts of political action in school and society.* Albany: State University of New York Press.

Wang, A.Y., & Thomas, M.H. (1995). Effects of keywords on long-term retention: Help or hindrance? *Journal of Educational Psychology, 87*, 468–475.

Webb, N., & Palincsar, A. (1996). Group processes in the classroom. In D.C. Berliner & R.C. Calfee (Eds.), *Handbook of educational psychology* (pp. 841–876). New York: Macmillan.

Weinstein, C.E. (1994). Learning strategies and learning to learn. *Encyclopedia of Education.*

Wexler, P. (1992). *Becoming somebody: Toward a social psychology of school.* London: Falmer.

Whitehead, A.N. (1929). *The aims of education.* New York: Macmillan.

Whiting, J.W.M., Kluckholn, R., & Anthony, A. (1958). The function of male initiation ceremonies at puberty. In E. MacCoby (Ed.), *Readings in social psychology.* New York: Holt.

Willis, P. (1983). Cultural production and theories of reproduction. In S.W.E.L. Barton (Ed.), *Race, class, and education.* London: Croom Helm.

Winne, P.H. (1995). Inherent details in self-regulated learning. *Educational Psychologist, 30,* 173–188.

Wolcott, H. (1994). Education as cultural transmission and acquisition, *International Encyclopedia of Education* (2nd ed.,).

Woolfolk Hoy, A., & Tschannen-Moran. M. (1999). Implications of cognitive approaches to peer learning for teacher education. In A. O'Donnell & A. King (Eds.), *Cognitive perspectives on peer learning* (pp. 257–284). Mahwah, NJ: Lawrence Erlbaum.

Yates, M., & Youniss, J. (1999). Promoting identity development: Ten ideas for school-based service-learning programs. In J. Claus & C. Ogden (Eds.), *Service learning for youth empowerment and social change.* New York: Peter Lang.

Youniss, J., & Yates, M. (1997). *Community service and social responsibility in youth.* Chicago: University of Chicago Press.

Zimmerman, B.J. (1998). Academic studying and the development of personal skill: A self-regulatory perspective. *Educational Psychologist, 33,* 73–86.

Zimmerman, B.J. (2000). Attaining self-regulation: A social cognitive perspective. In M. Boekaerts, P. Pintrich, & M. Seidner (Eds.), *Self-regulation: Theory, research, and applications* (pp. 13–39). Orlando, FL: Academic Press.

Zimmerman, B.J., & Martinez-Pons, M. (1988). Construct validation of a strategy model of student self-regulated learning. *Journal of Educational Psychology, 80,* 284–290.

Zimmerman, B.J., & Martinez-Pons, M. (1986). Development os a structured interview for assessing student use of self-regulated learning strategies. *American Educational Research Journal, 23,* 614–628.

Zimmerman, B.J., & Martinez-Pons, M. (1990). Student differences in self-regulated learning: Relating grade, sex, and giftedness to self-efficacy and strategy use. *Journal of Educational Psychology, 82,* 51–59.

Zimmerman, B.J., & Risemberg, R. (1997). Self-regulated dimensions of academic learning and motivation. In G.D. Phye (Ed.), *Handbook of academic learning: Construction of knowledge* (pp. 105–125). New York: Academic Press.

CHAPTER 6

Motivation in the Second Decade of Life

The Role of Multiple Developmental Trajectories

Akane Zusho and Paul R. Pintrich

INTRODUCTION

The motivation of adolescents is a key developmental question for parents and teachers as well as researchers. Many who work with adolescents are struck by the change in student motivation as elementary school children develop and make the transition to junior high school. There is a clear and well-documented decline in student motivation at the junior high school level (Eccles, Wigfield, & Schiefele, 1998). Parents and teachers are often left wondering what happened to the curious and energetic students they knew in elementary school as they now face the sullen and apathetic students populating so many junior and high school classrooms, and even college classrooms. At the same time, this general trend does not describe all students. There are students who are motivated for school in our secondary and post-secondary classrooms. There are students who do well and seem to enjoy their academic work and are not just consumed, as the old rock song goes, with "sex, drugs, and rock-n-roll."

This individual variation in the general developmental trajectory in motivation will be the main theme of our chapter. In other words, we will explore the potential that there are multiple developmental trajectories in adolescent motivation, not just a general decline trajectory. In addition, as our title denotes, we will consider adolescent motivation from late elementary school levels into the college years. We first begin with a general conceptual framework and definition of motivation. We will limit our discussion to the development of academic motivational beliefs such as control beliefs, self-efficacy, achievement goals, and values, although we are fully aware of the other developmental changes in social goals (see Wentzel, this volume), identity, and self-concept (Harter, 1999) that take place in the second decade of life. These general changes in self-concept and identity represent a self-constructed personal context that envelops and helps to define and shape the changes in academic motivation, but these general changes are beyond the scope of our chapter. In the second section of our chapter, we will then describe the general developmental trends that take place in student motivation over the course of adolescence from junior high through high school and on into the transition to college. Finally, in the last section of our chapter, we will explore the role of various personal and contextual characteristics that might moderate or change the nature of the general developmental decline in motivation.

ADOLESCENT MOTIVATION: WHAT DEVELOPS?

In discussing any developmental question, a key issue is to define "what develops," or what changes over the life course. In terms of this chapter, we will focus on adolescents' academic motivational beliefs. We take a general social cognitive perspective that assumes that student perceptions of themselves and of the academic tasks they confront in the classroom are important beliefs that change over time. Moreover, although we realize that these beliefs are contextualized and situated in different domains and contexts, we also assume that, like any cognition, they are internal representations that adolescents construct from the information in the setting as well as their own prior knowledge base (Pintrich, 2000a). As such, these internal representations not only change over time, but they also can have some stability over time within any individual. In other words, we reject any strong situated view of adolescent motivation that does not privilege an important role for internal representations of motivational beliefs that are carried by the individual. We focus on two global components of academic motivation, expectancy and value beliefs.

Expectancy Components

Expectancy components are adolescents "answer" to the question: "Can I do this task?" If students believe that they have some control over their skills and the task environment and that they have confidence in their ability to perform the necessary skills, they are more likely to choose to do the task, more likely to be involved in self-regulatory activities, and more likely to persist at the task. There are a variety of constructs that different motivational theorists have proposed that can be categorized as expectancy components. The main distinction is between how much control one believes one has in the situation and perceptions of efficacy to accomplish the task in that situation. Of course, these beliefs are correlated empirically, but most models propose separate constructs for control beliefs and efficacy beliefs.

Control Beliefs

There have been a number of constructs and theories proposed about the role of control beliefs for motivational dynamics. For example, early work on locus of control (e.g., Lefcourt, 1976; Rotter, 1966) found that students who believed that they were in control of their behavior and could influence the environment (an internal locus of control) tended to achieve at higher levels. Deci (1975) and de Charms (1968) discussed perceptions of control in terms of students' belief in self-determination. De Charms (1968) coined the terms "origins" and "pawns" to describe students who believed they were able to control their actions and students who believed others controlled their behavior. Connell (1985) suggested that there are three aspects of control beliefs: an internal source, an external source or powerful others, and an unknown source. Students who believe in internal sources of control are assumed to perform better than students who believe powerful others (e.g., faculty, parents) are responsible for their success or failure or those students who do not know who or what is responsible for the outcomes. Skinner (1995, 1996) has distinguished between means-ends beliefs, agent-ends, and agent-means beliefs in her model of perceived control. Means-ends beliefs are similar to outcome expectations in that the adolescent believes that if they do something, it will have an impact on ends or outcomes. Agents-means beliefs are similar to self-efficacy, and agent-ends beliefs involve the idea that the person can bring about desired outcomes. In the college classroom, Perry and his colleagues (e.g., Perry, 1991; Perry & Dickens, 1988; Perry & Magnusson, 1989; Perry & Penner, 1990) have shown that students' beliefs about how their personal attributes influence the environment, what they label perceived control, are related to achievement and to aspects of the classroom environment (e.g., instructor feedback).

In self-efficacy theory, outcome expectations refer to individuals' beliefs concerning their ability to influence outcomes, that is, their belief that the environment is responsive to their actions, which is different from self-efficacy (the belief that one can do the task, see Bandura, 1986; Pajares, 1997; Schunk, 1991). This belief that outcomes are contingent on their behavior leads individuals to have higher expectations for success and should lead to more persistence. When individuals do not perceive a contingency between their behavior and outcomes, this can lead to passivity, anxiety, lack of effort, and lower achievement, often labeled learned helplessness (cf. Abramson, Seligman, & Teasdale, 1978). Learned helplessness is usually seen as a stable pattern of attributing many events to uncontrollable causes which leaves the individual believing that there is no opportunity for change that is under their control. These adolescents do not believe they can "do anything" that will make a difference and that the environment or situation is basically not responsive to their actions.

The overriding message of all these models is that a general pattern of perception of internal control results in positive outcomes (i.e., more cognitive engagement, higher achievement, higher self-esteem), while sustained perceptions of external or unknown control results in negative outcomes (lower achievement, lack of effort, passivity, anxiety). Reviews of research in this area are somewhat conflicting, however (cf. Findley & Cooper, 1983; Stipek & Weisz, 1981) and some have argued that it is better to accept responsibility for positive outcomes (an internal locus of control) and deny responsibility for negative or failure outcomes (an external locus of control, see Harter, 1985). Part of the difficulty in interpreting this literature is the use of different definitions of the construct of control, different instruments to measure the construct, different ages of the samples, and different outcome measures used as a criterion in the numerous studies. In particular, the construct of internal locus of control confounds three dimensions of locus (internal vs. external), controllability (controllable vs. uncontrollable), and stability (stable vs. unstable). Attributional theory proposes that these three dimensions can be separated conceptually and empirically and that they have different influences on behavior (Weiner, 1986).

Attributional theory proposes that the causal attributions an individual makes for success or failure mediates future expectancies, not the actual success or failure event. A large number of studies have shown that individuals who tend to attribute success to internal and stable causes like ability or aptitude will tend to expect to succeed in the future. In contrast, individuals who attribute their success to external or unstable causes (i.e., ease of the task, luck) will not expect to do well in the future. For failure situations, the positive motivational pattern consists of, not an internal locus of control, but rather attributing failure to external and unstable causes (difficult task, lack of effort, bad luck) and the negative motivational pattern consists of attributing failure to internal and stable causes (e.g., ability, skill). This general attributional approach has been applied to numerous situations and the motivational dynamics seem to be remarkably robust and similar (Weiner, 1986).

It also is important to note that from an attributional analysis, the important dimension that is linked to future expectancies (beliefs that one will do well in the future) is stability, not locus (Weiner, 1986). That is, it is how stable you believe a cause is that is linked to future expectancies (i.e., the belief that your ability or effort to do the task is stable over time, not whether you believe it is internal or external to you). Attributional theory generally takes a situational view of these attributions and beliefs, but some researchers have suggested that individuals have relatively consistent attributional patterns across domains and tasks that function somewhat like personality traits (e.g., Fincham & Cain, 1986; Peterson, Maier, & Seligman, 1993). These attributional patterns seem to predict individual performance over time. For example, if adolescents consistently attributed their success to their own skill and ability as a learner, then it would be predicted that they would continually expect success in future classes. In contrast, if they consistently attribute success to other causes (e.g., the instructors are excellent, the material is easy, luck), then their expectations might not be as high for future classes.

Self-efficacy Beliefs

In contrast to control beliefs, self-efficacy concerns students' beliefs about their ability to just do the task, not the linkage between their doing it and the outcome. Self-efficacy has been defined as individuals' beliefs about their performance capabilities in a particular domain (Bandura, 1982, 1986; Pajares, 1997; Schunk, 1991). The construct of self-efficacy includes individuals' judgments about their ability to accomplish certain goals or tasks by their actions in specific situations (Schunk, 1991). This approach implies a relatively situational or domain specific construct rather than a global personality trait. In an achievement context, it includes adolescents' confidence in their cognitive skills to perform the academic task. For example, a college student might have confidence in their capability (a high self-efficacy belief) to learn the material for the chemistry test (i.e., "I can learn this material on stoichiometry.") and consequently exert more effort in studying. At the same time, if the student believes that the grading curve in the class is so difficult and that their studying won't make much difference in their grade for the exam (a low control belief, low outcome expectation) they might not study as much. Accordingly, self-efficacy and control beliefs are separate constructs, albeit they are usually positively correlated empirically. Moreover, they may combine and interact with each other to influence student self-regulation and outcomes.

An issue in most motivational theories regarding self-efficacy and control beliefs concerns the domain or situational specificity of the beliefs. As noted above, self-efficacy theory generally assumes a situation specific view. That is, individuals' judgment of their efficacy for a task is a function of the task and situational characteristics operating at the time (difficulty, feedback, norms, comparisons with others, etc.) as well as their past experience and prior beliefs about the task and their current beliefs and feelings as they work on the task. However, there may be generalized efficacy beliefs that extend beyond the specific situation which influence motivated behavior. Accordingly, students could have efficacy beliefs not just for a specific exam in chemistry, but also for chemistry in general, natural science courses in contrast to social science or humanities course, or for learning and school work in general. An important direction for future research will be to examine the domain generality of both self-efficacy and control beliefs.

Value Components

Value components of the model incorporate individuals' goals for engaging in a task as well as their beliefs about the importance, utility, or interest of a task. Essentially, these components concern the question: Why am I doing this task? In more colloquial terms, value components concern whether students "care" about the task and the nature of that concern. These components should be related to self-regulatory activities as well as outcomes such as the choice of activities, effort, and persistence (Eccles, 1983; Pintrich, 1999). Although there are a variety of different conceptualizations of value, two basic components seem relevant; goal orientation and task value.

Goal Orientation

All motivational theories posit some type of goal, purpose, or intentionality to human behavior, although these goals may range from relatively accessible and conscious goals as in attribution theory to relatively inaccessible and unconscious goals as in psychodynamic theories (Zukier, 1986). In recent cognitive reformulations of achievement motivation theory, goals are assumed to be cognitive representations of the different purposes students may adopt in different achievement situations (Dweck & Elliott, 1983; Dweck & Leggett, 1988; Ford, 1992). In current achievement motivation research, there have been two general classes of goals that have been discussed under various names such as target and purpose goals (e.g., Harackiewicz, Barron, & Elliot, 1998; Harackiewicz & Sansone, 1991), or task specific goals and goal orientations (e.g., Garcia & Pintrich, 1994; Pintrich & Schunk, 1996; Wolters, Yu, & Pintrich, 1996; Zimmerman & Kitsantas, 1997). The general distinction between these two classes of goals is that target and task specific goals represent the specific outcome the individual is attempting to accomplish. In academic learning contexts, it would be represented by goals such as "wanting to get an 85% out of 100% correct on a quiz" or "trying to get an A on a midterm exam," etc. These goals are specific to a task and are most similar to the goals discussed by Locke and Latham (1990) for workers in an organizational context such as "wanting to make 10 more widgets an hour" or to "sell 5 more cars in the next week."

In contrast, purpose goals or goal orientations reflect the more general reasons individual do a task and are related more to the research on achievement motivation (Elliot, 1997; Urdan, 1997). It is an individual's general orientation (or "schema" or "theory") for approaching the task, doing the task, and evaluating their performance on the task (Ames, 1992; Dweck & Leggett, 1988; Pintrich, 2000a, 2000b, 2000c). In this case, purpose goals or goal orientations refer to why individuals want to get 85% out of 100%, why they want to get an A, or why they want to make more widgets or sell more cars as well as the standards or criteria (85%, an A) they will use to evaluate their progress toward the goal. Given the focus of our own research on goal orientations in adolescence, we will focus on goal orientation in this chapter and discuss it in somewhat more depth than other constructs.

There are a number of different models of goal orientation that have been advanced by different achievement motivation researchers (cf. Ames, 1992; Dweck & Leggett, 1988; Harackiewicz et al., 1998; Maehr & Midgley, 1991; Nicholls, 1984; Pintrich, 1989, 2000a, 2000c). These models vary somewhat in their definition of goal orientation and the use of different labels for similar constructs. They also differ on the proposed number of goal orientations and the role of approach and avoidance forms of the different goals. Finally, they also differ on the degree to which an individual's goal orientations are more personal, based in somewhat stable individual differences, or the degree to which an individual's goal orientations are more situated or sensitive to the context and a function of the contextual features of the environment. Most of the models assume that goal orientations are a function of both individual differences and contextual factors, but the relative emphasis along this continuum does vary between the different models. Much of this research also assumes that classrooms and other contexts (e.g., business or work settings; laboratory conditions in an experiment) can be characterized in terms of their goal orientations (see Ford, Smith, Weissbein, Gully, & Salas, 1998 for an application of goal orientation theory to a work setting), but in terms of developmental changes, we will be concerned with personal goal orientations.

Most models propose two general goal orientations that concern the reasons or purposes individuals are pursuing when approaching and engaging in a task. In Dweck's model, the two goal orientations are labeled *learning* and *performance* goals (Dweck & Leggett, 1988), with learning goals reflecting a focus on increasing competence and performance goals involving either the avoidance of negative judgments of competence or attainment of positive judgments of competence. Ames (1992) labels them *mastery* and *performance* goals with mastery goals orienting learners to "developing new skills, trying to understand their work, improving their level of competence, or achieving a sense of mastery based on self-referenced standards" (Ames, 1992, p. 262). In contrast, performance goals orient learners to focus on their ability and self-worth, to determine their ability in reference to besting other students, surpassing others, and to receiving public recognition for their superior performance (Ames, 1992).

Maehr and Midgley and their colleagues (e.g., Anderman & Midgley, 1997; Kaplan & Midgley, 1997; Maehr & Midgley, 1991, 1996; Middleton & Midgley, 1997; Midgley, Arunkumar, & Urdan, 1996; Midgley et al., 1998) have mainly used use the terms *task* goals and *performance* goals in their research program which parallel the two main goals from Dweck and Ames. Task-focused goals involve an orientation to mastery of the task, increasing one's competence, and progress in learning which are similar to the learning and mastery goals of Dweck and Ames. Performance goals involve a concern with doing better than others and demonstrating ability to the teacher and peers, similar to the performance goals discussed by Dweck and Ames.

In a similar, but somewhat different vein, Nicholls and his colleagues (Nicholls, 1984, 1989; Thorkildsen & Nicholls, 1998) have proposed *task-involved* and *ego-involved* goals or *task orientation* and *ego orientation*. In this research, the focus and operationalization of the goals has been on when individuals feel most successful, which is a somewhat different perspective than the more general reasons or purposes learners might adopt when approaching or performing a task. Nevertheless, they are somewhat similar to the goals proposed by others in that task-involved goals are defined as experiencing success when individuals learn something new, gain new skills or knowledge, or do their best. Ego-involved goals involve individuals feeling successful when outperforming or surpassing their peers or avoiding looking incompetent.

Finally, Harackiewicz and Elliot and their colleagues (e.g., Elliot, 1997; Elliot & Church, 1997; Elliot & Harackiewicz, 1996; Harackiewicz, Barron, Carter, Lehto, & Elliot, 1997; Harackiewicz et al., 1998) have investigated two general goal orientations, a *mastery orientation* and a *performance orientation*. In their work, a mastery goal orientation reflects a focus on the development of knowledge, skill, and competence relative to one's own previous performance, and is thus self-referential. Performance goals concern a striving for demonstrating competence by trying to outperform peers on academic tasks. These two general orientations are in line with the other definitions of goals discussed in this chapter. More importantly, however, Elliot and his colleagues (e.g., Elliot, 1997; Elliot & Church, 1997) also make a distinction between two different types of performance goals, an *approach performance* goal and an *avoidance performance* goal. They suggest that individuals can be positively motivated to try to outperform others, to demonstrate their competence and superiority, reflecting an approach orientation to the general performance goal. In contrast, individuals also can be negatively motivated to try to avoid failure, to avoid looking dumb or stupid or incompetent, what they label an avoidance orientation to the performance goal.

In the same vein, Midgley her colleagues (Middleton & Midgley, 1997; Midgley et al., 1997, 1998) have separated out both approach and avoid ability goals, paralleling the work by Elliot and his colleagues on approach and avoid performance goals. Other researchers (e.g., Urdan, 1997; Wolters et al., 1996) have examined what they have called *relative ability goals* but this construct seems to reflect the same construct as the approach performance goal of Elliot and his colleagues. Finally, Skaalvik and his colleagues (Skaalvik, 1997; Skaalvik, Valas, & Sletta, 1994) also have proposed two dimensions of performance or ego goals, a *self-enhancing ego orientation*, where the emphasis is on besting others and demonstrating superior ability, as in the approach performance goal, and *self-defeating ego orientation* where the goal is to avoid looking dumb or to avoid negative judgments, as in the avoidance performance orientation. The approach performance orientation focused on besting others and superior performance relative to peers is similar to the performance and ego orientation in the models of Dweck, Ames, and Nicholls. In addition, although not formally separated out as two distinct performance or ego goals in the models of Dweck and Nicholls, both of those models did include concerns of avoiding judgments of incompetence or feeling dumb or stupid in their conceptualizations of performance and ego orientations, similar to the avoidance performance orientation of Elliot and Midgley or the self-defeating ego orientation of Skaalvik.

Given all these different goals and orientations which share some similar and some different features, future research needs to clarify the relations among these goals. At the same time, given space considerations in this chapter, the remaining discussion will focus on the role of mastery and performance goals and their approach and avoidance forms, which seems appropriate given that most of the research has addressed these two general goals. Pintrich (2000c) has proposed a general taxonomy to categorize mastery and performance goals and their approach and avoidance forms. Table 1 displays the taxonomy and the four goals. The columns in Table 1 reflect the general approach-avoidance distinction that has been a hallmark of achievement motivation research (Atkinson, 1957; Elliot, 1997; McClelland, Atkinson, Clark, & Lowell, 1953) since its inception as well as more recent social cognitive perspectives on approaching and avoiding a task (e.g., Covington & Roberts, 1994; Harackiewicz et al., 1998; Higgins, 1997). In particular, recent social cognitive models of self-regulation such as Higgins (1997) explicitly use this distinction of approach-avoidance (or promotion-prevention focus in his terms) to discuss different self-regulatory processes. An approach or promotion focus leads individuals to move toward positive or desired end-states, to try to promote them to occur, while an avoidance or prevention focus leads individuals to move away from negative or undesired end-states, to prevent them from occurring (Higgins, 1997).

Table 1. Two Goal Orientations and Their Approach and Avoidance Forms

	Approach Focus	*Avoidance Focus*
Mastery Orientation	Focus on mastering task, learning, understanding	Focus on avoiding misunderstanding, avoiding not learning or not mastering task
	Use of standards of self-improvement, progress, deep understanding of task (learning goal, task goal, task-involved goal)	Use of standards of not being wrong, not doing it incorrectly relative to task
Performance Orientation	Focus on being superior, besting others, being the smartest, best at task in comparison to others	Focus on avoiding inferiority, not looking stupid or dumb in comparison to others
	Use of normative standards such as getting best or highest grades, being top or best performer in class (performance goal, ego-involved goal, self-enhancing ego orientation, relative ability goal)	Use of normative standards of not getting the worst grades, being lowest performer in class (performance goal, ego-involved goal, self-defeating ego orientation)

The rows in Table 1 reflect two general goals that students might be striving for and represent the general goals of mastery and performance that have been proposed by every one of the different models discussed here. The cells in Table 1 include, in parentheses, some of the different labels that have been proposed for the two main goal orientations in the different models. All the models agree that mastery goals (learning, task, task-involved) are represented by attempts to improve or promote competence, knowledge, skills and learning and that standards are self-set or self-referential with a focus on progress and understanding. In all the models discussed, mastery goals have only been discussed and researched in terms of an approach orientation, that is, that students were trying to approach or attain this goal, not avoid it. As such, most models have only proposed the first cell in the first row in Table 1, but there is research emerging on the viability of an avoid mastery goal (see Elliot, 1999; Elliot & McGregor, 2001; Zusho & Pintrich, 2000).

An avoid mastery goal represents the occasions when students are focused on avoiding misunderstanding or avoiding not mastering the task. Some students that are more "perfectionistic" may use standards of not getting it wrong or doing it incorrectly relative to the task. These students would not be concerned about doing it wrong because of comparisons with others (an avoid performance goal), but rather in terms of their own high standards for themselves. Both Elliot and McGregor (2001) and Zusho and Pintrich (2000) have found that mastery avoid goal items do separate from the other three goals in Table 1 in factor analyses. Moreover, both of these studies show that mastery avoid goals have different outcomes (mainly negative) than the other three goals. Accordingly, there is some nascent evidence for these avoid mastery goals, but there is a clear need for more research on their role in motivation and learning.

The second row in Table 1 reflects the general performance goal orientation that all the models propose, but the approach and avoidance columns allow for the separation of the goal of trying to outperform or best others using normative standards from the goal of avoiding looking stupid, dumb, or incompetent relative to others. This distinction has been formally made in the work of Elliot, Midgley, Skaalvik and their colleagues, and all the studies have shown that there are differential relations between other motivational and cognitive outcomes and an approach performance goal and an avoidance performance goal (Harackiewicz et al., 1998; Middleton & Midgley, 1997; Midgley et al., 1998; Skaalvik, 1997). In Dweck's model the performance orientation included both trying to gain positive judgments of the self as well as trying to avoid negative judgments (Dweck & Elliott, 1983). In Nicholls' model, ego-involved or ego orientation also included both feeling successful when doing better than others or avoiding looking incompetent (Nicholls, 1984; Thorkildsen & Nicholls, 1998). Accordingly, most of the models did recognize the possibility that students could be seeking to gain positive judgments of the self by besting or outperforming others as well as trying to avoid looking stupid, dumb, or incompetent, although Dweck and Nicholls did not separate them conceptually as did Elliot, Midgley, and Skaalvik. In this case, within this performance row in Table 1, in contrast to the mastery row in Table 1, there is no doubt that both approach and avoidance goal orientations are possible and that students can adopt them and that they can have differential relations to other motivational or cognitive outcomes.

In the literature on mastery and performance goals, the general theoretical assumption has been that mastery goals foster a host of adaptive motivational, cognitive, and achievement outcomes, while performance goals generate less adaptive or even maladaptive outcomes (Midgley, Kaplan, & Middleton, 2001). Moreover, this assumption has been supported in a large number of empirical studies on goals and achievement processes (Ames, 1992; Dweck & Leggett, 1988; Pintrich, 2000c; Pintrich & Schunk, 1996), in particular the positive predictions for mastery goals. The logic of the argument is that when students are focused on trying to learn and understand the material and trying to improve their performance relative to their own past performance, this orientation will help them maintain their self-efficacy in the face of failure, ward off negative affect such as anxiety, lessen the probability that they will have distracting thoughts, and free up cognitive capacity and allow for more cognitive engagement and achievement. In contrast, when students are concerned about trying to be the best, to get higher grades than others, and do well compared to others under a performance goal, there is the possibility that this orientation will result in more negative affect or anxiety, increase the possibility of distracting and irrelevant thoughts (e.g., worrying about how others are doing, rather than focusing on the task), and that this will diminish cognitive capacity, task engagement, and performance.

More recently, however, there has been some empirical evidence emerging that performance goals are not necessarily maladaptive for all outcomes (Harackiewicz et al., 1998; Pintrich, 2000a, 2000b, 2000c). In this research, performance goals where students are trying to approach the goal of doing better than others, this competitive urge or goal, seems to be positively related to actual performance at least in terms of final course grade (Harackiewicz et al., 1998). In addition, these studies seem to show that there is not necessarily a decrement in cognitive engagement or self-regulation as a function of adopting a performance goal (Pintrich, 2000a, 2000b, 2000c). Finally, studies with younger students in junior high classrooms also have shown that students high in approach performance goals and high in mastery goals are not more anxious, do not experience more negative affect, and are equally motivated as those low in approach performance goals and high in mastery (Pintrich, 2000b). This recent research is leading to some reconceptualization of the general theoretical assumption that mastery goals are adaptive and performance goals are maladaptive, but this position is currently controversial and not supported by all researchers in the field (e.g., Midgley et al., 2001).

Task Value

Goal orientation can refer to students' goals for a specific task (a midterm exam) as well as a general orientation to a course or a field. In the same way, students' task value beliefs can be rather specific or more general. Three components of task value have been proposed by Eccles (1983) as important in achievement dynamics: the individual's perception of the importance of the task, their personal interest in the task (similar to intrinsic interest in intrinsic motivation theory), and their perception of the utility value of the task for future goals. These three value components may be rather parallel in children and adolescents, but can vary significantly in adults (Wlodkowski, 1988).

The importance component of task value refers to the individuals' perception of the task's importance or salience for them. The perceived importance of a task is related to a general goal orientation, but importance could vary by goal orientation. An individual's orientation may guide the general direction of behavior, while value may relate to the level of involvement. For example, a college student may believe that success in a particular course is very important (or unimportant) to them, regardless of their intrinsic or extrinsic goals. That is, the student may see success in the course as learning the material or getting a good grade, but they still may attach differential importance to these goals. Importance should be related to individuals' persistence at a task as well as choice of a task.

Student interest in the task is another aspect of task value. Interest is assumed to be individuals' general attitude or liking of the task that is somewhat stable over time and a function of personal characteristics. In an educational setting this includes the individual's interest in the course content and reactions to the other characteristics of the course such as the instructor (cf. Wlodkowski, 1988). Personal interest in the task is partially a function of individuals' preferences as well as aspects of the task (e.g., Malone & Lepper, 1987). However, personal interest should not be confused with situational interest which can be generated by simple environmental features (e.g., an interesting lecture, a fascinating speaker, a dramatic film) but which are not long-lasting and do not necessarily inculcate stable personal interest (Hidi, 1990). Schiefele (1991) has shown that student's personal interest in the material being studied is related to their level of involvement in terms of the use of cognitive strategies as well as actual performance. There is a current revival in research on the role of interest in learning after a hiatus in research on this important motivational belief (see Renninger, Hidi, & Krapp, 1992).

In contrast to the means or process motivational dynamic of interest, utility value refers to the ends or instrumental motivation of the student (Eccles, 1983). Utility value is determined by the individual's perception of the usefulness of the task for them. For students this may include beliefs that the course will be useful for them immediately in some way (e.g., help them get into college), for college students help them in their major (e.g., they need this information for upper level courses), or their career and life in general (e.g., this will help them in their jobs). At a task level, student may perceive different course assignments (e.g., essay and multiple choice exams, term papers, lab activities, class discussion) as more or less useful and decide to become more or less cognitively engaged in the task.

In summary, we define academic motivation in terms of these four general beliefs, control beliefs, self-efficacy beliefs, goal orientations, and task value beliefs. These beliefs can change over time and are important components of what develops in adolescent motivation. We now turn to describing the general developmental trends in these four beliefs over the course of the second decade of life.

GENERAL DEVELOPMENTAL TRAJECTORIES IN MOTIVATIONAL BELIEFS

The second decade of life spans the late elementary school years through junior high, high school, and college in terms of academic settings. These settings obviously provide different supports and constraints for the development of academic motivation. We assume that motivational beliefs are sensitive to contextual factors and we discuss some of these contextual factors in the third and last section of this chapter. However, in this section, we focus on the general developmental trajectories in motivational beliefs without concentrating on the contextual changes that are also taking place as adolescents move through these different contexts.

The Development of Control Beliefs

As noted in the previous section, control beliefs have been defined and researched in many different ways (cf. Connell, 1985; Skinner, 1995, 1996; Weiner, 1986), so it is somewhat difficult to summarize the developmental findings. Nevertheless, there are several general developmental trends that are important to note. First, there seems to be a general decline in the sense of omnipotence that many young children have that leads them to think they can control many events, even chance or luck events (Weisz, 1984). Accordingly, as children move into adolescence they come to better understand that some events or outcomes can be controlled through their own effort, skills, or actions and other events are more a function of luck or other external or unknown factors (Nicholls, 1990; Pintrich & Schunk, 1996). At the same time, while they are learning what they can and can't control, adolescents are also gaining more skills and expertise which allows them to exert more control over their own behavior. In addition, adolescents are allowed to have more actual control over their own behavior. For example, junior and senior high students are not left by their parents with babysitters any longer and college students (especially those living away from home) are given almost complete personal control over their time use and their daily life. In this sense of internal control, Skinner and Connell (1986) concluded that internal control beliefs increase with age. Heckhausen (1999) also suggests that primary control beliefs basically follow an inverted-U shape trajectory over the course of the life-span, showing a general increase over childhood and adolescence, peaking in middle age (30s–50s), and then declining in older adulthood.

As noted in the previous section, aspects of control beliefs are related to attributions and attributional thinking (Pintrich & Schunk, 1996; Weiner, 1986). Although the types of attributions that individuals make may be fairly situation-specific, there are important developmental differences in how individuals come to define ability, effort, luck, task difficulty and other causes for success and failure. Nicholls (1990) has summarized the phases of thinking that represent different schemas or "theories" for thinking about ability, effort, luck, and task difficulty. In this program of empirical work, Nicholls and his colleagues have (Nicholls, 1990; Nicholls & Miller, 1983, 1984a,b, 1985) shown that it is not until about 12–13 years of age that adolescents come to have completely differentiated views of ability, effort, and luck and can conceive of ability as capacity (Nicholls, 1990; Pintrich & Schunk, 1996). In other words, it is not until junior high school that adolescents understand that ability and effort actually covary inversely, with ability setting the upper limits on performance, and that when ability is low, effort needs to be high to achieve the same outcomes. Following the same logic, if the same outcomes are obtained, but one person uses less effort, then it is assumed that person has higher ability (Pintrich & Schunk, 1996).

In a related vein of research, Dweck and her colleagues (e.g., Dweck, 1999; Dweck & Leggett, 1988) have shown that individuals often adopt one of two theories of intelligence, an entity theory where ability is limited and fixed, and an incremental theory where ability is more malleable and can be changed through effort and learning. In this case, an entity theory of intelligence reflects the idea that ability is a stable, unchanging personal characteristic or trait, with little role for effort to play in learning. In contrast, under an incremental theory, effort can still play a role as one tries harder to learn and master the task, then one can still improve skills and abilities. In general, it would be expected that over the course of development, older adolescents would be less likely to be incremental theorists, while younger elementary school students would be more likely to be incremental theorists (Dweck & Leggett, 1988; Nicholls, 1990; Pintrich & Schunk, 1996). Developmentally, it makes sense that younger students who are constantly learning new skills in many domains, not just academic domains, would come to believe their skills and intelligence could improve. In contrast, with age and experience, all individuals come to understand that there may be some limitations on their intelligence, abilities, and skills.

The Development of Self-efficacy and Competence Judgments

The development of self-efficacy and competence judgments could show contrasting development patterns. On the one hand, very task specific judgments of efficacy might show a general increase over time as the adolescent gains more skill and expertise at the specific task. For example, self-efficacy measures are often very task or content specific (Pajares, 1997) such as judgments of being able to do two-digit math problems or quadratic equations in algebra. In this case, as adolescents work on these specific tasks and have some success, their judgments of efficacy should rise. Shell, Murphy, and Bruning (1995) found just this kind of developmental trend in their cross-sectional study of efficacy beliefs for specific reading and writing tasks (e.g., read a textbook; identify parts of speech; correctly punctuate a sentence). Fourth grade students had the lowest perceptions of efficacy, followed by seventh graders, and the highest efficacy beliefs were reported by tenth graders. In contrast, for example, in another cross-sectional study Pajares and Valiante (1999) found that sixth graders had the highest self-efficacy beliefs for writing, followed by eighth graders and that seventh graders had the lowest perceptions of self-efficacy. All these students were in a middle school, so the drop in seventh grade efficacy beliefs can't be explained by the transition to junior high/middle school. It may be that the writing tasks in seventh and eighth grade are more difficult than in sixth grade. The important point is that the development of specific self-efficacy judgments should be tied to actual experience on the task, not general developmental trends or age-related changes necessarily. This is quite a different developmental perspective than a focus on general competence perceptions.

On the other hand, research on general competence perceptions shows a very reliable and steady decline in adolescents' perceptions of their academic competence over time (Eccles et al., 1998). This research which has used longitudinal designs, not just cross-sectional designs, and has measured competence perceptions at a fairly global level (i.e., competence for school academics) or even at a domain-specific level (i.e., competence in math, reading, science), shows an average drop over time as students move from elementary school into junior high and high school contexts (Eccles et al., 1998). There has been very little longitudinal research that has followed students as they make the transition from high school to college settings. However, within the college literature (see Pascarella & Terenzini,

1991), there is some evidence to suggest that competence beliefs drop when adolescents enter college. This would fit prevailing wisdom as well in terms of the increased difficulty of college work and the increased competition among a more select group of generally academically able students. At the same time, the college literature suggests that competence perceptions do increase over the college years, following a pattern more like efficacy beliefs with a rise in competence as college students become more skilled at the tasks they encounter in the course of a college education.

The Development of Goal Orientation

Developmentally, there is little research on the age-related longitudinal changes in children's goal orientations (Eccles et al., 1998). This is partially due to the assumption that goal orientations are very contextually sensitive, not personal traits of the individual. In this case, it is more important to understand the nature of the context and how the contextual features shape the adoption of different goal orientations, than to understand how children's goal orientations change with age. Nevertheless, there may be both cognitive and contextual reasons to expect that mastery goals will become less dominant with age as performance goals become more salient to children. Dweck (1999; Dweck & Leggett, 1988) would predict that performance goals would become more important to children as they age given the increasing switch to entity theories of intelligence with age. In addition, there is evidence to suggest that classrooms become more competitive and performance goal-focused as students make the transition from elementary to middle school (Eccles et al., 1998). Both of these personal and contextual factors would contribute to the adoption of or emphasis on performance goals with age.

In terms of the general developmental progression of the four specific goal orientations outlined in Table 1, there may be some variability. It does seem likely that a general approach mastery orientation would show an age-related decline over adolescence, at least in terms of comparisons with the elementary school years. As the students move into the more competitive environments of junior high, high school, and college, the emphasis on grades and performance should increase. This contextual change has been well documented (Eccles et al., 1998; Maehr & Midgley, 1996) and it follows that students will be less likely to focus on approach mastery goals.

At the same time, given this contextual change, it would be expected that approach performance and avoid performance goals should increase with age. There should be more students concerned with trying to be better than others throughout adolescence. At the same time, given that not everyone can be the best and that achievement level differences can become more salient, there should be an increase in students adopting avoid performance goals. It seems likely that many secondary and even college students are very concerned with avoiding the appearance of looking stupid or dumb. This could lead to less self-regulation and help seeking (Newman, 2000; Pintrich, 2000a, 2000b, 2000c).

Finally, in terms of mastery avoid goals, it is unclear what the developmental trajectory might be over the course of adolescence. This is a new construct in goal theory and has only been examined empirically in college students and these studies have not been developmental. Elliot (1999) suggests that over the course of the life span that avoid mastery goals might increase as individuals age and realize they can't do what they used to do at the same level of competence. He uses the example of an aging Michael Jordan deciding that if he can't play basketball at the same level of competence as he did earlier in his life, he would adopt an mastery avoid goal toward basketball. This goal might lead him to choose to play basketball less often, or at least approach it with a different orientation of avoiding certain kinds of plays or moves since he realizes he can no longer perform them. On the other hand, it may be that within the more mastery-focused contexts of elementary school, there would be the potential for avoid mastery goals to arise. Young students may not be as concerned about how others are doing as under a performance goal, but they still may be concerned with mastery of the task or activity, and if they are not able to succeed, they might begin to adopt a mastery avoid goal of not wanting to do it incorrectly (Pintrich, 2000a,c). There is a clear need for more research on the development of avoid mastery goals.

The Development of Interest and Value Beliefs

From a developmental perspective, there is evidence that children's reports of their interest in and value for academic domains decline across the school years. It appears that elementary students report liking and valuing school work more than middle school and high school students in general (Eccles et al., 1998). Again, the developmental progression here is similar to that for self-efficacy and competence beliefs. If one examines the general interest in schoolwork or value for academic activities, there is a clear decline over the course of adolescence. On the other hand, similar to self-efficacy, from a developmental-task and individual differences perspective (Pintrich & Zusho, in press), there are clearly tasks and activities that individual students become very interested in as they grow older and begin to have some choices about how they spend their time. For example, a student that becomes very interested in athletics, or math, or science, may choose to spend more time on these activities and this can reinforce their interest and value for these activities. So, while there may be an overall general decline, there can be activity or task-specific increases in personal interest and value over the course of adolescence.

THE ROLE OF MULTIPLE TRAJECTORIES IN THE DEVELOPMENT OF MOTIVATION

The general decline in adaptive motivational beliefs and the potential rise in less adaptive beliefs (e.g., avoid performance goals) over the course of adolescence is a good summary of the extant research. This general decline also fits with our intuitive and personal experiences with adolescents and schooling. At the same time, there are clearly groups of adolescents who do not show this decline. Their motivational trajectories through school are quite different from the general developmental trend. The purpose of this section is to explore the personal and contextual factors that may promote a more positive trajectory. In other words, what characterizes these groups of individuals that make them more resilient or less "at risk" for showing the decline in motivation over the course of adolescence? Of course, there are always individuals who show different patterns, but the focus here will be on both personal and contextual factors that are associated with different trajectories for groups of adolescents. In particular, we focus on gender and we consider the role of multiple personal goals in students' motivational processes. Although we realize the importance of ethnicity, there is not as much research on ethnic differences, so we do not discuss it as a personal moderating factor. We also discuss how specific contextual factors might moderate the general negative trajectory in motivation over the course of adolescence.

The Role of Gender

Gender differences have been noted in both expectancy and value components of motivation. First, in terms of value-related constructs, Eccles, Wigfield and their colleagues have uncovered several gender-related differences in adolescents' valuing of certain subjects (Eccles et al., 1993; Wigfield & Eccles, 1992). For example, they found that girls typically valued instrumental music and English more than boys, while boys valued sports more than girls. Surprisingly, male and female adolescents did not differ in the relative value they attached to mathematics until they reached high school, when boys reported valuing math more than girls. Given these domain differences, gender can moderate the general negative trajectory in the development of value or interest, but the effect will vary by domain with males more "at risk" in writing or English, while females are more at risk for mathematics and sports over time.

As for expectancy constructs, males have been found to score lower on internal locus of responsibility measures than females. Males typically place less blame on themselves for failed outcomes, often attributing failures to lack of effort or bad luck (Dweck & Repucci, 1973; Meece, Parsons, Kaczala, Goff, & Futterman, 1982). This tendency among males to absolve themselves for failures has also been found to increase over time (cf. Crandall, Katkovsky, & Crandall, 1965), thus suggesting that males, in comparison to females, have relatively adaptive attributional styles, which can in turn "protect" them from developing motivational deficits such as learned helplessness. Indeed, some researchers have found males to display marked achievement strivings in the face of failure (Dweck & Repucci, 1973). However, it is not clear that males are less likely to be learned helpless than females, as males are more likely to be underachievers and drop out of school, although females are more likely to lower their expectations after failure and are more likely to avoid difficult and challenging tasks than males (Eccles et al., 1998).

Similarly, gender differences have been noted in students' ratings of their self-efficacy beliefs as well as their general perceptions of academic competence, with males usually displaying higher levels than females, especially in traditionally male-dominated fields such as science and mathematics (Eccles et al., 1998). Moreover, it has been found that this disparity in the competency ratings of boys and girls becomes even more pronounced following puberty. Researchers have typically accounted for such findings in terms of gender-role stereotyping and gender socialization. Eccles and her colleagues (Eccles et al., 1998) have asserted that while boys may hold higher competency ratings for athletics and mathematics, females often display higher ratings for subjects such as reading, English, and social studies. The magnitude of these differences, however, varies depending on the extent to which boys and girls actually endorse cultural values regarding gender-related superiority in these domains.

Taken together, these findings suggest that adolescent males may be more resilient than female adolescents in terms of the development of certain motivational beliefs. Interestingly, despite such gender disparities, investigators have found very little evidence suggesting that males actually outperform females academically (Eisenberg, Martin, & Fabes, 1996). This raises the issue of calibration, that is, the extent to which students' ratings of their motivational beliefs such as self-efficacy, accurately reflect their true level of motivation and achievement as measured by some external, objective standard. Some researchers have argued that males typically overestimate how well they think they will perform on future tasks, while females generally underestimate their abilities (Eccles et al., 1998). Likewise, a similar phenomenon has been noted among African American students. Despite generally low levels of achievement, African American students have been found to report remarkably high expectations for success, thus leading theorists to conclude that like males, African American students may tend to inflate their ratings of their academic abilities (Graham, 1994).

In line with a social-cognitive motivational perspective, one could argue that the actual relationship of these self-perceptions to some standardized measure of achievement is irrelevant and that being optimistic about one's abilities might in fact be beneficial in some situations. The positive psychology movement certainly attests to such an argument (cf. Chang, 2001). Some researchers, too, have documented higher levels of academic engagement and achievement among students who overrate their competence (Pintrich & Schunk, 1996). However, the question from a self-regulation perspective, not just a motivational perspective, is how much overestimation is too much? If a student consistently overestimates his academic prowess, might that not interfere with that student's perceived need to self-regulate his learning, or to engage in behaviors such as studying, that would be conducive to learning (Pintrich, 2000a, 2000c)? Similarly, other researchers have noted that explaining away failures, when taken to the extreme, can result in adverse consequences such as low expectations, avoidance of challenging situations, and ultimately, underachievement (Eccles et al., 1998). In general, these findings suggest that it is probably better to be somewhat optimistic about one's academic aptitude from a motivational perspective, but equally important from a self-regulation perspective is the ability to assess one's competence in a realistic and accurate manner.

To that end, it may be somewhat facile to conclude that males are in fact more "resilient" motivationally than females. Indeed, recent research examining gender differences in adolescents' self-efficacy beliefs in the domain of writing paints a more complicated picture. A series of studies conducted by Pajares and his colleagues examining elementary school, middle school, and high school students' writing-specific self-efficacy beliefs have uncovered no reliable gender differences, thus bringing to the fore the issue of domain-specific as well as task-specific gender disparities in motivation (Pajares & Johnson, 1996; Pajares, Miller, & Johnson, 1999; Pajares & Valiante, 1999). As Pajares and Valiante (1999) note, much of the gender-related research findings has been found in the domains of mathematics and science and more importantly focuses on students' ratings of their general academic abilities for those subjects rather than on students' task-specific self-efficacy beliefs. Females may perceive themselves to be inferior academically to males in general, but they may not necessarily perceive themselves to be lesser to males on certain academic tasks. In support of this conclusion, they found no differences in middle school girls and boys' mean-level judgments of their confidence in writing-related tasks such as composition, grammar, usage, and mechanical skills.

Furthermore, Pajares and Valiante (1999) raise another issue related to the assessment of adolescents' self-related motivational beliefs. In relation to gender differences in self-efficacy in particular, they suggest any such differences can be attributed in large part to the methodology employed. Specifically, they propose that girls and boys may be using a different metric when responding to traditional self-efficacy survey measures. To support this notion, they point to the fact that while they were unable to detect any gender differences in middle school students' self-efficacy ratings for writing, they found that middle school girls actually thought they were better writers than boys. In other words, they believe that the differences that might exist between the self-efficacy ratings of girls and boys are due to response bias, the use of different metrics, and some different psychological dynamics about what judgments mean in a relational context. While it seems somewhat peremptory to totally discount the validity of self-report measures (cf. Assor & Connell, 1992), Pajares and Valiante's suggestion of supplementing traditional survey items with additional items and techniques is an important one to consider. Moreover, their claim regarding the varying response styles of girls and boys is intriguing and certainly warrants further investigation.

The Role of Multiple Goals

There are very few reliable gender differences reported in the literature on adolescents' goal orientations. However, in discussing the role of multiple trajectories in the development of motivation among adolescents, it is important to acknowledge the recent work on multiple goals (Harackiewicz et al., 1998; Pintrich, 2000a,b,c). As we briefly reviewed in the first section of this chapter, this budding work contradicts, to a certain extent, normative goal orientation theory, which asserts that only those students who adopt a mastery goal orientation will generate positive motivational and learning outcomes. Rather, proponents of the multiple goals framework posit that it is possible to attain high levels of motivation and achievement through multiple pathways. More specifically, recent work seems to suggest that an endorsement of an approach performance goal is not entirely detrimental and in certain cases can even result in higher achievement levels (Harackiewicz et al., 1998; Pintrich, 2000b; Wolters et al., 1996).

It is possible to interpret such results in a manner as to discount the importance of mastery goals. We strongly believe that is not the intent of this work. In fact, advocates of the revised framework recognize firmly that mastery goals play an adaptive role in students' motivational processes. For example, Pintrich (2000b) proposes that students high in both mastery *and* performance goals should perform equally well as, if not better than, students high in mastery but low in performance goals, and certainly better than students who are only high in performance goals. Harackiewicz and her colleagues (1998), too, suggest that mastery goals can help students to foster and maintain an interest in the course work while performance goals can motivate students to focus on those aspects that will ensure their performance and thus, enable them to attain high grades. Furthermore, the positive relationship of approach performance goals to achievement is found most often in studies of college students (Harackiewicz et al., 1998; Pintrich, 2000b; Wolters et al., 1996). In this case, there may be a developmental self-selection bias operating, such that the students who go on to college are the ones who have been high achievers in junior high and high school. These students may be well equipped cognitively and motivationally to adopt performance goals. In contrast, the students who do not go on to college may be the ones who have more difficulty with performance goals in junior high and high school classrooms. In addition, the college context may be very performance-oriented in at least some college classrooms that may make the adoption of personal performance goals more adaptive. Accordingly, there is a need for more developmentally sensitive research on this issue, but it is clear that in some cases approach performance goals can be adaptive.

Nevertheless, it would stand to reason that this work on multiple goals is especially important when considering the adolescent population. In these times of rapid technological advances and the ever-growing societal demand for a skilled workforce, it is difficult to deny the importance of a college education. Unfortunately, it is still not possible to obtain that education without surmounting certain educational milestones, including scoring well on college entrance exams such as the SAT and other standardized measures of achievement. Given this reality, it does seem reasonable to propose that for college-bound adolescents, an adoption of a performance goal may not only be adaptive, but somewhat necessary not only to meet their short-term goal of attending college, but to also function effectively in our society in the long-term.

The important issue for future research is determining how multiple goals work and how they can have different effects on different outcomes over time and developmentally. Barron and Harackiewicz (2000, 2001) have suggested four possible patterns for multiple goal effects. First, they suggest that there may be an additive effect with both mastery and approach performance goals having main independent effects on the same outcome. For example, both mastery and approach performance goals may have positive, but independent effects on the use of cognitive and self-regulatory strategies by adolescents (e.g., Wolters et al., 1996). The second pattern is what they label the interactive pattern that is revealed by a significant two-way interaction between mastery and approach performance goals. In this case, students who are high in both goals may be particularly advantaged for an outcome. Pintrich (2000b) found this pattern for task value, such that adolescents who were high in both goals were higher on their ratings of task value in terms of their perceptions of utility, importance and interest in mathematics. The third pattern, the specialized goal pattern, represents the possibility that mastery and performance goals have main independent effects on two different outcomes. For example, in their work on college students, Harackiewicz and her colleagues (e.g., Harackiewicz et al., 1996) have found that mastery goals have a positive main effect on interest, while approach performance goals have a positive main effect on actual performance, such as grades or GPA. The final pattern is what they call the selective goal pattern, where students actively select different goals to focus on depending on the nature of the task and context (e.g., Zimmerman & Kitsantas, 1997, 1999). For example, when learning material, mastery goals may serve the student well, while performance goals may be helpful when studying for exams.

The implications of this multiple goals approach for adolescent motivation is that there is a need to examine different developmental pathways or multiple developmental trajectories for motivation through adolescence. The multiple goals approach highlights the importance of the general principle of equifinality (e.g., Ford, 1992; Shah & Kruglanski, 2000), or the idea that goals can be accomplished or attained in different ways. Mastery goals might be attained through different types of actions, behaviors, and outcomes, there is not necessarily one pathway to the realization of mastery goals. In the same manner, there may be more than one developmental pathway that is generated by performance goals. We need to understand these different developmental pathways, particularly in adolescence when there are many different options open for students to achieve their goals. There is a clear need for more research on how multiple goals can give rise to multiple developmental pathways.

In addition, this multiple goals perspective suggests that the principle of multifinality (Shah & Kruglanski, 2000) may be operative as well, such that different means can serve the same goal. For example, it may be that deeper processing or the use of self-regulatory strategies can serve both mastery goals and approach performance goals. In the one case, deeper processing is helping the adolescent achieve her goal of learning and understanding. In the other case, the same strategies or means are serving the goal of doing better than others. However, in both cases, the students are equally involved in processing the material cognitively. Of course, there is a need for research on how similar means or strategies become associated with multiple goals and if in fact, the strategies are identical, or if there are some subtle differences in how they are employed when serving different goals.

The Role of Contextual Factors

Throughout this paper, we have acknowledged that motivational processes are often context-sensitive. Researchers define "context" in myriad ways; for the purposes of this chapter, we will consider the role of classroom context, peers, as well as the home and family on adolescents' motivational development.

Classroom Context

There are a number of classroom contextual factors that are believed to influence students' motivational levels. Perhaps the most obvious is the actual nature of the academic task; this might include the form of the task, for example, whether students are asked to write reports or solve a problem set, the actual course content that is embedded in the task, as well as the level of difficulty of the task. Of course, task form often corresponds with specific subject domains; for instance, it is more common to find problem sets in mathematics and science than it is in English or social studies. These various types of tasks are thought to influence students' learning primarily by affecting the ways in which students process the material. Some tasks, like multiple-choice exams, have been criticized for encouraging students to study for breadth, but not particularly for depth.

In terms of motivation, some students might feel more comfortable with certain types of tasks, which should then influence their levels of self-efficacy, and perhaps affective components such as interest. Correspondingly, the actual subject matter can influence students' motivational levels; the difference in girls' and boys' ratings of their self-efficacy and values for mathematics and English is a good example (Eccles et al., 1998). Recently, there has been a push toward the increased use of "authentic" tasks, or those tasks that are connected to real-world events or situations and foster the kinds of thinking and problem-solving skills that are important in out-of-school contexts. Such tasks are thought to be valuable not only for its cognitive benefits; authentic tasks are also believed to be motivating in large part because they increase both students' utility value, interest, and perceived academic competence (Blumenfeld, Soloway, Marx, Krajcik, Guzdial, & Palincsar, 1991). Finally, task difficulty has also been found to influence students' level of motivation. Tasks that are perceived to be too easy may engender feelings of boredom, while tasks that are perceived to be too difficult can leave students feeling frustrated and can adversely affect students' self-efficacy beliefs and interest levels (Pintrich & Schunk,

1996). In this manner, classrooms that include tasks that are authentic, challenging, and interesting may help to buffer the general decline in adolescent motivation. At the same time, there is a need for more research on how these different task characteristics interact with the personal characteristics of students to shape multiple developmental trajectories. It may be that some of these tasks are much more difficult for some adolescents, and so may not have the intended positive main effect.

In addition to the task, the larger classroom context, including the overall reward and goal structures of the classroom, has been found to shape students' motivation (Ames, 1992; Pintrich & Schunk, 1996). Reward structures refer to how extrinsic rewards such as grades are distributed among students. They can be independent, as in the case when grades are assigned based solely on an individual's performance; cooperative, when one grade is given to a group of students for shared work; or competitive, when grades are based on an individuals' performance in relation to the rest of the class (i.e., based on a "curve"). Goal structures are related to reward structures, and refer to how various academic tasks are completed (e.g., alone, cooperatively, competitively). In general, the research shows that competitive reward and goal structures have detrimental effects on students' motivation by lowering levels of self-efficacy and feelings of self-worth (Ames, 1992; Covington, 1992). Cooperative goal structures, in contrast, have been found to foster increased levels of self-efficacy and interest (Ames, 1992; Covington, 1992). This research on reward and goal structures can explain, in part, the sudden drop in adolescents' motivational levels as they make the transition from elementary school to junior high school and beyond. Eccles and her colleagues have noted that as students progress through their schooling, they are exposed to increasing use of both competitive reward and goal structures. Again, classrooms that are more mastery-oriented and less competitive may help to stave off the seemingly inevitable decline in adolescent motivation.

At the same time, given the work on multiple goals, and the potential positive effects of performance goals, there is a need to examine how more performance-focused junior high and high school classrooms are negotiated by different types of students. It may be that some students, perhaps those who have more personal approach performance goals, are more likely to do well in classrooms that have a more congruent orientation with their own personal goals. This congruency hypothesis between personal goals and classroom goal stresses has not been tested in many studies. Newman (1998) did test it in a microgenetic experimental study on help seeking, but did not find much support for the congruency hypothesis, at least in terms of the personal performance goal-context performance goal relation. However, in more naturalistic classroom settings, where performance goals and reward structures are more meaningful, there may be a congruency effect. We need more research on this type of personal-contextual interaction and how they may create different developmental pathways for different types of students.

Finally, certain kinds of pedagogical techniques have been associated with increased levels of motivation. Specifically, students enrolled in classes where instructors encourage student participation, whether it is in the form of collaborative groups, discussion, or project-based learning, have been found to report higher levels of motivation. These instructional methods are motivating, in large part, because they increase students' perceptions of autonomy or control, by allowing students to make choices and take responsibility for their learning. However, it is also important to note that mere use of these student-centered instructional methods will not increase motivation in and of itself. Use of these methods requires a certain amount of pedagogical finesse in the form of increased demands for clarity, organization, pedagogical content knowledge, as well as the ability to scaffold students' knowledge effectively. Thus, it is imperative that the instructor is skilled in the use of these techniques. For example, inquiry learning, another form of student-centered instruction, has been popular in the domain of science for some time. This technique, in its purest form, encourages students to "discover" basic scientific principles with minimal teacher input or guidance. However, as one might expect, this form of unguided learning can prove to be frustrating for students, and unmanageable and unproductive for teachers.

Finally, there is a need for research that considers how these different classroom factors interact among themselves to influence the development of motivation. It is highly unlikely that we will be able to do "titration" studies where we can examine the independent main effects of these different classroom characteristics in isolation. It is clear that these factors are not completely orthogonal to one another in real classrooms. Accordingly, we have to develop ways to characterize classrooms along these different dimensions and to create profiles of the classrooms and then examine how these different profiles create and nurture different pathways. It may be that in some classrooms, some aspects of competition and performance-goal stresses can be positive. For example, if the tasks are not too interesting or boring to the students, then making them more interesting through the use of competitive game-like reward structures may facilitate motivation. In the same manner, some aspects of competition or performance-goal stresses may be positive, if combined with more authentic tasks or with teacher behaviors or affect that stress mastery and learning. We know very little about how these classroom features interact to produce student motivation. In addition, as Linnenbrink and Pintrich (2001) have pointed out, there is a need to understand how these actual contextual goal stresses (the alpha press of the classroom) are perceived and experienced by the student (the beta press) and how they interact to facilitate or constrain the development of motivation.

Peers

It is difficult to talk about adolescents without recognizing the strong influence their fellow peers have on their development. Motivation is certainly no exception. Peer groups can influence students' motivation in several ways. First, there has been considerable research examining the link between social competence and academic success. This body of work suggests that in comparison to socially rejected adolescents, adolescents who are accepted by their peers generally display elevated feelings of self-esteem, self-worth, as well as achievement (Brown & Lohr, 1987; Eccles et al., 1998). Numerous explanations have been proposed to explain this phenomenon; among them is the argument that adolescents who feel that they belong socially will have more resources at their disposal to devote to academics and learning (Osterman, 2000). For example, in one study of middle school students' motivation, researchers found that adolescents' sense of classroom belonging and support was associated with higher levels of expectancies for success and interest (Goodenow, 1993; see review by Osterman, 2000).

Peers can also positively influence students' motivational processes by supporting and extending the learning of their fellow classmates, as in the case of collaborative learning. In the previous section, we discussed how cooperative goal structures and use of student-centered instructional practices can influence students' learning and achievement. Peers are an integral part of this collaborative process. In such an environment, peers serve as "colearners," primarily by assisting their group members to understand and process the material more effectively, by sharing resources, and by modeling specific learning strategies (Eccles et al., 1998).

Finally, much of the extant literature on adolescent development focuses on negative influences of peer groups. However, the effect of peer groups on students' academic performance is not always negative. For example, Steinberg, Dornbusch, and Brown (1992) largely attributed the academic excellence of the Asian American adolescents in their sample to peer support. They found that in comparison to Hispanic and African American students, Asian students as well as Caucasian students reported having more friends who valued academic success. The work of Graham and her colleagues (cf. Graham, Taylor, & Hudley, 1998) offer additional support to such findings.

Such findings are in line with the work on peer groups as socializing agents of academic engagement and achievement (Ryan, 2000). This body of work suggests that peer groups can have a socializing influence on students' academic beliefs and behaviors. For example, investigators have found that students with high-achieving friends display greater achievement gains than students with low-achieving friends (Epstein, 1983). In terms of motivation, peer groups have been found to influence students' ratings of their intrinsic value for school, social, and cognitive competence, as well as achievement (Ryan, 2000). At the same time, as Ryan (2000) points out, investigators have yet to understand the mechanisms underlying the socialization influence of peer groups. While there is considerable evidence that peer groups share many characteristics, the extent to which peer groups actually change or reinforce the characteristics of its members is still unclear. For instance, a competing hypothesis would be that adolescents become friends with others who are similar to them to begin with. Thus, much work remains to be done in this area, but it seems clear that peer groups that value school can buffer the general decline in adolescent motivation.

Home and Family

The adolescent years typically are characterized as a time when activities shift from the family to the peer group. Nevertheless, the influence the home and family can have on the adolescent is considerable. Eccles and her colleagues have proposed one model of how various parental factors are related to students' achievement motivation. Given space constraints, we are unable to discuss their model in great detail. Accordingly, we direct those readers who are interested in a more comprehensive account of how parental beliefs affect students' motivational outcomes to their work (cf. Eccles et al, 1998).

Briefly, their model suggests that certain demographic characteristics (e.g., educational level, socioeconomic status, ethnicity) can influence, either positively or negatively, parents' general beliefs (e.g., gender-role stereotypes) as well as their perceptions of and expectations for their child. These general and child-specific parental beliefs are believed to have a direct effect on the child's motivational beliefs. Alternately, Eccles proposes that these parental beliefs can also affect specific parental behaviors, for example, the frequency and duration of time-use with the child, which in turn can also affect the child's motivation. For example, we have already discussed how general parental beliefs, such as gender-role stereotypes, can have profound influences on students' own motivational beliefs over time. Much of the work on Asian American students' educational success has also been framed in terms of the role of cultural and contextual influences related to the family (Chen & Stevenson, 1995; Sue & Okazaki, 1990). For example, Chen and Stevenson (1995) found that Asian American students were more likely to have parents with higher academic standards than European American students. The role of home seems to be an important factor for Asian American students, and it may play a similar role for other groups as well, but there is a need for more research that addresses this issue. There is little research that has examined how home and family factors interact with school and classroom factors to contribute to adolescent motivation development. This is an area that will become more important in future research.

CONCLUSIONS AND FUTURE DIRECTIONS

In summary, there is a general decline in students' motivation over the adolescent years. As students get older, they report less confidence in their academic abilities; they subscribe more to an entity theory of intelligence, and become less interested in and value school less in general. Adolescents also seem to become more concerned with outperforming their fellow students academically, as well as avoiding the appearance of looking dumb in comparison to their peers. This general developmental trajectory in adolescent motivation is not a very optimistic or favorable portrait of adolescents or the schools they inhabit.

At the same time, however, we have suggested that various personal and contextual characteristics can "protect" certain adolescents from this general decline trajectory. Specifically, it seems that being male buffers students from developing certain less adaptive motivational beliefs (e.g., decrease in self-efficacy, interest, and values). The adoption of multiple goals, specifically approach mastery and approach performance goals, also seems to be adaptive for some motivational and learning outcomes. Additionally, having support from parents and peers seems to contribute to the development of adaptive motivational beliefs. The classroom environment too, influences adolescents' motivation. Use of student-centered instructional techniques, authentic tasks, and cooperative goal structures, in particular seem to enhance students' motivation and appreciation for learning and can buffer the general negative developmental trajectory.

Taken together, these findings underscore the need to consider individual and contextual variation in the general developmental trajectory in adolescent motivation. It may not be that useful or instructive at this point in the development of motivational research to focus on the general negative decline in adolescent motivation. It seems more important to begin to research how different students construct their own developmental trajectories through adolescence and the school settings from junior high through college classrooms. There may be many different developmental trajectories and different personal and contextual factors that moderate the creation, shape, and maintenance of these trajectories. However, this emphasis on different developmental trajectories that run counter to the general negative decline trajectory may help us understand the role of different personal and contextual factors that contribute to more resilient adolescents. Moreover, this focus can provide insight and suggestions for the improvement of school settings for all adolescents.

The work on multiple goals in particular represents a promising area for future research. Currently, there is a debate in the literature concerning the potentially adaptive role of approach performance goals. To be sure, more work is needed on this topic before we can determine if, when, and for whom these goals can have potentially beneficial effects. More specifically, researchers need to address whether the adoption of specific goal orientations are more appropriate for certain populations or in certain types of contexts. For example, we have suggested that it may be particularly beneficial for college bound adolescents to adopt approach performance goals. However, not much is known about how performance goals would affect those adolescents who are not particularly invested in school and/or those who are considering alternative career trajectories. Additionally, more work is needed investigating the long-term effects of adopting approach performance goals and for what specific achievement outcomes these goals have positive effects. For example, are approach performance goals only useful in courses where learning is assessed with multiple-choice exams? Finally, it would be interesting to see how certain classroom contextual factors, in particular reward and goal structures, interact with the adoption of performance approach goals. Are students who adopt performance goals only rewarded with achievement gains in classroom environments that are congruent with their personal goal orientation?

There is also a need to examine more closely how personal characteristics, such as gender, moderate the relations between the various motivational constructs and outcome measures such as self-regulated learning and achievement. One the one hand, the research on gender differences in motivation seems to suggests that being male can make one less likely to develop motivational inadequacies such as maladaptive attributions and lower perceptions of academic competency. On the other hand, questions remain about the nature of these differences, and whether or not these disparities according to gender are in fact "real" or an artifact of methodology as Pajares and Valiante (1999) suggest. In the same manner, although we did not discuss it here, the role of ethnic differences as a moderator in these relations is an important avenue for future research. Of course, the home and family context is related to adolescent motivation and may interact in important ways with ethnic differences and so there is a need to examine how ethnicity, home and school cultures all interact to produce different developmental trajectories. Finally, given the extensive role peers play in adolescents' lives, investigating further the mechanisms underlying how peers influence the motivational trajectories of adolescents would be a fruitful area of research. Following these directions for future research should provide a much more accurate picture of adolescent development and the multiple pathways that adolescents can follow as they move through different schools contexts.

REFERENCES

Abramson, L., Seligman, M., & Teasdale, J. (1978). Learned helplessness in humans: A critique and reformulation. *Journal of Abnormal Psychology, 87,* 49–74.

Ames, C. (1992). Classrooms: Goals, structures, and student motivation. *Journal of Educational Psychology, 84,* 261–271.

Anderman, E.M., & Midgley, C. (1997). Changes in achievement goal orientations, perceived academic competence, and grades across the transition to middle-level schools. *Contemporary Educational Psychology, 22,* 269–298.

Assor, A., & Connell, J. (1992). The validity of students' self-reports as measures of performance affecting self-appraisals. In D.H. Schunk & J.L. Meece (Eds.), *Student perceptions in the classroom* (pp. 25–47). Hillsdale, NJ: Erlbaum.

Atkinson, J.W. (1957). Motivational determinants of risk-taking behavior. *Psychological Review, 64,* 359–372.

Bandura, A. (1982). Self-efficacy mechanism in human agency. *American Psychologist, 37,* 122–147.

Bandura, A. (1986). *Social foundations of thought and action: A social cognitive theory.* Englewood Cliffs, NJ: Prentice-Hall.

Barron, K., & Harackiewicz, J. (2000). Achievement goals and optimal motivation: A multiple goals approach. In C. Sansone & J. Harackiewicz (Eds.), *Intrinsic and extrinsic motivation: The search for optimal motivation and performance* (pp. 229–254). San Diego, CA: Academic Press.

Barron, K., & Harackiewicz, J. (2001). Achievement goals and optimal motivation: Testing multiple goal models. *Journal of Personality and Social Psychology, 80,* 706–722.

Blumenfeld, P.C., Soloway, E., Marx, R.W., & Krajcik, J.S., Guzdial, M., & Palincsar, A. (1991). Motivating project-based learning: Sustaining the doing, supporting the learning. *Educational Psychologist, 26,* 369–398.

Brown, B.B., & Lohr, M.J. (1987). Peer group affiliation and adolescent self-esteem: An integration of ego-identity and symbolic-interaction theories. *Journal of Personality and Social Psychology, 52,* 47–55.

Chang, E.C. (Ed.). (2001). *Optimism and pessimism: Implications for theory, research, and practice.* Washington, DC: American Psychological Association.

Chen, C., & Stevenson, H.W. (1995). Motivation and mathematics achievement: A comparative study of Asian-American, Caucasian-American, and East Asian high school students. *Child Development, 66,* 1215–1234.

Connell, J.P. (1985). A new multidimensional measure of children's perceptions of control. *Child Development, 56,* 1018–1041.

Covington, M.V. (1992). *Making the grade: A self-worth perspective on motivation and school reform.* Cambridge: Cambridge University Press.

Covington, M.V., & Roberts, B. (1994). Self-worth and college achievement: Motivational and personality correlates. In P.R. Pintrich, D.R. Brown, & C.E. Weinstein (Eds.), *Student motivation, cognition, and learning: Essays in honor of Wilbert J. McKeachie* (pp. 157–187). Hillsdale, NJ: Erlbaum.

Crandall, V.C., Katkovsky, W., & Crandall, V.J. (1965). Children's beliefs in their own control of reinforcements in intellectual-academic achievement situations. *Child Development, 36,* 91–109.

de Charms, R. (1968). *Personal causation: The internal affective determinants of behavior.* New York: Academic Press.

Deci, E.L. (1975). *Intrinsic motivation.* New York: Plenum.

Dweck, C. (1999). *Self-theories: Their role in motivation, personality, and development.* Philadelphia, PA: Psychology Press.

Dweck, C. ,& Elliot, E.S. (1983). Achievement motivation. In P.H. Mussen (Series Ed.) & E.M. Heatherington (Vol. Ed.), *Handbook of child psychology: Vol 4. Socialization, personality, and social development* (4th ed., pp. 643–691). New York: Wiley.

Dweck, C., & Leggett, E.L. (1988). A social-cognitive approach to motivation and personality. *Psychological Review, 95,* 256–273.

Dweck, C., & Repucci, N. (1973). Learned helplessness and reinforcement responsibility in children. *Journal of Personality and Social Psychology, 25,* 109–116.

Eccles, J. (1983). Expectancies, values, and academic behaviors. In J.T. Spence (Ed.), *Achievement and achievement motives* (pp. 75–146). San Francisco: Freeman.

Eccles, J., Wigfield, A., Harold, R., & Blumenfeld, P. (1993). Age and gender differences in children's self-and task perceptions during elementary school. *Child Development, 64,* 830–347.

Eccles, J.S., Wigfield, A., & Schiefele, U. (1998). Motivation to succeed. In W. Damon (Series Ed.) & N. Eisenberg (Vol. Ed.), *Handbook of child psychology: Vol. 3. Social, emotional, and personality development* (5th ed., pp. 1017–1095). New York: Wiley.

Eisenberg, N., Martin, C.L., Fabes, R.A. (1996). Gender development and gender effects. In D.C. Berliner & R.C. Calfee (Eds.), *Handbook of educational psychology* (pp. 358–396). New York: Simon & Schuster Macmillan.

Elliot, A.J. (1997). Integrating the "classic" and "contemporary" approaches to achievement motivation: A hierarchical model of approach and avoidance achievement motivation. In M.L. Maehr & P.R. Pintrich (Eds.), *Advances in motivation and achievement* (Vol. 10, pp. 143–179). Greenwich, CT: JAI Press.

Elliot, A.J. (1999). Approach and avoidance motivation and achievement goals. *Educational Psychologist, 34,* 169–189.

Elliot, A.J., & Church, M. (1997). A hierarchical model of approach and avoidance achievement motivation. *Journal of Personality and Social Psychology, 72,* 218–232.

Elliot, A.J., & Harackiewicz, J.M. (1996). Approach and avoidance achievement goals and intrinsic motivation: A mediational analysis. *Journal of Personality and Social Psychology, 70,* 461–475.

Elliot, A.J., & McGregor, H.A. (2001). A 2 x 2 achievement goal framework. *Journal of Personality of Social Psychology, 80,* 501–519.

Epstein, J. (1983). The influence of friends on achievement and affective outcomes. In J. Epstein & N. Karweit (Eds.), *Friends in school* (pp. 177–200). New York: McGraw Hill.

Fincham, F.D., & Cain, K.M. (1986). Learned helplessness in humans: A developmental analysis. *Developmental Review, 6*, 301–333.

Findley, M., & Cooper, H. (1983). Locus of control and academic achievement: A review of the literature. *Journal of Personality and Social Psychology, 44*, 419–427.

Ford, M. (1992). *Motivating humans: Goals, emotions, and personal agency beliefs.* Newbury Park, CA: Sage Publications.

Ford, J.K., Smith, E.M., Weissbein, D.A., Gully, S.M., & Salas, E. (1998). Relationships of goal orientation, metacognitive activity, and practice strategies with learning outcomes and transfer. *Journal of Applied Psychology, 83*, 218–233.

Garcia, T., & Pintrich, P.R. (1994). Regulating motivation and cognition in the classroom: The role of self-schemas and self-regulatory strategies. In D.H. Schunk & B.J. Zimmerman (Eds.), *Self-regulation of learning and performance: Issues and educational applications* (pp. 127–153). Hillsdale, NJ: Erlbaum.

Goodenow, C. (1993). Classroom belonging among early adolescent students: Relationships to motivation and achievement. *Journal of Early Adolescence, 13*, 21–43.

Graham, S. (1994). Motivation in African Americans. *Review of Educational Research, 64*, 55–117.

Graham, S., Taylor, A.Z., Hudley, C. (1998). Exploring achievement values among ethnic minority early adolescents. *Journal of Educational Psychology, 90*, 606–620.

Harackiewicz, J.M., Barron, K.E., Carter, S.M., Lehto, A.T., & Elliot, A.J. (1997). Predictors and consequences of achievement goals in the college classroom: Maintaining interest and making the grade. *Journal of Personality & Social Psychology, 73*, 1284–1295.

Harackiewicz, J.M., Barron, K.E., & Elliot, A.J. (1998). Rethinking achievement goals: When are they adaptive for college students and why? *Educational Psychologist, 33*, 1–21.

Harackiewicz, J.M., & Sansone, C. (1991). Goals and intrinsic motivation: You can get there from here. In M.L. Maehr & P.R. Pintrich (Eds.), *Advances in motivation and achievement: Goals and self-regulation* (Vol. 7, pp. 21–49). Greenwich, CT: JAI Press.

Harter, S. (1985). Competence as a dimension of self-evaluation: Toward a comprehensive model of self-worth. In R. Leary (Ed.), *The development of the self* (pp. 95–121). New York: Academic Press.

Harter, S. (1999). *The construction of the self: A developmental perspective.* New York: The Guilford Press.

Heckhausen, J. (1999). *Developmental regulation in adulthood: Age-normative and sociostructural constraints as adaptive challenges.* New York: Cambridge University Press.

Hidi, S. (1990). Interest and its contribution as a mental resource for learning. *Review of Educational Research, 60*, 549–571.

Higgins, E.T. (1997). Beyond pleasure and pain. *American Psychologist, 52*, 1280–1300.

Kaplan, A., & Midgley, C. (1997). The effect of achievement goals: Does level of perceived academic competence make a difference? *Contemporary Educational Psychology, 22,* 415–435.

Lefcourt, H. (1976). *Locus of control: Current trends in theory research.* Hillsdale, NJ: Erlbaum.

Linnenbrink, E.A., & Pintrich, P.R. (2001). Multiple goals, multiple contexts: The dynamic interplay between personal goals and contextual goal stresses. In S. Volet & S. Jarvela (Eds.), *Motivation in learning contexts: Theoretical advances and methodological implications* (pp. 251–269). Amsterdam: Pergamon Press.

Locke, E.A., & Latham, G.P. (1990). *A theory of goal setting and task performance.* Englewood Cliffs, NJ: Prentice-Hall.

Maehr, M.L., & Midgley, C. (1991). Enhancing student motivation: A school-wide approach. *Educational Psychologist, 26,* 399–427.

Maehr, M.L., & Midgley, C. (1996). *Transforming school cultures.* Boulder, CO: Westview Press.

Malone, T., & Lepper, M. (1987). Making learning fun: A taxonomy of intrinsic motivations for learning. In R. Snow & M. Farr (Eds.), *Aptitude, learning, and instruction: Vol. 3. Cognitive and affective process analyses* (pp. 223–253). Hillsdale, NJ: Erlbaum.

McClelland, D., Atkinson, J.W., Clark, R.A., & Lowell, E.L. (1953). *The achievement motive.* New York: Appleton-Century-Crofts.

Meece, J., Parsons, J., Kaczala, C., Goff, S., & Futterman, R. (1982). Sex differences in math achievement: Toward a model of academic choice. *Psychological Bulletin, 91,* 324–348.

Middleton, M., & Midgley, C. (1997). Avoiding the demonstration of lack of ability: An underexplored aspect of goal theory. *Journal of Educational Psychology, 89,* 710–718.

Midgley, C., Arunkumar, R., & Urdan, T. (1996). "If I don't do well tomorrow, there's a reason": Predictors of adolescents' use of academic self-handicapping strategies. *Journal of Educational Psychology, 88,* 423–434.

Midgley, C., Kaplan, A., & Middleton, M. (2001). Performance-approach goals: Good for what, for whom, under what circumstances, and at what cost? *Journal of Educational Psychology, 93,* 77–86.

Midgley, C., Kaplan, A., Middleton, M., Maehr, M. L., Urdan, T., Anderman, L. H., Anderman, E., & Roeser, R. (1998). The development and validation of scales assessing students' achievement goal orientations. *Contemporary Educational Psychology, 23,* 113–131.

Midgley, C., Maehr, M., Hicks, L., Roeser, R., Urdan, T., Anderman, E., Kaplan, A., Arunkumar, R., & Middleton, M. (1997). *Patterns of adaptive learning survey.* Ann Arbor: The University of Michigan.

Newman, R. (1998). Students' help-seeking during problem solving: Influences of personal and contextual goals. *Journal of Educational Psychology, 90,* 644–658.

Newman, R. (2000). Social influences on the development of children's adaptive help seeking: The role of parents, teachers, and peers. *Developmental Review, 20,* 350–404.

Nicholls, J. (1984). Achievement motivation: Conceptions of ability, subjective experience, task choice, and performance. *Psychological Review, 91,* 328–346.

Nicholls, J. (1989). *The competitive ethos and democratic education.* Cambridge, MA: Harvard University Press.

Nicholls, J. (1990). What is ability and why are we mindful of it? A developmental perspective. In R. Sternberg & J. Kolligian (Eds.), *Competence considered* (pp. 11–40). New Haven, CT: Yale University Press.

Nicholls, J., & Miller, A. (1983). The differentiation of the concepts of difficulty and ability. *Child Development, 54,* 951–959.

Nicholls, J., & Miller, A. (1984a). Development and its discontents: The differentiation of the concept of ability. In J. Nicholls (Ed.), *Advances in motivation and achievement: The development of achievement motivation* (Vol. 3, pp. 185–218). Greenwich, CT: JAI Press.

Nicholls, J., & Miller, A. (1984b). Reasoning about the ability of self and others: A developmental study. *Child Development, 55,* 1990–1999.

Nicholls, J., & Miller, A. (1985). Differentiation of the concepts of luck and skill. *Developmental Psychology, 21,* 76–82.

Osterman, K. (2000). Students' need for belonging in the school community. *Review of Educational Research, 70,* 323–367.

Pajares, F. (1997). Current directions in self-efficacy research. In M. Maehr & P.R. Pintrich (Eds.), *Advances in motivation and achievement* (Vol. 10, pp. 1–49). Greenwich, CT: JAI Press.

Pajares, F., & Graham, L. (1999). Self-efficacy, motivation constructs, and mathematics performance of entering middle school students. *Contemporary Educational Psychology, 24,* 124–139.

Pajares, F., & Johnson, M. J. (1996). Self-efficacy beliefs and the writing performance of entering high school students. *Psychology in the Schools, 33,* 163–175.

Pajares, F., Miller, M.D., & Johnson, M.J. (1999). Gender differences in writing self-beliefs of elementary school students. *Journal of Educational Psychology, 91,* 50–61.

Pajares, F., & Valiante, G. (1999). Grade level and gender differences in the writing self-beliefs of middle school students. *Contemporary Educational Psychology, 24,* 390–405.

Pascarella, E., & Terenzini, P. (1991). *How college affects students.* San Francisco: Jossey-Bass.

Perry, R. (1991). Perceived control in college students: Implications for instruction in higher education. In J. Smart (Ed.), *Higher education: Handbook of theory and research* (Vol. 7, pp. 1–56). New York: Agathon Press.

Perry, R., & Dickens, W. (1988). Perceived control and instruction in the college classroom: Some implications for student achievement. *Research in Higher Education, 27,* 291–310.

Perry, R., & Magnusson, J-L. (1989). Causal attributions and perceived performance: Consequences for college students' achievement and perceived control in different instructional conditions. *Journal of Educational Psychology, 81,* 164–172.

Perry, P., & Penner, K. (1990). Enhancing academic achievement in college students through attributional retraining and instruction. *Journal of Educational Psychology, 82,* 262–271.

Peterson, C., Maier, S., & Seligman, M. (1993). *Learned helplessness: A theory for the age of personal control.* New York: Oxford University Press.

Pintrich, P.R. (1989). The dynamic interplay of student motivation and cognition in the college classroom. In C. Ames & M.L. Maehr (Eds.), *Advances in motivation and achievement: Motivation enhancing environments* (Vol. 6, pp. 117–160). Greenwich, CT: JAI Press.

Pintrich, P.R. (1999). The role of motivation in promoting and sustaining self-regulated learning. *International Journal of Educational Research, 31,* 459–470.

Pintrich, P.R. (2000a). An achievement goal theory perspective on issues in motivation terminology, theory, and research. *Contemporary Educational Psychology.*

Pintrich, P.R. (2000b). Multiple goals, multiple pathways: The role of goal orientation in learning and achievement. *Journal of Educational Psychology, 92,* 544–555.

Pintrich, P.R. (2000c). The role of goal orientation in self-regulated learning. In M. Boekaerts, P.R. Pintrich, & M. Zeidner (Eds.), *Handbook of self-regulation* (pp. 451–502). San Diego, CA: Academic Press.

Pintrich, P.R., & Schunk, D.H. (1996). *Motivation in education: Theory, research and applications.* Englewood Cliffs, NJ: Prentice-Hall Merrill.

Pintrich, P.R., & Zusho, A. (In press). The development of academic self-regulation: The role of cognitive and motivational factors. In A. Wigfield & J. Eccles (Eds.), *The development of achievement motivation.* San Diego, CA: Academic Press.

Renninger, K.A., Hidi, S., & Krapp, A. (1992). *The role of interest in learning and development.* Hillsdale, NJ: Erlbaum

Rotter, J.B. (1966). Generalized expectancies for internal versus external control reinforcement. *Psychological Monographs, 80,* 1–28.

Ryan, A.M. (2000). Peer groups as a context for the socialization of adolescents' motivation, engagement, and achievement in school. *Educational Psychologist, 35,* 101–111.

Schiefele, U. (1991). Interest, learning, and motivation. *Educational Psychologist, 26,* 299–323.

Schunk, D.H. (1991). Self-efficacy and academic motivation. *Educational Psychologist, 26,* 207–231.

Shah, J., & Kruglanski, A. (2000). Aspects of goal networks: Implications for self-regulation. In M. Boekaerts, P.R. Pintrich, & M. Zeidner (Eds.), *Handbook of self-regulation* (pp. 85–110). San Diego, CA: Academic Press.

Shell, D., Murphy, C., & Bruning, R. (1989). Self-efficacy and outcome expectancy mechanisms in reading and writing achievement. *Journal of Educational Psychology, 81,* 91–100.

Skaalvik, E.M. (1997). Self-enhancing and self-defeating ego orientation: Relation with task and avoidance orientation, achievement, self-perceptions, and anxiety. *Journal of Educational Psychology, 89,* 71–81.

Skaalvik, E.M., Valas, H., & Sletta, O. (1994). Task involvement and ego involvement: Relations with academic achievement, academic self-concept and self-esteem. *Scandinavian Journal of Educational Research, 38,* 231–243.

Skinner, E.A. (1995). *Perceived control, motivation, and coping.* Thousand Oaks, CA: Sage.

Skinner, E.A. (1996). A guide to constructs of control. *Journal of Personality and Social Psychology, 71,* 549–570.

Skinner, E., & Connell, J. (1986). Control understanding: Suggestions for a developmental framework. In M. Baltes & P. Baltes (Eds.), *The psychology of control and aging* (pp. 35–69). Hillsdale, NJ: Lawrence Erlbaum Associates.

Steinberg, L., Dornbusch, S.M., & Brown, B.B. (1992). Ethnic differences in adolescent achievement: An ecological perspective. *American Psychologist, 47*(6), 723–729.

Stipek, D., & Weisz, J. (1981). Perceived personal control and academic achievement. *Review of Educational Research, 51,* 101–137.

Sue, S., & Okazaki, S. (1990). Asian-American educational achievements: A phenomenon in search of an explanation. *American Psychologist, 45,* 913–920.

Thorkildsen, T.A., & Nicholls, J.G. (1998). Fifth graders' achievement orientations and beliefs: Individual and classroom differences. *Journal of Educational Psychology, 90,* 179–201.

Urdan, T. (1997). Achievement goal theory: Past results, future directions. In M.L. Maehr & Pintrich, P.R. (Eds.), *Advances in motivation and achievement* (Vol. 10, pp. 99–141). Greenwich, CT: JAI Press.

Weiner, B. (1986). *An attributional theory of motivation and emotion.* New York: Springer-Verlag.

Weisz, J. (1984). Contingency judgments and achievement behavior: Deciding what is controllable and when to try. In J. Nicholls (Ed.), *Advances in motivation and achievement: The development of achievement motivation* (Vol. 3, pp. 107–136). Greenwich, CT: JAI Press

Wlodkowski, R. (1988). *Enhancing adult motivation to learn.* San Francisco: Jossey-Bass.

Wigfield, A., & Eccles, J. (1992). The development of achievement task values: A theoretical analysis. *Developmental Review, 12,* 265–310.

Wolters, C., Yu, S., & Pintrich, P.R. (1996). The relation between goal orientation and students' motivational beliefs and self-regulated learning. *Learning and Individual Differences, 8,* 211–238.

Zimmerman, B.J., & Kitsantas, A. (1997). Developmental phases in self-regulation: Shifting from process to outcome goals. *Journal of Educational Psychology, 89,* 29–36.

Zimmerman, B.J., & Kitsantas, A. (1999). Acquiring writing revision skill: Shifting from process to outcome self-regulatory goals. *Journal of Educational Psychology, 91,* 241–250.

Zukier, H. (1986). The paradigmatic and narrative modes in goal-guided inference. In R. Sorrentino & E.T. Higgins (Eds.), *Handbook of motivation and cognition: Foundations of social behavior* (pp. 465–502). New York: Guilford Press.

Zusho, A., & Pintrich, P.R. (2000). *Fear of not learning? The role of mastery avoidance goals in Asian-American and European-American college students.* Paper presented at the American Educational Research Association, New Orleans.

CHAPTER 7

The Effects and Implications of High-Stakes Achievement Tests for Adolescents

Marguerite Clarke, Lisa Abrams, and George Madaus

INTRODUCTION

A hearty perennial in the hothouse of educational change in the United States is test-driven reform. Policymakers mandate a test to gather information about student and school attainment and then use the information to hold students, educators, schools, or school systems accountable. Adolescents often bear the brunt of the high stakes associated with many of these testing programs. For example, graduation from high school is tied to passing a test in 18 states. Further, many adolescents must take the SAT (formerly known as the Scholastic Assessment Test) or the ACT (formerly known as the American College Test) as part of the college admissions process. Likewise, for most of this century, European adolescents have had to sit for exams to certify successful completion of secondary school, for admission to third-level education, or to qualify for jobs in the public and private sectors (Madaus & Kellaghan, 1991).

We know a lot about the effects of these high-stakes tests on adolescents. We have a wealth of evidence from two centuries of educational testing in Europe, the United States, and elsewhere. This knowledge comes from the testimony of teachers, administrators, and students, and from investigative panels and commissions; it comes from surveys and interviews of educators and students; it is embedded in a large corpus of popular literature—fiction, biography, poetry, drama—which describes how tests and examinations are experienced by teachers and students; and finally it can be found in empirical studies of the effects of testing.

In this chapter we begin with a discussion of arguments for and against high-stakes testing. We then expand on those arguments by examining research on the effects of these testing programs on adolescents. First, we explore research on the relationship between high-stakes testing and student motivation. We ask, "Who do these tests motivate?" and "What do they motivate them to do?" Next, we discuss five lines of evidence on the relationship between high-stakes testing and persistence/dropout rates among adolescents. Following this, we present data on the achievement gap on high-stakes tests and related access and equity issues for different student groups. Finally, we discuss how these testing programs might be better crafted to maximize the value and minimize the harm to adolescents.

ARGUMENTS FOR AND AGAINST HIGH-STAKES TESTING

Since 1983, most state-level education reform efforts have consisted of three components: educational goals or standards; a test designed to measure the degree to which these goals have been achieved; and a high-stakes piece (in the form of consequences attached to the test results) intended to influence the behavior of teachers and students. As of 2001, 49 states have standards-based testing programs. Of these, 39 have a high-stakes component, with rewards or sanctions imposed directly (e.g., promotion and graduation decisions) or indirectly (e.g., school accreditation) on students.

Proponents believe that these high-stakes testing programs are the driving force behind educational reform and are essential to promoting quality teaching and encouraging student achievement. Alternatively, opponents suggest that the rewards and sanctions tied to test performance only serve to undermine classroom instruction and student learning. The debate plays out daily in newspapers and on television as well as in the business, education, legal, political, and research communities. While opinions abound, they are generally focused on issues of student motivation and persistence, curriculum and instruction, and student learning or achievement. We discuss each issue briefly here, before looking at research on the effects of high-stakes testing on each.

Motivation and Persistence

Proponents of high-stakes testing programs suggest that punishments or rewards are necessary because they motivate teachers and students to work harder. Students exert more effort on the state-mandated test because their performance will determine if they are promoted to the next grade level, graduate from high school, or are suitable for employment. Teachers work harder so that they will receive a cash reward or so that their school will not lose its accreditation. In this way, the external motivation provided by the high-stakes attachment uses teachers' and students' self interest as a way to improve the overall educational system (Madaus, 1991).

Opponents argue that external motivators, such as high-stakes tests, can actually negatively motivate or de-motivate some students. As will be discussed later, this is because the motivating effect of the consequences associated with test performance is linked to a student's perceptions of his/her ability, the difficulty of the test, and the likelihood that he or she will succeed (Kellaghan, Madaus, & Raczek, 1996). Consequently, because of such individual variability, the motivating power of the consequences will not be the same for all students. Opponents also contend that the labeling associated with test results (e.g., "failing," or "needs improvement") can lower students' self esteem in addition to increasing their stress levels and feelings of inadequacy. An extension of this argument is that students who view these tests as insurmountable barriers may not only become de-motivated, but also give up and drop out of school. We discuss some compelling research evidence below that suggests a strong relationship between high-stakes tests and increased student dropout rates.

Curriculum and Instruction

The curriculum standards or frameworks at the core of most state education reform packages are intended to clearly define content and performance standards in various subject areas. Proponents claim that these standards establish a needed consensus on the knowledge and skills to be taught in a particular subject at a particular grade level since they often become the focus of classroom instruction. This is particularly the case if there is a high-stakes assessment based on the frameworks.

However, opponents note that in a high-stakes context, and when teachers do not have enough time to teach everything listed in the frameworks, the test effectively becomes the curriculum and instruction becomes test preparation. In this regard, Mehrens (1998) notes that "if stakes are high enough . . . curriculum and instruction are likely to change to reflect more closely the content sampled by the test." As a result, classroom activities may focus on rote memorization of isolated facts and lower-level thinking skills that are often the focus of state exams. In addition, teachers may change the format of their own classroom assessments to match that of the state test. This reality can directly conflict with the higher-level thinking goals embodied in the state curriculum standards or frameworks. Some proponents counter that this close alignment of teacher instruction and assessments with the state test is not necessarily bad and that it is possible to develop tests that tap into higher-level thinking skills, thereby reducing the conflict between test preparation and learning. In a later section, we discuss some of these issues in terms of what high-stakes tests motivate students (and teachers) to do.

Student Learning and Achievement

Proponents of high-stakes testing programs contend they are an objective, efficient, and equitable way to hold all students to the same standards and to measure whether teachers and schools are effectively utilizing the money and other resources made available to them. In addition, proponents contend that test results provide valuable information that enables educators to target the strengths and weaknesses of individual students and to plan instruction accordingly. The end result is a learning environment that narrows the performance gap between various student groups as well as types of school districts. Opponents argue the exact opposite, claiming that these testing programs, even when preceded or accompanied by an injection of money and resources, cannot narrow the achievement gap in the short amount of time given by impatient policymakers, and cannot narrow it enough to prevent the bulk of the negative consequences attached to doing poorly on the test from falling on minority, limited-English-proficiency, and low-socioeconomic-status students. In a later section, we discuss the minority achievement gap and its equity implications for two types of high-stakes tests—state-mandated graduation tests and tests required for college admissions.

Another argument made by proponents, particularly those in the business community, is that high-stakes testing will improve the basic job skills of high school graduates, enabling the United States to maintain its economic competitiveness in the world marketplace (Lehigh, 2001). The view that United States students are falling behind their international counterparts is based primarily on the results of international studies such as The Third International Mathematics and Science Study (TIMSS) and TIMSS-Repeat. TIMSS results released in 1996 ranked United States eighth grade students 12th in science and 18th in mathematics, lagging behind students in many European and industrialized Asian countries (Beaton et al.,

1996a,b). The findings of the repeat study showed a similar picture—United States eighth grade students ranked 18th in science and 19th in mathematics (Martin et al., 2000; Mullis et al., 2000). Opponents argue that these international comparisons should be interpreted with great care due to curricular and contextual differences among countries, and that the ranked nature of the data can obscure the fact that there may be no significant differences between the scores of neighboring countries (Bracey, 2000). In addition, opponents have made the point that the test score-productivity link is weak at best (Lehigh, 2001).

Clearly, there is a great divide with respect to opinions on the effects of high-stakes testing programs. These testing programs, along with the test scores that result, are powerful symbols for some of the extent to which teachers and students have applied themselves, and for others of the inequities of an educational system that punishes already-disadvantaged students and schools. In the next few sections, we evaluate the arguments made for and against these testing programs in light of what the research tells us.

MOTIVATION[1]

A growing body of research supports the view that motivation is an important determinant of school learning and achievement (Lens, 1994). It seems particularly crucial during the period of adolescence, at which time one finds evidence of students becoming increasingly involved in nonacademic activities at the expense of academic work (Anderman & Maehr, 1994). Though one may accept that motivation (and other non-cognitive factors) are important determinants of achievement, it is quite another matter to say that the introduction of a system or systems of high-stakes tests would solve the motivational problems of students. At the very least, a careful analysis of relevant issues and a consideration of the findings of empirical evidence are required before reaching such a conclusion.

In their review of the literature on motivation and student learning Kellaghan, Madaus, and Raczek (1996) conclude that high-stakes testing proposals fail to address the psychological complexity of motivation and the many personal and situational factors that can determine whether a student will be motivated or not. They conclude that high-stakes tests are likely to have motivating power, for at least some students, but go on to raise the question: What do such tests motivate them to do? Are they likely to promote high-quality learning, conceptual understanding, a valuing of education, and students' confidence in their own capacities and attributes? Or are they likely to have less desirable effects, indeed ones that might suggest that a high-stakes testing system may actually inhibit rather than support broader educational reform efforts?

Proposals to use tests as a motivating device often draw on concepts from motivation research. For example, if one interprets state content and performance standards as student goals, then this reform can be said to fall broadly within the ambit of goal theory (Locke & Latham, 1990). So too do the ideas that standards should be high and that they should be clear to individuals, and the idea that individuals should see the connection between endeavor and rewards (all found in the reform statements).

However, while research findings support the view that goal setting fosters achievement, the relevance of the findings to high-stakes tests cannot be assumed. It may be that the conditions that energized and regulated behavior in the research studies differ from those that operate in high-stakes testing contexts (Fisher, 1992). In particular, some of the conditions under which high-stakes tests operate would seem antagonistic to the development of motivation to succeed in all students. In the reform arguments, it is expected that students will exert effort once they recognize that they will be entitled to social, educational, or vocational rewards if they are successful on the test. That is, it is assumed that students will see a clear connection between doing well and attaining the reward of grade promotion, a diploma, a job, or entry to college. However, this chain of events may not work for a number of reasons. For example, students may perceive that there are not enough jobs or higher education opportunities for all, a situation that exists in most parts of the world today, where attaining certificates or credentials through examinations no longer guarantees employment or admission to third-level education (Edwards & Whitty, 1994; Hargreaves, 1989; Kariyawasam, 1993; Little, 1993). Indeed, high-stakes tests function in a way that ensures that some students will not be successful. Only some candidates get high grades and only some gain admission to further education. Many students will judge on the basis of their past record of achievement that they are not going to be the successful ones. This can be an alienating, not a motivating, experience (Broadfoot, 1979; Hannan & Shorthall, 1991). Some students may respond by indifference (Hargreaves, 1989), others by disappointment and anger (Edwards & Whitty, 1994), and in extreme cases, by discord and open rebellion (Kariyawasam, 1993; Little, 1993).

Where high-stakes testing proposals fall down most is in their failure to take account of the psychological processes that are involved in adaptive achievement behavior or to allow for the fact that the responses of some students may be maladaptive in terms of the long-term goal of improving achievement. While high-stakes tests are envisaged for all students in reform proposals, the research on motivation tells us that individuals' acceptance of and pursuance of goals can be affected by a variety of factors such as perceived competence, the perceived difficulty of a task, and the likelihood of their success. It may be that intention to try is a function of a cost-benefit analysis: if benefits are held constant, intention will increase with task difficulty up to the point at which the individual decides the potential benefit is not worth the effort (Brehm & Self, 1989).

A consequence of differences in students' perceptions of their personal characteristics is that the motivating power of a test will not be uniform for all students (Dweck, 1986; Dweck & Leggett, 1988). Since students differ in their views of their academic efficacy, they will also differ in their personal goal-setting. We should not be surprised then if students often do not adopt the high academic aspirations that are set for them. For example, how likely is it that a high-stakes test will motivate and change the behavior of students who are defined as helpless, who are low in confidence, or who believe their ability is low and non-malleable? The role of students' perceptions of their ability in arousing motivation, as described in attribution theory, would lead one to expect considerable variation among individuals in their reactions to the incentives posed by an external reward system, such as that provided by high-stakes tests. One would, for example, expect students who believe that they possess high ability, which they consider to be stable and non-controllable, to respond most positively to external incentives. Less positive responses would be expected from students who have low ability, coupled with a belief in ability as stable and non-controllable. Considerations such as these lead to the conclusion that efforts to foster academic achievement will need to do more than simply set demanding standards. There also will be a need to restructure the academic experiences of students in a way that will enhance their sense of academic efficacy (Zimmerman, Bandura, & Martinez-Pons, 1992), a much more difficult task than mandating tougher standards and a high-stakes test that is referenced to them.

Since environmental constraints affect subsequent intrinsic interest (Pittman & Heller, 1987), it is reasonable to expect that the social and cultural context in which students live would affect their motivation to pursue the goals set by high-stakes tests. Thus, in some social contexts, even if goals are accepted, we would expect students' willingness to make the necessary effort to be affected by local mores and norms. That such mores and norms vary across American classrooms is clear from many studies (see Jackson, 1990; Kidder, 1989; Kozol, 1991; Sizer, 1992). For one thing, achievement levels are much lower in some schools and classes than in others. We know that seeing others succeed can convey to students that they too are capable and can motivate them to attempt a task while the observance of failures may lower students' sense of efficacy and dissuade them from working on a task (Schunk, 1991). Further, the effort involved in half an hour's homework by some students may be exceptionally high in comparison to their peers in other communities, but may still be inadequate for success on a test (Dornbusch & Scott, 1975). The necessary effort may also be influenced by perceptions of whether students believe that school resources and teachers are adequate to help them attain the goal of examination success (Katzell & Thompson, 1990).

These considerations lead to the conclusion that high-stakes tests are likely to be perceived by some students as obstacles that they cannot overcome rather than as incentives to work harder. What consequences, one might ask, would be expected if students are not motivated by high-stakes tests? Would this mean that the tests would have no impact and that students would go on more or less as before? The answer would seem to be no. High-stakes tests change the culture of schools and, for students who are not likely to do well on the tests, there may be serious negative effects. For example, students who perceive high-stakes tests as insurmountable obstacles may react by avoiding achievement situations (e.g., by quitting school) in order to defend their self-esteem. We will examine this persistence/dropout issue in more detail in a subsequent section.

A survey of students in grades 2 through 11 in four large American states found that the "negative impact [of testing] on students can be summarized in three general trends: growing disillusionment about tests, decreasing motivation to give genuine effort [on tests], and increasing use of inappropriate strategies [to pass the test]" (Paris, Lawton, & Roth, 1991, p. 14). In a second survey in another state, the same investigators found that:

> the results of standardized tests become increasingly less valid for low achievers, exactly the group who are most at risk for educational problems and who most need diagnostic testing. Their scores may be contaminated by inappropriate motivation and learning strategies that further debilitate their performance and affirm a self-fulfilling prophecy of low scores. Apparently in their efforts to decrease personal anxiety and increase the protection of their own self-esteem, they relinquish effort and appropriate strategies on standardized achievement tests. (p. 16)

In extreme cases, in efforts to obtain high scores, students (and sometimes teachers and examination officials) resort to cheating, through copying, impersonation, or altering scores after the test has been taken (see Haney, 1993; Punjab. Commission for Evaluation of Examination System and Eradication of Malpractices, 1992, p. 61).

Appraisal of actual test questions and test performance indicates that for the most part students are asked to recall or recognize factual knowledge rather than synthesize material or apply principles to new situations. To prepare for this, students in test-dominated systems spend much of their time in school in rote memorization, routine drilling, and the accumulation of factual knowledge rather than in general reasoning and problem-solving activities (Brooke & Oxenham, 1984; Cambridge Educational Consultants, 1988; Little, 1982; Madaus & Macnamara, 1970). While reformers may argue that new performance assessments—"tests worth teaching to"—will overcome the negative aspects of the older multiple-choice standardized tests, we are aware of no evidence that would support the view that changing the format of assessments from a selection to a performance or supply mode would alter students' negative reaction to the high stakes associated with performance.

Finally, assumptions that the rewards and punishments attached to high-stakes tests will motivate students to learn fail to appreciate that breakdowns occur in volition in everyday life when we have difficulty in doing something that we want to do or not doing something that we do not want to do (Pervin, 1992). This fact of classroom life is captured in Kidder's (1989) *Among School Children.* Chris, the teacher, ruminating over whom in her fifth grade class would flunk the Basic Skills Tests, concluded that:

> Jimmy probably would if he took the test on a Monday, when he was always exhausted. She imagined Jimmy yawning and stretching right in front of her, just like a baby getting ready for a nap. That was one of the problems with tests. They tested things more basic than skills, and one of them was a good night's sleep. (p. 205)

Regarding another student, Chris observed that "Robert hadn't even bothered to read half of the questions; in Robert's case a standardized test merely measured the child's willingness to take a standardized test" (p. 205). A question for the reformers is: How will a high-stakes test measuring higher-order thinking skills change Robert's attitudes and behaviors?

In summary, Kellaghan et al. (1996) concluded that high-stakes testing proposals do not take account of the complexity of the intentionality of school learning. Second, they fail to recognize the personal and situational factors that may affect the fostering of motivation. Third, they fail to recognize the variety of types of motivation that may exist and that reasons for learning may be many and varied.

The heavy reliance on the use of extrinsic rewards to motivate students is particularly problematic if one's aim is to promote high levels of achievement and an interest in, and commitment to, learning (Deci & Ryan, 1985). For a variety of reasons, not least because adolescents who are intrinsically motivated and pursue knowledge for its own sake have higher academic achievement scores (Henderson & Dweck, 1990), the development of intrinsic motivation is to be preferred to the development of extrinsic motivation. It may be, of course, that the form of extrinsic motivation generated by high-stakes tests might in time lead some students to achieve higher degrees of self-determination or even intrinsic motivation. The odds would seem to be against that, however, since summative high-stakes tests do not convey information about competence during the course of an individual's studies, a condition that, if present, would be likely to enhance intrinsic motivation (Pittman & Heller, 1987). Further, high-stakes tests are likely to be perceived as controlling; that is, as indicating that behavior is being influenced or shaped by a reward, a condition that is associated with a decrease in intrinsic motivation (Pittman & Heller, 1987). While, by definition, the use of high-stakes tests to motivate students involves extrinsic rather than intrinsic motivation for learning, it is not possible in our present state of knowledge to say what conditions surrounding the administration of these tests might lead to the development of differing degrees of autonomy in the motivation that is fostered. The form of the tests and the stakes that are attached to performance might affect this process (Little, 1994).

Of perhaps even greater importance than the short-term effects of motivation on students' behavior are the long-term effects. However, we know practically nothing about what the long-term effects of an extrinsic motivation system on students' future work performance might be. On the basis of a rare study that attempted to link assessment procedures to after-school life, Little and Singh (1992) concluded that if individuals are motivated to learn at school through task-interest rather than to pass tests, they are more likely to be motivated by a desire to innovate at work. Until more evidence is available on these topics we have to accept the possibility that reforms in which student behavior is primarily a function of external regulation will have serious immediate and long-term disadvantages.

PERSISTENCE/DROPOUT RATES

An extension of the motivation argument is that students who become engaged in learning will be encouraged to persist in school as they focus on the goal of being promoted to the next grade-level, graduating from high school, or getting into college. Thus, dropout rates will drop and graduation rates will increase. But the evidence does not necessarily support this conjecture. It can even suggest the opposite. For example, Fine (1991) in her study of dropouts found a persistent belief in credentials, the value of a high-school diploma, and the pursuit of education as a prerequisite to success. But she also found that there "lingers too a more subtle cynicism about the likelihood of success" (p. 107). This cynicism is rooted in the belief of some students that educational credentials do not necessarily produce economic success. Fine notes that more than one of her interviewees observed that "the richest man in my neighborhood, the one with the fanciest car, he ain't got but an eight-grade education" (p. 107).

In a recent National Board on Educational Testing and Public Policy publication, we examine five lines of evidence on the relationship between high-stakes testing and dropout rates for adolescents (Clarke, Haney, & Madaus, 2000). Our conclusion is that high-stakes testing programs are linked to decreased rates of high school completion. The evidence is mainly correlational, but suggestive enough to warrant further research to clarify the role of high-stakes testing in decisions to drop out of school. We present the five lines of evidence here: The first two pieces are based on national data, the others focus on data for Florida and Texas.

Our first intriguing piece of evidence comes from the minimum competency testing era. A study of the ten states with the highest and the ten states with the lowest 1986 dropout rates found a strong link between attrition or dropout rates and the use of high-stakes minimum competency testing programs (Kreitzer, Madaus, & Haney, 1989). There was no minimum competency testing in half of the ten states with the lowest dropout rates. The other five had minimum competency testing programs that involved rather low stakes: four used the tests to decide about remediation; only one used them for accountability. Furthermore, in three of the latter five states, local, not state, education agencies set the standards. The states with the highest dropout rates had minimum competency testing programs with standards set at least in part by the state. Nine of the ten used the tests in decisions about high school graduation; four used them in decisions about promotion.

The study authors note that these data do not necessarily mean that high-stakes minimum competency testing programs increase dropout rates. The states with the highest dropout rates differed in obvious ways from those with the lowest. The latter were largely western and midwestern, with proportionately fewer minority and poor students. The authors conclude that high dropout rates may be symptoms of the educational system's failure that spurred legislation of minimum competency testing programs in the first place, or that minimum competency testing may have contributed in some way to the dropout problem. In any case, crude as these comparisons may be, they underline the need to explore further how high-stakes testing and dropping out are related.

A second piece of evidence, again correlational, comes from a study of the relationship between minimum competency testing in eighth grade and early high school dropout patterns (Reardon, 1996). Data from the 1988 and 1990 National Educational Longitudinal Surveys were examined to determine whether students who had to pass one or more minimum competency tests in eighth grade were more likely to have dropped out of school by tenth grade than students who did not. Results show that in schools with proportionately more students of low socioeconomic status that used high-stakes minimum competency tests, early dropout rates—between the eighth and tenth grade—were 4 to 6 percentage points higher than in schools that were similar but for the high-stakes test requirement. While there may be many reasons for this link (e.g., the higher dropout rates may be a symptom of other problems in these schools such as low student morale or lack of support programs), the data still suggest that more attention should be paid to identifying the possible differential impact of high-stakes testing policies on students from different socioeconomic groups.

A third piece of evidence suggests a more complex relationship between high-stakes testing and dropout rates (Griffin & Heidorn, 1996). In this study, based on records for grades 10, 11, and 12 in Florida, researchers sought to control for other factors associated with dropping out of high school, such as gender, grade point average, English language proficiency, and whether students were enrolled in dropout-prevention programs. Results show that students who performed poorly on Florida's high school graduation test were more likely to leave school, but that this relationship was affected by students' grades. For students with lower grades, there was no apparent relationship between failing the graduation test and the probability of dropping out. Only for students with moderately good grades (in the range of 1.5 to 2.5 on a 4-point scale) was failure on the test associated with a significant increase in likelihood of dropping out of school. Moreover, this study found that after controlling for grades, failing on the high-stakes test did not increase the likelihood of minority students' dropping out of high school any more than it did that of non-minority students.

A fourth line of evidence concerns the evolution of high-stakes testing in Texas and patterns of high school completion in that state over the last twenty years. Texas has had a statewide high school graduation test since the mid-1980s—first the Texas Educational Assessment of Minimum Skills (TEAMS) and then the Texas Assessment of Academic Skills (TAAS). The TAAS measures the Texas statewide curriculum in reading, writing, and mathematics at various grades between 3 through 8; at grade 10 students take the exit-level tests. Since 1991, a high school diploma requires satisfactory performance on the TAAS exit tests. Research findings suggest that because of this requirement some 40,000 of Texas's 1993 sophomores dropped out of school (Fassold, 1996). The dropout rates for black, Hispanic, and white students were about 25, 23, and 13 percent respectively. In addition, it was found that the average black or Hispanic student was three times more likely to drop out than the average white student, even controlling for socioeconomic status, academic track, language program participation, and school quality.

While these data concern just one cohort of Texas high school students, they fit well with Texas enrollment patterns over a 20-year period observed by our colleague, Walt Haney (Haney, 2000). Haney found that the ratio of high school graduates in a particular year to the number of ninth graders three years earlier declined only slightly between the late 1970s and 1991. For example, between 1978 and 1985–86, the ratio of high school graduates to grade 9 students three years earlier was in the range of 0.72 to 0.78 for white students and between 0.57 and 0.64 for black and Hispanic students. Between 1985–86 (the year the TEAMS graduation test was first administered) and 1989–90 these ratios fell very slightly for all ethnic groups. In other words, high school graduation testing in Texas in 1985 did not dramatically impede the progress of students from grade 9 to high school graduation. However, as Figure 1 shows, in 1990–91 (the year the new, more difficult TAAS high school graduation test was implemented), the ratios for all three groups evidenced the most precipitous drops in the entire 20 years and were about 50 percent greater for black and Hispanic than for white students. From full implementation of the TAAS as a requirement for high school graduation in 1992–93 until 1997–98, the ratio of high school graduates to grade 9 students three years earlier was just at or below 0.50 for black and Hispanic students, while it rebounded to around 0.70 for white students.

We discuss the Texas data in more detail below, but these patterns suggest that high school graduation testing in Texas affected the rates of high school completion differently in the 1990s than in the 1980s and that this impact was more severe for minority students. The fact that the less difficult TEAMS test did not dramatically affect completion rates seems at odds with the first piece of evidence presented. That evidence suggested that

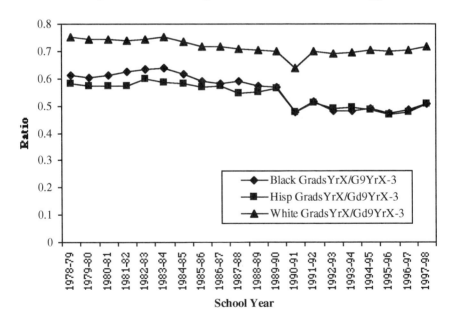

Figure 1.   Ratio of Texas high school graduates to grade 9 enrollment 3 years earlier, 1978–79 to 1997–98, by ethnic group.
Source: Haney, W. (2000). The myth of the Texas miracle in education. *Education Policy Analysis Archives, 8*(41). Available at http://epaa.asu.edu/epaa/v8n41

even tests of minimum competency are associated with higher dropout rates when used for high-stakes decision making. However, that study did not focus specifically on the effects of such tests when used as a graduation requirement (as is the case here).

A fifth line of evidence comes from research on the relationship between grade retention, being overage for grade, and dropout rates. Research on the effects of grade retention has generally concluded that, at least beyond the early elementary grades, its harms outweigh its purported benefits (Heubert & Hauser, 1999; Shepard & Smith, 1990). In particular, being overage for grade as a result of being held back eats away at students' sense of academic worth. Overage students are twice as likely as on-grade students to be retained in grade again (Texas Education Agency, 1996). In addition, many of them ultimately become disengaged and drop out (Alexander, Entwhistle, & Danber, 1994). In fact, being overage for grade predicts dropping out better than do below-average test scores (Texas Education Agency, 1996).

These findings are worth keeping in mind when looking at grade enrollment patterns in Texas. Figure 2 shows that the ratio of Texas ninth graders to eighth graders one year earlier increased steadily since the early 1980s for black and Hispanic students, while remaining relatively constant for white students. By the late 1990s, there were close to 30 percent more black and Hispanic students in grade 9 than in grade 8 the year before. While these progression ratios show a fairly consistent linear trend over the last two decades (one that does not appear to be dramatically affected by TEAMS or TAAS), they become more suggestive when combined with the information in Figure 3. Figure 3 shows grade progression ratios for grades 1 through 12 for black, white, and Hispanic students between 1996 and 1998. The dramatic upswing in the grade 9 to grade 8 ratio for black and Hispanic students and the dramatic downswing in the grade 10 to grade 9 ratio for the same groups of students suggest that many of these students were being held back in grade 9—the grade preceding the first administration of the TAAS graduation test. Given what we know about the effects of grade retention and of being overage for grade, it would be worth watching closely how such retention policies—informal or otherwise—affect rates of high school completion, and how they interact with graduation test requirements.

The Texas data also shed interesting light on the seemingly anomalous Florida study mentioned earlier. This was the study that suggested, contrary to most other literature, that failing that state's high school graduation test did not increase the likelihood of minority students' dropping out of high school. But recall that this study examined the records of only grade 10, 11, and 12 students. It turns out that Florida, like Texas, has unusually high rates of retention in grade 9 (Heubert & Hauser, 1999). It

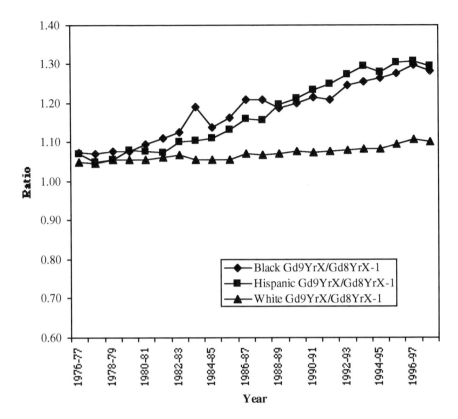

Figure 2.   Grade 8 to 9 progression ratio, 1976–77 to 1997–98, by ethnic group.
Source: Haney, W. (2000). The myth of the Texas miracle in education. *Education Policy Analysis Archives, 8*(41). Available at http://epaa.asu.edu/epaa/v8n41

also turns out that Florida, like Texas, has one of the lowest rates of high school completion—only about 80 percent—among the states (National Center for Education Statistics, 1997). However, it should be kept in mind that the low rates of high school completion in these states are not due simply to their high-stakes graduation tests; states in the South have historically had lower rates of high school completion than other regions of the country.

These five strands of evidence suggest that high-stakes testing, together with grade retention practices that may be affected, both directly and indirectly, is associated with increased dropout rates among adolescents. The evidence is divided on whether there is a differential effect by race. While the data are mainly correlational, they are compelling enough to warrant caution in the use of these tests alone to make important educational decisions about students.

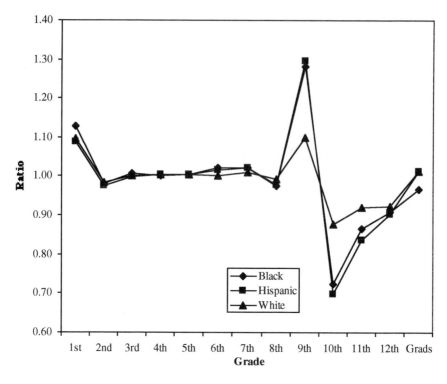

Figure 3.   Grade progression ratio 1996–97 to 1997–98, by ethnic group.
Source: Haney, W. (2000). The myth of the Texas miracle in education. *Education Policy Analysis Archives, 8*(41). Available at http://epaa.asu.edu/epaa/v8n41

THE ACHIEVEMENT GAP

It is a well-established fact that from the time children enter kindergarten, testing is strongly implicated in their life chances. Over time, educational testing, in its role as gatekeeper, has an additive effect in influencing life chances with respect to opening or closing doors of opportunity (National Commission on Testing and Public Policy, 1990). Decisions made on the basis of test scores at the elementary level can influence the type of secondary education one receives, and decisions at the high school level can either open or close doors of opportunity at the college level.

In order to understand the gatekeeping role of tests one must appreciate the implications of group differences on cognitive tests and how that plays out when tests become a principal criterion for making high-stakes decisions. Here we focus on differences in performance between minority (defined here as black and Hispanic) and non-minority adolescents. While gender, socioeconomic status, and other group differences exist on many tests, they are not as pervasive or large as those between minority and non-minority students (Jencks & Phillips, 1998). The implications of minority and non-minority performance differences are discussed in relation to tests required for graduation from high school and tests required for college admissions.

Graduation Tests

By 2005, half of all U.S. states will require students to pass a graduation test in order to receive their high school diploma (Olson, 2001). Students who fail the graduation test may be denied a diploma even if they have completed all required coursework and maintained a good grade point average. Much concern has focused on differential pass rates for minority and non-minority students on these tests. Two examples will suffice to illustrate the basis for this concern—the Massachusetts Comprehensive Assessment System (MCAS) and the TAAS.

Since the first administration of the MCAS in 1998, there has been a wide gap between the performance of minority and non-minority students on the mathematics, English language arts, science/technology, and history/social science tests (see http://www.doe.mass.edu/mcas/results.html). While statewide scores for 2000 showed slight improvement in most subjects for the fourth, eighth, and tenth grade students, minority failure rates remained high. Overall tenth grade failure rates in English language arts, and mathematics were 34 and 45 percent respectively, while Hispanic failure rates were 66 and 79 percent, black failure rates were 60 and 77 percent, and white failure rates were 27 and 38 percent. Beginning in 2003, public school students in Massachusetts must pass the tenth grade English language arts and mathematics tests in order to graduate. While some argue that failure rates will go down when the tests count (the motivation argument) and students have multiple opportunities to retake them, others are concerned that the test will demoralize and marginalize low achieving students, as well as those with limited English proficiency or in special education programs, eventually pushing them out of the education system.

The MCAS is viewed as one of the most difficult graduation tests in the country, but similar achievement gaps are seen on other graduation tests. For example, since becoming a graduation requirement in 1991, minority students have failed the TAAS exit-level test at a much higher rate than non-minority students (Haney, 2000). While this difference in pass rates has narrowed, some doubt the validity of the score gains involved (Klein, Hamilton, McCaffrey, & Stecher, 2000), pointing out a widening minority-non-minority achievement gap for Texas students on measures such as the National Assessment of Educational Progress and a smaller percentage of Texas high school graduates (overall and by racial group) taking the SAT-I or ACT (Fisher, 2000). Others have pointed to the previously discussed increased retention rates around grade 9 and the rising dropout rate as mechanisms that artificially raise tenth grade pass rates while masking negative fallout on minority students (Haney, 2000; McLaughlin, 2000).

The use of the MCAS and TAAS tests as gatekeepers to graduation is especially troubling because several national bodies, including the National Research Council (Heubert & Hauser, 1999), the American Educational Research Association, the American Psychological Association, and the National Council on Measurement in Education (AERA, APA, and NCME, 1999) have stated that high-stakes decisions of this type should not be made on the basis of a single test or test score. Instead, multiple measures of a student's abilities should be employed (e.g., Wisconsin is using this approach). Some experts also suggest using a "compensatory" model in which a student's strong performance in one area, such as coursework, could offset low performance in another, such as a graduation test (e.g., Indiana is using this approach). Others suggest providing "advanced" or endorsed diplomas to students who do well on such tests rather than withholding diplomas from students who fail the exams (e.g., Ohio and Connecticut are using this approach). Providing alternative ways for students to demonstrate their knowledge is particularly important given the higher failure rates for minority students as well as the flawed nature of the standard-setting process used to set the cut scores on many of these tests. An example of the latter is the MCAS standard-setting process, which has resulted in large numbers of students falling into the failure and needs improvement categories on the test despite contradictory standardized norm referenced data (Horn, Ramos, Madaus, & Blumer, 2000).

College Admission Tests

Similar minority-non-minority achievement gaps are seen on college admissions tests, with similar gatekeeping implications. Here, we focus on performance trends on the SAT-I and the ACT since they are the most commonly used standardized tests for admission to college.

The trend lines in Figures 4 and 5 provide a picture of how students from various racial and ethnic groups compare with their white counterparts on the SAT-I and ACT mathematics tests (similar trends can be seen on the other sections of these tests). The performance of white students for each year of a test is taken to be the zero point of the scale. Groups below the zero line do worse than whites, and groups above do better. Differences between groups are expressed in standard deviation units. (When differences are expressed in standard deviations, they can be compared across tests.)

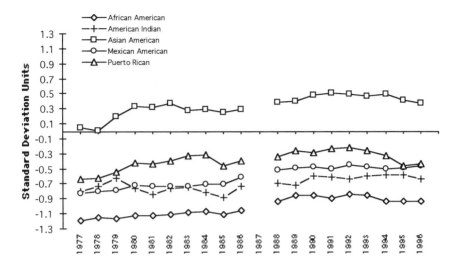

Figure 4.   Trends in racial/ethnic group differences: ACT mathematics–high school seniors.

Note: The performance of White students for each year is taken to be the zero point of the scale. Groups above the zero line perform better, groups below perform worse. Data were not available for 1987.

Sources: "ACT Math Scores and ACT Score Means and SDs for Successive Years of ACT-Tested College-Bound Seniors 10% National Sample" (Iowa City: American College Testing, undated and unpublished tabulations); James Maxey, American College Testing, personal communications (August-September, 1997).

The trend lines show that Asian American high school seniors were the highest performing group on both the SAT-I and ACT mathematics tests over the twenty or so years spanning 1976/77 to 1997/98. White high school seniors, the second highest performing group on both tests, achieved at average levels that were about 0.3 of a standard deviation unit lower than Asian American seniors. In other words, only about 35 percent of the white high school seniors performed at or above a level that was met or exceeded by 50 percent of the Asian high school seniors. The average performance of black students was consistently lower than all other groups on both tests and stood well below that of Asian American and white students (about one standard deviation unit below whites and 1.3 standard deviation units below Asian Americans on both tests). While Mexican American and Puerto Rican high school seniors performed somewhat better than black seniors on both tests, there was still a considerable gap between them and their white and Asian American counterparts. In addition, this gap began to widen again for Puerto Ricans on the ACT and for Mexican Americans on the SAT-I in the 1990s. (American Indian students showed a slow and somewhat erratic improvement on both tests over the twenty-year period.)

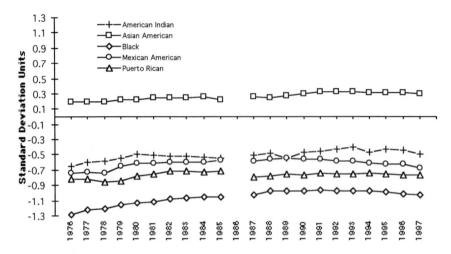

Figure 5.   Trends in racial/ethnic group differences: SAT-I mathematics–high school seniors.

Note: The performance of White students for each year is taken to be the zero point of the scale. Groups above the zero line perform better, groups below perform worse. Data were not available for 1986.

Source: College Entrance Examination Board (1972–1997).

While much has been written on the reasons for these gaps, we do not discuss them here. We present them merely to illustrate their magnitude and equity implications, particularly in an environment where 90 percent of colleges require applicants to submit SAT-I or ACT scores and test scores are often the second most important piece of information (after high school achievement) in making admission decisions (Breland, Maxey, McLure, Valiga, Boatwright, Ganley, & Jenkins, 1995).

The recent rollback of affirmative action in Texas (the Hopwood decision), California (SP-1 and Proposition 209), Washington (Initiative 200), and Florida (One Florida Initiative) brought these equity issues to the fore. What would happen to minority student access to college in these race-blind systems? In particular, how would minority students' lower average performance on college admission tests affect their admission chances at selective institutions? In order to answer these questions, National Board researchers conducted a study that looked at the effects of the repeal of affirmative action in California on minority access to the University of California (UC) system (see Koretz, Russell, Shin, Horn, & Shasby, 2001). Using a database of some 140,000 Californian students, the researchers asked the following: (1) What are the effects of different stages in the admissions process on racial and ethnic diversity in the student population?; (2) How does a race-neutral admissions model (using only test scores and grade point average (GPA) to predict admission to college) compare with actual post-affirmative action admission results in the UC system?; and (3) What are the effects of alternative approaches that take factors into account other than students' test scores and grades, but not their race or ethnicity? Given the logic of the analysis, we will take up the first two questions in a related way and then consider the third.

The effect of the admissions process on the diversity of the student population was examined by following this set of progressions: Given the percentage of Asian Americans, blacks, Hispanics, whites, and others in the graduating classes of California high schools in 1998, what percentage in each of these racial/ethnic categories

- took the SAT-I (a requirement for admission to the UC system);
- was eligible for admission to the UC system (based on a sliding scale of SAT-I and high school GPA);
- applied to a highly selective, moderately selective, or least selective campus (as measured by SAT-I scores sent to a campus);
- was admitted under a race-neutral model that employed only SAT-I/ GPA.

By adding a fifth progression, namely,

- was actually admitted in three selected years—1995 (before SP-1 and Proposition 209), 1997 (enactment of SP-1 and Proposition 209), and 1999 (implementation of SP-1 and Proposition 209)

the researchers were also able to compare the race-neutral admissions model they derived from the first four progressions with actual pre- and post-affirmative action results for the UC system.

Analyses showed that this set of progressions had the greatest impact on the racial and ethnic profile of students admitted to the most highly selective campuses in the UC system. The results for these campuses are shown in Table 1.

Focusing on progressions one through four outlined above, let us follow the table for Asians.

- In 1998, 15 percent of graduates of California high schools were Asian.
- They comprised 22 percent of SAT-I test-takers that year.
- 25 percent of those who were UC eligible were Asian.
- 36 percent of those who were both eligible for the UC system and actually applied were Asian.
- Asians constituted 38 percent of those who were admitted under a race-neutral model.

For the first research question—what are the effects of different stages in the admission process on racial and ethnic diversity in the student popula-

Table 1.   Racial/Ethnic Composition, Highly Selective Campuses: Actual and Estimated Using All Screens and SAT-I+GPA Admissions Model

	Asian, Asian American, Pacific Islander	Black or African American	Hispanic	White	Other	Decline to State
Graduates, 1998	15	7	31	45	1	NA
SAT-takers, 1998	22	7	19	42	6	3
UC eligible, 1998	*25*	*4*	*15*	*46*	*6*	*3*
Eligible and applied to high-selectivity school, 1998	*36*	*4*	*15*	*35*	*7*	*2*
Admitted by neutral model, 1998	*38*	*2*	*9*	*42*	*7*	*3*
1995 Admitted class	36	7	19	31	2	5
1997 Admitted class	38	6	15	33	2	6
1999 Admitted class	41	3	10	35	2	9

Note: Race/ethnicity is based on student self-reports for all rows except the "Graduates" row, which is based on reports by school administrators. Estimates are italicized; other numbers are actual counts. Percentages may not sum to totals because of the exclusion of American Indian students and rounding.

Sources: Estimates reflect National Board analysis; admission figures are published figures from UC (http://www.ucop.edu/pathways/infoctr/introuc/prof_engin.html); counts of SAT-I-takers are based on National Board tabulations of data provided by the College Board; counts of graduates are from California Department of Education, Educational Demographics Unit (http://data1.cde.gov/dataquest).

tion—we can see that for Asians, the effect is to over-represent their relative percentages in the population at each progressive stage of the admissions process. If we look at the last three entries for Asians in Table 1 (Asians constituted 36, 38, and 41 percent of the actual admitted class in 1995, 1997, and 1999), then we can see that they approximated (in 1995 and 1997) and then exceeded (in 1999) the relative percentage predicted by the race-neutral model.

If we follow these progressions for the other racial/ethnic groupings, we note that the admissions process decreased the percentage of blacks and Hispanics rather dramatically and that these outcomes are in line with post-affirmative action outcomes in the UC system's most selective institutions. For whites, the admissions process decreased some the percentage "eligible and applied." In addition, the percentage admitted by the race-neutral model over-predicted the percentage actually admitted post-affirmative action.

In sum, Asians have gained the most in the race-neutral admissions process and blacks and Hispanics have lost the most at the most selective institutions. Stated differently, the greater the reliance on testing the lower the percentage of the black and Hispanic student populations that gain admittance. Other analyses conducted show that these impacts are much less pronounced for the moderately selective and least selective schools in the UC system.

National Board researchers also attempted to assess the effects of alternative admissions approaches that take other factors into account in addition to test scores and grades, but not race or ethnicity. Several proxies for race were tried, including geographic location of the student's high school (preference given to urban or rural setting), parent education (preference given to less well-educated mother), parent income (preference given to low income), percent free and reduced lunch at the student's high school (preference given to high percent), percent graduating from the student's high school (preference given to low graduation rates), and the so-called X percent models (models tried include top 12.5 percent admitted across the state system of high schools; top 4 percent within a high school admitted; top 6 percent within a high school admitted; and top 12.5 percent within a high school admitted). We found that giving preference to students based on any of these variables decreased Asian representation and increased that of whites, blacks, and Hispanics. Giving preference to students whose mothers were less well educated or whose families were poor had the largest impact on the representation of black and Hispanic students. However, even the largest effects of giving preference to demographic variables did not come close to making the representation of black and Hispanic students in the admitted groups proportionate to their numbers in the pool of potential students.

The analyses summarized here suggest that race-neutral admission decisions have a large impact on black and Hispanic admit rates in highly selective academic environments. However, other analyses done show that black and Hispanic populations are also noticeably under-represented in the moderately and least selective levels of the UC system when compared with their presence in the California high school graduating pool. This under-representation is due to factors besides the actual admissions decision. The largest factors influencing this under-representation are related to a student's decision to take the SAT-I and whether they meet the minimum eligibility criteria for the UC system. Once students pass these two hurdles, the actual admissions decision only has a meaningful impact on the representation of black and Hispanic students at highly selective schools.

CONCLUSION

Tests have played a prominent role in the education of adolescents for centuries and will continue to do so for the foreseeable future. Their effects and implications for adolescents in a high stakes context have been outlined here. Our conclusions are that high stakes tests do not motivate all students to learn nor do they motivate students in the same way; that there is evidence to suggest a strong link between high stakes tests and increased dropout rates; and that high stakes tests do not necessarily narrow the minority achievement gap, but may withhold educational opportunities from these students.

If high-stakes testing programs are to be better crafted to maximize the value and minimize the harm to adolescents, the following six points should be kept in mind:

1. The school environment should be one that places student learning at the core of daily activity. The role, if any, of high-stakes testing in this environment needs to be carefully considered in terms of the extent to which it can foster and motivate that learning.
2. Tests are not perfect. Therefore, an educational decision that will have a major impact on a student should not be made on the basis of a single test score. Multiple measures of achievement should be used.
3. Educators should be involved in the development and implementation of any curriculum standards or frameworks that are to provide guidance for instruction and learning. If progress on these standards is to be measured with a test, the interaction between the stakes attached to the test results and the potential for negative impact on the curriculum should be carefully weighed and alternatives considered.
4. Teacher judgment and classroom assessment should be given a prominent role in high stakes testing programs since these types of student evaluations are linked to ongoing instruction and more likely to show what students know and can do.
5. Efforts to use high stakes tests as a way to narrow the achievement gap between different student groups should proceed cautiously. Current research shows that these tests do not narrow, and in some cases widen, the gap. Even if there is the potential to narrow or close some of these achievement gaps, sufficient resources should be poured into the system and enough time given before students or others are held accountable for the test results.
6. More attention needs to be given to the development of tests that tap into higher-level thinking skills and that allow students to show

what they know and can do in a variety of formats and contexts. While such tests would provide valuable information on student learning, care still should be taken when using them to make high-stakes decisions.

NOTE

1. The content of this section on motivation comes directly from T. Kellaghan, G.F. Madaus, and A. Raczek (1996), *The use of external examinations to improve student motivation*, Washington, D.C. American Educational Research Association. For a complete listing of references, please consult this source.

REFERENCES

Alexander, K.L., Entwisle, D.R., & Danber, S.L. (1994). *On the success of failure: A reassessment of the effects of retention in the primary grades*. New York: Cambridge University Press.

American Educational Research Association, American Psychological Association, & National Council on Measurement in Education. (1999). *Standards for educational and psychological testing*. Washington, DC: AERA.

Anderman, E.M., & Maehr, M.L. (1994). Motivation and schooling in the middle grades. *Review of Educational Research, 64*, 287–309.

Beaton, A., Mullis, I.V.S, Martin, M.O., Gonzalez, E.J., Kelly, D.L., & Smith T.A., (1996a). *Mathematics achievement in the middle school years: IEA's Third International Mathematics and Science Study*. Chestnut Hill, MA: Boston College.

Beaton, A., Martin, M.O., Mullis, I.V.S, Gonzalez, E.J., Kelly, D.L., & Smith T.A., (1996b). *Science achievement in the middle school years: IEA's Third International Mathematics and Science Study*. Chestnut Hill, MA: Boston College.

Bracey, G.W. (2000). The 10th Bracey report on the condition of public education. *Phi Delta Kappan, 82*(2), 133–144.

Brehm, J.W., & Self, E.A. (1989). The intensity of motivation. *Annual Review of Psychology, 40*, 109–131.

Breland, H., Maxey, J., McLure, G., Valiga, M., Boatwright, M., Ganley, V., & Jenkins, L. (1995). *Challenges in college admissions: A report of a survey of undergraduate admission policies, practices, and procedures*. American Association of Collegiate Registrars and Admissions Officers, American College Testing, The College Board, Educational Testing Service, and National Association of College Admission Counselors.

Broadfoot, P. (1979). Communication in the classroom: A study of the role of assessment in motivation. *Educational Review, 31*, 3–10.

Brooke, N., & Oxenham, J. (1984). The influence of certification and selection on teaching and learning. In J. Oxenham (Ed.), *Education versus qualifications* (pp. 147–175). London: Allen & Unwin.

Cambridge Educational Consultants. (1988). *The Ethiopian school leaving examination: A strategy for improvement.* Report for the Commission for Higher Education, Addis Ababa. Cambridge: Author.

Clarke, M., Haney, W., & Madaus, G. (2000). *High stakes testing and high school completion.* Chestnut Hill, MA: National Board on Educational Testing and Public Policy.

Deci, E.L., & Ryan, R.N. (1985). *Intrinsic motivation and self-determination in human behavior.* New York: Plenum.

Dornbusch, S.M., & Scott, W.R. (1975). *Evaluation and the exercise of authority.* San Francisco: Jossey-Bass.

Dweck, C.S. (1986). Motivational processes affecting learning. *American Psychologist, 41,* 1040–1048.

Dweck, C.S., & Leggett, E.L. (1988). A social-cognitive approach to motivation and personality. *Psychological Review, 95,* 256–273.

Edwards, T., & Whitty, G. (1994). Education: Opportunity, equality and efficiency. In A. Glyn & D. Milibrand (Eds.), *Paying for inequality* (pp. 44–64). London: Rivers Oram Press.

Fassold, M.A. (1996). *Adverse racial impact of the Texas Assessment of Academic Skills.* San Antonio, TX: Mexican American Legal Defense and Education Fund.

Fine, M. (1991). *Framing dropouts: Notes on the politics of an urban public high school.* Albany, NY: State University of New York Press.

Fisher, F. (2000). *Tall tales? Texas testing moves from the Pecos to Wobegon.* Draft paper.

Fisher, L.M. (1992, June 23). Sear's auto centers to halt commissions. *New York Times,* pp. D1, D5.

Griffin, B., & Heidorn, M. (1996). An examination of the relationship between MCT performance and dropping out of high school. *Educational Evaluation and Policy Analysis, 18,* 243–251.

Haney, W. (1993, April). *Cheating and escheating on standardized tests.* Paper presented at annual meeting of the American Educational Research Association, Atlanta.

Haney, W. (2000). The myth of the Texas miracle in education. *Education Policy Analysis Archives, 8*(41). Available at http://epaa.asu.edu/epaa/v8n41.

Hannan, D.F., & Shortall, S. (1991). *The quality of their education. School leavers' views of educational objectives and outcomes.* Dublin: Economic and Social Research Institute.

Hargreaves, A. (1989). The crisis of motivation and assessment. In A. Hargreaves & D. Reynolds (Eds.), *Educational policies: Controversies and critiques.* (pp. 41–63). New York: Falmer.

Henderson, V.L., & Dweck, C.S. (1990). Motivation and achievement. In S.S. Feldman & G.R. Elliot (Eds.), *At the threshold: The developing adolescent* (pp. 308–329). Cambridge, MA: Harvard University Press.

Heubert, J., & Hauser, R. (Eds.). (1999). *High stakes: Testing for tracking, promotion, and graduation.* Washington, DC: National Academy Press.

Horn, C., Ramos, M., Madaus, G., & Blumer, I. (2000). *Cut scores: Results may vary.* Chestnut Hill, MA: National Board on Educational Testing and Public Policy.

Jackson, P.W. (1990). *Life in classrooms.* New York: Teachers College Press.

Jencks, C., & Phillips, M. (Eds.). (1998). *The black-white test score gap*. Washington, DC: Brookings Institution Press.

Kariyawasam, T. (1993). *Learning, selection, and monitoring: Resolving the roles of assessment in Sri Lanka.* Paper presented at Conference on Learning, Selection, and Monitoring: Resolving the Roles of Assessment, sponsored by the International Centre for Research on Assessment, Institute of Education, University of London.

Katzell, R.A., & Thompson, D.E. (1990). Work motivation: Theory and practice. *American Psychologist, 45*, 144–153.

Kellaghan, T., Madaus, G.F., & Raczek, A. (1996). *The use of external examinations to improve student motivation.* Washington, DC: American Educational Research Association.

Kidder, T. (1989). *Among school children.* New York: Avon Books.

Klein, S., Hamilton, L., McCaffrey, D., & Stecher, B. (2000). What do test scores in Texas tell us? *Education Policy Analysis Archives, 8*(49). Available at: http://epaa.asu.edu/epaa/v8n49/

Koretz, D., Russell, M., Shin, D., Horn, C., & Shasby, K. (2001). *Testing and diversity in postsecondary education: The case of California.* Chestnut Hill, MA: National Board on Educational Testing and Public Policy.

Kozol, J. (1991). *Savage inequalities: Children in America's schools.* New York: Crown Publishers.

Kreitzer, A.E., Madaus, G.F., & Haney, W.M. (1989). Competency testing and dropouts. In L. Weis, E. Farrar & H.G. Petrie (Eds.), *Dropouts from school: Issues, dilemmas, and solutions* (pp. 129–152). Albany: State University of New York Press.

Lehigh, S. (2001, January 7). If our kids are such slackers, why has our economy done so well? *The Boston Globe*, pp. D1, D3.

Lens, W. (1994). Motivation and learning. In T. Husén & T.N. Postlethwaite (Eds.), *The international encyclopedia of education* (2nd ed., pp. 3936–3942). Oxford: Pergamon.

Little, A. (1982). The role of examinations in the promotion of "the Paper Qualification Syndrome." In *Paper Qualifications Syndrome (PQS) and unemployment of school leavers. A comparative sub-regional study* (pp. 176–195). Addis Ababa: Jobs and Skills Programme for Africa, International Labour Office.

Little, A. (1993). *Towards an international framework for understanding assessment.* Paper presented at Conference on Learning, Selection, and Monitoring: Resolving the Roles of Assessment, sponsored by the International Centre for Research on Assessment, Institute of Education, University of London.

Little, A. (1994). Types of assessment and interest in learning: Variation in the south of England in the 1980s. *Assessment in Education, 1*, 201–220.

Little, A.W., & Singh, J.S. (1992). Learning and working: Elements of the diploma disease thesis examined in England and Malaysia. *Comparative Education, 28*, 181–200.

Locke, E.A., & Latham, G.P. (1990). *A theory of goal setting and task performance.* Englewood Cliffs, NJ: Prentice-Hall.

Madaus, G.F. (1991, January). *The effects of important tests on students: Implications for a national examination or system of examinations.* Paper prepared for the American

Educational Research Association Invitational Conference on Accountability as a State Reform Instrument: Impact on Teaching, Learning, Minority Issues, and Incentives for Improvement. Washington, DC.

Madaus, G.F., & Kellaghan, T. (1991). Student examination systems in the European Community: Lessons for the Unites States. In G. Kuln & S.M. Malcom (Eds.), *Science assessment in the service of reform* (pp. 189–232). Washington, DC: American Association for the Advancement of Science.

Madaus, G.F., & Macnamara, J. (1970). *Public examination. A study of the Irish Leaving Certificate.* Dublin: Educational Research Centre.

Martin, M.O., Mullis, I.V.S., Gonzales, E.J., Gregory, K.D., Smith, T.A., Chrostowski, S.J., Garden, R.A., & O'Connor, K.M. (2000). *TIMSS 1999 international mathematics report: Findings from IEA's repeat of the third international mathematics and science study at the eight grade.* Chestnut Hill, MA: Boston College.

McLaughlin, D. (2000). *Protecting state NAEP trends from changes in SD/LEP inclusion rates.* Palo Alto, CA: American Institutes for Research.

Mehrens, W.A. (1998). Consequences of assessment: What is the evidence? *Education Policy Analysis Archives, 6*(13). Available at: http://epaa.asu.edu/epaav6n13.html

Mullis, I.V.S., Martin, M.O., Gonzales, E.J., Gregory, K.D., Garden, R.A., O'Connor, K.M., Chrostowski, S.J., & Smith, T.A., (2000). *TIMSS 1999 international science report: Findings from IEA's repeat of the third international mathematics and science study at the eight grade.* Chestnut Hill, MA: Boston College.

National Center for Education Statistics. (1997). *Dropout rates in the United States, 1996,* Report No. 98-250. Washington, DC: Author.

National Commission on Testing and Public Policy. (1990). *From gatekeeper to gateway: Transforming testing in America.* Chestnut Hill, MA: National Commission on Testing and Public Policy.

Olson, L. (2001). Finding the right mix. *Education Week, 20*(17), 12–21.

Paris, S.G., Lawton, T.A., & Roth, J.L. (1991). A developmental perspective on standardized achievement testing. *Educational Researcher, 20*(5), 12–20.

Pervin, L.A. (1992). The rational mind and the problem of volition. *Psychological Science, 3,* 162–164.

Pittman, T.S., & Heller, J.F. (1987). Social motivation. *Annual Review of Psychology, 38,* 461–489.

Punjab. Commission for Evaluation of Examination System and Eradication of Malpractices. (1992). *Report.* Report submitted to Mr Ghulam Hauder Wyne, Chief Minister of the Punjab. Lahore: Author.

Reardon, S.F. (1996, April). *Eighth grade minimum competency testing and early high school dropout patterns.* Paper presented at the Annual Meeting of the American Educational Research Association, New York.

Schunk, D.H. (1991). Self-efficacy and academic motivation. *Educational Psychologist, 26,* 207–231.

Shepard, L.A., & Smith, M.L. (1990). Synthesis of research on grade retention. *Educational Leadership, 48*(8), 84–88.

Sizer, T. (1992). *Horace's school: Redesigning the American high school.* Boston: Houghton Mifflin.

Texas Education Agency. (1996). *Comprehensive biennial report on Texas public schools: A report to the 75th Texas legislature.* Austin: Author.

Zimmerman, B.J., Bandura, A., & Martinez-Pons, M. (1992). Self-motivation for academic attainment: The role of self-efficacy beliefs and personal goal setting. *American Educational Research Journal, 29,* 663–676.

CHAPTER 8

Race and Gender Influences on Teen Parenting

An Identity-focused Cultural-Ecological Perspective

Margaret Beale Spencer, Lauren J. Silver, Gregory Seaton, Sharon R. Tucker, Michael Cunningham, and Vinay Harpalani

INTRODUCTION

Race and gender are widely recognized as central components of an individual's identity. Yet, scholarship on human development tends to neglect the integration of race and gender on identity formation processes. Considering the complexity of interactions between race and gender is central to understanding developmental processes and outcomes for majority and minority youth. Put simply, one cannot merely transfer assumptions about gender across racial/ethnic groups or vice versa; race and gender identity formation must be studied as culturally linked within-group processes, with a focus on the particular contexts that individuals are encountering. Identity processes

231

are particularly salient during adolescence, when major developmental tasks involving identity are typically negotiated as a normative feature of human development. Developmental stressors encountered by minority youth, resulting from particular ecological risks and, for many, impoverished conditions, pose threats to health and normative development. The interaction of race and gender identity formation, viewed in context, is central to understanding normative development among these youth.

One vantage point from which to consider these issues is the phenomenon of teen parenting. A growing body of scholarship on adolescent education has focused on this phenomenon, particularly among minority youth. Moreover, teen parenting is one example of how minority youth development has been viewed through a pathological lens, neglecting the viewpoint and resilience of many of these youth. Of course, major structural inequities do contribute to teen pregnancy among minority youth. Poverty is always a problem, and minority status exacerbates the experience. Growing up in poverty has been related to higher teen pregnancy rates among African Americans (Mayer & Jencks, 1989). More than one-half of African American children are born to unwed teen mothers; prenatal care in these situations is often characterized by poor nutrition and substandard medical care (Spurlock & Norris, 1991). Studies have also linked teen pregnancy to high school attrition and welfare enrollment among teen mothers, and several adverse life outcomes—such as poor school performance and criminality—for children of teen mothers (Card, 1999). Of importance, however, is that this work has often failed to consider the interaction between social context and identity formation. Teen parenting is a complex phenomenon, linking subtle cultural beliefs with structural inequities, all in the midst of normative identity formation for adolescents. More often than not, youth are not consciously aware of how structural inequities coerce reactions to normative adolescent challenges. Thus, teen parenting provides an interesting vantage point from which to consider race and gender identity development for minority youth.

TEEN PARENTING AND CONCEPTUAL FLAWS IN RESEARCH ON MINORITY YOUTH

Mainstream research on teen parenting reflects four major conceptual defects that have historically characterized scholarship on minority adolescents (Spencer & Harpalani, in press). First, these youth are often studied as isolated entities, without regard for the larger context in which they are growing, maturing and developing. Numerous manifestations of symbolic and structural racism, economic hardships, and related barriers often characterize the environments encountered by minority adolescents. These factors impact adolescent perceptions of self, other, and future life prospects and often influence behaviors such as sexual activity and perceptions of teen parenting.

Another major flaw in theorizing about minority adolescents is the lack of a developmental perspective. The normative developmental stressors experienced by minority youth, such as physical and social maturation and peer pressure, are compounded by the larger context. These normative adolescent developmental processes, in conjunction with encounters of stressful context, also influence the phenomenon of teen parenting; yet, one or both of these perspectives are often ignored in scholarship.

Another major shortcoming that characterizes scholarship on minority youth is a highly deficit-oriented perspective. Through this deficit-oriented lens, youth of color are viewed as pathological products of oppression (e.g., Kardiner & Ovesey, 1951), and only the negative outcomes attained by these youth are studied. This perspective ignores the resilience of those who do succeed in spite of tremendous barriers. On the other hand, it leaves the same issues generally ignored among non-minority youth (e.g., teen pregnancy for White female teenagers). Similarly, resilience among low-income minority youth is not well studied and often misunderstood (e.g., Fordham & Ogbu, 1986). For minority adolescents who become parents, a focus on resilience has important implications for both parent and child outcomes.

Finally, a fourth flaw is the general lack of cultural understanding and competence in scholarship on youth of color. Minority adolescents often grow up in a context of unique family structure and cultural practices, many of which are not understood by White American society and generally ignored in developmental science. These include norms and values associated with childbirth and parenting. Given these conceptual flaws and the growing need to understand the phenomenon of teen parenting, three primary issues merit our attention; these are discussed in the next section.

MITIGATING CONCEPTUAL SHORTCOMINGS

In order to remedy these traditional shortcomings, we recognize several important steps that must be taken. One is the need to focus on issues of race and ethnicity in terms of cultural differences, structural racism, and racial identity formation. These various perspectives are central to understanding the significance of race and ethnicity; yet they are seldom integrated in a single body of scholarship. Each perspective derives from a different disciplinary source; cultural differences are the realm of anthropology, structural racism is the domain of sociology, and racial identity formation falls under the rubric of psychology. An integrative approach, combining all three, is central to understanding issues of race and ethnicity in general, and, in this chapter, teen parenting and its educational implications in particular.

A second factor is the need to examine gender identity and its interaction with race. Typically, for Whites, gender issues are viewed in terms of barriers to attainment faced by women. While many of these issues are certainly applicable across ethnic groups, confounding factors create complex interactions between race and ethnicity. For example, Black males have always been viewed as particularly threatening to White male patriarchy. This created unique systems of oppression that impact gender identity formation and outcomes for both Black and White males and females. Moreover, this issue is particularly relevant to teen parenting, where the perspectives of teen fathers have been studied only sparsely.

The third primary issue is the need for developmentally sensitive theory that helps to integrate the various perspectives of race and ethnicity. Spencer's (1995) Phenomenological Variant of Ecological Systems Theory is employed as an overarching framework; it is a tool for examining human development, focusing on identity formation while taking into account structural factors, cultural influences, and individual phenomenological experiences and perceptions of these contextualized features.

In this chapter, we use our strategy to explore the issue of teen parenting, highlighting the interaction between social context and race and gender identity formation. Our approach considers the impact of normative developmental processes, proximal contextual influences including cultural values and social supports, and more distal, systemic influences such as the impact of the school and health care systems and other social institutions. Additionally, we explore the significance of teen parenting for both female and male adolescents, as the latter is often ignored in considerations of the issue. Spencer's PVEST model provides the overarching framework for our analysis. We will use ethnographic case studies to illustrate and contextualize various aspects of teen parenting and its implications, as experienced by youth. The case studies focus on African American youth, and, due to limitations of available research particularly on teen fathers, much of our analysis focuses on African American female adolescents, although we do cite other minority groups. All of our analysis focuses upon the larger social and contextual issues that impact the experience of teen parents, and we illustrate the educational implications of these experiences. Also presented are the broader implications of our analysis for policy and youth intervention.

PHENOMONOLOGICAL VARIANT OF ECOLOGICAL SYSTEMS THEORY (PVEST): AN IDENTITY-FOCUSED CULTURAL-ECOLOGICAL (ICE) PERSPECTIVE

Spencer's (1995) Phenomenological Variant of Ecological Systems Theory (PVEST) integrates a phenomenological perspective with Bronfenbrenner's (1989) ecological systems theory, linking context with perception. In doing so, it allows us to capture and understand the meaning making processes underlying foundational identity development and outcomes (Spencer, 1995, 1999; Spencer, Dupree, & Hartmann, 1997). Determining how minority youth view and comprehend family, peer, and societal expectations, as well as their prospects for competence and success, is central to understanding resiliency and devising interventions that promote it (Spencer, Harpalani, & Dell'Angelo, in press). As such, PVEST utilizes an *Identity-focused Cultural-Ecological* perspective, integrating issues of culture, social and historical context, and normative developmental processes involved in identity formation.

A systems theory, PVEST consists of five components linked by bidirectional processes (Figure 1); it is a cyclic, recursive model that describes identity development throughout the life course. The first component, *risk contributors,* consists of factors that may predispose individuals for adverse

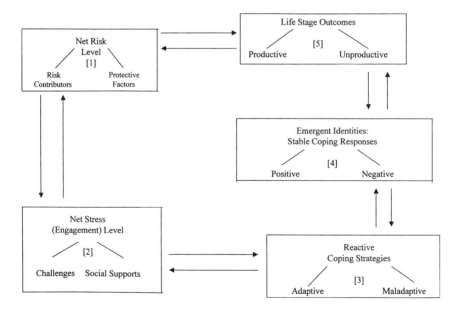

Figure 1.   Phenomenological variant of ecological systems theory (PVEST).

outcomes. The risks, of course, may be offset by protective factors (e.g., cultural capital). For urban minority youth, these include socioeconomic conditions such as poverty, sociocultural expectations such as race and sex stereotypes, and sociohistorical processes including racial subordination and discrimination. Additionally, factors such as single parent family background may be salient risks for teen parenting, and the experience of teen parenting creates risks that may compromise educational outcomes. Self-appraisal is a key factor in identity, and how minority youth view themselves depends on their perceptions of these conditions, expectations, and processes.

Net stress engagement, the second component of PVEST, refers to the actual net experience of situations that challenge one's psychosocial identity and well being. These are essentially risk contributors that are actually encountered and manifested in everyday life and may be offset or balanced by available supports. Experiences of discrimination, violence, and negative feedback are salient stressors for minority youth. Adult supports serve as protective factors. In conjunction with normative developmental processes, such as the expression of adolescent "male bravado" and sexuality, these stressful experiences may lead to teen parenting. Also, the phenomenon of teen parenting yields its own stressful experiences that may require specific supports.

In response to stress, *reactive coping methods* are employed to resolve dissonance-producing situations. Normative cognitive maturation makes awareness of dissonance unavoidable and acute. Reactive coping responses include strategies to solve problems that can lead to either adaptive or maladaptive solutions. In addition, a solution may be adaptive in one context, such as neighborhood, and maladaptive in another, such as school. While many consider teen parenting itself to be a maladaptive coping mechanism, this assumption will be explored, along with a variety of coping strategies that are utilized. The latter is important since individuals cope differently with the experience of becoming parents as teenagers.

As coping strategies are employed, self-appraisal continues, and those strategies yielding desirable results for the ego are preserved. Accordingly, they become stable coping responses, and, coupled together, yield *emergent identities.* Emergent identities define how individuals view themselves within and between their various contextual experiences. The combination of cultural/ethnic identity, sex role understanding, and self and peer appraisal all define one's identity. This paper explores how the identity of a teen parent, which is stigmatized in different ways, is expressed among minority youth.

Identity lays the foundation for future perception and behavior, yielding adverse or productive *life-stage, specific coping outcomes.* Productive outcomes include good health, positive relationships, and high self-esteem, while adverse outcomes include poor health, incarceration, and self-destructive behavior. Teen parenting is usually defined as an adverse, negative outcome; we explore this assumption and its implications.

The PVEST framework recycles and recourses through the lifespan as individuals balance new risks against protective factors, engage new stress levels, given challenges potentially offset by supporters, try different coping strategies, and redefine how they and others view themselves. We consider this process from the viewpoint of the teen parent, with particular attention to educational outcomes and the factors that effect educational attainment.

SOCIAL POLICY AND CONTEXTUAL INFLUENCES ON TEEN PARENTING

Generally, American attitudes concerning teenage sexuality have been criticized as ambivalent in nature; by sending mixed messages, they create a complex set of risk factors. While the media often emphasizes sexual themes in entertainment, our nation's policies concerning teenage sexuality take on a "moral" front as they often encourage abstinence instead of safer sex. These policies are in stark contrast to those in many other industrialized Western countries, which confront teenage sexuality openly and encourage sexual education at early ages (Furstenburg,1998). In their promotion of traditional morality, our nation's public policies on issues of teenage pregnancy do not always adequately address the needs of today's teenagers. Some of these policies, both economic and educational, will be discussed in further depth in this paper. In a society with a strong economy and increased life choices for men and women alike to become more educated, American public policy has been slow in responding to changing trends in sexuality, marriage, and childbirth. As Furstenberg (1998) argues, in America, "ideology is much more powerful than rationality in setting public policy" (p. 252).

Very often the "problem" of teenage pregnancy is painted as a recent phenomenon, as if teenagers have only begun having sex and becoming pregnant in recent years. This is not the case; in actuality, teenage pregnancy rates reached an all time high during the baby boom era, in the late 1950s and early 1960s. Despite the high rates of teenage pregnancy, it remained outside of public debate because such pregnancies were often followed by marriage and as such, were socially acceptable. Of course, there are problematic issues surrounding teenage pregnancy, such as adverse outcomes involved in adolescent childbearing. Teenage parents are less likely to graduate from high school and are more likely to live in poverty (National Campaign to Prevent Teen Pregnancy, 1997). Children of teenage parents also face more obstacles in life. Such children are more likely to have lower birth rates, more likely to remain in poverty, and more likely to do poorly in school (George & Lee, 1997; Maynard, 1996; Wolfe & Perozek, 1997). Thus, teen parenting can create multiple sets of risk factors, for both parent and child, throughout the life course.

A major policy initiative that affected teenage parents was the Personal Responsibility and Work Opportunity Reconciliation Act of 1996 (PRWORA). Provisions of this welfare reform act include $50 million spent on abstinence education, bonuses to states which rank the highest in decreasing out-of-wedlock births while also decreasing abortions, the requirement that national goals be created by the Department of Health and Human Services, and the enforcement of statutory rape laws. The enforcement of such laws came about in response to research findings indicating that the fathers of most teenage mothers under the age of 18 were in their 20s (Annie E. Casey Foundation, 2000).

In terms of actual welfare benefits, the law gives states the option to deny welfare benefits to unwed teenage parents under the age of 18 on the basis of school enrollment or the teenager's place of residence. All unmarried parents under the age of 18 must be enrolled in school or an alternative educational program to receive benefits. Such teenagers must also live at home, or at another adult-supervised setting, such as a Second Chance Home. Second Chance Homes are residences for teen parents and their children who may be at risk for abuse if they remain in their own homes. The 1996 welfare law makes provisions for the establishment of such homes that function to give teen parents guidance in parenting, health and nutrition, child development, budgeting practices, and methods for avoiding repeat pregnancies.

The rationale behind these restrictions was shaped by the belief that teenagers, despite their status as parents, should "stay teenagers" while they are still minors; they should live with their parents and not live independently; they should attend and graduate from high school to increase their future earning prospects, and not prematurely enter the workforce. Such aims seem supportive of adolescent development. They encourage the maintenance of adult supports that encourage and maximize children's developmental processes and progress. Moreover, teens who remain in a school setting may also be discouraged to have more children before they finish high school. In the view of policymakers, out-of-wedlock parents who live independently or do not attend school are more likely to be a greater burden on the system, either using benefits to pay for the costs of independent living, or potentially being a continued burden on the system if not better-equipped for the workforce with a high school degree.

From a PVEST perspective, one question we ask is what kinds of risk does our current welfare system contribute to becoming a teen parent? Although most research focuses on the systemic risks presents after the fact, PRWORA does pose risks for teenagers even before pregnancy and parenting, especially for children of color. Some of the basic tenets of the law were not funded, including the establishment of national goals and the enforcement of statutory rape laws. Without funding, the implementation of these policies is likely to lack rigor or comprehensiveness. The effectiveness of the law itself has come into question in 1998, when a report by the U.S. General Accounting Office investigated the effect of the 1996 welfare law in eight states that already had teen pregnancy prevention (TPP) programs in place. The report found that many states already enforced key provisions of the Personal Responsibility Act, including the requirement for minors to live at home and attend school in order to receive benefits, before the law was enacted. Further, the abstinence-focused aspects of the law may have been restrictive in their reach. Many state officials regarded the funding for abstinence education as too prescriptive, as such funds could not be used in programs that gave students information on both abstinence and contraception. Also, some states found that they were uncompetitive for the bonus program because they did not have accurate abortion data, or because state trends would decrease their eligibility for rewards. One such state, Georgia, may prove uncompetitive because most of its out-of-wedlock births occur among women 20 or older.

The provisions within the welfare law which address statutory rape as a factor in teen pregnancy may also be somewhat misguided. Questions have been raised about the connection between teenage motherhood and statutory rape, and some research has found contradictory findings. For example, data compiled by the U.S. General Accounting Office (1993) and other research groups found that the majority of teenage mothers are 18 years of age or older. In fact, birth rates for such women were more than double the rates for younger females. With this data in mind, the stereotypical image of a "teen parent" changes.

Much of the public, academic, and political discourse about the interaction between welfare and teenage pregnancy implies a causal interaction between the two phenomena. The myth of the "welfare queen" connects increased welfare benefits to subsequent out-of-wedlock pregnancies, the latter occurring only to receive greater benefits from the state. In such an interaction, welfare benefits represent an incentive for women to have additional children to receive more benefits. This notion has no grounding in actual research that explored this interaction. Current research has found no correlation between higher welfare benefits and women having children out-of-wedlock. Instead, research shows just the opposite: state comparisons show that out-of-wedlock births are more common in states with lower benefit levels (National Campaign to Prevent Teen Pregnancy, 1996). Moreover, other studies have found a race differential on this issue: White women in states with higher welfare benefits are slightly more likely to have children out-of-wedlock than white women in states with lower benefits. Such is not the case among Black and Latina women, whose pregnancy rates are not correlated with levels of welfare benefits (National Campaign to Prevent Teen Pregnancy, 1996).

In light of this research, why does public discourse and some policy makers see decreased welfare benefits as a method to decrease teenage pregnancy? Policymakers might do better to understand poverty as the main reason for teenage out-of-wedlock pregnancy. A body of research shows that although teen parents are more likely to live in poverty, it can be argued that such teenagers remain in poverty because of preexisting economic conditions. More than 80 percent of teenage mothers come from poverty or near-poverty home environments (Luker, 1996). Restricting welfare benefits to teenage parents in one form or another, and not addressing poverty as a core contributor to teenage pregnancy may perpetuate the generational cycle of teenage pregnancy.

The educational system also poses risks for teen pregnancy. While teen pregnancy and education are usually linked in terms of post-pregnancy outcomes (i.e., high dropout rates for teen parents and low educational outcomes for children of teen parents), the education system can also be understood as a risk contributor for teen pregnancy. Independent of poverty status, young women who are enrolled in college preparatory programs are less likely to become teen mothers, and this distinction is even greater within the African-American population (Luker, 1996). Thus, issues such as the academic tracking of students must be taken into account.

Although more research has yet to be conducted on the effect of being "disadvantaged and discouraged" on early pregnancy (Luker, 1996), studies do show that those students who feel strongly connected to their school and have higher grades are more likely to postpone sexual activity (Blum & Rhinehart, 1998). Therefore, a strong educational system, especially for minority populations at most risk, may decrease the effect of poverty on teenage pregnancy. Moreover, the school itself may also represent a place of support, as a recent study found that students consider teachers and counselors as reliable sources of sexually related information.

Questions have also been raised about the assumed cause-effect relationship between teenage pregnancy and dropout rates. This relationship is based on available data showing that once a child is born to teenagers, teen parents encounter difficulty trying to attend and graduate from high school. These findings contribute to the overall stigma of early teenage pregnancy as a contributor to continued poverty status. However, Luker (1996) notes that data used to imply a casual relationship between early pregnancy and dropout rates are unclear. Much of these data do not definitively show that teenagers drop out after pregnancy. In many instances, the reverse may be true; a teenage female may have become pregnant after attrition. Such findings call into question the conventional assumptions about school motivation as a primary factor in preventing teen pregnancy.

Like education, health care policy and teenage pregnancy are usually discussed in terms of post-pregnancy concerns, including infant mortality rates and children's physical wellness. However, health care does play a strong role in the prevention of teenage pregnancy with the widespread availability of contraception. Although contraception has been available to adult females for years without extensive debate, making contraception available to teens has been approached with much controversy. During the 1970s, when this issue was first at the forefront of public debate, unwed teenagers needed parental consent before receiving medical or surgical treatment. However, this came into question when research showed that women who had children as teenagers were poorer than those who waited until during their twenties. These findings encouraged family planning advocates to argue for the availability of contraceptives for teenagers as a way to avoid poverty.

Although contraceptives are now widely available for men and women of all ages, studies show that some teenagers remain unprotected during sexual activity. Three out of 10 teen girls were completely unprotected the last time they had sex. Moreover, of those teenagers who do use contraception, approximately one-third do not use it regularly (National Campaign to Prevent Teen Pregnancy, 2000).

INTERACTION OF RACE AND GENDER IDENTITY FORMATION: A COMPARATIVE ANALYSIS

In order to understand the phenomenon of teen parenting, we must consider not only the impact of social context and policy, but also the interaction of this context with identity formation among minority youth. This consideration must incorporate notions of race and gender identity and the interaction between the two. It is only by examining normative identity formation for both adolescent males and females, compounded by stressful contexts and given available support, that we can understand the subtleties of teen parenting.

African American males are probably the most highly stigmatized and stereotyped group in America. Whether it is with images of the super athlete, criminal, gangster, or hyper-sexed male, it seems that most of society's views of African Americans are defined by these stereotypes. The Black male has, in one way or another, captured the imagination of the media to such a wide extent that media representations create his image far more than reality does. Moreover, most of the images of the Black male denote physical prowess or aggression and downplay other characteristics. For example, stereotypes of Black athletic prowess can be used to promote the notion that Blacks are unintelligent (Harpalani, 2001). These societal stereotypes, in conjunction with numerous social, political, and economic forces, interact to place African American males at extreme risk for adverse outcomes and behaviors. Whether it is hostile encounters with law enforcement, lukewarm everyday interactions with strangers, or negative teacher perceptions (Spencer, 1999), Black male youth experience and develop within stress-filled contexts. Not only through numerous structural and economic inequities, but even for middle class Black males, there exists a societal ethos that defines them as dangerous, threatening, and unintelligent. All of these factors, in addition to normative developmental processes encountered by adolescents, impact identity formation among African American adolescent males (Cunningham, 1993).

Stevenson (1997) describes how African American youth are "missed" and "dissed" by mainstream American society, and how this treatment in conjunction with neighborhood factors relates to African American youth becoming "pissed" and managing their anger. Black youth are "missed" as stereotypical media-based images distort, usually in negative terms, the meanings of their social and affective displays. Hence, these unique cultural displays are devalued and viewed with insolence—"dissed." In conjunction with these misrepresentations, many Black youth reside in high-risk contexts where anger display may be an appropriate coping mechanism. Anger may indeed become a form of competence for social and emotional viability in certain high-risk contexts. Thus, misrepresentation, disrespect, and hazardous contextual factors interact in creating the anger of Black youth (i.e., "pissed").

Developmental stressors also compound identity development for adolescent females. This effect may be pronounced when fathers are absent. Fathers often serve as an initial "safe male" figure (Hetherington, Cox, & Cox, 1985), whose male feedback plays a role for girls in gender socialization. It may be from this feedback that girls understand and refine a sense of their own femininity. When the father is not present, girls may seek this feedback from their peers, which is not as "safe" an interaction. Risky sexual behavior and teen pregnancy are possible consequences of this interaction.

Moreover, this risk is increasing as girls are physically maturing at much younger ages. The average age of menarche has fallen from 17 to 13 between the mid-1800s and the mid-1900s. Today, 1 out of 7 White girls starts to develop breasts or pubic hair by the age of 8; for Black girls, nearly half start showing such signs of sexual maturity at this early age (Lemonick, 2000). By drawing more attention from older males, early maturation can increase the risk for earlier sexual activity and teen pregnancy, accordingly this effect is more pronounced for Black girls.

In fact, according to Ellis, McFadyen-Ketchem, Dodge, Petit, and Bates (1999), early sexual maturation is related to father absence. Analyzing data from a longitudinal study of 173 girls, the authors conclude that quality of fathers' relationships with daughters delayed the onset of puberty. These data are particularly salient for minority youth, as McLoyd (1990) notes that 50% of Black youth may remain with a single parent for their entire childhood, compared to only 15% of White youth. Also, Spencer and Dornbush (1990) note that single parenthood creates additional stress by giving children autonomy earlier. While this may facilitate the development of coping skills, it can also be associated with negative outcomes. Adolescents dealing with normative developmental issues may not have supports available to deal with the challenges of additional autonomy; this depends on the quality of resources and relationships available in school, community, and other contextual settings.

Additionally, in two parent families, African American fathers face additional pressures (e.g., racism, discrimination, negative stereotypes, and joblessness) that exacerbate the pressures of fatherhood. The role of being a father has sex role expectations of being the head or in charge of the family. Fathers are expected to be the financial support of the family, as well as the male model. But with unemployment rates continuing to rise for African American men, the pressure of being the financial support of the family increases, which adds to the pressures of everyday life. These factors may impinge upon the quality of father-daughter relationships, which as noted are related to timing of pubertal onset. Thus, the influence of family relationships and their interaction with contextual factors can compound risks posed by physical maturation, particularly for girls, and this may be related to teen pregnancy.

Another developmental issue that must be considered for girls (and also for boys, although not as well studied), particularly during adolescence, is body image. Research has indicated differences in body image perceptions between Black and White adolescent girls. For example, Parker et al. (1995) found that Black adolescent females do not typically have an ideal body image to which they aspire. Instead, they emphasize individually desirable features they possess. In contrast, many White adolescent females do have an ideal body image to which they aspire, the so-called "Barbie doll" image. These differing views of ideal body image have implications for gender identity in its various manifestations.

In addition to gender identity formation, the notion of privilege and its effects must be taken into account in the identity development of White youth. *Webster's Dictionary* defines the term *privilege* as "a special right or immunity granted to a person or group" (1996, p. 545). A privileged person is one that is not subject to the usual rules or penalties because of some *special circumstances*. It suggests a customary concession. That is, the obtainment of concessions is customary, as it is a function of something being "due." Privilege represents a perquisite (i.e., benefit or gratuity), a prerogative (i.e., a right, sanction or choice). It represents opportunity. When used in a legal sense, such status suggests immunity from disclosure. For North Americans, the special status of equal citizenship afforded to all "by law" is, in fact, obfuscated by the fact of unacknowledged privilege by particular members of the society. In fact, the special status and "privileging" of particular citizens is associated with color, gender, immigration status, ethnicity and race. In fact, the special and privileged status of white American males has just recently "enjoyed" a level of currency in the public discourse. The impact of a privileged status and its very existence for some, and absence in the lives of others, has been dire. The lack of equity and institutionalization of assumptive status and privilege has contributed to interseting outcomes. In general it results in an unrealistic life course analysis of all and the negative stereotyping of "ordinary citizens" or non-privileged minorities, women and immigrants. Although infrequently described as such, the student massacre at Columbine High School in Colorado, along with the recent white identity research, theorizing (e.g., Helms, 1990) and general whiteness discourse (e.g., Ignatiev, 1995), suggest that there is a downside of privilege. From a systems analysis (e.g., Spencer's PVEST formulation), privilege denies the opportunity to hone an individual's responsive coping repertoires to unavoidable and life course challenges. Similar to the development of language potential at birth, if a particular language is not used, one loses the early facility for every day linguistic options. Similarly, the downside of privilege, which offsets its many opportunities for expressed supports, is that individuals become more dependent upon the "built in and unacknowledged" concessions and supports that ultimately define one's potential for human growth, development, and interdependent and relationally focused (i.e., humane behavioral) life course outcomes (see Spencer, 2001).

Thus, although privilege may be viewed by some as a protective factor, buffering individuals from negative experiences, it can also have adverse consequences. Privilege can preclude individuals from learning the requisite coping skills necessary to function in situations of stress, particularly when social supports are lacking. On the other hand, the experiences of African American males represent the antithesis of privilege. They may develop "reactive coping" mechanisms in response to too much challenge and too little support. These factors must be taken into account when considering the experiences of all youth, including teen parents.

THE SIGNIFICANCE OF AN ICE PERSPECTIVE AND PVEST FRAMEWORK FOR INTERPRETING PATTERNED ADVERSE OUTCOMES

In our work with urban, extremely impoverished African American youth, my colleagues and I also struggle with the issue of youth stereotyping experiences. The education and psychology literatures continue to show a lack of understanding about youths' unique developmental processes and schooling experiences. Our work suggests that moral and sex role identity processes are inextricably linked to context character. For many urban youth, their environments represent hostile conditions. Chestang (1972) describes their developmental experiences and situation as character development in a hostile environment. The theoretical application of Chestang's notion suggests that both sex role and moral identity processes might be best understood from a view that explores linkages between identity, culture and context character.

Identity development during adolescence involves coming to understand oneself as a member of a society within a particular ethnic, cultural, religious, or political tradition. In addition, an orientation to habitual right action, as described by Youniss (1998), is fundamental to identity, insofar as defining oneself entails becoming part of a normative cultural tradition. Additionally, members of devalued sub-cultural groups may have very different experiences from those more mainstream. Given unavoidable cognitive maturation and attendant shifts in meaning making processes, youths may infer a need to react against (i.e., the deployment of maladaptive reactive coping methods) broader societal traditions. The reaction may suggest to some a lack of morality. The response may represent, in fact, an unconscious consideration of societal expectations for appropriate behaviors with the recognition that equitable access to social opportunities is lacking. Particularly, given the experiences of ethnic and racial minorities, the reaction may be plausible for those young people who generally remain outside the mainstream of American life. Accordingly, their orientation to habitual right action (see Youniss, 1998) may represent somewhat of a conundrum of competing allegiance to dual contexts of socialization, (see Boykin, 1986). In the case of African American boys who are generally viewed with some degree of dissonance and trepidation in many situations, including educational settings (see Cunningham, 1994; Spencer & Cunningham, in press), the task of managing an ego-supporting identity while coping with generalized negative imagery, at best, is daunting. The extra burden further influences the character and reaction to socialization efforts and particularly so in educational settings. The phenomenon and reactive responses to it compromise school adjustment and the possibility of maximizing learning opportunities.

The fact that these conditions and experiences are generally not formally recognized makes the individual's managing of normative developmental tasks more challenging (Havighurst, 1953). Specifically, those tasks associated with establishing a moral identity are particularly salient. Attendant stresses and coping behaviors might enhance school adjustment on the one hand, or may potentially provide fodder for further misinterpretation on the other. Youthful efforts to cope with normative tasks, with few resources and supports, often result in less than constructive coping. From the adolescent's perspective, the maladaptive reactive coping strategies may be experienced as emotionally comfortable in the short run. However, they only further exacerbate an already challenging situation in the long run. For some low-resource males, maladaptive, reactive coping methods are often linked to gender identity themes. In many cities, the dilemma has given rise to the initiation of single-gender schools that permit more generalized gender-associated socialization efforts and educational innovations. Clearly, gender themes require more careful attention particularly for low resource African American and Hispanic youth. However, Deyhle (1986) would add similar concerns about Native American youth, as would Sung (1985) for Chinese immigrant children.

In his discussion of gender-role socialization, Steinberg (1999) notes that Hill and Lynch (1983) have speculated about a "gender intensification hypothesis." They indicate that many of the sex differences observed between adolescent males and females are due, not to biological differences, but to an acceleration in the degree to which youngsters are socialized to act in stereotypically masculine and feminine ways (see Steinberg, 1999, p. 269). They suggest that, with adolescence, girls become more self-conscious and experience more disruption in the self-image than boys. Of course, they do not rule out contributions of biology but suggest that some areas of sex role socialization show intensification. For example, it may be more important to act in ways that are consistent with sex-role expectations and that meet with approval in the peer group (Steinberg, 1999, p. 267). More often than not, particularly for minorities and low-resource youngsters, given the problem of stigmatization, racism, and socioeconomic inequities, youth often infer a lack of respect frequently accorded others. These analyses may occur as they pursue an orientation of habitual right action, that is, consistently manifesting behavior narrowly equated with principled and moral values. As noted, these efforts frequently occur in hostile contexts or minimally supportive environments as youth develop greater independence and respond to autonomy needs.

The development of autonomy becomes a particularly critical developmental task during adolescence as youths find themselves moving into positions that demand responsible and independent behavior. One aspect of independence is "value autonomy." As described by Steinberg (1999), value independence is more than simply being able to resist pressures to go along with the demands of others; it means having a set of principles about what is right and what is wrong, about what is important and what is not (Steinberg, 1999, p. 278). It involves changes in youths' views about moral, political, ideological, and religious issues. In addition to greater abstract thinking, their beliefs are increasingly connected to general principles that represent ideological positions. Youth often believe that their academic efforts are not being respected by the school system or by their peers. Thus, the exaggerated sex role orientation (i.e., reactive coping method) often adopted by urban youth is conjured to demand respect and is assumed to be both okay and, in fact, principled behavior. Youth may infer that the response style is the only method for obtaining earned respect. Steinberg's view would indicate that the strategy insures that beliefs become nested in youths' own values as opposed to becoming a system of values merely handed from parents, teachers and other socializing adults (see Steinberg, 1999, pp. 297–298).

In sum, especially for many low-resource youth, the demand and demonstration of independence and responsibility occur early and are recognized in particular microsystems, such as family, community, and church. However, if respect from the broader society, and particularly school settings, is not generally forthcoming, the reactive coping response may require the adoption of habitual right actions that are polar opposite to those generally valued by society, anticipated by schools and associated with good school adjustment. For example, gender-intensified behavior and hypermasculinity may be seen by youth as potentially more effective in generating respect; when, in fact, it may add to group stigma and further undermine school adjustment.

Accordingly, given the growth in autonomy and the unavoidable changes in the understanding of moral, political, ideological issues, particularly those linked with social status, our empirical research takes a theoretically grounded approach with its use of a phenomenological variant of ecological systems theory (PVEST) (Spencer, 1995; Spencer, Dupree & Hartmann, 1997; Swanson, Spencer, & Petersen, 1998). As indicated, critical and implicit for the perspective is the acknowledged importance of the person's lived experience considered in context. As illustrated in Figure 1, PVEST affords an opportunity for understanding value autonomy as a process that identifies competing coping methods and attendant moral and school-linked identities. Coping methods and identities may, in fact, represent shared values and beliefs generally accepted across groups (e.g., academic achievement, good school adjustment and school completion). However, they are often coupled with behaviors that suggest a significant need for respect as a consequence of early demonstrated independence and responsibility that too frequently accompany human development processes originating in challenging settings. The situation of adolescent males represents a context shared with females. Thus, the experiences of females are inextricably linked to those of their male counterparts, with similar risks due to their low-resource and minority status and the reactive coping responses they develop and that contribute to identity processes.

ETHNOGRAPHIC CASE STUDY: AFRICAN AMERICAN TEEN MOTHERS

PVEST is a useful lens through which to examine the situation of teenage mothers. More specifically, by applying PVEST we can begin to explicate a mother's unique context, her personal perspective and the bidirectional process of engagement in which interaction occurs between a mother and her environment. Using PVEST as a theoretical frame allows us to perceive the young mother as an individual. Too often, the literature concerning teenage parenthood presents a composite picture of the teenage mother. The composite necessarily eliminates the complexity of each mother's unique circumstance and perspective, dissipating interactions of the young mother in her particular context, providing an image that is flat and unchanging. A PVEST perspective complicates the literature because it necessarily advocates an individual, contextually sensitive understanding of young mothers. However, only when the innate complexity of this issue is accurately explored will there be proper promotion of the type of advocacy needed for contextually based policy reform.

The demography of teenage childbearing is not pervasive and evenly distributed across the landscape of the United States. As noted earlier, it is a phenomenon that moves along the boundaries of poverty and inequality, following a predictable pattern. Luker (1996) contends that 80% of teenage mothers come from backgrounds of poverty, and Lawson and Rhode (1993) state that Black adolescents are two-and-a-half times more likely to bear a child than are white adolescents. Luker (1996) also suggests that teenagers from low-income families are nine times more likely than teenagers from higher-income families to have a child. Of course, data on the use of abortions is not considered generally, although the topic remains a politically "charged" concern. The term, *teenage mother,* is not devoid of moral implications, as it is invoked frequently with a sigh of disdain as one ponders the dysfunctional state of American families today. However, it is essential that a perspective of teenage motherhood go beyond an assumed image. While poverty appears to be the most salient common denominator, teenage mothers have distinct outlooks and engage in diverse situations while facing varied stressors and supports in their lives; there is no one composite "type" of teenage mother. Therefore, we cannot solve the "problem" of teenage parenthood by locating the behavioral mode among all teenage mothers and then presenting the composite for policy to negotiate. Rather, the diversity among young mothers' must be engaged, with consideration of their contextual surroundings, toward an understanding that the only policy that will solve the "problem" of teenage mothers is one designed to eliminate the common denominator of poverty.

Luker (1996) asserts that the more successful a young woman is, or expects to be, the more likely she is to seek an abortion. She also suggests that young women from affluent, White, and two-parent homes are far more likely to end their pregnancies than are women from poor, minority, and single-parent homes. Young women from families who are receiving Aid to Families with Dependent Children (AFDC) are also less likely to seek an abortion. Luker (1996) also includes neighborhood and familial factors in determining the likelihood that a teenager will seek an abortion. She states that the perspectives of family and friends toward abortion influence a young woman's decision in addition to whether the teenager is acquainted with girls who are already teenage mothers. If a teenager has peers who are teenage mothers, the young woman is less likely to have an abortion. Luker further contends that, among teenagers from disadvantaged backgrounds, those who do well in school, get better grades, and aspire to higher education for themselves are more likely to obtain an abortion than those who are less motivated.

Teen Parenting and Education

Conventional literature suggests that the composite young mother is a girl who is unmotivated, does not have a positive outlook on life, does not perform well in school, is perhaps immoral, and most importantly does not have a goal-oriented perspective for her future. Much literature also states that a discouraged adolescent will carry a baby to term simply because she perceives few opportunities in her future (Furstenberg, 1998; Luker, 1996; Mauldon, 1998). In other words, according to this view, an adolescent in such circumstances does not imagine a future much different from the life she lives today. For example, Furstenberg (1998) states, "the costs of early childbearing is not that great nor the benefits that large" (p. 249).

The literature presents the decision making process as to whether to carry a baby to term as a relatively straightforward calculation, implying that those young women who choose to bring their pregnancies to term do so because they do not perceive benefits of postponement (Anderson, 1999; Furstenberg, 1998; Luker, 1996; Mauldon, 1998). The decision to carry a baby to term is considered to be an outcome of discouraged circumstances. In contrast, young women who decide to abort their babies do so because of their relatively optimistic outlook on their future options.

Using ethnography as a methodology, Silver (2000) illustrates how the generalization of the teenage mother falls apart when the realities of the girls' lives are explored. For example, among the adolescents interviewed in the analysis, one of the young mothers is extremely successful at school and has very specific future goals, which include higher education. Another young mother explains that her desire to succeed in school was ignited following the birth of her daughter. After being placed at a state-supported group home because of truancy, she has returned to high school and has maintained honor roll status for each consecutive grading period. What characteristics of her educational context did not encourage school success prior to her impetus to support her child? PVEST is a useful theoretical lens for framing ethnographic and qualitative data and provides a heuristic device that illuminates the limitations in the literature. Research in this field has predominately searched for the reasons why certain types of teenagers decide to carry a pregnancy to term. The PVEST perspective suggests that we cannot find simple answers to this question. The decision-making process is complex, interactive, and intricate and, in fact, different for each young woman. It is influenced by many factors including a girl's own beliefs about abortion, her feelings of readiness about being a parent and her relationship with the baby's father in addition to his feelings about abortion and having a baby. The perspectives of her friends, family and community also influence an adolescent's decision. However, the literature tends to present the decision-making process as straightforward and preordained by whether the girl's circumstances are fortunate versus unfortunate or privileged versus economically challenging (Furstenberg, 1998; Luker, 1996; Mauldon, 1998).

These qualitative inquiries illustrate that the question of why teenagers become mothers is embedded within a context that is framed and understood differently by different individuals. Teenage mothers represent different types of adolescents with diverse perspectives and unique situations. Silver (2000), one of the authors, conducted qualitative interviews, during which the young mothers talk about a multitude of reasons why teenagers decide to have babies. During discussion, the mothers speak about a desire to obtain commitment from a baby's father, to experience motherhood before perceived old age (given the life expectancies of Black men and woman), and to enjoy the attention gained from motherhood. The young mothers also suggest that adolescent childbearing can result as a consequence of sexual abuse, early physical maturity, and the absence of a father figure. These are some of the more tangible reasons; however, the girls also discuss the barriers and constraints in their lives. They mention the broader, contextual issues that are correlated with teenage pregnancy, such as growing up with crack-addicted mothers and living in contexts where one must fight to defend oneself. The girls deal with jealousy from other girls and sexual proposals from guys, resisting drugs and the threat of AIDS, and watching friends die. They also mention societal disparities and prejudice as well as the differences they have witnessed between education in the inner city and in the suburbs. A plethora of stressors and barriers frame their lives. However, despite these pressures, the young women continue to assert an active ability to handle their lives. While expressing the reality of the environments that structure their experiences, they also reiterate their personal control. Their stories suggest resiliency and courage as each young woman carves her individual path through the world, making decisions through lenses that have been shaped by context and the barriers of life.

Ethnographic Findings

Veronica and Danita, two teenager mothers, talk about the issue of responsibility in regards to motherhood and the connection between education and supporting one's child. It is interesting to note that Veronica begins this discussion by asserting that, "just because you a teen mom don't mean that you're a bad person or your life is over. Like people say you can't get your education, cause you have a child." This initial phrase indicates her awareness of the stereotype of the teenage mother and Veronica counters this image by stating that having her child has enabled her to value her education more strongly. She contends that having a dependent has made her find merit in education as it will allow her to provide for her daughter. As noted earlier, Luker (1996) suggests that the relationship between teenage pregnancy and school dropout is not clearly evident. In early studies during the 1950s and 1960s, pregnancy was elucidated as a common cause of school dropout among adolescent girls. However, Luker (1996) argues that many of these statistical figures of school dropout among adolescent girls do not indicate whether withdrawal from school occurred prior to or after pregnancy. Further, Luker (1996) indicates that in more recent studies, as researchers have been able to control more effectively for differences in ability, motivation, and family background, the disparity in the educational levels of teenage mothers and older mothers has diminished considerably.

Luker (1996) also suggests that the factor of race influences school withdrawal. Black teenage mothers are more likely to graduate from high school than are white teenage mothers. This finding can be related to the downside of privilege noted earlier, as youth who do not develop responsive coping skills may not be able to effectively negotiate the challenges of teen parenting.

Several issues complicate the association between teenage motherhood and dropping out of school. More recent studies indicate that many teenage mothers drop out of school before becoming pregnant, and that relative to adolescents who remain childless, in similar conditions of poverty, they may not fare significantly worse in terms of educational outcomes. A study by Stevenson, Maton, and Teti (1998) indicates that value is placed on schooling, even among students of low socioeconomic status. Veronica and Danita talk about their impressions of their schooling and they discuss the disparities they find evident in the educational system.

Veronica: It's still . . . racial issues. When I graduated out of elementary, I went to a school, a gifted school for children. [Inaudible] which was all white. So, I was like almost the only black child there and that's what my trouble started from. Because it was a lot of prejudice and all that, you know, and then when I look back at everything, my elementary school . . . was in my neighborhood and this, one wasn't in my neighborhood. It was totally different learning. It was two different environments. They teach you all different things, you know. What you (she is referring to the researcher's previous description of her high school experience) all learn, we don't learn. You all might have 16 kids in a classroom. We got forty kids in a classroom. How you supposed to learn? You know, so when I got to the other school and I had seventeen kids in my classroom, it was unusual to me . . . the learning was different. It wasn't hard and it wasn't easy but it was different. It was a different way of learnin. So that's why, you know, it's the environment that you're—the society and the neighborhood you in. But you get taught different things, so some people—if you in this environment, which is our environment, you're not getting taught to be ahead. You're getting taught to be behind. And if you in that society which you were raised, you didn't have to go through this, you getting taught to be ahead.

(Discourse not included.)

Danita: . . . So when I—I think Philly schools is so much easier than suburb schools. I swear to god. Because the suburb schools are so organized. That's the way it is. I don't know why it is. The suburb schools is so organized. They have everything planned out. They have everything computerized—everything. Like I could ask my teacher on the same day, what was my grade. My teacher had . . . our grade posted on the wall. When I went to Philly school, I ask them what's my grade, "Oh, Danita, I don't know." "Oh, what's this?" "Oh, I don't know." I mean I had to, you know, I mean—I wasn't used to being around Black people, a lot of them in a classroom. I was not used to that.

Veronica: That's—that's the system and [inaudible] the system and society the way they got it goin, they—that's goin back way, way, way back when they done put Blacks behind and you know White people ahead.

Danita: Slavery and stuff.

Veronica: And that's another reason why Blacks got so much hate in them from learnin about all this and goin on. And that's another reason cause Black people was taught not to learn. So you know its still carrying on, its still goin on, just because they in school, don't mean they learnin. Because I don't see how you can learn in a class with forty students.

Veronica: Because you know why they give more money to them schools then they do to our schools. So, you know, they want us behind. You know, you got kids, you got people that graduate from our middle schools and got straight A's and got straight A's since they been in school. And they will go to a school like Martin Luther King and get … a scholarship. People, I think really it's only what you make it…

The girls discuss differences between city and suburb schools, which include distinctions in financial resources, class size, learning styles, organization, planning and teacher involvement. However, this conversation is not only a commentary about the differences between suburb and city schools. Underlying these differences are notions more intangible in character such as racism and White privilege. The girls invoke ideas of race and economics in framing the differences between city and suburb schools. They attempt to locate the root of the differences between White and Black learning opportunities. Veronica and Danita locate this divergence historically, finding its roots in the foundation of slavery. Veronica notes that while Black children are in school, they are not necessarily learning or getting taught to "be ahead."

This comment complicates a notion of school access. Veronica claims that Black children have the opportunity to attend school. However, she clarifies that attendance at *a* school does not necessitate an equivalent (compared to the suburbs) quality of educational experience. Metz (1989) argues that the literature refers to a "common script" of schooling, which has created the notion of a "real school," in which high schools generally have the same form across the United States. However, she argues that this notion of sameness depoliticizes the disparities between privileged high schools and disadvantaged high schools. Veronica and Danita's comments indicate the differences in educational quality and resources between high schools that serve different populations of students. They characterize this population difference by race. The girls contend that this disparity has been internalized by Blacks and has developed into hatred. Veronica and Danita locate the impetus of this disparity within the evasive, all-encompassing term—society. The girls locate the root of this disparity in history and society and suggest that it is perpetuated through economics and education. However, Veronica ends this discussion by shifting her focus in the opposite direction. She makes the conversation more tangible as she individualizes it. Veronica cites the hypothetical example of a student from a high school in Philadelphia winning a scholarship to collage. She states, "...I think it's only what you make it," she pulls us away from the barriers that exist and shows us that in spite of these obstacles, some teenagers, through their own initiative, are able to succeed in the educational system.

As a theoretical framework, Spencer's PVEST model fosters an understanding of agency and makes room for resiliency by linking the young mothers' stressful experiences and interpretations into coping strategies, and then transforming them into a resilient identity of their own. In spite of an abundance of obstacles both within educational systems and within the realities of their contexts, some low-income black students, including teenage mothers are able to succeed in the educational system.

ETHNOGRAPHIC CASE STUDY: AFRICAN AMERICAN TEEN FATHERS

Despite the fact that there is an abundance of research that focuses on the general topic of adolescent pregnancy, further research is required. Existing research in this field is extremely myopic in character. Comparatively speaking, very little is known about adolescent fathers; the bulk of research has concentrated on adolescent mothers. In order to provide a more complete and accurate picture of adolescent pregnancy, future research must focus on the roles of males in this phenomenon. In particular, careful attention must be paid to the role of education in the lives of young urban fathers. Such research offers an important opportunity to understand the role of job marketability and availability in determining the familial participation of fathers. The reasons for this omission of men in the discourse are numerous; females are more likely to have custody of the child and are more likely to seek help from social support agencies. Thus, we must examine the roles of African American adolescent and young adult fathers in the context of education. To do so, ethnographic data collected by one of the authors (Seaton, 1994) will be presented. Seaton (1994) observed group sessions of the Fathers Initiative Program (FIP), a Philadelphia-based program designed to increase the familial participation of African American fathers. Additionally, the role of curriculum in educating diverse populations such as teenage and young adult fathers will also be discussed.

The limited research, which is available on adolescent fathers, appears to agree that there is nothing inherently wrong with parenting a child as an adolescent. Literature on the topic of adolescent and young adult fatherhood explicitly conveys that fatherhood only becomes problematic if it is incongruent with the larger social context in which it occurs. For example, in an agrarian society having a child as an adolescent would not be problematic, because more people are needed to increase agricultural productivity. In fact, adolescent pregnancy would be a plus. The exact opposite is true of societies such as present-day America, of which economic mobility is positively correlated with educational attainment. Parenting a child as an adolescent is problematic because the responsibility that accompanies giving birth to a child may greatly hinder one's educational attainment. Consequently, parenting a child as an adolescent may greatly decrease one's own economic mobility. The incongruence between society and adolescent/young adult fathers is particularly problematic for African Americans.

Father research has been framed in terms of the traditional roles associated with fatherhood—provider, protector and, to a lesser extent, nurturer. McAdoo (1993) contends that this limited view tends to merely conclude that Black men are failing at the provider role. This contention is made without careful examination of process or a consideration of the variance among Black fathers. He further, contends that fathers need to be examined from an ecological framework. Ecological theory assumes that fathers of all ethnic groups play various roles in the family and community, roles that can lead to positive or negative family outcomes. Additionally, this perspective considers the effects of economic, educational, and social institutions in functioning as protective or inhibiting factors to fathers fulfilling their familial role.

Research has primarily focused on child outcomes when fathers are absent from the family. The well-being of fathers has largely been neglected. Studies have demonstrated that children bear the brunt of the social and economic repercussions of father absenteeism as mothers tend to be under greater stress meeting family financial and psychological needs (McLoyd, Jayaratne, Caballo, & Borquez, 1994). However, the prevailing thought is that children reared in single parent households are more likely to experience risk factors that are highly correlated with negative life outcomes, particularly boys (Johnson, 1996). For example, boys reared in father absent homes are more vulnerable to aggressive behaviors and sex role confusion (Montare & Bonne, 1980). Further, studies have demonstrated that active fathers, particularly middle class, serve important roles of nurturer and provider. The primary tenant of ecological systems theory is that nothing exists in isolation. Changes in one are of a system has impact and influence in other seemingly unrelated areas of the system. PVEST highlights the role of ecological risks and how they are understood by the individual as one of the primary determinants of life outcomes. In the case of fathers in the (FIP), the risks were numerous and primarily centered around their identity as Black males rather than fathers. This trend tends to follow the development of research literature as much of the father literature has its genesis in the research on Black males (Gadsden & Smith, 1995).

Race and gender are the primary components of the social glue that bonded the group members at FIP together. By providing the young men a forum to share and express ideas as it relates to them and those who are similar the fathers are enabled to bring about a change in their lives. According to Seaton (1994), the most memorable night of a year long ethnographic study was a discussion of police brutality in the Black community. There were at least fifteen Black males who could all recall at least one incident of being wrongly accused or harassed by the police. Although there were some group members who were previously involved in illegal activities, they proclaimed their innocence at the time they were approached by the police. One father, in tears told how his incident with the police has "scarred his daughter for the rest of her life":

> **Nate**:   I went over my baby's mom's house to see my little daughter, right. So I come in and (a tear began to roll down Nate's face, the room becomes still with motionless silence) my daughter is standin' there in her underwear and she is hiddin' somethin' behind her back. So I say to her, "come here let me see what you got behind your back." So she comes and she . . . hidin' a gun behind her back. So I go to take it from her and she won't let me. She said that she needed it to shoot the cops when they come beat daddy again. Man, they just came in the house . . . and started beatin' me down. If they had to fu__ me up like that they didn't have to do it in front of my three-year-old daughter.

As we consider the location of Nate's beating, it is only then that we fully comprehend the tensions between the roles of protector that fathers are supposed to fulfill. Nate was beaten by the police in his home—a place where one finds solitude, safety and comfort. Nate was arrested because he met the profile of a robbery suspect. Ultimately, he was not convicted of the crime as he was working at the time. To be sure, Nate was not the only one affected. His daughter was greatly impacted by witnessing her father being beaten by the cops that is evident by her usage of the toy gun.

Another compelling example of how one is challenged by their context is the experience of one young father's encounter with the criminal justice system. During the sharing portion of a group session, Derek expressed his happiness not to be behind bars and explained to the rest of the group of how he managed the challenge of a racially biased judicial system.

> Derek: Man I was in that courtroom. Man I was scared. Mr. Brown was there with me. It was nothing' but Black and Puerto Ricans up in there. And all the other people like the judge and the uhm, uhm bailiff and the guy that took you in back to the holdin' cell were White. (All around the table people were shaking their heads slowly not of disbelief, but of pity.) I was scared man. Everybody that came before was locked up. I'm like the eighth one right. Up in Jersey they do not play yo' Black a—walk in, but you won't be walkin' out! (there is an outburst of laughter around the room as someone comments "Damn, sounds like a roach motel.) So it's my turn, I go up there man, I ain't talkin' no slang—I was like, "Yes sir. No sir.". And this time I didn't go in no jeans, Tee-shirt, or sneaks. I went and bought some clothes and put a pair of dress pants in the cleaners. (There is another outburst of laughter as someone comments, "Oh they wasn' t keepin' you there huh?") Naw man. I had my shirt and tie and everything. I was the only one that came in like that. I told 'em that I was in this program and that I was tryin' to get my life together. And, I think the fact that George was there every time I went up there helped out too. Cause the judge was asking him questions about me.

Through this experience Derek has learned that tee-shirts, jeans, and sneakers will not afford him the level of social acceptability required to remain free. In order to retain his freedom, he becomes what he thinks the judge wants him to be—a reformed young Black man in a suit. Unfortunately, there was greater emphasis on the suit rather than reformation.

To adequately address the needs of fathers, or any population for that matter, one must understand that learning is not bound to a specific location. Learning takes place across multiple context. Dewey (1938) captures the dynamic between learning and context:

> Since in reality there is nothing to which growth is relative save more growth, there is nothing to which education is subordinate save more education. It is a commonplace to say that education should not cease when one leaves school. The point of this commonplace is that the purpose of education is to insure the continuance of education by organizing powers that insure growth. The inclination to learn from life itself and to make the conditions of life such that all will learn in the process of living. (Dewey, 1938, p. 51)

Dewey (1938) does not limit learning to the actual school building. Learning takes place in many different contexts and is influenced by many different actors. He asserts that a school merely facilitates growth by

encouraging life long learning. Learning occurs through the lived experience of different opportunities or possibilities. Life's experience is at the
crux of learning. Sound curriculum acknowledges the lived experiences of
the learner as it attempts to expose the learner to additional experience
that will promote growth. All sound curriculums are based on research and
give some forethought as to how the pupil is to be engaged as well as their
past learning experiences. Accordingly, curriculum must address much
more than the actual subject matter, it must also attempt to at least
acknowledge the multiple ecologies in which students exist.

The formal curriculum for the Father's Initiative Program appears to
meet these requirements. However, the curriculum did not address the
challenges faced by many of the fathers. Before moving to the actual book
learning there were some other needs that had to be met. Often it is the
challenge of curriculums to consider the multiple ecologies of the learner.
One of the unwritten objectives of (FCP.) is to inform African American
fathers of their heritage and the racist context in which they live. This is an
unveiled attempt to use knowledge as a protective factor to cope with or
avoid stressful situations.

For example, during a group session Mr. Brown posed the following
question in a preacher-like fashion:

> If you know they wanna lock your a–– up why you do sh–t to get yourself in
> trouble? There is nothing more that the Cops wanna do than throw your
> Black a–– in jail. What good are you to your family? Your community? Your-
> self? If you see a pothole in the road, what, you gonna go through it or are
> you going to go around it.

The room was silent as he spoke. All eyes were trained on him as he vented
frustrated by the arrest of one of the group members who was caught with
drugs. There is no way that one could be 100% certain that Mr. Brown's
homily caused group members to stop selling drugs, but the incidence of
"stopped selling drugs due to the program" self reports went from 0 to 3
within the next four weeks.

Mr. Brown, the program director, would probably contend that a lot of
Black young adult and adolescent fathers do not participate in their children's lives due to the inability to cope with the stresses of racism and poverty. Thus, there is serious role constraint.

When first granted permission to enter what the group termed the
"house"—a high-rise office room equipped with conference table, T.V. and
V.C.R., Seaton (1994) was surprised by the word used to refer to the conference room—"house." Typically when one thinks of the word "house" feelings of freedom, power, and sanctity come to mind.

Throughout the entire session, Seaton (1994) anxiously anticipated discussions on changing diapers, preparing formula, and helpful hints for diaper rash. Those discussions never came. Instead, there were discussions on the problems that one encountered through the week a viewing of *Eyes on the Prize* (Williams, 1987), a documentary detailing the trials and triumphs of African Americans during the Civil Rights Movement. After being in the house for two weeks, Seaton realized that the curriculum was Afrocentric as opposed to "father centric" in nature.

That is, rather than having discussions limited to what it is to be a father, the discussion hinged upon what it is to be a Black male who is a father. The latter more specifically addresses the challenges and risks that the men faced by virtue of being African American.

When asked why the curriculum did not include items such as diaper changing, or child dietary needs the director responded:

Mr. Brown: All that stuff is in there (pointing to a large three ringed curriculum guide book on a shelf). But that study ain't gonna do these guys no good. Most of 'em took care of their brothers and sisters when they were younger or get more that one child. They know that stuff already. They need to know what's really going on out there in the world. Do you have any brothers or sisters? (looking at me as if he had proven a major point) Did you ever feed them or change diapers?

Seaton (abruptly and with certainty):   Yeah!

Mr. Brown: So you already know about diapers and formula.

Seaton: Yeah, I guess that you are right.

Mr. Brown: It is the same with these guys.

The curriculum serves as a protective factor as it provides a forum for young Black men to discuss the many roles and how they make sense of them. Additionally, the family like atmosphere provides a source of challenge, recognition and accountability.

The viewing of series such as *Eyes on The Prize*, and discussions such as the following provide a historical context for the challenges that men face. From a PVEST perspective, it also highlights positive coping strategies that the young men may employ to overcome challenges in their own lives and in their communities. Anthony, 20, a father of two, probes the group as to why many communities lack solidarity:

Anthony: Why do y'all think that nobody organizing against stuff no more—like that woman in the tape (Fannie Lou Hammer). She stood up to a crowd of thousands of White people and now days, we won't even stand up to three dealers on the corner. As soon as somebody get a degree or somethin', they moving out the neighborhood. They should at least stay and try to be examples or role models.

Frank: Just like Mr. Brown said, 'They suffer from the illusion of inclusion."

Mr. Brown: Well just think about it. How can somebody organize if they are high or been drinking malt liquor all day? Why do you think that they put that stuff in your neighborhoods? How many Stop and Go's (neighborhood stores that primarily carry alcohol, cigarettes, and fast food) do you see around your block?

Many of the young men answer at once, "Four, three, five, six…"

Mr. Brown (continues):   When you drive out to the Northeast (a predominately White section of town) how many do you see?

Many of the young men again speak at once. Two responses stood out over the others, "None" and "They ain't got sh-t up there."

The discussion which ensued after watching "Eyes on the Prize" motivated many to reconsider some of the social roles that they play. "Der he," the television blared as an elderly Black man boldly stood up and pointed out the White murderer of young Emmit Till, a thirteen-year-old Black boy who was murdered in Mississippi.

Mr. Brown: I just want you to realize how much courage it took for this man to point out a White man and accuse him of murder, the man was brave…

Bill: That's just like today you got people who scared to death of tryin' to tell drug dealers "get off the corner." They scared to turn him in. And the drug dealer is less likely to hurt you than the White man who wants to string you up.

Shawn: That's how I'm raisin' my son to be better than me. He's going to stick up for what he believes in. Just like the old man. My mom used to say, "that if you don't stand for something you'll fall for anything." My son is gonna stand for the right.

In addition to impacting fathering, F.I.P has also impacted the way individuals see their roles as members of the Black community. They now play a more active role in the community. For example, two brothers in the program have turned into community activists and coach a football team (which incidentally made it to the playoffs). When the season ended the team will turn into an after-school interest group. One of the fathers who used to sell drugs has taken the role of drug activist trying to persuade those who do sell to stop. Brian describes his attempt to convince others to stop selling drugs:

> **Brian**:   When I go around the way and see some of the boys that I used to be out there in the game with. I try to talk them out of it. I don't tell 'em they wrong or bad or nothin' because I was out there just like them … sellin' poison to people. But dat ain't no way to live.

Another young man as part of his own recovery from drugs speaks at local school and for various social service agencies. He describes his experience:

> **James**:   Man it ain't nothing like recovery! I can remember when I was just out there sellin weed, powder (cocaine), caps (crack cocaine). You name it, I had it. Then I started usin' the sh–t. I started sellin' it to get high myself. It did not matter to me how old the people was either man. Young bols (boys) or old heads, I sold it to them. Now man that I am recovering from my sickness (pointing to his head), I can go out there and tell other people that sh–t ain't worth it. I suppose to go talk to this group of about forty-five young people … delinquents in trouble with the law … I feel like I am paying some of my debt off. I know that I ain't gonna be able to reach all of them, but if I reach jus one, it will be worth it.

Overall, the case studies from the Father's Initiative Program highlight the multiple layers of risks and stress engagement encountered by Black adolescent males. These factors compound the normative challenges faced by adolescents males, particularly those who are fathers.

CONCLUSION AND IMPLICATIONS

To adequately address the issue of teen parenting, the emphasis must be not just on prevention; it must incorporate a cultural and developmental understanding of the phenomenon in context and also seek to support teen parents. The influence of race and gender identity development must be considered, as numerous factors create specific situations of stress for minority youth. This paper has noted the impact of several needed social justices, including reducing poverty, reexamining academic tracking, and combating police brutality, which may not seem directly related to teen pregnancy.

Intervention and policy innovations designed to address teen parenting must provide support at multiple levels: federal, state, and local; similarly, they must focus not only on teen parenting, but also on the broader range of contextual experiences faced by youth. There are different support systems for teenage parents through every level of the government. In terms of current policy initiatives, each level's response to teenage pregnancy must be considered.

Federal Level

Earlier in this paper the 1996 welfare reform act as discussed and its implications for teenage pregnancy were outlined. However, other federal initiatives also impact teenage pregnancy. One such initiative, Title IX of 1972, prohibited the exclusion of pregnant or parenting teens from educational programs and activities.

State Level

Although the level of programming for teenage pregnancy varies from state to state, Lesko (1995) argues that, overall, programs that deal with teenage pregnancy at the state level often act in "the mode of crisis intervention" (Lesko, 1995, p.188). These programs are short-term in nature, and usually include little or no follow-up with young mothers. Such programs range in their comprehensiveness: some cover prevention and support a wide variety of services to teenagers, and others provide job training alone in an attempt to prevent students' premature departure from school. Typically, states provide very little leadership concerning program implementation, and much is left on the shoulders of individual districts.

Local Districts

Some districts are moving toward more comprehensive approaches to teenage pregnancy. These programs are housed in supportive environments and allow students to work flexibly. They address the educational, medical, counseling, and child care services that young parents often need. Although many of these programs successfully address the needs of teen parents, they often suffer from unstable funding and lack dependable political support.

A number of recommendations can also follow from this analysis:

- *Inter-generational solutions.*   As discussed earlier, teen parents are often children of former teen parents. This fact makes the issue of teenage pregnancy an inter-generational one. The PRWORA addresses this fact in its requirement that teen parents who receive Temporary Assistance for Needy Families (TANF) must live with their parents in most circumstances. These youth must also attend school in order to receive funding. For these reasons, supports need to be provided to the parents and grandparents in a teen parent's family, as they often need to assume different roles (caregiver, income-bearer, etc.) to support the needs of the teen's child.

- *Parenting.*   Schools should offer classes in parenting, which would inform young parents about the health, social and psychological needs of their children. Such programs can better equip a young parent as each moves into adulthood and continues responding to child care needs. Moreover, as illustrated by the Father's Initiative Program, such programs must take into account the broader social and community context and aim for the development of competent and resilient identities.

- *Child care.*   Funding for child care is an important support for teen parents. Since young parents are required to attend school to receive TANF payments, the needs of their children must be met during the school day. Stable funding must be provided, either in the form of provider or consumer-based subsidies, which can make the cost of child care affordable or cost-free for young parents.

- *Supportive schools.*   Even in the absence of teen pregnancy, most populations who are at risk of early pregnancy (minorities in particular) usually experience high attrition rates from high school. Teenage parenting exacerbates this problem. Schools must implement systems that help support young parents' graduation from high school. Such support may require the creation of a flexible school day for parents. Moreover, alternative schools may offer a more supportive educational environment for teens who may not be able to fit normal school standards and expectations.

- *Health Care.*   Pregnant teens need access to quality health care during and after their child is born. School-based programs may provide these services to make then more accessible for young mothers. These services may include prenatal care, nutrition education, and counseling support. These services can also be helpful in preventing pregnancies in the greater school population.

Of course, general improvement of economic opportunities will help address the poverty that is associated with teen parenting and remains a major risk factor for numerous adverse outcomes. In conjunction with creating educational options, post-secondary opportunities for both work and education must be expanded.

Additionally, social support is vital, as teens need programs that address the risks they face, many of which have been illustrated in this paper. Such programs may address early teenage sexual activity, drug and alcohol abuse, domestic and community violence, among others. Many young women who become teenage mothers have early links with public agencies in some way before their pregnancy (Institute for Educational Leadership, 1999). Therefore, once a child is in the system, he or she should be targeted for additional social support. Furthermore, after their pregnancies, some young mothers may need safe housing. Although the PRWORA offers funding for "second chance homes," this funding is scarce and available houses are few.

To be effective potential interventions should represent standards of cultural competence, and seek to understand the meanings of both sexuality and parenthood to male and female adolescents growing up in particular social and cultural contexts. As noted, both structural racism and racial stereotyping add another level of complexity to these issues. While the ideas posed in this paper go beyond the conventional realm of thought on teen parenting, such an extension is necessary to adequately address the underlying issues. It is only by considering the complex interactions between structural factors, policy influences, cultural values and beliefs, and normative processes of race and gender identity development that responsive supports can adequately and competently address the phenomenon.

NOTE

1 This paper was prepared with funding provided to the first author by the National Institutes of Mental Health, National Science Foundation, Office of Educational Research Improvement (Field-Initiated-Studies), and the Ford and Kellogg Foundations.

REFERENCES

Anderson, E. (1999). *Code of the street.* New York: W.W. Norton & Company.

Annie E. Casey Foundation. (2000). *Kids count data book: State profiles on child well-being.* Baltimore, MD: The Annie E. Casey Foundation.

Blum, R., & Rhinehart, P. (1998). *Reducing the risk: Connections that make a difference in the lives of youth.* Minneapolis: University of Minnesota.

Boykin, A.W. (1986). The triple quandary and the schooling of Afro-American children. In U. Neisser (Ed.), *The school achievement of minority children* (pp. 57–92). Hillsdale, NJ: Lawrence Erlbaum Associates.

Bronfenbrenner, U. (1989). Ecological systems theory. In R. Vasta (Ed.), *Annals of child development* (pp. 187–248). Greenwich, CT: JAI Press.

Card, J.J. (1999). Teen pregnancy prevention: Do any programs work? *Annual Review of Public Health, 20,* 257–285.

Chestang, L.W. (1972). *Character development in a hostile environment.* Occasional Paper No. 3 (Series), (pp. 1–12). Chicago: University of Chicago Press.

Cunningham, M. (1993). African American adolescent males sex role development: A literature review. *Journal of African American Males Studies, 1*(1), 30–37.

Cunningham, M. (1994). *Expressions of manhood: Predictors of educational achievement and African-American adolescent males.* Dissertation abstracts International, 34(5-A), (University Microfilms No. 1223).

Dewey, J. (1938). *Experience and Education.* New York: Macmillan.

Deyhle, D. (1986). Break dancing and breaking out: Anglos, Utes, and Navajos in a border reservation high school. *Anthropology and Education Quarterly, 17,* 111–127.

Ellis, B.J, McFadyen-Ketchum, S., Dodge, K.A., Pettit, G.S., & Bates, J.E. (1999). Quality of early family relationships and individual differences in the timing of pubertal maturation in girls: A longitudinal test of an evolutionary model. *Journal of Personality & Social Psychology* 77(2), 387–401.

Fordham, S., & Ogbu, J. U. (1986). Black students' school success: Coping with the "burden of 'acting White.'" *The Urban Review, 18*(3), 176–206.

Furstenberg, F. (1998). When will teenage childbearing become a problem? The implications of western experience for developing countries. *Studies in Family Planning, 29*(2), 246–253.

Gadsen, V., & Smith, R. (1994). African American Males and Fatherhood: Issues in Research and Practice. *Journal of Negro Education, 63(4),* 634–648.

George, R.M., & Lee, B.J. (1997). Abuse and Neglect of Children. In R.A. Maynard (Ed.), *Kids Having Kids: Economic Costs and Social Consequences of Teen Pregnancy* (pp. 205–230). Washington, DC: The Urban Institute Press.

Harpalani, V. (2001, April). *Racial stereotyping and Black athletic achievement: Developmental and ethical considerations.* Presented at the 2001 Biennial Meeting of the Society for Research in Child Development (SRCD), Minneapolis, MN.

Havigurst, R.J. (1953). *Human development and education.* New York: McKay.

Helms, J. (Ed.). (1990). *Black and White racial identity: Theory, research, and practice.* Westport, CT: Greenwood.

Hetherington, E.M., Cox, M., & Cox, R. (1985). Long-term effects of divorce and remarriage on the adjustment of children. *Journal of American Academy of Psychiatry, 24,* 518–530.

Hill, J.P., & Lynch, M.E. (1983). The intensification of gender-related role expectations during early adolescence. In J. Brooks-Gunn & A.C. Petersen (Eds.), *Girls at puberty: Biological and psychosocial perspectives* (pp.201–228). New York: Plenum Press.

Ignatiev, N. (1995). *How the Irish became White.* New York: Routledge.

Institute for Educational Leadership. (1999). *School-based and school-linked programs for pregnant and parenting teens and their children.* Washington, DC: National Institute on Early Childhood Development and Education.

Johnson, D. (1996). *Father presence matters: A review of the literature.* Philadelphia: National Center on Fathers and Families.

Kardiner, A., & Ovesey, L. (1951). *The mark of oppression: Explorations in the personality of the American Negro.* New York: W.W. Norton.

Lawson, A., & Rhode, D. (Eds.). (1993). *The politics of pregancy: Adolescent sexuality and public policy.* New Haven: Yale University Press.

Lemonick, M. D. (2000, October 30). Teens before their time. *Time, 66–74.*

Lesko, N. (1995, Summer). The leaky needs of school-aged mothers: An examination of U.S. programs and policies. *Curriculum Inquiry, 25*(2), 177–205.

Luker, K. (1996). Dubious conceptions: The politics of teenage pregnancy: London: Harvard University Press.

Mauldon, J. (1998). Families started by teenagers. In M. Mason, A. Skolnick, & S. Sugarman (Eds.), *All our families: New policies for a new century.* (pp. 39–65). New York: Oxford Press.

Mayer, S.E., & Jencks, C. (1989). Growing up in poor neighborhoods: How much does it matter? *Science, 243,* 1441–45.

Maynard, R.A., (Ed.). (1996). *Kids having kids: A Robin Hood Foundation Special Report on the Costs of adolescent childbearing.* New York: Robin Hood Foundation.

McAdoo. (1993). The roles of African American fathers: An ecological perspective. *The Journal of Contemporary Human Services, 53,* 28–34.

McLoyd, V. (1990). The impact of economic hardship on Black families and children: Psychological distress, parenting, and socio-emotional development. *Child Development, 61,* 311–346.

McLoyd, V., Jayaratne, T., Ceballo, R., & Borquez, J. (1994). Unemployment and work interruption among African American single mothers: Effects on parenting and adolescent socio-emotional functioning. *Child Development, 65,* 562–589.

Metz, M. (1989). Real School: a universal drama amid disparate experience. *Politics of Education Yearbook,* 75–91.

Montare, A., & Bonne, S. L. (1980). Aggression and paternal absence: Racial-ethnic differences among inner-city boys. *The Journal of Genetic Psychology, 137,* 223–231.

National Campaign to Prevent Teen Pregnancy. (1996). *Teenage pregnancy provisions in the welfare reform bill.* Available <http://www.teenpregnancy.org/WelSum.html> (20 June 2001).

National Campaign to Prevent Teen Pregnancy. (1997). *Whatever happened to childhood? The problem of teen pregnancy in the United States.* Washington DC: Author.

National Campaign to Prevent Teen Pregnancy. (2000, May). *Fact sheet: Recent trends in teen pregnancy, sexual activity, and contraceptive use.* Available <http://www.teenpregnancy.org/rctrend.htm> (20 June, 2001).

Parker, S., Nichter, M., Nichter, M., Vuckovic, N., Sims, C., & Ritenbaugh, C. (1995). Body image and weight concerns among African American and White adolescent females: Differences that make a difference. *Human Organization 54*(2); 103–113.

Seaton, G. (1994, March). *"Boys two men": An ethnographic investigation of maleness and fatherhood.* Paper presented at the University of Pennsylvania Urban Ethnography Forum, Philadelphia, PA.

Silver, L.J. (2000). *Being a teen mom: Multiple angles.* Unpublished manuscript, University of Pennsylvania.

Spencer, M.B. (1995). Old issues and new theorizing about African American Youth: A phenomenological variant of ecological systems theory. In R.L. Taylor (Ed.), *Black youth: Perspectives on their status in the United States* (pp. 37–70). Westport, CT: Praeger.

Spencer, M.B. (1999). Social and cultural influences on school adjustment: The application of an identity-focused cultural ecological perspective. *Educational Psychologist, 34*, 1, 43–57.

Spencer, M.B. (2001). Identity, achievement, orientation and race: "Lessons learned" about the normative developmental experiences of African American males. In W. Watkins, J.H. Lewis, & V. Chou, (Eds.), *Race and education* (pp. 100–127). Needham Heights, MA: Allyn & Bacon.

Spencer, M.B., & Cunningham, M. (in press). Patterns of resilience and vulnerability: Examining diversity within African American youth. In G.K. Brookins & M.B. Spencer (Eds.), *Ethnicity and diversity: Minorities no more.* Stamford, CT: JAI Press, Inc.

Spencer, M.B., & Dornbusch, S. (1990). American minority adolescents. In S. Feldman & G. Elliot (Eds.) *At the threshold: The developing adolescent* (pp. 123–146). Cambridge, MA.: Harvard University Press.

Spencer, M.B., Dupree, D., & Hartmann, T. (1997). A phenomenological variant of ecological systems theory (PVEST): A self-organization perspective in context. *Development and Psychopathology, 9,* 817–833.

Spencer, M.B., & Harpalani, V. (in press). African American adolescents, Research on. In R.M. Lerner & J.V. Lerner (Eds.), *Today's teenager: Adolescents in America.* Denver, CO: ABC-CLIO.

Spencer, M.B., Harpalani, V., & Dell'Angelo, T. (in press). Structural racism and community health: A theory-driven model for identity intervention. In W. Allen, M.B. Spencer, & C. O'Connor (Eds.), *New perspectives on African American education: Race, achievement, and social inequality.* Stamford, CT: JAI Press.

Spurlock, J., & Norris, D.M. (1991). The impact of culture and race on the development of African Americans in the United States. *American Psychiatric Press Review of Psychiatry, 10,* 594–607.

Steinberg, L. (1999). *Adolescence.* New York: McGraw-Hill.

Stevenson, H.C. (1997). "Missed, dissed, and pissed": Making meaning of neighborhood risk, fear and anger management in urban Black youth. *Cultural Diversity and Mental Health, 3*(1), 37–52.

Stevenson, W., Maton, K., & Teti, D. (1998). School importance and dropout among pregnant adolescents. *Journal of Adolescent Health, 22,* 376–382.

Sung, B.L. (1985). Bicultural conflicts in Chinese immigrant children. *Journal of Comparative Family Studies, 16*(2), 255–270.

Swanson, D.P., Spencer, M.B., & Peterson, A. (1998). Identity formation in adolescence. In K. Borman & B. Schneider (Eds.), *The adolescent years: Social influences and educational challenges,* Ninety-seventh Yearbook of the National Society for the Study of Education (Part 1, pp. 18–41). Chicago: University of Chicago Press.

U.S. General Accounting Office: Health, Education, and Human Services Division. (1998). *Teen mothers: Selected socio-demographic characteristics and risk factors.* Report to the Honorable Charles B. Rangel, House of Representatives. (GAO/ HEHS Publication No. 98-141). Washington, DC: Author.

Webster's II New Riverside Dictionary. (1996). Boston: Houghton Mifflin.

Williams, J. (Producer). (1987). *Eyes on the prize: America's civil rights years, 1954–1965.* [Film].

Wolfe, B., & Perozek, M. (1997). Teen children's health and health care use. In R.A. Maynard (Ed.), *Kids having kids: Economic costs and social consequences of teen pregnancy* (pp. 181–203). Washington, DC: The Urban Institute Press.

Youniss, J. (1998, February). *Symposium submission summary statement.* Unpublished submission statement for the Identity and Moral Life of Adolescents symposium panel, Society for Research on Adolescence Conference, San Diego, CA.

CHAPTER 9

Dropping Out of High School

Detours in the Life Course

Phillip Kaufman

INTRODUCTION

Adolescence is a time of transition—from a period of dependence on others to one of self-sufficiency (Keniston, 1970). One of the most critical transition points is graduation from high school. Without completing high school, it is difficult for young people to become autonomous members of society and achieve the independence that marks adulthood. In today's economy, employers demand the aptitudes that a high school diploma signals. Young people without these credentials are locked out of many jobs that could give them economic independence (Murnane & Levy, 1996). When dropouts do find employment, they earn substantially less than high school completers. For example, the Census Bureau estimates that more than one-third of all high schools dropouts who were employed full-time in 1990 worked at low wage jobs—those that paid below the poverty level for a family of four (U.S. Bureau of the Census, 1992). In 1998, dropouts earned 25% less per year than did workers with only a high school credential. Dropouts earned less than 70% of what workers with just some college, but no degree, earned (National Center for Education Statistics, 1999).

Economic hardship is not the only consequence of adolescents failing to complete high school. Dropouts are also more likely to have health problems, and are also more likely to receive public assistance than high school graduates who do not go on to college (Rumberger, 1987). This increased reliance on public assistance is likely due, at least in part, to the fact that young women who drop out of school are more likely to have children at younger ages and more likely to be single parents than high school graduates (McMillen & Kaufman, 1996). Dropouts also make up a disproportionate percentage of the nation's prison and death row inmates. Estimates indicate that one-quarter of federal and one-half of state prison inmates are high school dropouts (Harlow, 1994).

This chapter examines the causes and consequences of dropping out of high school for young people in the United States. I begin with a brief description of the historical context of early school leaving—dropping out of high school has not always been such a critical transition for adolescents as it is today. I follow this overview with a discussion of the issues involved in measuring who drops out of school—no easy task for something that seems so simple. I then discuss what is known about the causes of dropping out of high school in late twentieth-century America, using several theoretical frameworks to examine the antecedents to dropping out of school. I follow with an examination of the power of these models to predict which students will drop out of school and why these models do not always work well. This discussion leads to the consideration of resiliency and protective factors. I end with a discussion of what can or should be done about the dropout problem as currently defined.

HISTORICAL CONTEXT

Graduation from high school has not always been seen as the norm for adolescents in this country. At the beginning of the 20th century most young people stopped their formal education well short of a high school diploma. Few students at the time attended high school, let alone graduated (Dorn, 1996). In 1909 only about 10% of 17 year olds had graduated from high school (National Center for Education Statistics, 1999). Even as late as 1950, only about half of all 17-year-olds earned a diploma. However, over the last half of the twentieth century graduation from high school rapidly became the norm—with well over 70% of all 17-year-olds earning diplomas by the end of 1999 (Figure 1).

This increase in high school attendance and graduation in the twentieth century was due to several convergent forces: the enforcement of child labor laws, the passage of compulsory school age laws, the rise of the corporation, and the increase in the credentialing effect of a high school

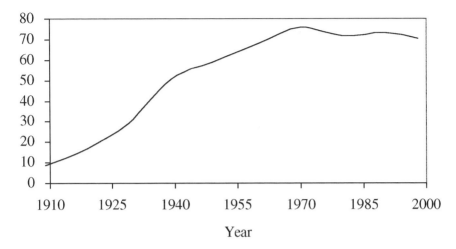

Figure 1.   Proportion high school graduates to the 17-year old population 1909 to 1999.

Source: National Center for Education Statistics (1999)

diploma (Dorn, 1996). Consequently, high schools, rather than the farm or the factory, became the dominant environment shaping the lives of adolescents. Today, attendance at school defines adolescents' lives both socially and economically. For the vast majority of young people, graduation from high school has become the rite of passage from childhood to adulthood— one marked by formal commencement ceremonies.

Yet non-completion of high school remains a prominent policy concern. Ironically, it is the success of high school completion for the majority of students that makes dropping out of high school all the more of a concern for these young people that *do* drop out. When half of all students did not complete high school dropping out was not a problem. When a small minority fails to reach this goal, it becomes a crisis. As high school has become the social norm and as high school diploma signals the larger society that the adolescent is ready to take on adult roles (however limited), those who fail to achieve this norm are all the more at a loss.

Moreover, the current enthusiasm in most states for high school exit exams has prompted concerns about the adverse effects these examinations might have on high school completion (Hebert & Hauser, 1999). Some have thought that the implementation of such tests will make it more likely that students will drop out of school rather than face the consequences of failure on these exams. For example, Bonsteel and Rumberger warn that the twin horns of the end of social promotion and the beginning of high school exit exams will greatly increase the number of high school dropouts (Bonsteel & Rumberger, 1999).

Concerns have also been raised that these tests will particularly affect the graduation rates of minority students. While overall rates of high school dropout may seem to be at historical lows, dropout rates for minorities are still unacceptably high and may be headed even higher. Figure 2 shows some well-recognized differences among racial/ethnic groups in the dropout rates. These data come from the Current Population Survey, a household survey conducted by the U.S. Bureau of the Census. These data show that an estimated 5% of students dropped out of school in 1999 (Figure 2). As is well known, black and Hispanic students are more likely than white students to drop out of school. Low-income students are also more likely than middle- or high-income students to drop out of school.

As stated above, these groups that now drop out at the greatest rate may be those most likely to feel the impact of high stakes graduation examinations. For example, in Texas, the most visible state using such tests, the on-time graduation rate for Latino and black students dropped dramatically after the implementation of high school graduation examinations (Haney, 2001).

Thus while dropout rates may be at all time lows, concern over dropouts has rarely been higher. The increasing importance of a high school diploma, added to the concern that high stakes testing will lead to more students dropping out of school, results in an increased interest in the "dropout problem."

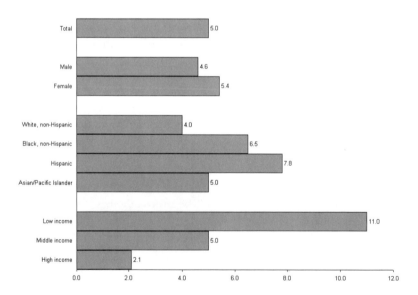

Figure 2.   Percentage of 16- through 24-year-olds who dropped out of grade 10 through 12 in 1999.

Source: Kaufman, Kwon, Klein, and Chapman (2000)

However, assessing (1) the extent and size of the problem; and (2) the causes and solutions to the problem requires reliable statistics on recent trends in high school completion and dropout. Unfortunately, despite decades of collecting data on completers and dropouts, this still remains no easy task. The relatively limited resources that go into the collection of high school completion and dropout data produce data that provide more heat than light on some rather basic questions on high school completion—how many students drop out in any given year and how many students complete high school. The next section of this chapter discusses the measurement issues in dropout research.

MEASUREMENT ISSUES IN DROPOUT RESEARCH

There are numerous ways in which dropout rates are calculated in the research literature and in official statistics. For example, most official state and federal dropout and completion rates differ significantly from one another and are not easily "translatable" into one another (Kaufman, 2001). This may lead to the appearance that these give different answers and make it difficult for policy makers to sort out the magnitude of the dropout "problem." As I will show, differences in rates primarily arise from two sources:

- Different rates are based on different populations; and
- Different rates are derived from different definitions.

For example, the data in Figures 1 and 2 show two of the various methods of presenting information on high school completion and dropping out. The first displays the percentage of the 17-year-old population that hold a high school diploma. It shows that in 1998 about 71% of 17-year-olds in the United States had graduated from high school. However, this does not mean that 29% of 17-year-olds (i.e., 100%-71%) were dropouts. Many of the 29% were still enrolled in school; some had completed high school with an alternative credential (i.e., a GED). Furthermore, not all those who were dropouts had dropped out from U.S. schools. Some portion of the 17-year-old dropout population may be immigrants who were never enrolled in school in the U.S. but had dropped out of school in their native country. Therefore, one needs to be clear on what is being measured before interpreting these data.

The data in Figure 2 illustrate another way of measuring dropouts. These data, based on the Current Population Survey (CPS), measure what proportion of a cohort of 16- to 24-year-olds had dropped out of school in a single year. That is, by asking respondents if they had graduated from high school, and if not, whether (1) they are currently enrolled in school, and

(2) were enrolled in school last year, one can calculate what proportion dropped out of high school last year. Rather than inferring a dropout rate from a completion rate, these data promise to supply a direct measure of dropping out of school. However, these data are also not without measurement issues. For example, the CPS survey covers only the civilian, non-institutionalized population. It therefore does not survey young people in the military or in prison. This has consequences for interpreting these data. For example, a person in prison is less likely to have completed high school than a person in the general population. Thus, if young black males are more likely to be incarcerated than young white males, the dropout rates from CPS will underestimate the difference in dropout rates between white and black males in the total population. If the proportion of blacks being incarcerated changes over time, then the CPS will underestimate the gap in the dropout rates of blacks and whites over time.

One other difference in the statistics reported in Figures 1 and 2 is how high school completion is defined. The data in Figure 1 report only on high school graduates (i.e., those with high school diplomas). However, the dropout rate shown in Figure 2 counts anyone with a high school diploma or a GED as a high school completer and thus not a dropout. These differences were trivial 20 years ago when relatively few alternative credentials were awarded. However, over the last two decades more and more young people are opting for a GED-based credential rather than completing the requisite coursework for a regular diploma. Recent studies estimate that about 1 in 5 high school completers finish high school with a GED (Kaufman et al., 2000). The GED Testing Service reports that during the late 1990s, more than 500,000 adults had earned a high school credential based on passing the GED tests (GED Testing Service, 2000). This was about an 18% increase over the number of credentials awarded in 1990.

In recent years, research on the adult outcomes for GED credential holders, as compared with dropouts on the one hand, and regular diploma recipients on the other, has fueled a debate over the value of the GED credential. There is conflicting evidence in the research literature concerning the effects of having a GED credential on labor force participation, employment, earnings, wage rates, post-secondary program participation, and persistence in post-secondary programs (Murnane, 1995).

Clearly these differences in rates are not just methodological technicalities, but have real impacts on the interpretation of research based on the data. Most researchers in the field recognize this and provide in their research detailed definitions of how they counted dropouts. Others, not as familiar with the field, need to be cautious in interpreting dropout statistics and the research based on them. Is the problem those students who are not enrolled in school and do not have a regular diploma? Do GEDs count? Or is the problem the number of students who fail to graduate from high school in some reasonable amount of time? Different data definitions will frame the problem in different ways.

However, getting the data clearly defined is just the first step in a research program that seeks understanding of why certain students "drop out" of school and designing interventions to help prevent them from doing so. That understanding comes from careful empirical analysis—analysis based on both clear definitions of what it means to drop out of school and a clear idea about the process being investigated. A great deal of thought has been devoted to conceptualizing the process of dropping out of school. Lately, a convergence of thought has occurred among researchers on dropping out of high school and common frameworks have emerged that combine the insights from several fields of thought. A review of these frameworks is presented next.

FRAMEWORKS ON ADOLESCENCE AND DROPPING OUT OF SCHOOL

One of the problems with any theoretical framework is the issue of boundaries. Too narrow a focus runs the risk of ignoring important aspects of the problem—too broad a focus runs the risk of needless abstraction. Henry James once made the observation that "Really, universally, relations stop nowhere, and the exquisite problem of the artist is eternally but to draw, by a geometry of his own, the circle in which they shall happily appear to do so." So it is with social science research. Different social or behavioral scientists will draw the circle at different points—depending on their purpose. To understand general social or developmental processes—such as adolescence in general—the circle may be drawn fairly large. This macro level (or large) theory provides frameworks for researchers to outline the overall conceptual domains within which they will place their own specific inquiry.

However, when examining particular aspects of their own research, large theory may be too broad to be of great use. In this case it is more useful to draw the circle a little tighter. For example, in attempting to explain the particulars of specific processes—in this case dropping out of school—more precise theories of that particular process are needed. In this instance, small theory rather than large theory is more important (Lipsey, 1993).

Recently, the life course perspective has provided the overall theory for framing the research on high school dropouts. Within this general theory or perspective, smaller models of the dropout process itself have been developed. After describing the life-course perspective, I briefly describe two related models of early school leaving.

The Life Course Perspective

Over the past decade, researchers on adolescence have begun to focus their inquiry on the settings in which young lives are shaped rather than solely on the individual characteristics of youth (National Research Council, 1995). The life-course perspective provides an overall framework that places schooling within the larger context of adolescent development with the role of student being just one phase in the totality of one's life. Within this framework, the role of student is seen as a transitional role compared with more enduring roles of parent, worker, and spouse (Marini, 1984). The sequencing of events is also important in this perspective (Pallas, 1993). This sequencing emphasizes the orderly process of adolescents' development as an adult rather than any one event in itself. In the context of schooling, the life-course perspective views dropping out as the culmination of a process of school disengagement, rather than a sudden event. As we will see later when discussing specific models of dropping out of school, early school leaving is seen from the life course perspective as one step in the course of one's life that may have started early in the child's development. (However, we will also see that this model does not fit *every* dropout.) Alexander (1997) found antecedents to dropping out of school as early as the first grade. The decision to drop out of school can thus be rooted in the child's earlier experiences at school, in the family, or in the community.

As stated above, while this overall perspective is useful in developing ways of thinking about the contexts within which students drop out of school, it is too general to be of great worth in helping policymakers build programs that address their concerns about dropouts. However, this overall framework for adolescent development *is* useful in thinking about specific models, or small theory models, that can be used in research on high school dropouts (Rumberger, 2000). Two of these small theory models are discussed below.

Specific Models of Early School Leaving

There are two models that are commonly used to understand the particular process of dropping out of school. These models are the participation-identification model and the frustration/self-esteem model.

The Participation/Identification Model

Finn (1989) describes this withdrawal process as both a behavioral response—actual physical participation in school—and as an emotional response—identification with school. Students can participate in a wide variety of activities at school—from academic activities to sports and other social activities. Participation in these events builds attachments to school that can be seen as part of the process of social integration into the school environment described by Tinto (1975) and Spady (1971). Their research examining educational persistence in post-secondary education was based on a conceptual scheme centered on two distinct dimensions of the school environmental system: the academic system and the social system. A student's lack of integration into either one of these systems results in the student's withdrawal from school. Tinto states that "given individual characteristics, prior experiences and commitments, it is the individual's integration into the academic and social systems of the [school] that most directly relate to continuance" in school (p. 52).

In this model, students begin withdrawing from school by curtailing their active participation in the academic and social environments at school. This leads to further loss of identification with the academic and social activities of school that in turn leads to lower levels of participation. It culminates in dropping out of school altogether.

The Frustration/Self-esteem Model

A related model is the frustration-self esteem model, in which students' unsuccessful school experiences lead to lowered feelings of self worth which in turn lead to dropping out of school. Being poorly prepared academically, these students fail to achieve school-normed status. The students' response to their status deprivation is withdrawal from school.

Consequently, in the life course perspective, the study of why students drop out of school involves the search for attitudes and experiences of young people before they drop out of school rather than the mere listing of structural variables (such as race and socioeconomic status) that are associated with dropping out.

Summary

To briefly summarize, the frustration/self esteem model describes dropping out of school as the culmination of the student's frustration with failure at school, and the resulting loss of self-esteem. This cycle leads to a desire for escape, most easily accomplished by dropping out. The participation-identification model also sees dropping out of school as the culmination of a cycle rooted in the students earlier school failure. However, it uses a slightly different lens to look at this cycle. The participation-identification model views dropping out as an interaction between the student's failure in school, the resulting avoidance of school related activities, and finally, a reduction of identification with schooling and the goals of schooling altogether.

However, as will be shown later, not all dropouts fit easily into these models and not all students whose profiles fit these models drop out. Some students drop out of school with little or no signs of frustration or failure in school while some students stay in school despite repeated failures and frustrations. Some adolescents seem to be almost invulnerable to the traumas of their lives (Anthony, 1987). These young people seem to be resilient to the processes described in the frustration/self esteem and the participation/identification models.

However, as I will try to show, dropping out of school is seen in all of these models (even the resiliency models) as a process that is set firmly in the life course perspective. Within the frustration/self esteem and the participation/identification models, school leaving "happens" within several environments and is just the final stage of a student's frustration and disengagement with school—one that ends in withdrawal from school altogether. In the resiliency model described below, students accumulate protective factors in their life course that protect them from the harmful effect of these frustrations.

These various frameworks have led researchers to a variety of factors related to the dropout process and the individual student, the schools that the student attends, and the families and communities in which the student lives. I describe the research that supports the frustration/self esteem and the participation/identification models first before turning to research on protective factors and resiliency.

RESEARCH SUPPORTING MODELS OF ENGAGEMENT AND FRUSTRATION

A good deal of empirical research has been conducted over the years in identifying individual factors that are associated with increased likelihood of dropping out of school. I will not attempt to provide an exhaustive list of these factors here. Those interested in a more comprehensive list should consult Rumberger (2000) Rather, I outline below some of the research that supports the two small theoretical models discussed above—the frustration/self-esteem model and the participation/identification model.

The Frustration/Self-esteem Model

In support of the frustration/self esteem model, a variety of individual social/psychological indicators have been shown to be associated with dropout decisions. For example, a student's self-esteem and feelings of depression have been shown to be related to leaving school early. In a now classic study on high school dropouts, Bachman (1971) estimated that "one fourth of students lowest on self-esteem scale dropped out of high school, whereas dropping out occurred only half as often among those highest in self-esteem" (p. 80). He also found that those who reported the highest levels of negative affect (depression) had the highest dropout rates. Gottfredson (1982) found three factors that she labeled commitment, anxiety, and extroversion were related positively to persistence in education. Other researchers have reached similar conclusions, seeing dropping out as a reaction to loss of self-esteem, and damage to self-concept and feeling of self worth (Cervantes, 1965; Elliot, Voss, & Wendly, 1966).

In my own research with the High School and Beyond (HS&B) survey, I found that students' self concept when they were sophomores was related to whether or not they dropped out of school (Kaufman, 1988). The size of this effect was rather small, however. Also, the direction of causality was not clear in this study; lack of school success may have affected self-esteem as much as a lack of self-esteem affected school success. Nevertheless, persons with higher self-concept as sophomores were more likely to complete on time.

However, other researchers have found little evidence of a relationship between dropping out of school and self-esteem. For example, neither Wehlage and Rutter (1986), nor Ekstrom et al. (1986) found that the change in self-esteem for dropouts over the two years between their sophomore and senior years was no different from the change for students who went on to college.

In terms of the "frustration" part of the frustration/self-esteem model, Bachman (1971) found that students who felt powerless to control their own fate, those toward the external control end of Rotter's Internal-External Control (I-E) Scale (1966), were twice as likely to drop out as were students toward the internal end. Earlier, in another classic study, Coleman (1966) also found that "the extent to which an individual feels that he has some control over his destiny" had important positive effects on school achievement.

One of the sources of students' feelings of powerlessness and frustration may come from their being retained in grade. It is one of the more noticeable signs of their failure in school. Fine (1991) reported that a sizeable portion of the dropouts she interviewed said that being held back in grade had "contributed significantly to their decision to drop out of school" (p. 77). One familiar comment among her narratives was that students who were held back "felt kind of left out." Other researchers have found similar results in terms of the negative impact of grade retention on student outcomes. For example, using the Current Population Survey data my colleagues and I found that in 1995 about 13% of all 16- to 24-year-olds had been held back at least one time before the 12th grade (McMillen, Kaufman, & Klein, 1997). Of those who had been retained, about one in four had not completed school compared with about 10% who had not been held back. Similarly, using the National Education Longitudinal Study of 1988, we found that after controlling for sex, race–ethnicity and socioeconomic status, 8th graders who were overage for their grade (and presumably had been retained) were 8 times more likely to have dropped out of school (Kaufman & Bradby, 1992).

Another potential source of frustration for poor-performing students comes from the increased use of high school exit exams. In an effort that many thought would hold schools accountable and insure that students gained knowledge and skills during high school, students in some states were required to show mastery of basic skills before receiving a diploma. By 1998, 18 states had such exit exams with the promise that other states would soon follow.[1]

The increase in the enthusiasm for high school exit exams has prompted concerns about the adverse effects that these exams might have on high school completion (Heubert & Hauser, 1999). As mentioned previously, some have thought that the implementation of such tests will make it more likely that students will drop out of school rather than face the frustration of failure on these exams.

The Participation/Identification Models

The concepts embedded within the participation/identification model have also had empirical support. A growing body of research has shown that the withdrawal from participation in school has antecedents that reach well back into the elementary grades (Alexander, 1997; Roderick, 1993). For example, Alexander and Entwisle (in press) found that in their sample of first graders in Baltimore, those who eventually dropped out averaged 16.5 absences in the first grade. In the middle years of school, eventual dropouts averaged 28 absences a year (compared with 12 for eventual completers). In the first year of high school dropouts averaged more than 47 absences a year—nearly one day out of every four. These children do not drop out of school; as Alexander et al. state it, they "fade out" (Alexander et al., in press, p.1).

In my own work with the HS&B data I measured the commitment of 10th graders to school by looking at their responses to three items: (1) How many times have you been absent but not ill?; (2) How many times have you been late to school?; and (3) How interested are you in school? (Kaufman, 1988) Not surprisingly, commitment to school was highly predictive of whether or not a student dropped out of school. Less than 6% of students with high commitment to school, compared to almost 27% of students with low commitment to school, dropped out. This relationship was statistically significant even after family background and other factors were held constant.

One measure of commitment to school that has sometimes been over-looked is student mobility. Rumberger (1998) has argued that student mobility—changing schools more often than thought "normal"—not only is a predictor of dropping out of school, but also is a form of student disen-gagement or withdrawal from school. Using the NELS:88 data, a colleague and I found evidence that family mobility, measured by the number of times a student had changed schools, was indeed associated with poor edu-cational outcomes (Kaufman & Bradby, 1992).[2] Compared with students who had never changed schools, students who had changed schools twice were almost two and one-half times as likely to drop out, those who had changed schools three times were three times as likely, and students who had changed schools four times were four times as likely to drop out. While from these observational studies it is unclear whether student disengage-ment leads to changing schools or whether changing schools leads to stu-dent disengagement, the point seems clear; moving around a good deal lessens students' attachment and identification with school thus increasing the chances that they will drop out of school.

So far in this section I have focused on the academic integration of stu-dents into school. Some researchers have found that the *social* integration of students is also a powerful agent of engagement in school. In particular, participation in extracurricular activities (including sports) has been shown by some researchers (Otto & Alvin, 1977) to build attachments to school and provide alternative avenues for school-based success. In my own early work with the HS&B data, I found that 10% of students (both male and female) who had participated in sports during high school dropped out as opposed to 15% of those who did not participate in sports (Kauf-man, 1988). (Furthermore, over half of those active in sports who did drop out later returned to school.) Participation in other extracurricular activi-ties also had a weak association with dropping out. About 16% of those who did not participate in any extracurricular activities dropped out between the 10th and 12th grades, compared to only 11% who had a high level of participation in extracurricular activities.

More recently, Mahoney and Cairns (1997) found in a longitudinal study of 7th graders that participation in extracurricular activities reduced the odds of a student dropping out of school by the 12th grade. The effect appeared to be most pronounced for those students most at risk of drop-ping out in the first place. More academically competent students had less positive effects of participation in extracurricular activities. Much like the earlier study by Otto and Alvin, Mahoney and Cairns argue that these activ-ities enhance the positive associations that students—especially marginal students—have with school. As they explain: "Extracurricular involvement, particularly for persons at risk for dropout, may be one component of that [developmental] transition that could help shift the balance toward greater engagement in school" (Mahoney & Cairns, 1997, p. 250).

RISK AND RESILIENCE

To this point, I have focused on models of who is at risk of dropping out. The primary purpose of this line of research is predicting and explaining who drops out and why—who is at risk? However, while research has been fruitful in predicting which students are more likely than others to drop out, these predictions are not always as precise as one would like. There are two reasons for this. One is that while many dropouts display the characteristics and behaviors described in the frustration/self-esteem model and the participation/identification models, not all dropouts can be so described. Another is that while many who display these characteristics do dropout, not all do.

That is, while these models "work" for many dropouts, they do not work for all. Students can drop out of school for a variety of reasons, not all of which fall nicely into either of these models. While for the majority of adolescents dropping out of school is the culmination of a long process of disengagement and alienation from school, for some it is indeed a sudden event (e.g., some drop out of school because of sudden changes in their life circumstances). If not for these changes, they would have stayed in school. Thus, in an analysis of the NELS:88 data, we found that about 34% of dropouts said they dropped out because of pressing family concerns such as they needed to support their family, had to care for a family member, or got married (Berktold, Geis, & Kaufman, 1998). About 27% of the females that dropped out said they dropped out because they were pregnant. Altenbaugh, Engel, and Martin (1995) found that almost half of the female urban school dropouts they studied dropped out because they were pregnant.

While early pregnancy may itself be a response to earlier disengagement with school, some portion of pregnant dropouts would have stayed in school if it were not for their pregnancy. They may not have been disengaged at all, but the immediate circumstances of their lives led them away from school. As one of the young women in the Altenbaugh et al. study stated:

> If I hadn't gotten pregnant, I would still be in school. I felt uncomfortable. . . When I was pregnant, during the whole nine months, I stayed sick all morning long. If I stayed in school, I would have been throwing up and uncomfortable and miserable. (p. 116)

Consequently, not all dropouts conform to the generalizations that guide much of the research into dropping out of school—not all dropouts are "at-risk" students. Likewise, although at-risk students drop out at higher rates than students deemed not at risk, not all students identified as at risk drop out of school. For example, again using the NELS:88 data, my colleagues and I examined dropout rates for students who had multiple factors that would predict their leaving school early. The list of factors was fairly extensive and included both family risk factors and academic risk factors. Family risk factors included: lowest quartile of socioeconomic status; non-intact family composition; parent's education of high school graduate or less; having own child living at home; mother's expectation of less than high school or only high school graduate; not having a specific place to study; and having none of the types of reading materials at the home. Academic factors included: watching more than 5 hours of TV per day; working more than 20 hours per week; doing no homework per week; often or sometimes attending class without books; often or sometimes attending class without paper or pencil; low math test scores; D and below average grades; below 5 credits earned by end of 10th grade; taken remedial math; taken remedial English; ever repeated a grade.

Not surprisingly, we found that the number of risk factors to be highly associated with the odds of dropping out of school (Figure 3). For example, only about 3% with no risk factors dropped out of school whereas about 25% of those with 4 or more academic risk factors dropped out and about 16% with 4 or more family risk factors dropped out. However, this also means that over 70% of students with 4 or more risk factors *did not* drop out of school, but were somehow able to overcome the odds and stay in school.

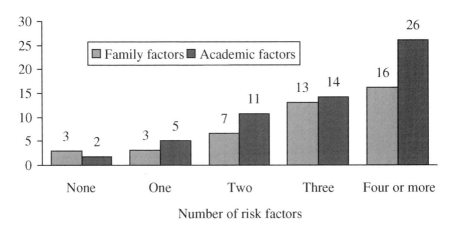

Figure 3.   10th to 12th grade dropout rates by number of family and academic risk factors present.

Source: Kaufman, McMillen, and Sweet (1996)

These were results from a national survey, but even in individual schools with high dropout rates, not all students at high risk drop out of school. For example, in Baltimore, Alexander et al. (in press) found that well over 50% of high-risk students dropped out of school—an alarming rate of school failure. However, even here a significant portion of high-risk students in an inner city school did not drop out.

These observations have resulted in an awareness among researchers that many children, despite impediments associated with social, economic, and educational disadvantages, do not succumb to these disadvantages by curtailing their education prematurely. Rather, they persist and graduate from school. This led some to explore why these children can "make it" and others cannot and what makes them resilient to the risks in their lives. This, in turn, has led to the development of related theoretical concepts— resilience and protective factors.

The term *resilience* refers to the process, phenomenon, or outcomes of successful adaptation despite risk, adversity, or challenging circumstances (Masten, Best, & Garmezy, 1990). Specifically, it is often used to describe three types of phenomena (Masten, 1994). The first type of resilience occurs in people from high-risk groups who display better-than-expected outcomes. The second type describes sustained competence or good adaptation in the presence of chronic or major life stresses. The third type refers to recovery from trauma. Among the three resilient phenomena, the first one is most relevant to the dropout issue. It can be adapted to describe students who persist in high school despite the fact that they have encountered many adversities that make them at risk of dropping out of school.

The concept of *protective factor* is often linked to the notion of resilience and risk. Past research often operationalizes resilience as the outcome of specific protective factors or mechanisms. Masten (1994) described protective factors as "either individual or environmental characteristics that facilitate better outcomes in people at risk or exposed to adversity" (p. 7). Rutter (1990) also defined a factor as *protective* if it exerts a buffering effect on the influence of risk. Simply put, protective factors operate only when a risk is present. To the extent that a protective factor is operative, it attenuates, balances, or insulates against the effects of risk factors, and facilitates better outcomes in people at risk than they would be if the protective factor were not present (Garmezy, 1985).

However, risk and protective factors are not always "self-contained" variables. Sometimes protective factors can be viewed as the opposite of risk factors, or vice versa (Stouthamer-Loeber et al., 1993). In other words, a single variable may be viewed as a protective factor at one pole and as a risk factor at the other (e.g., the variable of parenting style can vary from caring at one end to neglecting at the other).

Research Supporting Resilience and Protective Factors

There has been a good deal of research that supports the notion of resiliency and protective factors. Below I provide a partial description of the family, individual, school and peer group characteristics that may ameliorate the frustration/disengagement process that leads to dropping out of school.

Family Characteristics

Family provides the first protective agents in the child's life, and the quality of parenting is particularly important to children who grow up in dangerous environments (Wang, Haertel, & Walberg, 1994). Several studies have considered the role of families as protective factors under socioeconomic hardship. Lewis and Looney (1983) examined family qualities in relation to competence in adolescents. They found that low-SES black children were more likely to adapt well if they lived in families where the parents had good marital relationships, family members were close, and the family was connected with extended family members, friends, and community. Other studies investigating family aspects found that at-risk children who developed well tended to live in caring, warm, and structured home environments (Garmezy, 1991; Resnick, Harris, & Blum, 1993); and had formed a strong and close bond with at least one caregiver who gave them needed attention and support (Benard, 1991; Rutter, 1990). Within the family, parents set up high goals for their children (McMillan & Reed, 1994); consistently enforced family rules (Bennett, Wolin, & Reiss, 1988); regularly monitored their children's activities (Masten et al., 1990; Patterson & Stouthamer-Loeber, 1984); regularly interacted with their children (Westfall & Pisapia, 1994); encouraged participation in family and household activities (Benard, 1991); provided adequate learning materials (e.g., books, encyclopedias, magazines, or computers), and were actively involved in school activities (Peng, Wang, & Walberg, 1992). It is suggested that these family characteristics are among the factors that can help protect children against adversity.

In our own research on resilience, Xianglei Chen and I used the NELS:88 database to match students who dropped out of school with students with similar at-risk characteristics (Chen & Kaufman, 1999). Those who did not drop out but had at-risk characteristics we called resilient students. We compared these resilient students and dropouts in their family background, individual attributes, school experiences, and peer groups. The findings revealed many significant differences between the two groups, though they had similar risk factors that link to the high probability of dropping out. As earlier studies have shown, families of resilient students appeared closer, warmer, and more structured than dropouts' families.

These findings are, of course, in line with 25 years of research on the characteristics of effective parenting (Darling, 1993). That is, the collection of parent attributes that seem to more likely to be present in the homes of resilient adolescents is associated with Baumrind's (1991) work on "authoritative" parents. These attributes include emotional support, high standards, appropriate autonomy giving, and clear communications. Thus, by providing guidance in developing autonomy and strong emotional support, authoritative parents may be supplying their children with the tools they need to survive traumas in their lives.

Individual Attributes

In addition to family characteristics, resilient children often display a set of unique personal traits that may promote their school success regardless of risks in their lives (Garmezy, 1985). A profile of resilient children has emerged from numerous studies. For example, resilient children tend to have positive expectations about their abilities and high motivation to do well in school (Westfall & Pisapia, 1994); are generally optimistic about the future and maintain a positive vision of a meaningful life despite the hardship (Rutter, 1987; Worrell, 1996); are able to elicit help from others when needed; and are actively involved in the activities that provide a sense of support, success, and recognition, such as hobbies, volunteer work, and community or religious activities (Masten, 1994; Peng et al., 1992). These studies pointed out that these personal characteristics may act as protective factors that alter or reverse expected negative school outcomes and enable at risk children to manifest resilience.

In the study with the NELS:99 data (Chen & Kaufman, 1999), we also found certain individual characteristics that seemed to ameliorate the effects of being at-risk. Again consistent with past findings, resilient students are optimistic about the future, particularly their education. When asked about the chance to graduate from high school, 85% of resilient students said that the chance was high, compared with 63% of dropouts who said so. When asked about the chance to go to college after high school graduation, 51% of resilient students responded that the chance was high, compared with only 32% of dropouts who said so. Resilient students were also more likely than dropouts to believe that they have a high chance to get a well-paid job and to had a happy family life in the future. These results suggest that resilient students are different from dropouts in many personal traits, and that positive individual attributes such as having high goals for education, self-efficacy, self-worth, expectations of success, and hopefulness may act as protective agents that enable resilient students to believe in education and persist in school, despite negative circumstances in their lives.

Research is less clear on why some adolescents, placed in similar circumstances, are more optimistic about their future than their peers. Murphy (1987) speculates that some people have an "optimistic bias," an emotional orientation that is often expressed as "latching on to any excuse for hope..." (p. 102). This optimistic bias may be rooted in the earliest developmental stages of the child, when the infant's needs are repeatedly gratified and the infant comes to expect life to feel good. These early experiences, when negative, may lead to a "negative bias" in which the child comes to expect the worse.

School Factors

One area that researchers have focused on in looking for protective factors is the school environment. In addition to family and individual characteristics, schools, where students spend most of their time during the day, are also important. Perhaps school connectedness is the most salient protective factor against "acting out" behaviors (Clark, 1995). Various research has found that resilient students generally like school and are interested in learning there (Wang et al., 1994). Most of these children attend school regularly, engage in classroom discussions and activities, participate in extracurricular events in school, and expect to graduate from high school and receive further education after high school (McMillan & Reed, 1994; Peng et al., 1992). Werner (1990) also found that among the most frequently encountered positive role models in the lives of resilient children, outside of the family circle, is a favorite teacher who is not just an instructor for academic skills but also a confidant and positive model for personal identification. Other studies (Geary, 1988; Pisapia & Westfall, 1994) found that resilient students often interact with teachers who care about them, respect them, listen and talk to them, take them seriously, and provide personal encouragement and support.[3] In sum, high motivation to go to school, positive attitudes toward learning, along with a school setting where children can connect with caring, supportive, and competent adults, may play an important role in the success of resilient students.

Peer Association

Peer groups can exert significant influence on students' learning attitudes and behaviors (Epstein & Karweit, 1983). Past research suggested that resilient students had more close friends than children who did not adapt as successfully (Werner, 1990). In addition to the number of friends, the type of friends is also important. Clark (1991) reviewed research on friendship patterns and suggested that close friendship, particularly with those who value education, plays an important role in fostering resilience. Patchen (1982) found that students with peers who value education spent more time on homework, finished more of their homework assignments, attended school more regularly, were tardy less often, and missed class without permission fewer times than those who had fewer of these peers. Chen (1997) found that students with friends who care about learning had better educational outcomes; in particular, they were less likely to drop out, and more likely to graduate from high school and continue their education after graduating. In sum, opportunities to interact with peers who have high achievement motivation and positive attitudes toward school may be beneficial to students who are considered at risk.

In our own study of resilient students (Chen & Kaufman, 1999), we found that resilient students had more positive peer influences than dropouts: They had more friends who emphasized education, planned to go to college, offered encouragement to them to attend college as well. On the other hand, they had fewer friends who had dropped out before or who were engaged in risk behaviors.

TRANSLATING DROPOUT RESEARCH INTO ACTION

Over the years hundreds of dropout prevention programs have been developed. Most of these programs have not proven to be successful at preventing high-risk students from dropping out of school (Slavin, 1998). In particular, programs that isolate dropping out of school as a separate problem of schooling have not enjoyed much demonstrated success (Dynarski & Gleason, 1998). However, from the discussion of at-risk students in this chapter, it should be clear why these programs do not seem to work. First, it is not possible with any accuracy to identify who will drop out. At-risk factors, as currently measured, do not predict with much accuracy who will actually drop out. Some students so identified will not need dropout prevention services; some of those *not* identified, will. Secondly, school is only one of several environments that have an impact on adolescents' lives. Dropout prevention programs will be less effective if they do not take into account the larger circumstances of students' life course—their work, family, and community environments.

In contrast, the most promising approaches have viewed dropping out of school in the larger contexts of students' lives. These programs build on what is known about adolescents' risks and resiliency—and have concentrated on restructuring schools to provide a more caring and supportive environment that will foster resiliency to external stressors, increase students' participation and identification with school, and lessen the frustration that some students have felt with the traditional high school (Dynarski & Gleason, 1998). These programs are in line with the models of the dropout process outlined in this chapter and are in line with the best knowledge of adolescent development.

For example, one approach that has shown encouraging results is the Achievement for Latinos Through Academic Success (ALAS) (Gandara, 1998). ALAS stresses the importance of academic achievement to the student's entire environment—the individual student, the family, the school, and the community—in designing an intervention for high-risk Latino students. It emphasizes the "psycho-social" aspects of students' lives as much as the academic. The student component focuses on problem solving skills, self-esteem, and school affiliation. The family component focuses on the direct instruction and modeling for parents of parenting skills. The school component focuses on improving teacher/student communication as well as on intense attendance monitoring. The community component focuses on enhancing the collaboration among community-based organizations that can help the students and their families. Data from evaluations of ALAS has shown positive effects on student mobility, attendance, and course credits (Gandara, 1998).

Another approach to school reform that shows promise in preventing dropping out of school is the Career Academy model (Stern, 1992). Career Academies combine both academic and occupational learning in an applied environment. Academies also develop partnerships with local businesses to provide career awareness and employment opportunities for their students. This emphasis on applied learning is targeted at increasing the students' interest and engagement with the curriculum—making it more relevant to their own experiences and lives.

Career academies are also organized around smaller organizational units, enrolling only 250 to 350 students in each academy. Academies may be housed at a separate site or may be schools within schools. Some whole schools are organized around career academies, the "wall to wall" model (McPartland, 2001). Regardless of the physical layout, these smaller learning environments serve several purposes. Because all students within the academy attend classes together with the same faculty, closer relationships among students and between students and teachers are facilitated. This allows for closer monitoring of students by teachers (students do not become lost in large impersonal schools), closer relationships among students (facilitated by group projects), and greater collaboration among faculty and staff (common planning time creates the conditions for greater teamwork).

Controlled experiments have demonstrated the effectiveness of this model (Kemple, 2000). For high-risk students in particular, career academies reduced dropout rates, improved attendance, increased academic course taking, and increased the likelihood of graduating on time. Academies that were most successful produced particularly dramatic enhancements in the interpersonal support that students received from teachers and peers.

These two examples demonstrate that programs can be effective when they are based upon established empirical evidence regarding the dropout process and have a strong "theory of action" that guides the implementation of the intervention (McPartland, 2001). Thus, by putting into practice the best knowledge of adolescent development, dropout prevention programs can make improvements to the prospects for at-risk students. Still, even in these successful programs, large numbers of high-risk students drop out of school. For example, Kemple et al. (2000) found that dropout rates for Career Academy students were substantially less than students in their control group. However, 21% of students in the Career Academies still dropped out of school before the 12th grade.

CONCLUSION

In this chapter I have tried to outline what is currently known about what causes some students to leave school before they graduate from high school. The research on high school dropouts has a long tradition, and I have organized the review of what is known about dropouts around related theoretical models of why some students drop out—the frustration/self-esteem and participation/identification models—and why some students *do not* drop out—the resiliency model. I have tried to show how these models can be placed within the context of life-course research.

The best evidence then, from both a theoretical and empirical view, is that dropping out of school for most adolescents is just one visible event in a life-long struggle in school. However, the empirical evidence also shows that for some portion of dropouts, the act of dropping out appears to be indeed a sudden event with no apparent prior warnings. Adolescents with good grades, good behavior, and with all the outward signs of being engaged in school, nevertheless drop out of school. For example, Wehlage et al. (1989) describe one young girl, Evelyn, who was bright and ambitious, whose mother was active in the school's PTA, and whose family was relatively affluent. Evelyn nevertheless found herself pregnant and a school dropout. In my own experience as a high school teacher, I ran across students who had been exemplary students in earlier grades, were involved in extra curricular activities, but nevertheless, over a very short period of time, disengaged from school and dropped out. Some of these students had become suddenly involved in drugs or other problem behaviors and their life course took an abrupt turn for the worse—culminating in their dropping out of school.

This is not to say that schools could not do more for these kinds of young people. To the contrary, it is the interaction between the school environment and the student's resiliency to sudden events that lead students to drop out of school. Anthony (1987, p. 10) uses the analogy of three dolls to illustrate this point. One doll is made of glass, one of plastic, and one of steel. Each is exposed to a blow from a hammer. The first doll breaks completely, the second one cracks, while the third gives out a "fine metallic sound." Of course, Anthony states, "the outcome for the three dolls would be different if their 'environments' were to buffer the blows from the hammer by interposing some type of 'umbrella' between the external attack and the recipient" (Anthony, 1987. p. 10). Schools, like those built around the Career Academy model, can supply these umbrellas by providing the support systems that sustain all students when their own individual life courses come off track.

NOTES

1. Rolf Blank, CCSSO, personal communication.
2. In counting the number of times the student had changed schools, movements resulting from a promotion and movements between schools within a single school district were dismissed.
3. This finding is particularly relevant to the study of dropouts. According to Wehlage and Rutter (1986), one of the primary reasons dropouts gave for leaving school was that they could not get along with their teachers. They found that dropouts were more likely than other students to perceive their teachers lacking interest in students. This finding was confirmed by our analysis of the dropout survey in the NELS:88 data (Berktold et al., 1998).

REFERENCES

Alexander, K.K. (1997). From first grade forward: Early foundations of high school dropout. *Sociology of Education, 70,* 87–107.

Alexander, K.L., Entwisle, D.R., & Kabbani, N. (In press). The dropout process in life course perspective: Risk factors at home and school. *Teachers College Record.*

Altenbaugh, R.J., Engel, D.E., & Martin, D.T. (1995). *Caring for kids: A critical study of urban school leavers.* Washington DC: The Falmer Press.

Bachman, J.G., Green, S., & Wirtamen, I.D. (1971). *Dropping out—problem or symptom?* Ann Arbor, MI. Institute for Social Research, University of Michigan.

Benard, B. (1991). *Fostering resiliency in kids: Protective factors in the family, school, and community.* ERIC Document Reproduction Service.

Bennett, L., Wolin, S., & Reiss, D. (1988). Cognitive, behavioral, and emotional problems among school-age children of alcoholic parents. *American Journal of Psychiatry, 145,* 185–190.

Berktold, J., Geis, S., & Kaufman, P. (1998). *Susequent educational attainment of high school dropouts.* U.S. Department of Education, National Center for Education Statistics. Washington, DC: U.S. Government Printing Office.

Bonsteel, A., & Rumberger, R. W. (1999, May 16). Get ready for dropout shock. *Los Angeles Daily News.*

Cervantes, L.F. (1965). *The dropout.* Ann Arbor, MI: University of Michigan Press.

Chen, X. (1997). *Students' peer groups in high school: The pattern and relationship to educational outcomes.* U.S. Department of Education, Office of Educational Research and Improvement, NCES. Washington, DC: U.S. Government Printing Office.

Chen, X., & Kaufman, P. (1999). *Risk and protective factors: The effects on students dropping out of high school.* Unpublished manuscript.

Clark, M. (1991). Social identity, peer relations, and academic competence of African-American adolescents. *Education and Urban society, 24,* 41–52.

Clark, P. (1995). *Risk and resiliency in adolescence: The current status of research on gender differences.* ERIC Document Reproduction Service No. ED 387 714.

Coleman, J. (1966). *Equality of educational opportunity.* Washington, DC: U.S. Government Printing Office.

Dorn, S. (1996). *Creating the dropout: An institutional and social history of school failure.* Westport, CT: Praeger.

Dynarski, M., & Gleason, P. (1998). *How can we help? What we have learned from Federal dropout-prevention programs.* Princeton, NJ: Mathematica Policy Research, Inc.

Ekstrom, R.B., Goertz, M.E., Pollack, J.M., & Rock, D.A. (1986). Who drops out of high school and why? Findings from a national study. *Teacher's College Record, 87,* 356–373.

Elliot, D.S., Voss, H.L., & Wendly, A. (1966). Capable dropouts and the social milieu of the school. *The Journal of Educational Research, 60,* 180–186.

Epstein, J.L., & Karweit, N. (1983). *Friends in schools: Patterns of selection and influence in secondary schools.* New York: Academic Press.

Fine, M. (1991). *Framing dropouts.* Albany: State University of New York Press.

Finn, J.D. (1989). Withdrawing from school. *Review of Educational Research, 59*(2), 117–142.

Garmezy, N. (1985). Stress-resistant children: The search for protective factors. In J.E. Stevenson (Ed.), *Recent research in developmental psychopathology: Journal of child psychology and psychiatry book* (pp. 212–233). Oxford: Pergamon Press.

Garmezy, N. (1991). Resiliency and vulnerability to adverse developmental outcomes associated with poverty. *American Behavioral Science, 34,* 416–430.

Geary, P.A. (1988). *Defying the odds?: Academic success among at-risk minority teenagers in an urban high school.* ERIC Document Reproduction Service No. ED 296 055.

Gottfredson, D.C. (1982). Personality and persistence in education: A longitudinal study. *Journal of Personality and Social Psychology, 43,* 532–545.

Harlow, C.W. (1994). *Comparing federal and state prison inmates, 1991.* U.S. Department of Justice, Office of Justice Programs, Bureau of Justice Statistics. Washington, DC: U.S. Government Printing Office.

Heubert, J., & Hauser, R.M. (1999). *High stakes testing for tracking, promotion and graduation.* Washington, DC: National Academy Press.

Kaufman, P. (1988). *Dropouts that return to school.* Unpublished Dissertation, Claremont Graduate School, Claremont Ca.

Kaufman, P. (2000). *Calculating high school dropout and completion rates: The complexities of data and definitions.* Paper presented at the The National Academies' workshop on School Completion in Standards-Based Reform: Facts and Strategies, Washington, DC.

Kaufman, P., & Bradby, D. (1992). *Characteristics of at-risk students in NELS:88.* National Center for Education Statistics. Washington, DC: U.S. Government Publishing Office.

Kaufman, P., Kwon, J., Klein, S., & Chapman, C. D. (2000). *Dropout rates in the United States: 1999.* U.S. Department of Education, National Center for Education Statistics. Washignton DC: U.S. Government Printing Office.

Kaufman, P., McMillen, M. M., & Sweet, D. (1996). *A comparison of high school dropout rates in 1982 and 1992.* U.S. Department of Education, National Center for Education Statistics. Washignton, DC: U.S. Government Printing Office.

Keniston, K. (1970). Youth as a stage of life. *American Scholar, 39*, 631–654.

Lewis, J.M., & Looney, J.G. (1983). *The long struggle: Well-functioning working class Black families.* New York: Brunner/Mazel.

Lipsey, M.W. (1993). Theory as method: Small theories of treatments. In l.B. Sechrest & A.G. Scott (Eds.), *Understanding causes and the generalizing about them* (Vol. 57). San Francisco: Jossey-Bass.

Mahoney, J.L., & Cairns, R.B. (1997). Do extracurricular activities protect against early school dropout? *Developmental Psychology, 33*, 241–253.

Marini, M.M. (1984). Age and sequencing norms in the transition to adulthood. *Scocial Forces, 63*, 229–244.

Masten, A.S. (1994). Resilience in individual development: Successful adaptation despite risk and adversity. In M.C. Wang & E.W. Gordon (Eds.), *Educational resilience in inner-city America: Challenges and prospects.* Hillsdale, NJ: Lawrence Erlbaum Associates.

Masten, A.S., Best, K.M., & Garmezy, N. (1990). Resilience and development: Contributions from the study of children who overcome adversity. *Development and Psychopathology, 2*, 425–444.

McMillan, J.H., & Reed, D.F. (1994). At-risk students and resiliency: Factors contributing to academic success. *The Clearing House, 67*, 137–140.

McMillen, M., & Kaufman, P. (1996). *Dropout rates in the United States: 1994.* U.S. Department of Education, National Center for Education Statistics. Washignton, DC: U.S. Government Printing Office.

McMillen, M.M., Kaufman, P., & Klein, S. (1997). *Dropout rates in the United States: 1995.* Washington DC: U.S. Government Publishing Office.

Murnane, R.J., & Levy, F. (1996). *Teaching the new basic skills: Principles for educating children to thrive in a changing economy.* New York: Free Press.

National Center for Education Statistics. (1999). *Digest of education.* Statistics. U.S. Department of Education, National Center for Education Statistics. Washington, DC: U.S.Government Printing Office.

National Research Council. (1995). *Losing generations: Adolescents in high-risk settings.* Washington, DC: National Academy Press.

Otto, L.B., & Alvin, D.F. (1977). Atheletics, aspirations, and attainments. *Sociology of Education, 42*, 102–113.

Pallas, A. (1993). Schooling in the context of human lives: The social context of education and the transition to adulthood in industrial society. *Review of Educational Research, 63*(4), 409–447.

Patchen, M. (1982). *Black-white contact in schools: Its social and academic effects.* West Lafayette, IN: Purdue University Press.

Patterson, G.R., & Stouthamer-Loeber, M. (1984). The correlation of family management practices and delinquency. *Child Development, 55*, 1299–1307.

Peng, S.S., Wang, M.C., & Walberg, H.J. (1992). *Resilient students in urban settings.* Paper presented at the Annual Meeting of American Educational Research Association, San Francisco, CA.

Pisapia, J., & Westfall, A. (1994). *Developing resilient schools and resilient students.* ERIC Document Reproduction Service No. ED 411 343.

Resnick, M.D., Harris, I.J., & Blum, R.W. (1993). The impact of caring and connectedness on adolescent health and well-being. *Journal of Pediatrics and Child Health, 29*, 83–98.

Roderick, M. (1993). *The path to dropping out.* Westport, CT: Auburn House.

Rumberger, R.W. (1987). High school dropouts: A reveiw of issues and evidence. *Review of Educational Research, 57*, 107–121.

Rumberger, R.W. (2000, July 17–18). *Who drops out and why.* Paper presented at the National Academy of Sciences' Committee on Education Excellence and Testing Workshop.

Rumberger, R.W., & Larson, K.A. (1998). Student mobility and the increased risk of high school drop out. *American Journal of Education, 107*, 1–35.

Rutter, M. (1987). Psychosocial resilience and protective mechanisms. *American Journal Orthopsychiatry, 57*, 316–331.

Rutter, M. (1990). Psychosocial resilience and protective mechanisms. In A.S.M.J. Rolf, D. Cicchetti, K.H. Neuchterlein, & S. Weintraub (Eds.), *Risk and protective factors in the development of psychopathology* (pp. 191–214). New York: Cambridge University Press.

Spady, R. (1971). Dropouts from higher education: Towards an empirical model. *Interchange, 2*, 38–62.

Stouthamer-Loeber, M., Loeber, R., Farrington, D.P., Zhang, Q., Van Kammen, W., & Maguin, E. (1993). The double edge of protective and risk factors for delinquency: Interrelations and developmental patterns. *Development and Psychopathology, 5*, 683–701.

Tinto, V. (1975). Dropout from higher education: A theoretical synthesis of recent research. *Review of Educational Research, 49*, 89–125.

U.S. Bureau of the Census. (1992). *Workers with low earnings.* Washington, DC: U.S. Government Publishing Office.

Wang, M.C., Haertel, G.D., & Walberg, H.J. (1994). Educational resilience in inner cities. In M.C. Wang & E.W. Gordon (Eds.), *Educational resilience in inner-city America: Challenges and prospects.* Hillsdale, NJ: Lawrence Erlbaum Associates.

Wehlage, G.G., & Rutter, R.A. (1986). Dropping out: How much do schools contribute to the problem? *Teachers College Record, 87*, 374–392.

Werner, E.E. (1990). Protective Factors and Individual Resilience. In S.J.M. a. J.P. Shonkoff (Ed.), *Handbook of early childhood intervention* (pp. 97–116). Cambridge: Cambridge University Press.

Westfall, A., & Pisapia, J. (1994). *At-risk students: Who are they and what helps them succeed?* ERIC Document Reproduction Service No. ED 411 341.

Worrell, F.C. (1996). *The risk-resilience paradigm in research on dropping out.* ERIC Document Reproduction Service No. ED 407 624.